KJV Version

Very exciting Bible School® Curriculum

Senior Product Manager: Janet Lee
Product Development Manager: Karen Pickering
Cover Design: idesignetc
Cover Illustration: Ron Adair
Interior Design: idesignetc
Illustrations: Ron Adair, Aline Heiser
Writers: Judy Gillispie, Gail Rohlfing, Karen Schmidt, Sheila Siefert, Karla Warkentin
Music: Music Precedent, Ltd.

4050 Lee Vance View • Colorado Springs, CO 80918-7100 • Colorado Springs, CO/Paris, Ontario
www.CookMinistries.com/NexGen

Printed in China

ISBN: 0-7814-4209-5

104035

Table of Contents

Kids will learn the wisdom and joy in

following God's 10 Commandments and related Bible stories through exploring five historic sites.

As a result the kids will deepen and improve their relationships with God, family, and friends.

Time-Stone Travelers™ is a Very exciting Bible School® curriculum based on Psalm 119:33-34:

"Teach me, O Lord, the way of thy statutes; and I shall keep it unto the end. Give me understanding, and I shall keep thy law; yea, I shall observe it with my whole heart."

Each of the *Time-Stone Travelers*™ site Introductions features a skit involving one or two Leaders and the puppet dog or interaction between two Leaders.

Five separate Discovery Sites have been developed, based on the locations in the *Time-Stone Travelers*™ youth book series. At each Discovery Site the children will learn how to relate to God and others in respectful and loving ways.

○ Mayan Jungle

There is only one God.

From the first two commandments and the Bible story of the three men in the fiery furnace, children will learn that the one true God alone is to be worshiped.

○ Medieval Castle

God deserves our worship.

Through the third and fourth commandments and the account of Jesus' healing the crippled woman on the Sabbath, the children will study how to respect the Lord's name and set aside time to worship Him.

○ Ancient Laboratory

Honor your father and mother.

Studying the fifth commandment and Jesus' example as a boy at the temple will help children understand the need to honor and obey their parents.

○ Hawk's Village

God wants us to treat others with kindness.

The children will learn to be careful to not hurt others, as they study commandments 6, 7, 8, and 9 and Jesus' story of the Good Samaritan.

○ Hawaiian Volcano

God wants us to be happy with what He has given us.

The children will examine their attitudes about possessions, greed, and contentment as they study the tenth commandment and the Bible story of Naboth's vineyard *(and in Preschool the birds and the flowers in Matthew 6)*.

Every site includes a take-home paper called "The Quest Continues." Copy these pages to give to the kids before they leave each site. The take-home papers will inform parents about what their child learned and help parents get involved in their child's spiritual growth. Please note that there are separate take-home papers for elementary and preschool children.

Introduction to VeBS®

Kids love activity! This adventure will take the kids both around the world and through history while they learn Bible stories about how to relate to God and others. Exploring the Scriptures through fun-filled activities while "visiting" exotic locations, your children will gain new insights into loving God, their families, their friends, and others around them.

Visiting five Discovery Sites, the children will open the Scriptures to learn to love and worship God alone, to respect and obey their parents, to be kind to everyone around them, and to examine their inner attitudes about their material possessions.

Learning Models

For Small Groups:

If your total VBS attendance is expected to be small, or if you have trouble recruiting enough leaders to assist you, you may choose to present each Discovery Site separately—one each day of the week.

For Large Groups:

If your total VBS attendance is large enough, and if you have plenty of Helpers, you may opt to hold each session simultaneously at five locations in your church building or auditorium. A unique feature of this VBS learning model is that each Leader *(or pair of Leaders)* prepares ONLY one lesson. That lesson is presented by the same Leader*(s)* every day to a different group of children. All the activities for the day, including the interactive Bible story, crafts, activities, games, and snacks, can all be done at this one location. There is no particular order for the visits, but by the end of the week, each of the five groups will have visited all five sites. This method allows the children to be immersed in single environments where all aspects of the lesson tie together and reinforce one core concept. It also gives the Leaders the freedom to focus on the needs of the kids, not the clock.

These five sites remain intact for the entire week. If you wish, divide children into five groups by age or grade. Key Verses and materials for each site have been age-graded as follows:

PRESCHOOL—children who have completed preschool or have not yet attended school.

EARLY ELEMENTARY—children who have completed kindergarten or first grade.

ELEMENTARY—those who have completed second or third grade.

UPPER ELEMENTARY—those who have completed fourth or fifth grade. Alter these divisions if needed.

Discovery Sites

Regardless of the learning model you choose, each Discovery Site will present an exciting experience for your kids to learn about the Lord. Each Discovery Site will be decorated according to the day's mini-theme to give the children a setting in which to learn about the 10 Commandments.

Goals

- ○ **Introduce children to the 10 Commandments as wise rules that will help them love God and others.**
- ○ **Change children from the inside out as their hearts are transformed by God's love for them and the security He offers through His good teachings in the Bible.**
- ○ **Develop in children an understanding of the relationship God wants to have with them through stories from the Bible.**
- ○ **Match Leaders' abilities with tasks so they are free to enjoy the children.**
- ○ **Develop meaningful relationships between Leaders and children in an interactive environment.**
- ○ **Build a bridge between church and home as families are encouraged and challenged by the VBS ministry.**

We hope these are your goals, too, as you seek to provide your kids with the best VBS program possible. Have fun as you join with your kids on an adventure to understand God's good rules for them.

Custom VeBS® Options

Are you looking for a new way to maximize your Bible school investment? Do you see needs in your church and community that would be better met with a different format than the standard five-day Bible school? Look no further! Here are some helpful tips for customizing our VBS to meet those needs. Be creative and make it your own!

Backyard Bible Club

Backyard Bible clubs are an excellent way to do outreach and you can easily customize this VBS program to meet the unique needs of this setting. Backyard Bible clubs take place in the neighborhoods of people in your church. *Time-Stone Travelers*™ is designed so that you can set up all the Discovery Sites at once, one Discovery Site each day, or create a general setup with small changes each day. If your schedule does not allow for five meetings, you can cut it down to meet your schedule— each lesson stands alone so children will have a complete experience in one day or five!

The Purpose

Outreach: Backyard Bible clubs provide a unique opportunity for outreach into your community. Instead of asking people to come to the church, the church is going to them. Children are invited into a neighbor's home, a safe and fun place where they can learn about the love of Jesus. Backyard Bible clubs also provide a unique opportunity for outreach to parents who can be casually involved in what their child is doing without the commitment of being a church volunteer.

Evangelism: Backyard Bible clubs are a great way to reach kids who do not usually attend church with the good news of salvation in Jesus. Because the invitations are sent out into the neighborhoods, many families are introduced to the love of Jesus Christ for the first time through backyard Bible clubs.

Church Growth: Backyard Bible clubs often bring new people to your church. When new families in the area are introduced to the church and develop relationships with people in the church, they are likely to get involved in other ways as well. Instead of taking away from another church's membership, backyard Bible clubs are a way to grow the church with new Christians who might not otherwise attend any church at all.

The benefits of backyard Bible clubs are great. Kids have a fun, safe setting in which to learn about Jesus, parents get involved and are introduced to the church and the Christian community, and most importantly, children and adults alike are introduced to Jesus and to a church family in which meaningful relationships can continue to grow after VBS is over.

How It Works

A backyard Bible club is just what it says it is— a Bible club that is held in someone's backyard. So the only real differences in implementing a backyard Bible club instead of a traditional VBS are the location and the use of facilities and materials.

One option is to have five backyard Bible clubs going on in neighborhoods during one week, set up and run just like VBS, except there will only be one Discovery Site set up per session. Each backyard Bible club teacher develops only one Discovery Site. This includes collecting all of the materials, creating the site scene, and so on. On the first day of VBS, each backyard Bible club teacher runs the Discovery Site he or she developed. Later in the day, all five teachers meet to exchange materials so each Bible club teacher does another Discovery Site on the second day. The teachers continue exchanging materials until all have done each Discovery Site. This way, the work of developing the Discovery Site is divided between five leaders.

Another option is to run separate clubs throughout the summer. This way, each club will get all the materials at once and then pass them on to the next club when they have finished all five sessions.

Who You Need

Backyard Bible clubs are a wonderful way to match people with jobs that fit their spiritual gifts! Each person involved has specific responsibilities that allow him or her to use their gifts to honor God and serve others.

The first thing you need is a host*(ess)*. This person is a member of the church who has the gift of hospitality and desires to open his or her home and life to others. The size of the home is not important as long as there is space to tell the story, a place to do crafts and have snacks, and an open area in the yard or even in a nearby park for kids to play games. It is good if this person is already a respected and trusted member of the neighborhood or community, but it is also a great way for someone who is new to an area to develop relationships with neighbors.

You will also need a Leader for the backyard Bible club. This person should have the gifts of teaching and shepherding as his or her attention will be focused on helping the kids learn about Jesus and applying the lessons to their own lives. It is also helpful for this person to be gifted in administration, as he or she will coordinate and facilitate the overall program. If your church is running multiple clubs at one time, you may also need a director to oversee the coordination and staffing of all the club programs.

Finally, you will need some Helpers, based on the number of children attending the backyard Bible club. This is a wonderful chance to get parents and others from the neighborhood involved! They are there to do just what their name says—help. Each site needs three or four Helpers who can play the characters in the Introduction and Application times. Extra hands are always helpful, and it is a great opportunity to build relationships with neighborhood adults as well as children.

Individual Responsibilities

Host(ess):

○ **Pray for the children and families of the neighborhood and for the staff involved.**

○ **Hand out invitations to parents in the neighborhood, inviting kids to take part.**

○ **Host a meeting for the Leader and Helpers in his or her home a couple of weeks before the backyard Bible club begins.**

○ **Provide a safe, clean place for the kids to come each day of the backyard Bible club.**

○ **Provide snacks each day of the club.**

○ **Follow up with families and continue to build relationships after the club is over.**

Leader: *(If your clubs have a director, he/she would share some of these responsibilities.)*

○ **Understand and facilitate each step of the schedule.**

○ **Provide all needed supplies and props.**

○ **Lead a planning meeting with all staff before the backyard Bible club begins.**

○ **Present the Discovery Site materials and Bible story to the children.**

○ **Lead or make sure that someone is prepared to lead the other sections of the lessons.**

○ **Make sure the host's/hostess's home is clean and in good shape after the backyard Bible club.**

○ **Follow up with the kids and families after the club has ended.**

Helpers:

○ **Follow the direction of the Leader in whatever capacity has been decided on.**

○ **Assist children who need extra attention.**

○ **Build relationships with and love the children.**

○ **Play characters in the skits, as needed.**

Helpful Hints:

Send invitations and then have a registration day in a nearby park or common area. Make it fun with games, balloons, and so on. Even those in the area who did not receive invitations will be drawn to this and it gives parents a safe, non-threatening place to ask questions and find out about your backyard Bible club.

Always make sure that the parents register their kids—it is important that the parents know where the child is and have given their permission.

Follow up with the children and the parents! Hand out invitations to your church with the location and service times on the card. Provide a way for the families to go along with someone they have met during the backyard Bible club. You may also want to follow up with the parents by having dinner or coffee and dessert in the host's/hostess's home sometime after the club ends. You might even consider starting a neighborhood Bible study!

Intergenerational Option

To involve more of your church in the excitement of VBS, shape your activities to include the diverse and valuable people within your church body. While "intergenerational" may mean different things to different people, the basic idea of several generations learning God's Word together is a great way to get involved and learn from each other.

What Is Intergenerational?

The most direct use of "intergenerational learning" in the Bible is found in Deuteronomy 6:6-7: "And these words, which I command thee this day, shall be in thine heart: And thou shalt teach them diligently unto thy children, and shalt talk of them when thou sittest in thine house, and when thou walkest by the way, and when thou liest down, and whe thou risest up."

Parents have been given an immense responsibility to teach and instruct their children. This responsibility extends even beyond the parents to other members of the family of God. In the church, we often divide the family into different "age levels." The goal of intergenerational learning is to bring many people back together to share in a common learning experience centered around God's Word. Intergenerational learning activities enable you to include adults, senior citizens, youth, and children in one dynamic learning environment. In that one learning environment, they can learn from the teacher and also from the wealth of experience and new perspectives that old and young alike can bring.

How Does It Work?

Intergenerational activities are fun and challenging. Often the real challenge is not convincing people that it is a good idea, but showing them how it can work. To have a successful intergenerational component to your

VBS activities, remember that the teaching will be primarily focused on the children. Keep in mind that the passage from Deuteronomy is written for the instruction of the child. The youth and adults, however, will also benefit from the teaching. It is often the simple messages that we learn as children that we go back to time and again because they are foundational to our faith. It may be a re-learning for some of the older participants, but it can still be a meaningful and life-changing experience.

There are a number of ways that you can incorporate intergenerational learning into your VBS program. If the intergenerational learning model is new for your church, you may choose to do VBS just for the kids but use the intergenerational options presented in the Closing Program included in this *Time-Stone Travelers*™ book. Or you may want to design VBS so that families are together during the opening and closing assembly times but break into age groups for the Bible story and main activity times.

Another option is to teach just one of the Discovery Sites to an intergenerational group. Invite the members of children's families to come to VBS on the day that their child or children will be in that particular Discovery Sites. This option could easily be combined with the opening and closing assembly option. You may also choose to do a one-day event where all the Discovery Sites are set up as learning centers and families are free to travel to each one in one-hour intervals, participating in the activities, games, and Bible stories at each.

Finally, the youth, adults, and kids of your church will get excited about an entire intergenerational VBS. Read on for ideas and tips to make your intergenerational event run smoothly.

What Does a Five-Session, Intergenerational Program Look Like?

Preparation for this intergenerational VBS will follow the same basic steps outlined for the traditional VBS, including planning, recruiting, training, promoting, and so on. Set up your registration and attendance just as you would for the traditional VBS, assigning families to different groups that will rotate to a different Discovery Site each day. You will need one Leader and three or four Helpers/Actors in each Discovery Site, as well as one Helper to travel with each group. Since parents will be in the Discovery Site with their kids, you will want to communicate to them from the beginning that their participation with activities and discipline will keep things running smoothly.

Before VBS begins, talk to five families who will be involved and ask them for their help in the opening assemblies. Give each of the five families one of the songs on the *Time-Stone Travelers*™ CD and ask that they learn it, come up with some hand motions, and be ready to teach it to the others at VBS during the opening assembly time. If you have a number of families willing to participate, you may also want to write a short *(five-minute)* skit for each day and have families act it out.

In the Discovery Site each day, the activities and Bible story will be presented just as they are for the traditional VBS. Encourage the Leaders to choose the games and crafts that will appeal to the widest variety of ages. Parents and youth should participate in making the crafts but may need to be reminded that it is the process of the whole family doing it together, not the best finished product, that is most important. For some of the crafts, you may want to assign different steps to different age levels so that each person contributes a specific thing to the final product.

The Bible Memory activity will be a great time for all age levels to participate together, as many of the youth and adults may not already know the Key Verse for the day. Use the Bible Memory activities suggested in the Discovery Sites. You may want to divide your group into families or age levels. If the groups are made up of families, they should learn the verse that corresponds to the age of the youngest child.

Since VBS is designed so all of the activities of one session happen in the individual Discovery Sites, there is a great deal of flexibility in adapting the program to meet your schedule. An intergenerational learning time can last between one hour and three hours simply by picking and choosing the games and crafts that you would like to do in each Discovery Site. Feel free to adapt the materials to meet your needs and enjoy the process of learning together.

Above all, keep in mind that the church is about bringing people together. As the writer of Hebrews put it, "Not forsaking the assembling of ourselves together, as the manner of some is; but exhorting one another: and so much the more, as ye see the day approaching." *(Heb. 10:25).*

As you prepare for your VBS, look for ways to teach the entire church about God's love for His children— even the adults!

Outdoor Option

Kids love to be outdoors! If the weather in your area permits and you have a park or open area nearby, consider doing an outdoor VBS. Being outside will help kids feel part of the outdoor settings and give them even more opportunities for experiential learning. If you choose this custom option, the program can be used exactly as it is described in the Director's Guide section—but outside!

Be sure to think through the following issues:

- **If you are using a public park, does the area need to be reserved or do you need a permit?**
- **Does your schedule need to change at all to allow more time for transitions?**
- **How will you transport the items needed?**
- **Is there a covered, secure area where you can set things up and leave them during VBS?**
- **Is there a place at the church where you can store items before and during VBS?**
- **Do you have plenty of water for the kids to drink throughout the days of VBS?**
- **Do you have plenty of sunscreen for the kids and leaders?**
- **What is the backup plan in case the weather turns bad?**

If this custom option sounds good to you but you can't work out all the details, you might try one of these ideas: Simplify the outdoor option by having only a couple of Discovery Sites outside; hold a one-day VBS where all the Discovery Sites are set up outside for a day; or have an area where kids from any of the Discovery Sites can go outside for some of the crafts, activities, and games. Even a few minutes of fresh air during a game can make the day more fun and exciting. Be creative and enjoy the beautiful world around you that God created!

Camp

Time-Stone Travelers™ is a great curriculum to use for camp! It is easy to expand and fits well into a camp setting. The VBS part of the camp can run just as a basic VBS would run in a church. The Discovery Sites can remain set up all week and groups of kids can rotate between them during the VBS time. You will want to add some camp activities as well. Below is a sample of what a VBS camp schedule might look like.

Use the people and resources in your church and at your camp to come up with the sports activities and electives for the afternoon time.

Alternative Schedules:

Besides the more extensive custom options mentioned here, there are many ways to adapt the VBS schedule to meet your needs. Here are some sample adaptations of the basic VBS schedule. Feel free to mix and match until your VBS is the way you like it.

Daily schedule for camp

7:45	Rise and Shine!
8:15	Breakfast
9:00	Cleanup time
9:15	Leaders meet for prayer
9:30	Opening assembly with singing
10:00	VBS sites
12:00	Lunch
1:00	VBS wrap-up and closing assembly
1:30	Rest and reflection time
2:00	Sports activities and electives
4:00	Singing and preparation for closing program
5:30	Cleanup
6:00	Dinner
7:30	Evening entertainment/campfire
8:30	Small group prayer time in cabins
9:00	Lights out

Five Consecutive Saturdays

If time, space, or staffing are issues for you, consider doing VBS on five consecutive Saturdays! This will spread out the time for preparation and allow working adults to participate. You may set up all five Discovery Sites and leave them set up for the five weeks, or set up one Discovery Site for each Saturday. If you choose to set up only one Discovery Site per week, you will need to consider that all of your kids will be in one place and how to move them all smoothly through the Discovery Site.

Evening VBS

Evening VBS is also an excellent way to get volunteers involved who may work during the day. You can use the basic three-hour schedule *(given on page D.26)* and adapt it to fit into the evenings. This is also a great way to provide VBS for the entire family. By using the free, downloadable Youth and Adult Guides that correlate with *Time-Stone Travelers*™ *(see www.cookvbs.com)*, family members will all be studying the same lessons. You may want to hold VBS from 5:30–8:30 p.m. to make sure that people have time to make it after work but end before it gets dark or too late for younger kids.

One-Day VBS

A one-day VBS can be a big hit! Because each of the Discovery Sites stands alone, children can participate in any of the Discovery Sites during the day and still have a great time. If space is limited, you may want to choose three Discovery Sites and have children rotate

One-day VeBS schedule

8:30	Staff meets for prayer and devotion
9:00	Opening ceremony and group formation
9:45	Rotation to one of three sites *(Intro and Bible Story, Game, Craft, or Snack)*
11:00	Rotation to another of three sites *(Intro and Bible Story, Game, or Craft)*
12:15	Gather for box lunch
1:00	Rotation to last of three sites *(Intro and Bible Story, Game, or Craft)*
2:45	Gather for cafeteria style snacks
3:00	Wrap-up and closing assembly
3:30	Dismissal

throughout the day. Here is a suggested one-day schedule using three of the Discovery Sites.

10-Day VBS

Expanding VBS is simple! There are plenty of crafts and games to choose from, and children often like playing a favorite game or doing a favorite activity more than once! To expand this VBS, you can present the opening activity and the Bible story, plus choose a craft and a game from those provided in the Discovery Site. On the second day, do a review of the Bible story and then start with the Bible Memory activity and finish out the lesson using the crafts and games that you did not use during day one. Children will spend two days in each Discovery Site, reinforcing the lesson and the Key Verse for that site. To make up time that would have been spent on the whole lesson in the Discovery Site, consider spending part of each day preparing for the closing program or extending the missions and/or singing time each day.

Alternative Uses

Children's Church

Time-Stone Travelers™ is a great curriculum to use in your children's church ministry. It's easy to expand and fits well into a children's church setting. Each VBS site can be set up to use for two weeks. There are plenty of crafts and games to choose from, and children often like playing a favorite game or doing a favorite activity more than once! On the first Sunday for each Discovery Site, you can present the opening activity and the Bible story, plus choose a craft and a game from those provided. On the second Sunday, do a review of the Bible story and then start with the Bible Memory activity and finish out the lesson using the crafts and games that you did not use the previous week. Children will spend two days in each Discovery Site, reinforcing the lesson and the Key Bible Verse for that site. On the eleventh and twelfth Sundays of the quarter, consider spending time preparing for a program to present to parents. The children can work on the songs and Key Bible Verses. Older children or Helpers can work on the puppet skits as shown for the closing program. Then on the last Sunday of the quarter, invite the parents to join the children for a time of worship as the children present their program.

Christian School Bible Study

Time-Stone Travelers™ would also be an excellent way to involve your students in a Christian school setting to make discoveries about God's good rules for them. Involve your class in creating the murals for each of the Discovery Sites. A team-teaching approach to this would work well if several classes joined together. Each classroom could be responsible for creating a mural and decorating for one of the Discovery Sites. Each teacher could prepare to teach the Bible story for that Discovery Site. Then each class could rotate on a following day *(or week)* to one of the other classrooms to learn about the Bible truths taught in that lesson. At the end of five days *(or weeks)* the children will have covered all the material. The curriculum could also be expanded to fit a 10-day schedule.

VeBS® as Outreach

Time-Stone Travelers™ is designed as a fun-filled experience that draws children into understanding the 10 Commandments. The fun aspect of this time-travel theme will appeal to unchurched children in your community. Children come for the fun, but discover the love and grace of the Lord while being challenged to follow Him. VBS is about outreach and discipleship.

This VBS book provides two resources to help your Leaders and Helpers talk with children who are seeking salvation. One resource is the Leader Hint "How to lead children to Jesus and into God's family" *(page R.12)*. The second is the "Discovering Jesus as Your Savior" brochure on pages R.82-83. Copy the

"Discovering Jesus" path for Leaders to use and then give to children to take home. The parent letter on the back will help parents understand and support decisions their child has made. The blank area on the back side can be customized to provide information about the worship and Bible study opportunities at your church. You might include an invitation too! Use the space to inform new Christians and their families on how your church can support them in their growing faith.

Online Resources

Valuable resources for you, your VBS leaders, plus your kids and their families are online now at **www.cookvbs.com**. Leaders will find spiritual encouragement, practical teaching tips, and helpful printable resources. When your VBS gets underway, tell your kids and their families about the web site. They'll find additional resources to help parents lead their families to discover Jesus. Get connected and explore the many ways God can work through VBS.

VBS for Youth

Most young people want to win in life, but many aren't sure how. *Time-Stone Travelers*™ *Youth Guide* is the VBS youth guide that correlates to the *Time-Stone Travelers*™ VBS. This resource helps church leaders teach teens about God's wise teaching for their lives. *Time-Stone Travelers*™ *Youth Guide* will lead your teens, and the friends they invite to VBS, to explore Bible stories that teach about the benefits of following God's 10 Commandments. Teens will encounter the truth that God's Word is an excellent guide. *"Teach me, O Lord, the way of thy statutes; and I shall keep it unto*

the end. Give me understanding, and I shall keep thy law; yea, I shall observe it with my whole heart" **—Psalm 119:33-34**. *Time-Stone Travelers*™ *Youth Guide* is available free, online, through the Cook Communications Ministries' VBS web site, www.cookvbs.com. When you log on, the home page will show an icon for the *Time-Stone Travelers*™ *Youth Guide* for use with *Time-Stone Travelers*™ VBS. Click on the *Time-Stone Travelers*™ *Youth Guide* icon and follow the instructions for downloading and printing.

Each *Time-Stone Travelers*™ *Youth Guide* session is based on high-energy games and real small-group discussion. Your students will be challenged to Reach In and deepen their own commitments to Jesus through personal Bible study and reflection. *Time-Stone Travelers*™ *Youth Guide* also challenges kids to Reach Out and get involved in leading their friends to Christ. Your students will belong and take ownership of their youth ministry as well as take the lead in inviting their friends into a relationship with Christ. *Time-Stone Travelers*™ *Youth Guide* leads your youth to take Bible truths and put them into faithful action by developing a relationship with God and trusting His commandments as they develop healthy relationships with family, friends, and others.

VBS for Adults

There might be some parents who would like to stick around while their kids are in VBS. Some of them might like to be in a study of their own. If this happens, we have FREE Bible studies just for adults that correspond with the five Training Camps in *Time-Stone Travelers*™

VBS, so parents and kids will have something to talk about on the way home from VBS. As with all Cook materials, these studies are age-appropriate, and tackle relevant issues that many "grown-ups" face today. You can find a link to download the studies on Cook's VBS site, **www.cookvbs.com**. When you log on, you'll see an icon for the adult guides. Click on the icon and follow the instructions for downloading and printing your own copy of the *Time-Stone Travelers*™ VBS Adult Guide. **www.cookvbs.com**

Using This Guide

There are many tasks and responsibilities on the shoulders of a director, so we have given you a guide to take you through VBS from beginning to end without a hitch. The resources and information in this step-by-step guide will help you with all your key responsibilities as a director. From Introduction to Closing Program you will be guided step-by-step through the events of *Time-Stone Travelers*™ and what needs to be done in each area. The Planning Calendar *(on pages D.13-14)* will help you to plan out your time and manage the different aspects of directing VBS.

Referring to the Table of Contents you will notice that each section starts with a unique prefix:

D	—	(Director's Guide)
E1	—	(Site 1 Guide)
E2	—	(Site 2 Guide)
E3	—	(Site 3 Guide)
E4	—	(Site 4 Guide)
E5	—	(Site 5 Guide)
P1	—	(Preschool Site 1 Guide)
P2	—	(Preschool Site 2 Guide)
P3	—	(Preschool Site 3 Guide)
P4	—	(Preschool Site 4 Guide)
P5	—	(Preschool Site 5 Guide)
R	—	(Reproducible Resources)

There are four sections featuring a durable, colorful, tabbed section divider for the Director's Guide, Elementary Sites, Preschool Guide, and Reproducible Resources. Page numbers for each section run sequentially starting with the first page of each section. However, notice that the Elementary and Preschool Site Guides are numbered individually to assist the Leaders as they work with each of them.

Comprehensive Supply Lists

You will find a comprehensive general supply list on pages D.17-24 for the five Elementary Sites, and a list of Preschool supplies on pages P.4-11. These lists are broken down by Sites and by activity *(e.g., crafts, snacks, etc.)*, allowing you to coordinate your supply needs before requesting donations or making purchases. For your Leaders' convenience, each Site section lists the supplies needed for that particular Site.

Everything in this guide is fully reproducible for use in the purchaser's VBS program. Pages have been perforated for your convenience and ease of use. Feel free to make this book your own! Add your own flair and ideas to it as you develop the program best suited to the kids who regularly attend your church and live in the community around your church.

Finally, trust God, and have fun! And before you go any further in this guide, stop and ask God to help you throughout this process. Then prepare to see Him touch the hearts of children with the knowledge that they can learn and grow in their walk with Jesus.

Quick View Icons

The icons shown below will help Leaders and Helpers quickly get to specific points in their lesson. The Preschool Guide will use some different/additional icons as noted below.

 **Bible Memory Time**

 **Bible Story Time**

 **Music Time**

 **Game Time**

 **Snack Time**

 **Craft Time**

 **Application Time**

 **Time-Stone Take Off**

 **Site Supplies**

PRESCHOOL ICONS

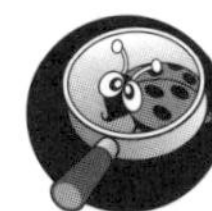 **Hands-on Exploration**

 **Take-Home Bible Verse**

 **Home Activity**

Electronic Clip Art

In addition to the lively music on the *Time-Stone Travelers*™ CD, we've added a collection of electronic images for use in creating your promotional materials. Images are accessible by Macintosh or PC users. Thumbnail representations of the images are printed on the inside front cover of this guide.

Please consult your software manual for the proper way to import images.

In addition to the clip art images, we've also included editable PDF documents so that you can "fill-in-the-blanks" with specific event information. These include a full-color poster, bulletin insert, doorknob hangers, name badges, postcards, and certificate of completion.

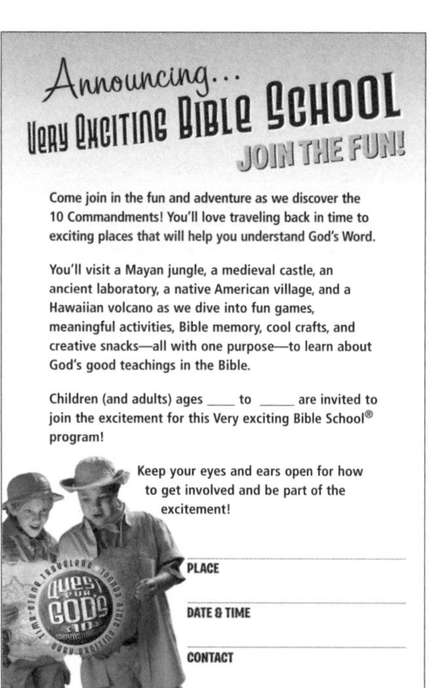

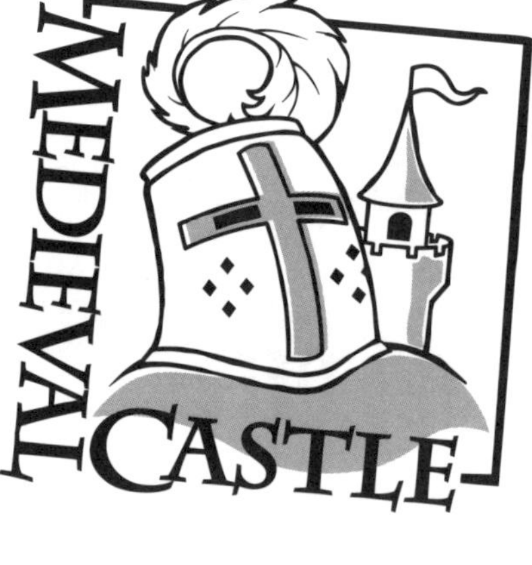

Planning Calendar

4 Months Prior

- ○ Begin praying for the Leaders and children who will be part of VBS.
- ○ Establish a VBS planning committee and/or select the director *(page D.14)*.
- ○ Establish the VBS dates on your church's calendar.
- ○ Establish a working budget for VBS *(page D.16)*.

3 Months Prior

- ○ Begin holding regular planning meetings. Assign responsibilities to the members of the VBS committee. Smaller churches can ask one person to fill multiple positions. *(Refer to Recruit section on pages D.56-62 for recruitment resources and descriptions of all positions.)*
- ○ Recruit someone to oversee setup of all Discovery Sites. *(See Creating Discovery Sites on page D.29.)*
- ○ Choose Leaders and Helpers *(one Helper per 6 to 8 kids plus three to four "actors")* for each site.
- ○ Recruit someone to be in charge of daily opening assembly time when all children meet together *(page D.29)*.
- ○ Recruit someone to be in charge of the Closing Program *(page D.50)*.
- ○ Recruit someone to be responsible for nursery and preschoolers.
- ○ Recruit craft coordinators *(one per Discovery Site would be ideal, but since all crafts are done within the Discovery Sites, Helpers can also fill this role).*
- ○ Recruit someone to be in charge of snacks. *(Again, use your Helpers in this area.)*
- ○ Recruit outreach and publicity staff.
- ○ Recruit someone to coordinate registration.
- ○ Recruit people to pray, to provide transportation, and to do follow-up.

2 Months Prior

- ○ Have the Leaders who are responsible for each Discovery Site select committees to plan how each environment will be created. *(See Creating Discovery Sites on page D.29.)*
- ○ Make assignments for each Discovery Site, such as one person to organize and order craft materials, someone to be in charge of props, refreshments, etc.
- ○ Begin publicity within your church. *(See Promote beginning on page D.71.)*
- ○ Begin holding regular staff training sessions. *(See Training beginning on page D.59 for information, training resources, and meeting agendas.)*

6 Weeks Prior

- ○ Begin community publicity through posters, newspapers, and "community events" radio spots *(page D.71-73)*.
- ○ Make sure committees continue to meet regularly.
- ○ Make sure Leaders are beginning to prepare.
- ○ Continue training for all VBS staff.

4 Weeks Prior

- ○ Make announcements in your church to create interest and enthusiasm *(page D.72)*.
- ○ Begin a registration drive. As kids are registered, decide how you will group them *(by age, grade, mixed ages, etc.)* and assign them to a team of children. *(Registration on page D.25)*
- ○ Begin preparing for the closing program and decide which option to use. *(See page D.50.)*
- ○ Double-check all props, costumes, music, snacks, and so on.
- ○ Continue training for all VBS staff.
- ○ Make sure the Helpers playing characters are beginning to prepare.

1 Week Prior

○ Review details with Leaders and committees.

○ Make signs to help the first day go smoothly ("Check-in," "Registration," and so on).

○ Prepare a checklist for each Discovery Site, detailing all items that will be needed the first day of VBS.

○ Make copies of the take-home pages and Travel Journals for each Discovery Site *(based on the number of registered children)* and distribute to Leaders.

○ Prepare for a devotion time with staff before VBS each day *(pages D.64-69)*.

Day Before

○ Set up the sites and make sure everything is ready for the first day!

○ See that final plans have been made for the closing program at the end of VBS.

○ Meet with the VBS staff for prayer.

1 Week After

○ Families, staff, and director complete evaluations *(pages R.42-44)*.

○ Activate the follow-up committee *(pages D.74-75)*.

○ Review your budget and keep information along with other general comments on file for next year's VBS director.

○ Update the name and address list of Leaders and children for follow-up as well as next year's registration and promotion.

Key Players

Use the following information as you look for people to be key players in VBS. This information will help you as you plan and will give people a good idea of what you are asking them to do as they consider their involvement in VBS. *(See pages D.56-57 for more information on recruiting staff.)*

VBS Director

This person oversees the entire VBS, coordinating and helping the staff as needed with promotion, preparation, and follow-up.

Leaders (2 per Discovery Site)

Leaders should be people who enjoy interacting with or leading groups. They will remain at their designated Discovery Sites and should portray only one role during VBS. The two Leaders per Discovery Site work as a team to present the activities and Bible story. The Leaders prepare only one lesson and give that lesson to each of the five groups of kids.

Leaders and Helpers should dress in character for the site they are working in. Suggestions for appropriate attire are listed at the beginning of each site *(See Site Coordinators.)* Keep your attire comfortable while enhancing the theme.

Helpers

Recruit three or four Helpers for each site who can play the roles of Josh, Will, Ellen, and at some sites one more character. They should be able to either learn or read the brief skit at the start and end of each lesson. In addition, recruit one Helper for every six to eight children. As children go to a different Discovery Site every day, they are accompanied by the same Helper. As the children arrive, Helpers should gather their groups, go with them to opening assembly, accompany them daily to each site, and assist as needed. Mature junior high and senior high young people make excellent Helpers. The Helpers have the unique and exciting opportunity to build meaningful relationships with the children and guide them toward God's love through their actions and informal teaching times.

Other Staff

Depending on how many volunteers you use, you could have people coordinate snacks or crafts. You may also want people to create the Discovery Sites and to promote and follow up within the church and your community. You can also rely on volunteers to gather props before VBS. Refer to page D.56 for more information on recruiting people based on their spiritual gifts.

Overview Chart

SITE	Mayan Jungle	Medieval Castle	Ancient Laboratory	Hawk's Village	Hawaiian Volcano
BIBLE STORY	Honor God; Commandments 1, 2 (Exod. 20:3-4)	Honor God; Commandments 3, 4 (Exod. 20:7-8)	Honor your father and mother; Commandment 5 (Exod. 20:12)	Don't hurt others; Commandments 6, 7, 8, 9 (Exod. 20:13-16)	Be happy with what you have; Commandment 10 (Exod. 20:17)
KEY VERSE	*"My soul, wait thou only upon God; for my expectation is from him. He only is my rock and my salvation: he is my defence; I shall not be moved."* —Psalm 62:5-6	*"There remaineth therefore a rest to the people of God. For he that is entered into his rest, he also hath ceased from his own works, as God did from his."* –Hebrews 4:9-10	*"Children, obey your parents in the Lord: for this is right."* –Ephesians 6:1	*"Thou shalt love the Lord thy God with all thy heart, and with all thy soul, and with all thy strength, and with all thy mind; and thy neighbour as thyself."* –Luke 10:27	*"Therefore I say unto you, Take no thought for your life, what ye shall eat; neither for the body, what ye shall put on. The life is more than meat, and the body is more than raiment."* –Luke 12:22-23
CONCEPT	There is only one God.	God deserves our worship.	Honor and obey your father and mother as God has commanded.	God wants us to treat others with kindness.	God wants us to be happy with what He has given us.
RESPONSE	Children will believe that there is only one God and they should worship only Him.	Children will learn to use the Lord's name only with respect and will set aside time to worship God.	Children will understand that they should respect, honor, and obey their father and mother because God has given parents the responsibility of taking care of their children.	Children will learn not to hurt others, but to treat others with kindness as God wants them to.	Children will take steps to be satisfied with the things they have and not want the things that others have.

Budget

DIRECTOR'S GUIDE

Developing a budget is one of the most important things you will do to plan your VBS.

Most churches will already have an amount budgeted for VBS. Once you know the total amount, it is a good idea to break down how much of that budget will be spent in each of the areas of VBS. Whether your budget is large or small, good planning means that money is available right up to the end of VBS. If VBS has been done in your church in previous years, the budgets from those VBS programs will be your best tools.

To develop your budget, it is a good idea first to make a list of all the categories in which money could be spent and break those down into specifics. Next, determine how many children you will have and how much income *(if any)* there will be from registration or other sources. Use the budget chart *(see page R.2)* to help you plan your budget. Some of the main expenses are listed. List any other main categories you can think of that apply to your situation and then break them down into specifics and keep track of money spent as you go.

Keeping track of a budget is as important as creating one, but sometimes more difficult—especially if there are a number of people involved. If other people from your VBS team are purchasing props or supplies, be sure they know how much to spend and how to report to you the amount spent. The reimbursement form *(see page R.3)* is one way to handle reimbursement records. This form can be copied and handed out to VBS staff at the beginning of the program or as needs arise.

The records that you keep will be very valuable to next year's director, so do your best to keep them accurate. Make notes on the budget at the end of VBS for next year!

Funding Ideas

- Take a VBS offering in your church.

- Hold a fund-raising event.

- Get supply donations.

- Get snack donations.

- Allow church members to sponsor a child by giving a certain amount to VBS. *(This is also a great way to get people without kids involved in VBS—you may want to choose the intergenerational option for the closing program so they can see what the child they sponsored has been doing all week!)*

- Choose ways of showing appreciation and doing follow-up using the services of people in the church rather than purchasing and giving gifts.

- Network with other churches in your area that are doing *Time-Stone Travelers*™ to see if there are ways to share props and supplies.

Supplies

All of the supplies for *Time-Stone Travelers*™ are common items and easy to obtain. This may seem to be a daunting task; however, with the aid of some organized volunteers and the comprehensive supply list below, you'll have it done in no time!

Your church may already have some supplies available for your use during VBS. For the remaining supplies, you may want to get donations from church members by sending out a list of needed supplies. After donations have been gathered, purchase the remaining items on the list.

Each activity, craft, game, and snack in this *Time-Stone Travelers*™ Step-by-Step Guide has a corresponding list of supplies that are referenced in the PG *(page number)* column in the compiled list below. You may want to cross off the items you already have on hand, and pencil in the quantities you need for each item based on the estimated number of children attending your VBS.

Supplies for Activities, Games, Snacks and Crafts have been placed in categories denoted by the prefix A, G, S, or C in front of each item. Numerals are listed after the prefix to keep all the supplies needed for a specific game, craft, or snack together *(C1)*. If you choose not to use a particular craft, game, or snack option, you can simply ignore the list of supplies needed for that particular option.

Supplies for Discovery Site decorations will vary, depending on your VBS plan. Please refer to suggested Discovery Site decorations in the **Setting the Scene** section of each site for recommended items and tips.

NOTE: The number of supplies listed in the TOT *(Total)* column will vary depending on the number of children attending each site, and/or the total number of teams that children are divided into. These quantities will need to be calculated when VBS registration is complete. You may want to have some extra supplies on hand for walk-in attendees.

CATEGORY & ITEM	PG	QTY	/UNIT	TOT	HAVE	NEED	✓
Common Supplies needed at each site							
Bibles		1	/site	5			
Time-Stone Travelers™ CD *(Duplicate CDs or cassettes)*		1	/site	5			
CD player or cassette player		1	/site	5			
Song lyrics on overhead transparencies		1	/site				
Overhead projector		1	/site				
Scissors, pens, pencils and colored markers		1	ea./child				
Glue, transparent tape, masking tape, stapler, hole punch							
Paper plates, cups, napkins, and utensils for snacks		1	ea./child/site				
Newspaper for table protection and paper towels for cleanup							

SITE 1: MAYAN JUNGLE

CATEGORY & ITEM	PG	QTY	/UNIT	TOT	HAVE	NEED	✓
Mayan Jungle Mural	R.70						
Copy of "The Quest Continues" student take-home paper	E1.12	1	/child				
Copy of "Travel Journal" for each child (pages R.59-66)	E1.11	1	each/child				
(A1) Large, foam-core board "replica" of the 10 Commandments tablet with the first two commandments clearly printed on it	E1.4	1	each/site				
(A1) Realistic looking, colorful, pretend snake	E1.4	1	each/site				
(A1) Soccer ball	E1.4	1	each/site				
(A1) Beautiful piece of girls' clothing`	E1.4	1	each/site				
(A1) Video game	E1.4	1	each/site				
(A2) Yellow, bigger-than-life statue (of cardboard, foam, etc.)	E1.6	1	each/site				
(A2) Bible-time clothes and throne	E1.6	1	each/actor/site				
(A2) Toy instruments (tambourines, horns, kazoos, bells, drums, etc.)	E1.6	1	each/child				
(A2) Room divider or large appliance box (to serve as fiery furnace)	E1.6	1	each/site				
(A2) Something to make sound effects of crackling fire	E1.6	1	each/site				
(A2) Yellow and red lights (can be flashlights with colored film over the lenses)	E1.6	1	each/site				
(A2) Life-size cardboard shape of a person	E1.6	1	each/site				
(A2) Ropes or binding	E1.6	1	each/actor				
(A3) Yellow banana-shaped sheets of construction paper, each with a word of the verse on it	E1.7	1	set/site				
(A3) Key Bible Verse poster on an easel	E1.7	1	each/site				
(A3) Key Bible Verse cards (page R.58)	E1.7	1	set/child				
(G1) Empty boxes and cardboard containers, taped closed	E1.8	1	set/5-7 children				
(G1) Beanbags or small foam balls	E1.8	2	ea./5-7 children				
(G2) Numerous small toys and other items (such as wooden blocks, miniature stuffed animals, etc.)	E1.9	1	assortment/site				
(G2) Blindfolds	E1.9	1	each/2 children				
(S1) Bananas or celery sticks	E1.9	1/2	each/child				
(S1) Peanut butter or cream cheese	E1.9	1	Tbsp/child				
(S1) Raisins	E1.9	5-6	pieces/child				
(S2) Banana chips	E1.9	1	Tbsp/child				
(S2) Dried pineapple pieces	E1.9	1	Tbsp/child				
(S2) Dried apricots, chopped	E1.9	1	Tbsp/child				
(S2) Dried cranberries	E1.9	1	Tbsp/child				
(C1) Blank stationery or card stock, cut/folded to fit into envelopes	E1.10	3	each/child				

CATEGORY & ITEM	PG	QTY	/UNIT	TOT	HAVE	NEED	✓

SITE 1: MAYAN JUNGLE *(continued)*

CATEGORY & ITEM	PG	QTY	/UNIT	TOT	HAVE	NEED	✓
(C1) Envelopes	E1.10	3	each/child				
(C1) Colored chalk	E1.10		variety/site				
(C1) Water	E1.10	several	cups/site				
(C1) 9" x 13" foil pans	E1.10	1	3-4/children				
(C1) 150 sand paper, cut into 2" squares	E1.10	1	piece/chalk				
(C1) White card stock, cut into 3" heart shapes *(or a size that will look nice on your blank stationery)*	E1.10	3	each/child				
(C2) Mailing tube 1 1/2" x 15" with end stoppers	E1.10	1	each/site				
(C2) Uncooked rice	E1.10	1	half cup/site				
(C2) Nails 3/4" - 1"	E1.10	80-100	each/site				
(C2) Brown, self-adhesive paper, 15" x 6"	E1.10	1	each/site				
(C2) Funnel	E1.10	1	each/site				
(C2) Green construction paper *(two different shades)*	E1.10	8-10	sheets/site				
(C2) Hammer	E1.10	1	each/site				
(C2) Key Bible Verse printed on a 6" x 2" paper	E1.10	1	each/site				
(C2) Yarn in various colors *(optional)*	E1.10		variety/site				
(A5) Piece of artificial fruit	E1.10	1	each/site				
(A6) Clean stones for the Time Stones	E1.12	1	each/child				

SITE 2: MEDIEVAL CASTLE

CATEGORY & ITEM	PG	QTY	/UNIT	TOT	HAVE	NEED	✓
Medieval Castle Mural	R.71						
Copy of "The Quest Continues" student take-home paper	E2.12	1	/child				
Copy of "Travel Journal" for each child *(pages R.59-66)*	E2.11	1	each/child				
(A7) Large, foam-core board "replica" of the 10 Commandments tablet with Commandments 3 and 4 clearly printed on it	E2.4	1	each/site				
(A7) Toy swords and shields	E2.4	2	set/site				
(A7) Pillows or cushions	E2.4	2	each/site				
(A7) Wall calendar	E2.4	1	each/site				
(A8) Simple Bible-time costumes	E2.6	1	each/actor				
(A9) Key Bible Verse poster on an easel	E2.7	1	each/site				
(A9) Key Bible Verse cards *(page R.58)*	E2.7	1	set/child				
(A9) Card stock sheets, each with one word of the verse in block printing	E2.7	1	set/team				
(G3) Something to serve as a "castle wall" *(large screen, blanket draped over a rope, plywood board securely propped up, stacked boxes, etc.)*	E2.8	1	wall/team				
(G3) Soft lobbing objects *(foam balls, bean bags, water balloons, etc.)* in buckets or boxes	E2.8	1	set/team				
(G3) Beach towels, blankets, or burlap bags	E2.8	1-3	each/team				

CATEGORY & ITEM	PG	QTY	/UNIT	TOT	HAVE	NEED	✓

SITE 2: MEDIEVAL CASTLE *(continued)*

CATEGORY & ITEM	PG	QTY	/UNIT	TOT	HAVE	NEED	✓
(G4) Colorful index cards with a name of God on each	E2.9	1	set/team				
(G4) Cotton swabs	E2.9	1	handful/team				
(G4) Boxes or other containers	E2.9	4	each/team				
(S3) French bread cubes	E2.9	several	each/child				
(S3) Cheese cubes	E2.9	2-4	each/child				
(S3) Pewter or wooden plates, goblets, and bowl	E2.9	1	set/site				
(S3) Tapestry table runner *(optional)*	E2.9	1	each/site				
(S4) Apples, sliced	E2.9	1	slice/child				
(S4) Pears, sliced	E2.9	1	slice/child				
(S4) Plums, sliced	E2.9	1	slice/child				
(S4) Seedless grapes	E2.9	2-3	each/child				
(S4) Small doilies	E2.9	1	each/child				
(C3) Fleece cut in 16" x 18" pieces	E2.10	2	each/child				
(C3) Straight pins	E2.10	several	each/site				
(C3) Sliver of soap bar or chalk	E2.10	1	each/site				
(C3) Fiberfill stuffing	E2.10	4-6 oz.	each/child				
(C4) Poster board in various colors	E2.10	1	2-3/children				
(C4) Clear packing tape	E2.10	1	roll/site				
(C4) Assortment of 1" pom-poms	E2.10	6	each/child				
(A11) Pillows *(may be towels stuffed in pillow cases)*	E2.11	1	each/child				
(A12) Clean stones for the Time Stones	E2.12	1	each/child				

SITE 3: ANCIENT LABORATORY

CATEGORY & ITEM	PG	QTY	/UNIT	TOT	HAVE	NEED	✓
Ancient Laboratory Mural	R.72						
Copy of "The Quest Continues" student take-home paper	E3.12	1	/child				
Copy of "Travel Journal" for each child *(pages R.59-66*	E3.11	1	each/child				
(A13) Non-breakable, clear beaker of colored fluid	E3.4	1	each/site				
(A13) Dried plants still on the stems	E3.4	1	handful/site				
(A13) Thick book covered in brown paper *(covered with powder for dust)*	E3.4	1	each/site				
(A13) Fountain pen and parchment paper	E3.4	1	set/site				
(A14) Copies of the Bible story, cut to fit inside a Bible	E3.6	3	each/site				
(A14) Large, foam-core board "replica" of the 10 Commandments tablet with Commandment 5 clearly printed on it	E3.4	1	each/site				
(A15) Poster board puzzle of the Key Bible verse	E3.7	2	each/site				
(A15) Key Bible Verse poster on an easel	E3.7	1	each/site				
(A15) Key Bible Verse cards *(page R.58)*	E3.7	1	set/child				
(G5) Plastic jars half full of colored water	E3.8	1	each/team				

SITE 3: ANCIENT LABORATORY (continued)

CATEGORY & ITEM	PG	QTY	/UNIT	TOT	HAVE	NEED	✓
(G5) Cans of dried plant material *(leaves, twigs, etc.)*	E3.8	1	each/team				
(G5) Paper lunch bags filled with wood chips or pebbles	E3.8	1	each/team				
(G5) Fabric bags of dirt	E3.8	1	each/team				
(G5) Tongs	E3.8	1	each/team				
(G5) Stuffed critters *(snake, lizard, alligator, etc.)*	E3.8	1	each/team				
(G5) Laundry baskets or boxes	E3.8	1	each/team				
(G6) Signs that read Respect/Disrespect	E3.8	1	set/site				
(S5) Instant gelatin in various flavors	E3.9	1/2	cup/child				
(S5) Whipped topping	E3.9	1/4	cup/child				
(S5) Various cake-decorating sprinkles in fun shapes	E3.9	1	Tbsp./child				
(S6) Animal cookies or other small shortbread or sugar cookies	E3.9	4-5	each/child				
(S6) Variety of creative dipping toppings *(yogurt, whipped cream, flavored sauces, melted butterscotch chips)*	E3.9	4-5	each/site				
(C5) Cardboard boxes with lids, about 4" x 5" x 1"	E3.10	1	each/child				
(C5) Poster paint or spray paint	E3.10	1	each/site				
(C5) Felt rectangles, 1/4" smaller than the boxes	E3.10	1	each/child				
(C5) Colorful paper, 1/2" smaller than the boxes	E3.10	1	each/child				
(C5) Paint pens in assorted colors	E3.10	1	set/site				
(C6) Potpourri ingredients *(dried rose pedals, dried orange slices, lemon peels, cloves, cinnamon sticks, dried straw flowers)*	E3.10	1	handful/child				
(C6) Fragrant oil	E3.10	2-3	drops/child				
(C6) Paper plates	E3.10	1	each/child				
(C6) Small jars with 3" diameter opening	E3.10	1	each/child				
(C6) White netting, cut in 6" squares	E3.10	1	each/child				
(C6) 1/4" ribbon, 22" long	E3.10	1	each/child				
(C6) Rubber bands	E3.10	1	each/child				
(A17) Clean stones for the Time Stones	E3.12	1	each/child				

SITE 4: HAWK'S VILLAGE

CATEGORY & ITEM	PG	QTY	/UNIT	TOT	HAVE	NEED	✓
Hawk's Village Mural	R.73						
Copy of "The Quest Continues" student take-home paper	E4.11	1	/child				
Copy of "Travel Journal" for each child *(pages R.59-66)*	E4.10	1	each/child				
(A18) Rustic baskets	E4.4	1	each/site				
(A18) Wigwam	E4.4	1	each/site				
(A19) Cloth or bandanna	E4.5	1	each/site				
(A19) Towels in different colors	E4.5	2	each/site				

SITE 4: HAWK'S VILLAGE *(continued)*

CATEGORY & ITEM	PG	QTY	/UNIT	TOT	HAVE	NEED	✓
(A19) Strips of fabric or rope	E4.5	2	each/site				
(A19) Coins	E4.5	a few	each/site				
(A19) Small jug	E4.5	1	each/site				
(A19) Donkey or horse *(rocking horse, cardboard replica)*	E4.5	1	each/site				
(A19) Large, foam-core board "replica" of the 10 Commandments tablet with Commandments 6, 7, 8, 9 clearly printed on it	E4.5	1	each/site				
(A20) Key BIble Verse poster on an easel	E4.6	1	each/site				
(A20) Key Bible Verse cards *(page R.58)*	E4.6	1	set/child				
(A20) Four extra verse cards, written and underlined as directed	E4.6	1	set/site				
(G7) Playground balls	E4.7	1-3	each/wite				
(G8) Bean bags	E4.7	1	each/site				
(G8) Bag of small treats *(such as individually wrapped candies, stickers, etc.)*	E4.7	1	each/site				
(G8) Construction paper sheets, each naming a category of person	E4.7	6-8	each/site				
(S7) Fish crackers	E4.8	1	handful/child				
(S7) Small, new fishnet *(the kind used for scooping aquarium fish)*	E4.8	1	each/site				
(S7) Large, clear glass or plastic bowl	E4.8	1	each/site				
(S7) Clear, plastic cups	E4.8	1	each/child				
(S8) Store-bought or homemade blueberry muffins	E4.9	1	each/chld				
(S8) Fresh or frozen blueberries in a bowl	E4.9	1	Tbsp/child				
(S8) Hand wipes for blueberry stains	E4.9	1	each/child				
(C7) Sandpaper, 4 1/2" x 5 1/2"	E4.9	1	each/child				
(C7) Jute or leather lacing, cut in 12" strips	E4.9	1	each/child				
(C7) Examples of historic Native American artwork	E4.9	2-3	example/site				
(C7) Scrap paper	E4.9	1	each/child				
(C7) Paintbrushes	E4.9	1	each/child				
(C7) Water	E4.9	a few	Tbsp/site				
(C7) Colored craft sand in a variety of colors	E4.9	1	set/site				
(C7) Foil	E4.9	several	each/site				
(C7) Disposable cups	E4.9	several	each/site				
(C8) Clear, bowl-shaped plastic lids, 8"-10" in diameter	E4.9	1	each/child				
(C8) Clear, flat plastic lids, 4" in diameter	E4.9	1	each/child				
(C8) 12" long dowels or sticks, small than 1/8" in diameter	E4.9	12	each/child				
(C8) Jute, 2' long	E4.9	3	each/child				
(C8) Zipper-closure plastic bags filled with birdseed	E4.9	1	each/child				
(A23) Clean stones for the Time Stones	E4.11	1	each/child				

CATEGORY & ITEM	PG	QTY	/UNIT	TOT	HAVE	NEED	✓
SITE 5: HAWAIIAN VOLCANO							
Hawaiian Volcano Mural	R.74						
Copy of "The Quest Continues" student take-home paper	E5.11	1	/child				
Copy of "Travel Journal" for each child *(pages R.59-66)*	E5.10	1	each/child				
(A24) Binoculars	E5.4	1	each/site				
(A24) Cell phone	E5.4	1	each/site				
(A25) Bible-time costumes for Naboth, Elijah, and Ahab--simple for Naboth and Elijah, royal for Ahab	E5.6	1	each/actor				
(A25) Bunch of fake grapes with a few leaves	E5.6	1	each/site				
(A25) Piece of burlap or torn cloth	E5.6	1	each/site				
(A25) Large, foam-core board "replica" of the 10 Commandments tablet with Commandment 10 clearly printed on it	E5.6	1	each/site				
(A26) Key Bible verse poster on an easel	E5.7	1	each/site				
(A26) Key Bible verse cards *(page R.58)*	E5.7	1	set/child				
(G9) Crumpled-up newspaper balls	E5.8	several	each/child				
(G9) Large container *(such as a garbage can)* covered in shelf paper to look like a volcano	E5.8	1	each/site				
(G9) Timer	E5.8	1	each/site				
(G9) Wet/dry shop vacuum, leaf blower, or air compressor	E5.8	1	each/site				
(G9) Baskets *(laundry, wicker, etc.)*	E5.8	several	each/site				
(G10) Inflated purple and green balloons	E5.8	several	each/child				
(S9) Grapes	E5.9	5-10	each/child				
(S9) Chilled fruit dip *(1 cup vanilla yogurt, 1 cup whipped topping, 1 tsp. almond flavoring, 1/2 tsp. lemon juice)*	E5.9	1	Tbsp./child				
(S10) Pineapple chunks	E5.9	2	each/child				
(S10) Grapes, red and green	E5.9	4	each/child				
(S10) Skewers, kabobs, or 4" toothpicks	E5.9	1	each/child				
(C9) Yellow tennis balls	E5.9	1	each/child				
(C9) Screw eyes	E5.9	1	each/child				
(C9) Yellow feathers	E5.9	3	each/child				
(C9) 1/4" movable eyes	E5.9	2	each/child				
(C9) Orange felt cut into 1/2" squares	E5.9	1	each/child				
(C9) String cut into 6' lengths	E5.9	1	each/child				
(C10) White matt boards, 5" x 7"	E5.10	1	each/child				
(C10) Small mirrors, 4" x 6" or smaller	E5.10	1	each/child				
(C10) Small seashells	E5.10	1	assortment/site				
(C10) Faux pearls	E5.10	1	assortment/site				

SITE 5: HAWAIIAN VOLCANO *(continued)*

CATEGORY & ITEM	PG	QTY	/UNIT	TOT	HAVE	NEED	✓
(A28) Three small suitcases or carry-on bags	E5.10	1	each/actor				
(A28) Vacation photos	E5.10	3-4	items/site				
(A28) Tropical or island postcards	E5.10	3-4	items/site				
(A28) Glass jar partially filled with sand	E5.10	1	each/site				
(A29) Clean stones for the Time Stones	E5.11	1	each/child				

DIRECTOR'S GUIDE

Registration

Registering kids for your VBS is another very important step in planning. Once registration starts, it is important to have a system to track each student and his or her information. Use the registration card, or design a similar card with the specific information that your church needs. *(See page R.4.)* Be sure to have one file that contains a card for each child attending VBS. Along with a registration card, you need to have a medical release form for each child, signed by a parent or guardian. This allows the VBS staff to obtain medical help for a sick or injured child. Check with your church and/or local government for the information and format they recommend.

Attendance

Once VBS begins, you will need a system for tracking attendance and knowing which kids are in the different Discovery Sites each day. Following the instructions below will help make the first day, including last minute registrations, run smoothly. This will also give you an ongoing record of the location of each child.

Once the majority of children have been registered, the director should divide the children into five groups and assign a color to each group. Reproduce the Group Color attendance sheet on page R.5, making a separate chart for each group in your VBS. On the first few lines of the chart write in the names of the Leaders for that group of kids, then list the children's names. *(Use as many pages as necessary if you have more children in a group than spaces on the chart.)* At the top of each chart are five boxes, noting the order in which that group will go to the Discovery Site. Fill in the days that your VBS sessions will be held and the order that the group will go through the Discovery Sites. *(Example: The red group might go through Discovery Sites 1-5; group yellow would then start with Discovery Site 2 and go through Discovery Site 5 and then to Discovery Site 1.)*

When your charts are complete, make name tags for the children. You may want to choose electronic clip art on the *Time-Stone Travelers*™ CD to create custom name tags that tie into the *Time-Stone Travelers*™ theme, or use the name tag layout provided on the CD. Write each child's name using the color of marker that matches the color of the group he or she is assigned to. Put the name tags all together in one box, alphabetized, regardless of color. Then make a photocopy of the chart pages and hand them off to the person in charge of registration and attendance during VBS. Also give this person extra name tags and the markers used to write the names.

For the first session, each child will come to the attendance desk and tell the VBS staff his or her name. The VBS staff will find the child's name tag in the box and give it to the child. Then the VBS staff will look at the list that corresponds to the name tag color and mark the child present for that session. The VBS staff can then direct the child to the area where he or she is to meet the rest of his or her group. If any new children come, they should fill out a registration card. The VBS staff will then assign them to a group, write each child's name on the appropriate attendance page, and make a name tag using the corresponding color. Once all the children have arrived, the VBS staff in charge of attendance should give any new names to the Director to add to his or her lists.

Schedule

Time-Stone Travelers™ is flexible enough to fit the most diverse schedules and needs. Adjust the program as you wish. A typical morning schedule might look like this:

8:15	Staff meets for prayer and devotions
8:30	Leaders and Helpers organize kids into their groups
8:45	Opening Assembly
9:15	Children dismissed to go to their Discovery Sites
11:15	Closing Assembly
11:30	Dismissal

The schedule for each Discovery Site is loaded with activities that are designed to last two hours. Leaders may find that they don't have enough time for everything. They should decide in advance which activities are optional. It's better to have too much planned than too little. But do avoid rushing children through activities. If you find that your location requires extra time for transitions, be sure to build this into your schedule by extending it by a few minutes at the beginning or end.

If you decide not to include the missions project in your opening assembly, you may want to adopt the following schedule since you may not need as much time in the Opening Assembly:

8:30	Staff meets for prayer and devotions
8:50	Leaders and Helpers organize kids into their groups
9:00	Brief Opening Assembly
9:15	Children dismissed to travel to their Discovery Sites
11:15	Closing Assembly
11:30	Dismissal

Time-Stone Travelers™ is also designed to give you flexibility within the lessons as well. If your schedule only allows for a shorter VBS, you can easily take time from each of the five Discovery Sites by cutting back on the number of activities or games. The Leaders have the flexibility to decide which activities to keep and which to cut in order to meet the time requirements and the skill level of the children. If, however, the needs of your church require a completely different format and schedule, see Custom VeBS® Options on pages D.3-8 for more ideas for creative VBS formats.

Puppet Option

Many children's ministries have found puppets to be effective ministry tools, capturing attention, and adding fun and variety to lessons and programs. That's why this year's VBS program offers you a creative Puppet Option.

The Puppet Option is a lively enhancement to existing program material. The puppet can be used to enhance all opening and closing skits. And puppets can be used to interact with the Leader during the time in each Discovery Site, leading the children to activities, leading the children during the music time, etc.

The VBS Puppet Option includes an easy, enlargeable puppet pattern, featuring *Time-Stone Travelers™* puppet named FINNEGAN. See the resources section *(pages R.53-57)* for the pattern to make your own puppet to use during *Time-Stone Travelers™*.

The puppet may be operated from behind a simple detective's desk, a sheet draped over chairs, or even behind a church piano. Use your imagination, and you'll come up with a great idea for each Discovery Site that's tailored to your own facilities and resources.

Puppeteers
(Consider youth participation)

While some tireless VBS Leaders can switch between puppeteering and handling other aspects of the programs, there may be options available for those who cannot. Consider that some of the best church and ministry puppeteers come from preteen and youth groups. If you have a group of motivated teenagers, they may add a wonderful, energetic dimension to your VBS program. Let them participate in the VBS effort by rehearsing and performing with the puppet. In addition, they can assist in other practical ways, such as serving snacks and monitoring games. By working together in this way, they will experience the reward of being a part of a vital community effort! Plus, they'll have a great time doing it.

Motivating Ideas for Young Puppeteers:

○ **Provide uniforms such as identical T-shirts or polo shirts and jeans.**

○ **Plan the schedule of who operates the puppet for each session. Be sure to give everyone a chance to participate during the week!**

○ **Schedule rehearsals with pizza.**

○ **Give your troupe an official name.**

Puppets can both entertain and teach. On the hand of a skillful puppeteer, the puppet becomes alive, and its message will most likely be remembered for a long time.

Puppetry Basics

Get to know the puppet well. What is its personality? What are its likes and dislikes, its characteristics, and the sound of its voice? Remind the puppeteers repeatedly that they need to speak very loudly in order for the audience to hear. Even if using a microphone backstage, the reader should speak more slowly and clearly than in normal conversation.

When the audience laughs, have the puppet pause in speaking so parts of the dialogue are not missed. To make the puppet look like it's talking *(realistically)*, open the puppet's mouth on each syllable spoken. This takes much practice, and at first it will feel unnatural. If the puppet's mouth doesn't move, work the head and arms appropriately to simulate movement while speaking. Puppets who are "listening" should turn to face the speaker. They should hold their heads up—no drooping hands inside of the puppets—to show they are attentive. Puppets onstage that are not speaking should hold completely still, unless otherwise indicated in the script. Otherwise, the audience gets confused about which puppet is speaking. Remember that the puppet is a role model. Avoid having the puppet display negative behavior *(such as fighting)*, use bad grammar, or rude language.

In addition, do these helpful things for the puppeteers:

Make a copy of the skit for each puppet handler. To help readers keep their place on the page, use highlighter markers to designate a character's name each time it appears. You could use a different color for each character.

Give copies of the scripts to the puppeteers at least a week before they are to do the presentation.

Encourage the puppeteers to practice at home in addition to set rehearsal times together. Send the skit home so they can practice with their parents or other family members. Be sure to send along a parent note explaining what to do.

Have the puppeteers use one of the skits included on pages D.32-55 to practice with. Then have them actually perform the skit for each other to learn how to do these things.

For inexperienced puppeteers, you could have one child work the puppet while another reads the script.

Making a Puppet Stage

A puppet stage can be as simple or elaborate as you wish to make it. Use or adapt one of the ideas below to create a stage that works well with your group and the class space.

Cardboard Box Theater

Obtain a large cardboard box from an appliance store. Cut a hole four inches from the top in the front of the box at least 18 inches wide by 8 inches high. Then cut off the flap of the box that hangs down in the back. Cut the stationary part of the rear of the box straight down the middle to create "swing doors" for the puppeteer to enter and exit.

Decorate the exterior of the box as you desire to make it into the room represented in each Discovery Site. Use paint, wallpaper, colorful adhesive paper, or fabric. Pleat and staple fabric to the front of the stage for curtains. A glue gun also works well to attach the curtain fabric across the top.

Garment Rack Theater

Buy a metal garment rack. Many of these have rollers or wheels on the bottom to make moving the theater simple. Slipstitch a length of curtain to the top of the rack to make a valance *(or use a shower curtain cut to fit along with shower curtain rings)*. Place curtains behind the valance so they can be opened and closed for the stage. Include strips of fabric or ribbon for each side so they can be tied back when the puppets are performing. Attach a piece of fabric to the bottom half of the garment rack to cover the area where the puppeteer sits. This can be hung by slipping a dowel or tension rod through a hem at the top of the fabric.

Doorway Theater

You will need a tension rod a little wider than the door opening and some fabric for this theater. Stitch a casing along the back of the fabric and insert the tension rod. Or use a shower curtain and rings. Place the curtain in the doorway at a height that will hide the puppeteer. Puppeteers can crouch down or sit on a chair behind the curtain.

Creating Discovery Sites

In each Discovery Site, there are specific suggestions for creating the learning environment for that Discovery Site. Transparencies found in the Reproducible Resources section contain art, directions, and suggestions to enhance your sites.

You may want to involve your whole church! Invite youth, Bible study groups, senior citizens, and others to help create the Discovery Sites. Be sure to have materials ready for your "paint party" and serve light refreshments if you like. Many props for the Discovery Sites can also be borrowed or rented. Be as creative as you'd like in order to give a "feel" for the various settings. The most important thing is that it is safe, colorful, fun, and kid-friendly.

Opening and Closing Assemblies

The Opening and Closing Assemblies are the times in the VBS when all the kids are together, doing the same things, and learning the same things. This is a great time to make announcements, celebrate birthdays, etc. This is also a time to get excited about VBS by singing the songs on *Time-Stone Travelers*™ CD. Be sure to sing the Theme Song, *Time-Stone Travelers,* each day. Kids will enjoy learning the songs together and singing them throughout all of VBS. You may also want to add some songs that are well known to the kids.

There are two versions of each Opening Assembly skit—one with only people and one using the puppet. Along with the opening assembly skits provided on the following pages, the Opening Assembly time is a great chance to practice the songs and skits in preparation for the Closing Program. The Opening Assembly is also designed as an opportunity to include a missions emphasis in your VBS. This year's missions project is called **Project Timeless Truth** and is a partnership with Cook Communications Ministries International. Through this program, your VBS can send New Testament Picture Bibles to kids in South America, Africa, the Middle East, Asia, or India who would not otherwise be able to have a Bible. Pages D.78-79 further explain the mission project.

Because the children rotate through the Discovery Sites simultaneously, the skit for each day may not match their Discovery Site. That is okay because they'll be learning more about the overall program and the 10 Commandments with each presentation.

The Closing Assembly is designed as a wrap-up of the day and a chance to communicate any information that needs to be given to all the children and leaders. Since the children have all been to a different Discovery Site each day, this is a good time to reinforce the overall theme for VBS and review the song*(s)* learned in the Opening Assembly.

Assembly Decorations

Decorate the assembly area with a welcome banner. Organize groups of kids by assigning a different color or group name to each. *(See Attendance on page D.25.)* Make matching group banners and attach them to seat sections in the assembly area so kids can easily find places to sit with their group. Encourage Helpers to dress in their group colors, or provide colored VBS T-shirts. Have music from *Time-Stone Travelers*™ CD playing as children arrive.

Introductory Letter from Josh

Hi, Everybody!

My name is Josh Mackenzie, and I'm the main character in the *Time-Stone Travelers*™ books. Right now I'm on a missions trip in Mexico with my mom and dad, my big sister Ellen, and my twin brother Will. He gets annoying sometimes because he's a big chicken and he likes school way more than I do. And Ellen's really great sometimes — when she's not bossing me around! We even brought our dog, Finnegan, because we couldn't bear to leave her behind. She got into trouble yesterday when she cornered a rat that was as big as a cat. The rat nipped the end of her nose. Now she sticks really close to me wherever I go!

I don't know if you've ever been to Mexico before, but it's great here. On the map it's underneath the United States — that's south. It's part of Latin America. And it's way hotter than where I live in Canada. (That's north of the United States.) The main reason we're here is to learn about Spanish-speaking countries that don't have Bibles. Lots of people in Latin America are very poor and can't afford a Bible. My family is giving out Spanish *New Testament Picture Bibles* here, and we're helping to send them to kids all over Latin America, too. These great Bibles will help the kids learn who Jesus is and how to follow Him.

Our whole missions trip got started because of my Time Stone. One day I found a rock partly buried under the grass in our front yard. It had strange symbols carved into it. When I touched it, it gave me a shock! Finnie barked like crazy when she saw the stone. It was the strangest thing! Will and Ellen helped me dig the dirt away from around the stone. We used a stick and my mom's oven mitts so we wouldn't get another shock! Then we pried it out and showed it to my parents. But we couldn't bring it in the house. My mom made us leave it in the garage.

Later that night, Will and I snuck down to the garage to look at it some more. When I aimed my flashlight at the stone, it made a quiet whirring noise and a hole opened in its side. A light shone out and started projecting pictures onto our garage wall. It was so weird! There were pictures of a jungle, a castle, an island — 10 scenes in all. And then they repeated over and over again.

We didn't know what to do, so we woke up Ellen and brought her out to the garage. Everything was going fine until I touched the stone when it was showing the jungle picture. A big shock ran up my arm. I was so surprised that I grabbed onto Will and Ellen. And just in time, too, because a whirlwind swept into our garage and carried us away! We landed in the Mayan jungle in Mexico. We had actually gone back in time thousands of years! We made some friends and had an incredible adventure.

The thing that really bugs me about the Time Stone is that it only turns on when it wants to. I wish it would work when I feel like going time traveling. So far it has sent us to five places — the Mayan jungle, a medieval castle, an ancient laboratory, a native American village, and an island volcano. On every trip we've had to do hard things. But we've learned a lot, especially about God. He's always with us, no matter what.

Anyhow, getting back to our family missions trip. . . . My parents didn't know what to think about this whole Time-Stone thing. They thought we were making it all up. I have a good imagination, but not that good! So when my dad found out about this missions trip, he decided that our family should go along. That way we could see Mexico together AND learn about Spanish-speaking countries that need Bibles.

I don't know much about the Time Stone or how it landed on our front yard. All I know is this: Every time we come back from a trip, one of the 10 symbols on the stone disappears. We're down to five now. I don't know what we're going to do when the rest are gone. Life will sure be boring if we don't get more trips!

I think the symbols on the stone are numbers. I was at the library the other day and found a book of ancient Phoenician writing that looks just like the symbols on the stone. I haven't told Will about it, though, because it'll bug him when he finds out I discovered it first.

The other thing you need to know is what the symbols stand for. If God's using the stone to teach me something, then maybe the 10 symbols on the stone have to do with 10 of something in the Bible. Can you think of anything in the Bible that has 10 parts? I bet some of you know — the 10 Commandments! That means that on each time-travel adventure, we learn about one of the 10 Commandments. That's what you're going to learn about at this Vacation Bible School, too.

My Sunday school teacher loves the 10 Commandments. She says you can divide them into two groups. The first four tell us how we should treat God. The last six tell us how we should treat others. All together, they teach us about the kind of people God wants us to be. God gave us the commandments because He loves us and He wants us to understand the best way to live. I know you're going to like learning about them, too.

Well, I'd better go. My hand is getting sore from writing this long letter. And besides, I need to go give out some more *New Testament Picture Bibles*. I'm sure we'll see each other a few more times this week. And you'll get to meet my brother, Will, and my sister, Ellen, too.

Bye for now!

Your friend,

Josh Mackenzie

Opening Skit – Day 1

CAST: Sightseer, Tourist

PROPS: Rubber band, travel brochure

SCENE: Sightseer and Tourist are onstage.

SIGHTSEER: Hi, Travelers! *(Waits for children to respond.)* **It's good to see you.**

TOURIST: Hello! My name is *(Tourist's name).*

SIGHTSEER: My name is *(Sightseer's name).* **Today we're in Mexico, looking at Mayan ruins—that's what's left of their buildings from hundreds of years ago.** *(Looks at travel brochure.)* **This is called Tulum, and we're in front of the steps of the Castillo.**

TOURIST: More stairs?

SIGHTSEER: Only 24 to reach the top.

TOURIST: How am I going to climb more stairs?

SIGHTSEER: *(To kids.)* **Travelers, let's show** *(Tourist's name)* **how to climb them. Stand up and do what I do.** *(Steps up and down in place 24 times.)* **Great job!**

TOURIST: Hold on! Everyone sit down. *(Waits for kids to sit down.)* **I've got a problem.**

SIGHTSEER: What's the matter, *(Tourist's name)***?**

TOURIST: I don't get it. God gave the Mayans vines that are stretchy like rubber bands.

SIGHTSEER: *(Shoots rubber band at Tourist.)* **God has an awesome imagination.**

TOURIST: I guess.

SIGHTSEER: I guess? *(To kids.)* **Travelers, do you think it would be fun to swing on a vine that is stretchy like a rubber band?** *(Waits for kids to say yes.)* **So do I.** *(Tourist's name)* **and I spent yesterday morning swinging on them.**

TOURIST: I got tangled in the vines and kept boing-ing up and down until you untangled me.

SIGHTSEER: That was really funny.

TOURIST: God also gave the Mayans cenotes [seh-NOTE-ez].

SIGHTSEER: Cenotes are deep pools of water that are so clear you can see the bottom. *(To kids.)* **Travelers, do you like splashing around in water?** *(Waits for kids to say yes.)* **So do I.** *(Tourist's name)* **and I spent yesterday afternoon swimming in a cenote.**

TOURIST: I forgot to hold my breath and got water in my nose.

SIGHTSEER: While you swam to shore, I searched for underwater caves.

TOURIST: God gave the Mayans vines, cenotes, and also the knowledge to build all these buildings.

SIGHTSEER: Which, unfortunately, the Mayans used to serve other gods.

TOURIST: That's wrong.

SIGHTSEER: I agree. God gave the Mayans so much, and they chose to use His gifts to honor make-believe gods.

TOURIST: *(Looks at steps and shakes head.)* **How could they do that!**

SIGHTSEER: I don't know. The first two commandments tell us to serve God and only God.

TOURIST: You're missing the point.

SIGHTSEER: Which is?

TOURIST: I had fun bouncing on vines God made even though I was upside-down most of the time. I had fun swimming in the

cenotes God made even when I got water in my nose. But people made steps. I DO NOT LIKE CLIMBING STEPS!

SIGHTSEER: *(Laughs.)* **You must be getting tired,** *(Tourist's name)*. *(To kids.)* **Travelers, when you move to different groups today, show** *(Tourist's name)* **how much you like climbing steps by lifting your legs high and pretending you're climbing even when you're not. Do this.** *(Demonstrates how to lift legs high when walking.)* **Now, Travelers, it's time for you to do some traveling!**

Opening Puppet Skit – Day 1

CAST: Leader, Finnegan puppet

PROPS: Rubber band, travel brochure

SCENE: Leader and Finnegan are onstage.

LEADER: Hi, Travelers! *(Waits for children to respond.)* It's good to see you.

FINNEGAN: Hello! My name is Finnegan.

LEADER: My name is *(Leader's name).* Today we're in Mexcio looking at Mayan ruins—that's what's left of their buildings from hundreds of years ago. *(Looks at travel brochure.)* This is called Tulum, and we're in front of the steps of the Castillo.

FINNEGAN: More stairs?

LEADER: Only 24 to reach the top.

FINNEGAN: How am I going to climb more stairs?

LEADER: *(To kids.)* Travelers, let's show Finnegan how to climb them. Stand up and do what I do. *(Steps up and down in place 24 times.)* Great job!

FINNEGAN: Hold it! Wait just a minute! Everyone sit down. *(Waits for kids to sit down.)*

LEADER: What's the matter, Finnegan?

FINNEGAN: I don't get it. God gave the Mayans vines that are stretchy like rubber bands.

LEADER: *(Shoots rubber band at Finnegan.)* God has an awesome imagination.

FINNEGAN: I guess.

LEADER: I guess? *(To kids.)* Travelers, do you think it would be fun to swing on a vine that is stretchy like a rubber band? *(Waits for kids to say yes.)* So do I. Finnegan and I spent yesterday morning swinging on them.

FINNEGAN: I got tangled in the vines and kept boing-ing up and down until you untangled me.

LEADER: That was really funny.

FINNEGAN: God also gave the Mayans cenotes [seh-NOTE-ez].

LEADER: Cenotes are deep pools of water that are so clear you can see the bottom. *(To kids.)* Travelers, do you like splashing around in water? *(Waits for kids to say yes.)* So do I. Finnegan and I spent yesterday afternoon swimming in a cenote.

FINNEGAN: I forgot to hold my breath and got water in my nose.

LEADER: While you dog paddled to shore, I searched for underwater caves.

FINNEGAN: God gave the Mayans vines, cenotes, and also the knowledge to build all these buildings.

LEADER: Which, unfortunately, the Mayans used to serve other gods.

FINNEGAN: It's wrong.

LEADER: I agree. God gave the Mayans so much, and they chose to use His gifts to honor make-believe gods.

FINNEGAN: *(Looks at steps and shakes head.)* How could they do that?

LEADER: I don't know. The first two commandments tell us to serve God and only God.

FINNEGAN: You're missing the point.

LEADER: Which is?

FINNEGAN: I had fun bouncing on vines God made even though I was upside-down most of the time. I had fun swimming in the

cenotes God made even when I had to
sneeze. But people made steps. I DO NOT
LIKE CLIMBING STEPS!

LEADER: *(Laughs.)* **You are a lazy dog,
Finnegan.** *(To kids.)* **Travelers, when you move
to different groups today, show Finnegan
how much you like climbing steps by lifting
your legs high like this and pretending
you're climbing steps even when you're not.**
(Demonstrates how to lift legs high when walking.)
**Now Travelers, it's time for you to do some
traveling.**

Opening Skit – Day 2

CAST: Sightseer, Tourist

PROPS: Travel brochure

SCENE: Sightseer and Tourist, acting like tourists, look around and point at things.

TOURIST: *(Sightseer's Name)*, **would you look at that.** *(Points to the floor.)*

SIGHTSEER: *(Looks.)* **Why are you looking at a stone floor when we could be looking at something important in this castle?**

TOURIST: I'm not pointing to the floor; I'm pointing to a bed.

SIGHTSEER: *(Looks at the floor from one direction and then another. Shakes head no.)* **I'm missing something.** *(To kids.)* **Do you see a bed or a floor, Travelers?** *(Pauses for response.)*

TOURIST: Wait. Whoever thinks that what I was pointing to was a bed, yell, "bed," when I count to three. Okay? One, two, three! *(Let Travelers yell "bed!")*

SIGHTSEER: Now, whoever thinks that where *(Tourist's Name)* **was pointing was the floor, yell, "floor," when I count to three. One, two, three!** *(Let Travelers yell "floor!")*

TOURIST: Bed!

SIGHTSEER: Floor!

TOURIST: Look in your brochure.

SIGHTSEER: *(Reads brochure.)* **You're right. It is a bed. The brochure says that the personal servant to the Lord and master of the castle slept with the family.**

TOURIST: He didn't even get a bed?

SIGHTSEER: It says here that he would use the floor.

TOURIST: Without any covers?

SIGHTSEER: Well, he did have a heavy cloak that he used as both a coat and covers.

TOURIST: How could he rest like that?

SIGHTSEER: There are many ways to rest.

TOURIST: Show me.

SIGHTSEER: I didn't mean sleep. I said, "Rest." In His commandments, God tells people to rest one day a week.

TOURIST: He doesn't say to rest on the floor.

SIGHTSEER: No, it's a different kind of rest. God wants people to stop working and spend more time with Him.

TOURIST: If I were sleeping on the floor, I'd be thinking about Him a lot.

SIGHTSEER: You would?

TOURIST: I'd be thinking, "God, why do I have to sleep on the floor?"

SIGHTSEER: *(Laughs.)* **We're like that medieval servant, only we're servants to the Lord Jesus Christ. That's why when we say God's name, we only say it respectfully, as a servant would to a master.**

TOURIST: I'm glad Jesus doesn't make us sleep on the floor.

SIGHTSEER: *(Tourist's Name)*, **you go camping a lot, don't you?**

TOURIST: So?

SIGHTSEER: Don't you sleep in a sleeping bag on the ground? It's the same thing.

TOURIST: *(Thinks for a moment.)* **Good point. Now I'm curious. I wonder if I could sleep on a stone floor.** *(Curls up, yawns, goes to sleep, and starts to snore.)*

SIGHTSEER: *(Whispers.)* **Okay, Travelers.** *(Tourist's Name)* **has fallen asleep. So as you head out today, make sure you're very quiet. Let's take a rest with the noise, and see if we can keep** *(Tourist's Name)* **asleep for a long time.**

Opening Puppet Skit – Day 2

CAST: Leader, Finnegan puppet

PROPS: Travel brochure

SCENE: Leader and Finnegan, acting like tourists, look around and point at things.

FINNEGAN: *(Leader's Name)*, **would you look at that.** *(Points to the floor.)*

LEADER: *(Looks.)* **Why are you looking at a stone floor when we could be looking at something important in the castle?**

FINNEGAN: I'm not just pointing to the floor; I'm also pointing to a bed.

LEADER: *(Looks at the floor from one direction and then another. Shakes head no.)* **I'm missing something.** *(To kids.)* **Do you see a bed or a floor, Travelers?** *(Pauses for response.)*

FINNEGAN: Wait. Whoever thinks that what I was pointing to was a bed, yell, "bed," when I count to three. Okay? One, two, three! *(Let Travelers yell.)*

LEADER: Now, whoever thinks that where Finnegan was pointing was the floor, yell, "floor," when I count to three. One, two, three! *(Let Travelers yell "floor!")*

FINNEGAN: Bed!

LEADER: Floor!

FINNEGAN: Look in your brochure.

LEADER: *(Reads brochure.)* **You're right. It is a bed. The brochure says that the personal servant to the Lord and master of the castle slept with the family.**

FINNEGAN: He didn't even get a real bed?

LEADER: It says that he would use the floor.

FINNEGAN: Without any covers?

LEADER: Well, he did have a heavy cloak that he used as both a coat and covers.

FINNEGAN: How could he rest like that?

LEADER: There are many ways to rest.

FINNEGAN: Show me.

LEADER: I didn't mean sleep. I said, "Rest." In His commandments, God tells people to rest one day a week.

FINNEGAN: He doesn't say "Rest on the floor."

LEADER: No, it's a different kind of rest. God wants people to spend more time with Him.

FINNEGAN: If I were sleeping on the floor, I'd be thinking about Him a lot.

LEADER: You would?

FINNEGAN: I'd be thinking, "God, why do I have to sleep on the floor?"

LEADER: *(Laughs.)* **We're like that medieval servant, only we're servants to the Lord Jesus Christ. That's why when we say God's name, we only say it respectfully, as a servant would to a master.**

FINNEGAN: I'm glad Jesus doesn't make us sleep on the floor.

LEADER: Finnegan, you've forgotten who you are.

FINNEGAN: I'm not the floor-sleeping-servant-to-the-lord-of-the-castle. That's who I'm not.

LEADER: You're a dog.

FINNEGAN: So?

LEADER: You always sleep on the floor.

FINNEGAN: *(Thinks for a moment.)* **Oh, yeah— I forgot! That floor doesn't look so bad. Maybe I'm just tired. I'd better take a little rest.** *(Curls up, yawns, and goes to sleep.)*

LEADER: *(Whispers.)* **Okay, Travelers. Finnegan has fallen asleep. So as you head out today, make sure you're very quiet. Let's see if we can keep Finnegan asleep for a long time.**

Opening Skit – Day 3

CAST: Sightseer, Tourist

PROPS: Two small clear containers, water, drink mix or dye

SCENE: Tourist carefully pours colored water from the container in his hands to a container in front of him. The Sightseer enters and watches Tourist. Tourist puts down the container he is pouring and picks up the other one.

SIGHTSEER: What're you doing, *(Tourist's Name)*?

TOURIST: Just a minute. *(Tourist pours the water from the container now in his hands into the one in front of him.)*

SIGHTSEER: Are you making something?

TOURIST: Yes. *(Continues pouring.)*

SIGHTSEER: You look like an alchemist.

TOURIST: What's that?

SIGHTSEER: An alchemist was a kind of scientist in the old days. He was always experimenting. He would stir and mix all sorts of things together.

TOURIST: Just like what I'm doing.

SIGHTSEER: Only alchemists wanted to turn things into gold.

TOURIST: Oh. Is that all? *(Goes back to pouring water from one container to the other.)*

SIGHTSEER: Is that all? *(To kids.)* *(Tourist's Name)* **must be doing something spectacular. What do you think he's making, Travelers? Window cleaner? The cure for the common cold?** *(Calls on children to name what they think Tourist is making. After each response, say, "That's a good idea.")* **Whatever he's doing, it has to be within the laws of nature.**

TOURIST: This is beyond nature. *(Continues pouring.)*

SIGHTSEER: Beyond nature? Does your mother know you're doing this?

TOURIST: Yes.

SIGHTSEER: Did she give you permission?

TOURIST: Yes.

SIGHTSEER: Does your father know you're doing this?

TOURIST: Yes.

SIGHTSEER: Did he give you permission?

TOURIST: Yes. He even gave me this container.

SIGHTSEER: Then I guess it's okay. It's very important to obey parents, so important that God gave us a commandment that tells us to honor our parents.

TOURIST: I honored my parents. I asked, and they gave me permission. *(Continues pouring the colored water back and forth.)*

SIGHTSEER: Then I guess it's okay.

TOURIST: They've done what I'm doing. Now it's my turn.

SIGHTSEER: What are you making? One of the kids thought it was *(what one thought it was)*.

TOURIST: No. I'm not making *(what one thought it was)*.

SIGHTSEER: Someone else thought it was *(what another thought it was)*.

TOURIST: No, not that either. *(Speaks slowly.)* I'm making the perfect—

SIGHTSEER: Way to fight disease?

TOURIST: No, the perfect mixture—

SIGHTSEER: To fight crime?

TOURIST: No. The perfect combination of flavoring, water, and sugar.

SIGHTSEER: That sounds like a drink mix.

TOURIST: Exactly. I've just completed the perfect cup of raspberry-flavored lemonade. And now I'm going to bring a cup to my mom. Bye!

(Tourist exits.)

SIGHTSEER: *(Calls after him.)* Wait! I'm thirsty. Can I have some too?

(Sightseer hurries after Tourist.)

Opening Puppet Skit – Day 3

CAST: Leader, Finnegan puppet

PROPS: Two small containers, water, drink mix or dye

SCENE: Finnegan carefully pours colored water from the container in his hands to a container in front of him. The leader enters and watches Finnegan. Finnegan puts down the container he is pouring and picks up the other one.

LEADER: What're you doing?

FINNEGAN: Just a minute. *(Finnegan pours the water from the container now in his hands into the one in front of him.)*

LEADER: Are you making something?

FINNEGAN: Yes. *(Continues pouring.)*

LEADER: You look like an alchemist.

FINNEGAN: What's that?

LEADER: An alchemist was a kind of scientist in the old days. He was always experimenting. He would stir and mix all sorts of things together.

FINNEGAN: Just like what I'm doing.

LEADER: Only alchemists wanted to turn things into gold.

FINNEGAN: Oh. Is that all? *(Goes back to pouring water from one container to the other.)*

LEADER: Is that all? *(To kids.)* **Finnegan must be doing something spectacular. What do you think he's making, Travelers? Window cleaner? The cure for the common cold?** *(Calls on children to name what they think Finnegan is making. After each response, say, "That's a good idea.")* **Whatever he's doing, it has to be within the laws of nature.**

FINNEGAN: This is beyond nature. *(Continues pouring.)*

LEADER: Beyond nature? Does your mother know you're doing this?

FINNEGAN: Yes.

LEADER: Did she give you permission?

FINNEGAN: Yes.

LEADER: Does your father know you're doing this?

FINNEGAN: Yes.

LEADER: Did he give you permission?

FINNEGAN: Yes. He even gave me this container.

LEADER: Then I guess it's okay. It's very important to obey parents, so important that God gave us a commandment that tells us to honor our parents.

FINNEGAN: I honored my parents. I asked, and they gave me permission. *(Continues pouring the colored water back and forth.)*

LEADER: Then I guess it's okay.

FINNEGAN: They've done what I'm doing. Now it's my turn.

LEADER: What are you making? One of the kids thought it was *(what one thought it was).*

FINNEGAN: No. I'm not making *(what one thought it was).*

LEADER: Someone else thought it was *(what another thought it was).*

FINNEGAN: No, not that either. *(Speaks slowly.)* I'm making the perfect—

LEADER: Way to fight disease?

FINNEGAN: No, the perfect mixture—

LEADER: To fight crime?

FINNEGAN: No. The perfect combination of flavoring, water, and sugar.

LEADER: That sounds like a drink mix.

FINNEGAN: Exactly. I've just completed the perfect cup of raspberry-flavored lemonade. And now I'm going to bring a cup to my mom. Bye!

(Finnegan exits.)

LEADER: *(Calls after him.)* Wait! I'm thirsty. Can I have some too?

(Leader hurries after Finnegan.)

Opening Skit – Day 4

CAST: Sightseer, Traveler, Tourist

PROPS: Three lunch bags and four sandwiches

SCENE: Tourist and Sightseer are walking together; Traveler is behind them.

TOURIST: Why did she have to come with us?

SIGHTSEER: I thought you liked *(Traveler's Name)*.

TOURIST: I do, but I thought that just the two of us were going to explore Hawk's Village.

SIGHTSEER: The more, the merrier.

TRAVELER: Just think, the Native Americans from Hawk's Village probably walked these trails.

TOURIST: I wonder if they got as hungry as I am now.

SIGHTSEER: *(Laughs.)* Is that a hint that you want to stop for lunch?

TOURIST: Exactly! I have a great lunch. *(Opens his lunch bag.)* What did you bring?

SIGHTSEER: A sauerkraut and strawberry jam sandwich with pickles.

TOURIST: Yuck!

TRAVELER: I have two peanut butter and jelly sandwiches.

TOURIST: I like PBJs, but I also like bologna. That's what I have. What else did you bring?

SIGHTSEER: I just brought one sandwich. That's all I usually eat.

TOURIST: One sandwich?

SIGHTSEER: And water.

TRAVELER: I brought a couple bags of chips and sodas. I knew I would be really hungry.

TOURIST: That's not hungry. That's being a pig.

SIGHTSEER: *(Tourist's Name)*!

TOURIST: I'm sorry. I brought a sandwich, water, pretzels, and a granola bar. But I dropped the granola bar on our way here. And I ate the pretzels before we started.

TRAVELER: *(Continues looking in her bag.)* I brought granola bars, too, and some candy to keep up my strength. *(Walks toward Tourist, still looking in her bag.)*

TOURIST: *(Holds up sandwich.)* Bologna sandwiches might not be PBJs, but they're still good. *(Tourist drops sandwich, and Traveler steps on it by accident.)*

TRAVELER: Oh, no!

TOURIST: My sandwich!

SIGHTSEER: Don't worry, Tourist. I'll share mine with you.

TOURIST: I'd rather starve.

TRAVELER: I have enough for both of us. I did bring two of everything.

TOURIST: But then you won't be able to keep up your strength.

TRAVELER: If I'd eaten all that food, I'd have had a tummyache.

SIGHTSEER: That's real nice of you. Many of the 10 Commandments deal with treating each other well.

TOURIST: So sharing your lunch pleases not only my stomach, but also God.

TRAVELER: I never thought of it that way.

SIGHTSEER: Whenever we treat people with kindness, our actions do please God.

TOURIST: Didn't Jesus sum up the commandments?

SIGHTSEER: He said that first we should love Him, and then we should love each other.

TOURIST: Even when we're wet?

SIGHTSEER: What do you mean?

TOURIST: Those are rain clouds.

TRAVELER: That was a raindrop.

SIGHTSEER: Grab your stuff, and run for it!

(They all run offstage.)

Opening Puppet Skit – Day 4

CAST: Leader, Traveler, Finnegan puppet

PROPS: Three lunch bags and four sandwiches

SCENE: Finnegan and Leader are walking together with Traveler is behind them. Each holds a lunch bag with a sandwich in each *(two in Traveler's)*.

FINNEGAN: Why did *she* have to come with us?

LEADER: I thought you liked *(Traveler's Name)*.

FINNEGAN: I do, but I thought that just the two of us were going to explore Hawk's Village.

FINNEGAN: The more, the merrier.

TRAVELER: Just think, the Native Americans from Hawk's Village probably walked these trails.

FINNEGAN: I wonder if they got as hungry as I am now.

LEADER: *(Laughs.)* Is that a hint that you want to stop for lunch?

FINNEGAN: Exactly! I have a great lunch. *(Opens lunch bag.)* **What did you bring?**

LEADER: A sauerkraut and strawberry jam sandwich with pickles.

FINNEGAN: Yuck!

TRAVELER: I have two peanut butter and jelly sandwiches.

FINNEGAN: I like PBJs, but I also like bologna. That's what I have. What else did you bring?

LEADER: I just brought one sandwich. That's all I usually eat.

FINNEGAN: One sandwich?

LEADER: And water.

TRAVELER: I brought a couple bags of chips and sodas. I knew I would be really hungry.

FINNEGAN: That's not hungry. That's being a pig.

LEADER: Finnegan!

FINNEGAN: I'm sorry. I brought a sandwich, water, pretzels, and a granola bar. But I dropped the granola bar on our way here. And I ate the pretzels before we started.

TRAVELER: *(Continues looking in bag.)* **I brought granola bars, too, and some candy to keep up my strength.** *(Walks toward Finnegan, still looking in bag.)*

FINNEGAN: *(Holds up sandwich.)* **Bologna sandwiches might not be PBJs, but they're still good.** *(Drops his sandwich, and Traveler steps on it by accident.)*

TRAVELER: Oh, no!

FINNEGAN: My sandwich!

LEADER: Don't worry, Finnegan. I'll share mine with you.

FINNEGAN: I'd rather starve.

TRAVELER: I have enough for both of us. I did bring two of everything.

FINNEGAN: But then you won't be able to keep up your strength.

TRAVELER: If I'd eaten all that food, I'd have had a tummyache.

LEADER: That's real nice of you. Many of the 10 Commandments deal with treating each other well.

FINNEGAN: So sharing your lunch pleases not only my stomach, but also God.

TRAVELER: I never thought of it that way.

LEADER: Whenever we treat people with kindness, our actions do please God.

FINNEGAN: Didn't Jesus sum up the commandments like that?

LEADER: He said that first we should love Him and then we should love each other.

FINNEGAN: Even when we're wet?

LEADER: What do you mean?

FINNEGAN: Those are rain clouds.

TRAVELER: That was a raindrop.

LEADER: Grab your stuff, and run for it!

(They all run offstage.)

Opening Skit – Day 5

CAST: Sightseer, Tourist

PROPS: Magazine, lawn chair

SCENE: Tourist intently reads a magazine. Sightseer sits in a lawn chair as if soaking up the sun with eyes closed.

SIGHTSEER: I love being on the beach. *(Pauses.)* **Don't you,** *(Tourist's name)***?** *(Pauses.)* *(Tourist's name)***?** *(Opens eyes and looks over at Tourist.)* **What are you reading?**

TOURIST: *(Face is completely covered by the magazine.)* **It's the newest issue of my favorite magazine.**

SIGHTSEER: You should be relaxing. We're on a beach in Hawaii.

TOURIST: I am relaxing. This is how I relax. *(Pauses.)* **Will you look at that!** *(Points to something in magazine.)*

SIGHTSEER: *(Leans over to look.)* **What?**

TOURIST: A candy-studded, black velvet, secret spy case that opens only by voice command.

SIGHTSEER: You're not a spy. You'd never use it.

TOURIST: You never know. *(Turns page.)* **Look at this!**

SIGHTSEER: *(Looks over.)* **What now?**

TOURIST: It's a super-sized, Egyptian-encoded, high gloss, aluminum cup with a secret compartment.

SIGHTSEER: A cup? Why do you need a secret compartment in your cup?

TOURIST: To hide secret messages, of course.

SIGHTSEER: You don't get secret messages.

TOURIST: A minor detail. *(Turns another page.)* **Wow! Have you ever seen one of these before?**

SIGHTSEER: *(Looks.)* **No. What is it?**

TOURIST: A supersonic, stealth, sensor-operated volcano that explodes on command.

SIGHTSEER: You can't even tie your shoelaces. Why would you want to be in charge of an exploding volcano?

TOURIST: *(Sighs.)* **I'll never be happy again! I don't have any of this neat stuff!**

SIGHTSEER: The tenth commandment tells us to be happy with what we have.

TOURIST: Impossible. I want—

(Sightseer grabs Tourist's magazine and throws it to the side.)

TOURIST: *(Rubs eyes.)* **What happened? Where am I? Where'd my magazine go?**

SIGHTSEER: Without that magazine, I think you'll enjoy life a lot more.

TOURIST: What's there to enjoy?

SIGHTSEER: We're in Hawaii.

TOURIST: Boring.

SIGHTSEER: Next to a volcano.

TOURIST: Ho hum! *(Yawns.)*

SIGHTSEER: We're on vacation, *(Tourist's name)***. Travelers, help me. What are some things that** *(Tourist's name)* **might enjoy?** *(Have the kids give answers, and have Tourist repeat the answers and then for each one say something like, "That's not boring," or "I like that.")*

TOURIST: *(Looks around.)* *(Sightseer's name)***, did you say that we're next to a volcano?**

SIGHTSEER: Yeah. It's not an active one, which means it won't explode on us, but it used to be.

TOURIST: What are we doing sitting here when we could be hiking up the volcano? It's not too far away. I can see it from here. I'm going up, *(Sightseer's name)*. **This is a great vacation!** *(Tourist hurries offstage.)*

SIGHTSEER: Wait for me, *(Tourist's name)*! *(Picks up lawn chair and hurries after Tourist.)*

Opening Puppet Skit – Day 5

CAST: Leader, Finnegan puppet

PROPS: Dog magazine, lawn chair

SCENE: Finnegan intently reads a dog magazine. The Leader sits in a lawn chair as if soaking up the sun with eyes closed.

LEADER: I love being on the beach. *(Pauses.)* **Don't you, Finnegan?** *(Pauses.)* **Finnegan?** *(Leader opens eyes and looks over at Finnegan.)* **What are you reading?**

FINNEGAN: *(Face is completely covered by the magazine.)* **It's the newest issue of Golden Retriever Monthly.**

LEADER: You should be relaxing. We're on a beach in Hawaii!

FINNEGAN: I am relaxing. This is how I relax. *(Pauses. Points to something in magazine.)* **Will you look at that!**

LEADER: *(Leans over to look.)* **What?**

FINNEGAN: A candy-studded, black velvet collar that keeps the fleas away.

LEADER: Seems like the candy would keep bugs around you. What's wrong with your collar?

FINNEGAN: Nothing. *(Pauses. Flips a page.)* **Look at this!**

LEADER: *(Looks over.)* **What now?**

FINNEGAN: It's a super-sized, Egyptian-encoded, high gloss, aluminum water dish with a secret compartment.

LEADER: A dog dish is a dog dish. Why do you need a secret compartment anyway?

FINNEGAN: To hide bones.

LEADER: That is one big secret compartment. What's wrong with your water dish?

FINNEGAN: Nothing, I suppose. *(Pauses.)* **Wow! Have you ever seen one of these before?**

LEADER: *(Looks.)* **No. What is it?**

FINNEGAN: A supersonic stealth sensor that lets you know if a cat is within a mile of you.

LEADER: There's nothing wrong with the basic instinct that God gave you.

FINNEGAN: *(Sighs.)* **Maybe not, but I'll never be happy again!**

LEADER: Why not?

FINNEGAN: I don't have all this neat stuff!

LEADER: The tenth commandment tells us to be happy with what we have.

FINNEGAN: Impossible. I want—

(Leader grabs Finnegan's magazine and throws it to the side.)

FINNEGAN: *(Rubs eyes.)* **What happened? Where am I? Where'd my magazine go?**

LEADER: Without that magazine, I think you'll enjoy life a lot more.

FINNEGAN: What's there to enjoy?

LEADER: We're in Hawaii.

FINNEGAN: Boring.

LEADER: Next to a volcano.

FINNEGAN: Ho hum! *(Yawns.)*

LEADER: We're on vacation, Finnegan! Travelers, help me. What are some things that Finnegan can enjoy? *(Have the kids give answers, and have Finnegan repeat the answers and then for each one say something like, "That's not boring," or, "I like that.")*

FINNEGAN: *(Sniffs the air.)* **What's that smell?**

LEADER: I don't know. Maybe it's the sweet and sour pizza I had for lunch.

FINNEGAN: No, it's better than that.

LEADER: The sweet and sour pizza I had for breakfast?

FINNEGAN: No. It's a cat, and it's not too far away. I'll see you later, *(Leader's name).* **This is a great vacation!** *(Runs offstage.)*

LEADER: Wait for me, Finnegan!

(Picks up lawn chair and hurries after Finnegan.)

Closing Program

As the finale for the *Time-Stone Travelers*™ experience, this program is designed to celebrate the goodness of God. It encourages program participants and the audience to respond to the gifts of God's grace, and presents a great opportunity for your church to reach out to neighborhood families who have sent their children to your VBS but do not attend church regularly. The skits offer relevant principles that children and their parents can easily recognize and apply to their lives. And the participation by the children is just plain fun! Make sure the children invite their parents, friends, and neighbors to share in this celebration! The traditional program is designed to follow this basic schedule:

10 minutes:	Welcome by Director
5 minutes:	Prayer by Pastor
60 minutes:	Closing Program
30 minutes:	Awards, missions, refreshments

Fifteen minutes before the closing program begins, play music from the *Time-Stone Travelers*™ CD or some other Christian children's music softly through the sound system.

When it is time to begin, play the VBS theme song, "Time-Stone Travelers" while the children enter from the back of the sanctuary or auditorium. Children can step in time with the music and line up in front of the church, facing the audience. *(If a particularly ambitious group of young performers happens to be among your attendees, they might choose to choreograph the processional to this song during the week and perform it while the other children are entering, lining up, and singing.)*

At this point, the Director welcomes the audience, followed by prayer by the pastor. The pastor should introduce *Time-Stone Travelers*™ program, which starts on the next page. You will need to select the version of the program you desire to use—the version with only people or the version which includes FINNEGAN the puppet.

Closing

The Director might give each child who attended VBS a Certificate of Completion *(on the CD, or see page R.9)*. The Director should thank the children and their families for participating. Close with a prayer followed by a reprise of the children singing this year's VBS theme song, "Time-Stone Travelers."

During a time for greeting people and enjoying refreshments, you might provide Family Evaluation forms *(see page R.42)* and invite families to give you their feedback by completing a form.

Intergenerational Option

This option allows for a fun two-hour family experience! *(Note: There are 10 extra minutes in this two-hour schedule to allow for transitions.)*

Follow this schedule:

15 minutes: As families arrive, greet them and place them into five groups. If any children do not have family present, team them up with a friend's family. Assign two Leaders to each group. Leaders should remain in costume.

75 minutes: Have each group start at one Discovery Site. Groups then rotate through each of the five Discovery Sites *(15 minutes each)* until each group has visited all five.

At each Discovery Site, the families will watch the Opening Assembly Skit for that Discovery Site *(see skits on pages D.32-49)*, hear children recite the Bible verse, and sing the song that was learned at that site. The Director should keep time and give a signal for the groups to move on to the next Discovery Site.

20 minutes: Gather the groups together for a closing awards assembly and refreshments. See the Closing suggestions given above.

Closing Skit

CAST: Sightseer, Tourist

PROPS: Blindfold, box with pennies inside, map

SCENE: Tourist is blindfolded. Sightseer is reading directions from a map.

SIGHTSEER: Take five steps to your left, *(Tourist's name)*.

TOURIST: Am I there yet, *(Sightseer's Name)*?

SIGHTSEER: No. Now take six steps to your right. *(Tourist moves accordingly.)*

TOURIST: Am I there now?

SIGHTSEER: Almost. Take another step to your left. *(Tourist moves accordingly.)*

TOURIST: I have to be almost there. Am I? Am I almost there?

SIGHTSEER: Only one more step straight in front of you. *(Tourist moves accordingly and then bends down to pick up a box.)*

TOURIST: It doesn't feel like a treasure chest.

SIGHTSEER: To find the treasure, you'll have to open it. *(Tourist takes the lid off the box.)* Now reach inside. *(Tourist reaches inside the box.)* What's inside? Is it a treasure?

TOURIST: Yes! Yes! *(Tourist pulls out a handful of pennies.)* I did it! *(Sightseer takes the blindfold off of Tourist.)* It's money! And it's mine, all mine. I'm rich.

SIGHTSEER: You were very good at following directions.

TOURIST: Thanks for telling me where to go. I couldn't see anything. I couldn't have done it without you.

SIGHTSEER: You followed my directions just as we all should follow the 10 Commandments.

TOURIST: It's not the same thing. Those are rules, and this was a treasure hunt with a real treasure at the end.

SIGHTSEER: They're both treasures maps, *(Tourist's name)*. Remember the Mayan Jungle? Travelers, what did we learn at the Mayan Jungle? *(Help the children express the concept: I will worship the one true God.)*

TOURIST: There's no treasure there.

SIGHTSEER: No? Who wants to tell *(Tourist's name)* what happened to Shadrach, Meshach, and Abednago when they were thrown into the fiery furnace because they refused to worship another god? *(Have children tell how the Bible characters were not burned by the fire.)*

TOURIST: That was a really cool thing that God did, but that was just one site. We only went over the first two commandments on that day.

SIGHTSEER: Travelers, what did we learn at the Medieval Castle? *(Help the children express the concept: I will use the Lord's name only with respect and will set aside time to worship God.)*

TOURIST: The Medieval Castle was cool.

SIGHTSEER: And we learned that God deserves our worship. Travelers, how did you learn to worship God? *(Choose a few of the children to answer how they learned to worship.)*

TOURIST: Worship was fun, but rules will never be the same as a treasure map.

SIGHTSEER: The 10 Commandments are exactly like a treasure map. Remember when I told you to take five steps to the left so you wouldn't run into anything?

TOURIST: Yeah. Although I was blindfolded and couldn't see anything, I did what you said and didn't run into a single thing.

SIGHTSEER: It's the same with worship. If you worship the one true God, you keep from running into all sorts of things that will hurt you. Too often you can't see those things, but God does.

TOURIST: Really?

SIGHTSEER: Definitely.

TOURIST: So what did we learn at the Ancient Laboratory?

SIGHTSEER: Travelers? *(Help the children express the concept: I will respect, honor, and obey my father and mother because God has given them the responsibility to take care of me.)*

TOURIST: Another rule.

SIGHTSEER: Another step. How did Jesus obey His parents, Travelers? *(Choose a few of the children to answer how Jesus obeyed Mary and Joseph.)*

TOURIST: When do we get to the treasure?

SIGHTSEER: Soon. What did we learn at Hawk's Village, Travelers? *(Help the children express the concept: I will not hurt others but will treat them with kindness as God wants me to.)*

TOURIST: I remember that. We studied the Good Samaritan that day.

SIGHTSEER: Exactly.

TOURIST: Are we almost there?

SIGHTSEER: Almost. From the Good Samaritan we learned how to be kind to others. What are some of the things you learned about being kind, Travelers? *(Choose a few of the children to answer.)*

TOURIST: Are we at the tenth commandment yet?

SIGHTSEER: Yes, we are. That was at the Hawaiian Volcano.

TOURIST: But that means we're done! The treasure has to come soon!

SIGHTSEER: It does. Kids what did we learn at the Hawaiian Volcano? *(Help the children express the concept: I will be satisfied with the things I have and not want the things that others have.)*

TOURIST: That's the last step. Where's the treasure?

SIGHTSEER: I'll show you. Travelers, if you have a song you want to sing, a memory verse to share, a project to show, or a story, raise your hands. Let's show *(Tourist's name)* just a couple of the jewels that came out of this week.

(Allow time for the kids to come up to show their item or sing or recite what they know. If there are too many children, have teachers pick a few of the children who would like to share.)

TOURIST: Wow! That was amazing. The treasure was not in a box. It was in the lives of people. What we saw were the rewards for following God's map for only one week.

SIGHTSEER: Did you know that the more you follow the 10 Commandments, the bigger your treasure will grow?

TOURIST: You get more the longer you follow God's map?

SIGHTSEER: Exactly. It's a treasure map that will help people live happy lives even when bad things happen.

TOURIST: Wow! That is an unbelievable treasure.

SIGHTSEER: And God wants to give His treasure map to each Traveler here.

TOURIST: Does He have enough for everyone?

SIGHTSEER: Definitely.

TOURIST: Do you all have God's treasure map in your heart? *(Wait for kids to answer yes.)* **I couldn't hear you. Let's try it again. Do you have God's treasure map?** *(Let kids shout yes!)*

SIGHTSEER: Travelers, as we finish today, don't forget to take God's treasure map home. Follow the 10 Commandments, and you'll receive many treasures no matter where you travel in your life. Goodbye!

(They exit.)

Closing Puppet Play

CAST: Leader, Finnegan puppet

PROPS: Blindfold, box with a dog bone inside, map

SCENE: Finnegan is blindfolded. The Leader is reading directions from a map.

LEADER: Take two steps forward, Finnegan. *(Finnegan moves accordingly.)*

FINNEGAN: Am I there yet, *(Leader's Name)*?

LEADER: No. Now take one step to your left. *(Finnegan moves accordingly.)*

FINNEGAN: Am I there now?

LEADER: Almost. Take another step forward. *(Finnegan moves accordingly.)*

FINNEGAN: I have to be almost there. Am I? Am I almost there?

LEADER: Only one more step to your left. *(Finnegan moves accordingly and then bends down to pick up a box.)*

FINNEGAN: It doesn't feel like a treasure chest.

LEADER: To find the treasure, you'll have to open it. *(Finnegan takes the lid off of the box.)* Now reach inside. *(Finnegan reaches inside the box.)* What's inside? Is it a treasure?

FINNEGAN: Yes! Yes! *(Finnegan pulls out a dog bone.)* I did it! *(Leader takes the blindfold off of Finnegan.)* It's a bone! And it's mine, all mine. It smells so good.

LEADER: You were very good at following directions. Now the treasure is all yours.

FINNEGAN: Thanks for telling me where to go. I couldn't see anything. I couldn't have done it without you.

LEADER: You followed my directions just as we all should follow the 10 Commandments.

FINNEGAN: It's not the same thing. Those are rules, and this was a treasure hunt with a real treasure at the end.

LEADER: They're both treasures maps, Finnegan. Remember the Mayan Jungle? Travelers, what did we learn at the Mayan Jungle? *(Help the children express the concept: I will worship the one true God.)*

FINNEGAN: There's no treasure there.

LEADER: No? Who wants to tell Finnegan what happened to Shadrach, Meshach, and Abednago when they were thrown into the fiery furnace because they refused to worship another god? *(Have children tell how the Bible characters were not burned by the fire.)*

FINNEGAN: That was a really cool thing that God did, but that was just one site. We only went over the first two commandments on that day.

LEADER: Travelers, what did we learn at the Medieval Castle? *(Help the children express the concept: I will use the Lord's name only with respect and will set aside time to worship God.)*

FINNEGAN: The Medieval Castle was cool.

LEADER: We learned that God deserves our worship. Travelers, how did you learn to worship God? *(Choose a few of the children to answer how they learned to worship.)*

FINNEGAN: Worship was fun, but rules will never be the same as a treasure map.

LEADER: The 10 Commandments are exactly like a treasure map. Remember when I told you to take a step to the left so you wouldn't run into anything?

FINNEGAN: Yeah. Although I had a blindfold and couldn't see anything, I did what you said and didn't run into a single thing.

LEADER: It's the same with worship. If you worship the one true God, you keep from running into all sorts of things that will hurt you. Too often you can't see those things, but God does.

FINNEGAN: Really?

LEADER: Definitely.

FINNEGAN: So what did we learn at the Ancient Laboratory?

LEADER: Travelers? *(Help the children express the concept: I will respect, honor, and obey my father and mother because God has given them the responsibility to take care of me.)*

FINNEGAN: Another rule.

LEADER: Another step. How did Jesus obey His parents, Travelers? *(Choose a few of the children to answer how Jesus obeyed Mary and Joseph.)*

FINNEGAN: When do we get to the treasure?

LEADER: Soon. What did we learn at Hawk's Village, Travelers? *(Help the children express the concept: I will not hurt others but will treat them with kindness as God wants me to.)*

FINNEGAN: I remember that. We studied the Good Samaritan that day.

LEADER: Exactly.

FINNEGAN: Are we almost there?

LEADER: Almost. From the Good Samaritan we learned how to be kind to others. What are some of the things you learned about being kind, Travelers? *(Choose a few of the children to answer.)*

FINNEGAN: Are we at the tenth commandment yet?

LEADER: Yes, we are. That was at the Hawaiian Volcano.

FINNEGAN: But that means we're done! The treasure has to come soon!

LEADER: It does. Kids what did we learn at the Hawaiian Volcano? *(Help the children express the concept: I will be satisfied with the things I have and not want the things that others have.)*

FINNEGAN: That's the last step. Where's the treasure?

LEADER: I'll show you. Travelers, if you have a song you want to sing, a memory verse to share, a project to show, or a story, raise your hands. Let's show Finnegan just a couple of the jewels that came out of this week.

(Allow time for the kids to come up to show their item or sing or recite what they know. If there are too many children, have teachers pick a few of the children who would like to share.)

FINNEGAN: Wow! That was amazing. The treasure was not in a box. It was in the lives of people. What we saw were the rewards for following God's map for only one week.

LEADER: Did you know that the more you follow the 10 Commandments, the bigger your treasure will grow?

FINNEGAN: You get more the longer you follow God's map?

LEADER: Exactly. It's a treasure map that will help people live happy lives even when bad things happen.

FINNEGAN: Wow! That is an unbelievable treasure.

LEADER: And God wants to give His treasure map to each Traveler here.

FINNEGAN: Does he have enough for everyone?

LEADER: Definitely.

FINNEGAN: Does you all have God's treasure map in your heart? *(Wait for kids to answer yes.)* I couldn't hear you. Let's try it again. Do you have God's treasure map? *(Let kids shout yes!)*

LEADER: Travelers, as we finish today, don't forget to take God's treasure map home. Follow the 10 Commandments, and you'll receive many treasures no matter where you travel in your life. Goodbye

(They exit.)

Spiritual Gifts

One of your most important jobs as VBS Director is recruiting your volunteers. God has already given your church the very best people to help you this summer, and now it's your task to find them and put them in the right jobs!

Pray—While you most certainly have already started to do this, add this next line to your prayer requests: "Lord, help me see how You have gifted people." Too often, recruiting is seen as the necessary filling of slots with warm bodies. But God's Word treats serving in the body of Christ much differently. First Corinthians 12:4-7 says, "Now there are diversities of gifts, but the same Spirit. And there are differences of administrations, but the same Lord. And there are diversities of operations, but it is the same God which worketh all in all. But the manifestation of the Spirit is given to every man to profit withal." Paul was writing about the fact that God has created us all in special ways to build up and support God's works in the church. And VBS is work that you cannot do alone. That's why you must start seeing people as vital members of a dynamic ministry community.

Seek—Ironically, the first step in recruiting is watching. Think of the people in your church. Who offers to come early to set up for your church's functions? Who loves to teach others about God's Word? Who offers to help with food? Who is gifted in arts or crafts? If you were to ask these people why they do what they do, most, if not all of them, will tell you that they help in certain areas because they enjoy it. That's one of the amazing things about spiritual gifts—people enjoy working in the areas in which God has gifted them. Your job as VBS Director is to help people identify the jobs they can do that match their gifts. There may also be people in your church that you do not know but who would enjoy being part of VBS. To locate these people and get them involved, you can make announcements during worship services as well as distributing a volunteer flyer where people can express interest in helping with VBS. *(See page R.11.)*

The chart on the next page gives a brief overview of key questions to ask yourself, how they match spiritual gifts, and how that might translate into a role for VBS. You may want to copy it and give it to others who may be helping with recruiting or considering volunteering.

Ask—Once you have prayed about your staff of volunteers and looked for their spiritual gifts and talents, you are in a position to ask them to help. When you approach potential volunteers, make sure you tell them the specific job duties and responsibilities that you have in mind for them, and why you think they would be a good fit for a specific task. Be sure to listen as they respond—they certainly know themselves better than you do!

Spiritual Gifts Chart

GIFT	QUESTIONS	POSSIBLE ROLE
	Based on: Romans 12; 1 Corinthians 12:28	
Helper	Who is always willing to lend a hand? Who thinks of ways to support and give, even when it is not asked of him or her?	Craft helper Snack coordinator Supply gatherer
Exhorter	Who is encouraging to be around? Who greets others with a smile and has a kind word, no matter who the person is?	Greeter Team leader Follow-up leader
Administration	Who is looking for ways to organize programs? Who seems to be organized and able to help others because of it?	Craft/Snack coordinator Registration Assistant director
Giver	Who is always willing to give to your ministries? Who looks to fill the needs of those around him or her?	Craft/Snack donation Closing Program sponsor
Mercy	Who is willing to reach out to others who are hurting or in crisis? Who is motivated to show God's love to others?	Greeter Team leader
Server	Who is willing to stay in the background, content to help in other ways?	Snack preparer Craft coordinator
Leader	Who likes to tell others about God's Word? Who is primarily interested in how God changes others' hearts by revealing His Word?	Leader Team leader

Note: *While this list is not exhaustive, it can provide a good starting point to ask key questions about the gifts and abilities of those in your church. For other listings of gifts, see also Ephesians 4:11 and 1 Corinthians 12:8-10.*

Volunteers

In addition, make sure that your church is protected from liability by screening your volunteers. Hopefully you will personally know all the people who volunteer. However, some churches do not always have this luxury. Use your children's ministry's existing volunteer application or create one that asks for a volunteer's history of work with children, an official form of identification, Social Security number, and other information such as address and phone number*(s)*, a brief testimony, and references. Unfortunately, these sorts of precautions are now standard in churches today, and VBS is no exception. Be sure that you talk with your pastor or Children's Minister to make sure you have met your church's screening standards so you can have the safest, most enjoyable VBS possible!

Personnel Chart

As you recruit and select team members for your VBS, the chart below will help you keep track of who is doing what and which positions still need to be filled.

SITE 1
MAYAN JUNGLE — There is only one God.

Leader 1	
Leader 2	
Location	
Other staff	

SITE 2
MEDIEVAL CASTLE — God deserves our worship.

Leader 1	
Leader 2	
Location	
Other staff	

SITE 3
ANCIENT LABORATORY — Honor your father and mother.

Leader 1	
Leader 2	
Location	
Other staff	

SITE 4
HAWK'S VILLAGE — Treat others with kindness.

Leader 1	
Leader 2	
Location	
Other staff	

SITE 5
HAWAIIAN VOLCANO — Be happy with what God has given us.

Leader 1	
Leader 2	
Location	
Other staff	

Training Your Staff

One of the many things your volunteers need to take with them as they set out to affect the lives of God's children is a trained mind. Training is one of the most important and stabilizing components to a successful VBS. Not only do your volunteers need to know what the VBS is all about, they need to know the specifics of their jobs and the best way to do their jobs. Make sure you schedule at least two training opportunities before the VBS begins so your volunteers can get to know each other and become a team, as well as become familiar with the roles they will perform.

As you recruit VBS staff, you will probably know who your Leaders will be before you have recruited all the people to be Helpers *(those who travel with each group of kids.)* These two groups of workers have different roles and will need some slightly different training for the jobs they will be doing. Included below are two meeting agendas: one for the Director and Leaders and one for all of the VBS staff. Each meeting is designed to last two hours. *(Note: You may want to ask your Leaders to come only to the second half of the second meeting or to help lead parts of the first half.)* Adjust these agendas to match the number of meetings you are able to have and the length of your VBS meetings. You may want to combine this time with other planning meetings, but be sure to set aside the specific time to spend on training.

Agenda 1 | Director and Leaders

10 min.	Welcome, prayer, introductions
15 min.	Team Building activity *(Page D.63.)*
10 min.	Review all VBS materials and resources that are available to the teachers.
10 min.	Discuss the role of the Leaders. *(See **Key Players**, page D.14.)*
15 min.	Overview of age-level characteristics *(see **Age Characteristics Charts**, pages R.17-20)* and how to adapt teaching to different age levels.
10 min.	BREAK
40 min.	Break into teaching teams *(two Leaders per Discovery Site)* to work on lesson preparation.
10 min.	Wrap-up discussion, questions, prayer

Agenda 2 | Director and all VBS Staff

10 min.	Welcome, prayer, introductions
15 min.	Team Building activity *(Page D.63.)*
10 min.	Review all materials and resources.
10 min.	Discuss the roles of the different staff who are present. *(See **Key Players**, page D.14.)*
10 min.	Discuss the logistics of how VBS will run in your particular setting.
15 min.	Overview of relationship building and the age-level characteristics *(See **Age Characteristics Charts**, pages R.17-20.)*
10 min.	BREAK
20 min.	Overview of Leader Hints *(See **Leader Hints**, pages R.12-16.)*
10 min.	Overview of important information *(include emergency procedures, safety tips, special education issues, and legal responsibilities)*
10 min.	Wrap-up discussion, questions, prayer

Inviting the middle school and high school youth to assist in your VBS program gives them a unique way to learn about God and minister to younger children. As they prepare and help lead, they will be listening and thinking more carefully about the Bible truths being taught. As they help and serve, they will be developing their Christian character. As they interact with you and other teachers, along with the younger children, they will be developing bonds in the body of Christ and friendships within your congregation.

In addition, lessons are much easier to teach with helpers along. With extra hands, feet, and voices, you will be much better able to befriend, teach, and meet the needs of the preschool and early elementary children. And when a lesson calls for extra helpers, the VBS Helpers will conveniently be available to lend a hand.

Finding and Recruiting Helpers

First, establish with your church's childrens ministries' team what age group you will be recruiting as your Helpers. Be sure to follow your church's screening procedures and rules for those who work with young children.

○ **Have the middle school and high school Sunday school announce the opportunity for youth to participate as VBS Helpers.**

○ **Send flyers home with the youth explaining the opportunity so it can be discussed with parents.**

○ **Host a short reception or "VBS Helpers' Party" and invite the youth of your church to come and find out what it's all about. Keep it fun and brief. Clearly define the jobs of a VBS Helper.**

○ **Present the opportunity to work as a VBS Helper as a positive experience rather than a chore for kids with "nothing else to do" during your VBS program. Make participation as a VBS Helper a big deal.**

○ **Be sure to emphasize the benefits of being a VBS Helper: a chance to gain experience** working with and caring for younger children, an opportunity to assist your church in reaching out to others in your community, a fun way to learn more about God and the Bible, and a chance to practice some acting skills.

Making It Fun

If you make participation as a VBS Helper an opportunity that offers both responsibility and fun, the youth will show more commitment and better attitudes. Consider some of these ideas:

○ **Using the VBS *Time-Stone Travelers*™ logo, design a badge, T-shirt, or vest for the VBS Helpers to wear. This will help the younger children identify who the responsible Helpers are when they need help.**

○ **Assign various job titles similar to the titles used by the adults helping in the program: Travel Helper; Craft Helper; Game Helper, Character Actor, etc.**

○ **Include Helpers in the Discovery Site planning meetings so they feel the responsibility and inclusion in the program.**

Training the Helpers

Training is essential if you want your VBS Helpers to be effective during the VBS program. It doesn't have to be long—and it can be fun! Here are some suggested ways to train.

○ **Plan a time that is convenient for both the youth and their parents. Consider a time that is just before or after another youth activity. It wouldn't have to take longer than 30 minutes.**

○ **Call the training session a "party." Keep the kids thinking, moving, and participating during most of the training. Use a lot of visuals.**

○ **Walk the kids through one of the Discovery Sites. At each section of the Discovery Site, explain what the Site Leader might need help with. (See the complete list below.)**

There are two main areas to stress during your training: responsibility and kindness.

Responsibility: The VBS Helpers need to show responsibility to the Site Leader by arriving on time, paying attention during class, remembering and carrying out duties, and looking for extra *(unasked for)* ways to help as they arise.

Kindness: The VBS Helpers need to be kind to the younger children they are helping. Kindness includes patience and being a good example at all times. If a discipline problem arises with the younger children, the Helpers should show kindness as they take the problem to an adult.

Jobs of the Helpers

The responsibilities you choose for the VBS Helpers will depend on your specific church and class needs. Here are ideas for how the youth in your church can help, serve, and learn during the *Time-Stone Travelers*™ VBS program.

○ **Help set up the classroom and gather supplies before the children arrive.**

○ **Welcome the children—make sure they have a name tag and get to the right group.**

○ **Welcome visitors—help them find a "buddy" to guide them during the day's activities.**

○ **Take part in the skits or role-playing as assigned by the Site Leader.**

○ **Lead the children from one activity to another as directed by the Site Leader.**

○ **Help with the CD player or other audio visual equipment as needed.**

○ **Participate with and/or help lead the singing.**

○ **Help non-readers with writing/reading activities.**

○ **For snacks: Wash and wipe tables before and after snack time, gather supplies and set up the snacks, help with hand-washing, refill cups, etc.**

○ **For games: Do preparation, gather supplies, help the children understand the rules, be a partner to reluctant children, etc.**

○ **For crafts: Arrange supplies, help younger children with assembly or writing on crafts, check to be sure all crafts have names on them, move completed crafts to a safe area until the end of class, clean up craft tables.**

○ **Oversee classroom cleanup.**

○ **Pass out take-home papers and crafts at the end of each day.**

Tips for Problem Solving

Discipline problems, emergencies, and unexpected incidents are bound to arise. A responsible and well-trained VBS Helper can be a big help during these times. Be sure your training session includes a time to cover this.

Discipline

The VBS Helpers should know that all discipline is handled by adults. However, the Helpers can be a big help in setting a good example for the younger children and by helping in the following ways:

○ **When a child loses attention or starts to play or talk during the lesson, the VBS Helper can quietly go and sit by that child. Usually that is all that will be needed to draw the child's attention back to the lesson, along with an occasional "shhh" or cheery reminder to "let's not miss what the teacher's saying!"**

○ **If a child becomes unruly or wants to wander off during transitions, the VBS Helper can gently hold the child's hand and walk alongside.**

○ **If a child becomes disruptive during a craft or game, it may be because the child doesn't understand what to do, has finished early, or is frustrated. The VBS Helper can sit by the child and offer encouragement, instruction, or a friendly conversation that focuses the child back on the task.**

Emergencies

Even with every detail planned and everything in place, emergencies do occur. How these emergencies are handled can make the difference between a slight inconvenience and a major upset in the classroom.

Make sure the VBS Helpers know where the nearest first-aid kit is kept so they can retrieve it for the Site Leader. Be sure to have a plan so that VBS Helpers know how to find the staff member in charge of VBS in case a parent needs to be contacted.

VBS Helpers should walk through your church's fire escape procedures so they could help lead the children outdoors in the event of a fire alarm.

Expecting the Unexpected

Younger children may need to use the restroom at any point during the lesson. Instruct the VBS Helpers to be on the lookout for any children with this need and to be prepared to quietly lead the child to and from the restroom. Boys should always escort boys and girls should always escort girls.

Some children may be unwilling to leave their parents when they arrive for VBS. They may cry or show stubbornness. A VBS Helper can join the child with a smile, offer to be a friend or buddy, and help the child get started on a transitional activity. Sometimes a VBS Helper may need to be assigned to one child for the whole class.

Visitors feel better when they have a friend, so a VBS Helper can take on that role. He or she can show the visitor where activities take place and explain what is happening during each part of the lesson.

Training Your Church's Youth Leaders

The youth who participate as your VBS Helper will be your church's future adults and leaders in the next few years. You have a wonderful opportunity, not just to have useful helpers in the classroom, but to make an important spiritual impression on these young people. Now is the time to help them form connections with your church, build relationships with Christian adults *(like yourself)*, and develop a commitment to God that goes beyond their parents' responsibility to bring them to the church doors each week. By having useful and age-appropriate responsibilities, these VBS Helpers will recognize and have an outlet for their God-given talents and interests. They will learn what it means to be part of the body of Christ. Their participation as VBS Helpers will develop spiritual maturity that will help them understand and draw closer to the Lord.

With this in mind, plan to meet with your VBS Helpers. Listen to their interests and concerns. Try to assign them duties that fit with their personalities and interests. Be sure they understand and are comfortable with their assignments and know who to contact during the VBS program in case of illness or unforeseen difficulties that could prevent them from participating. Pray with them about this opportunity for service.

Team Building

Use these team-building activities to develop friendships and a good working relationship among your staff.

Global God

Hang a length of mural paper on the wall. Sketch the outlines of the continents on it so it resembles a world map. Explain that since the *Time-Stone Travelers*™ VeBS® takes the kids around the world, the staff will encourage one another with God's work across the map. Ask everyone to think of answered prayers or news of God's work that they might have heard from missionaries, traveling friends, or newsletters and newspapers. Let volunteers briefly share what they know about God's work in those places and then draw a heart on the map at that spot. Then spend time as a group thanking God for His work around the world and in the lives of the kids you will teach.

Sharing Kid Connections

Find tokens or candies of three different colors (such as red, blue, and yellow), and place them in a container. Have the leaders take turns reaching into the container without looking and pulling out a token. The color determines what "kid connection" they will then share with the rest of the group:

- **Red—Share a joy you've experienced while working with kids.**
- **Blue—Share a challenge you've experienced while working with kids.**
- **Yellow—Share a memorable moment you've experienced with kids.**

Teamwork Refreshments

Divide the group into five teams, and assign each team a simple food to prepare related to one of the five sites. Everyone on the team must help with the preparation. Assign each team a spot to work. When all are finished, enjoy the refreshments together.

Mayan Jungle—Provide powdered drink mixes, sugar, and water for this group to create their own "bug juice." Or let this group use a blender to mix a variety of sub-tropical fruits with a little yogurt to make "goat's milk" smoothies.

Medieval Castle—Provide uncut loaves of bread (wheat, rye, etc.), cutting boards, knives, and serving trays. Include a variety of bread "toppings," such as chunk cheese, flavored cheese spreads, and meat pátés. This group should create flavored, open-face bread treats (cut in any shapes they wish).

Ancient Laboratory—Provide a variety of fruits that would have been found growing in historic Eastern Europe—berries, apples, cherries, and so on—for the group to chop and mix. As "science experiment" options, offer yogurt or sweetened condensed milk for this group to mix with different combinations of fruit.

Hawk's Village—Provide fresh vegetables for this group to chop into bite-size pieces, along with cream cheese and various spices for team members to mix together to create their own dip. Or have the group make a cold corn and bean salad with a simple vinegar and oil dressing.

Hawaiian Volcano—Provide softened chocolate ice cream, chocolate brownies, and cherry pie filling. This group mixes together crumbled brownies and ice cream, molds it into a mountain shape—with a volcano crater in the top—and refreezes it on a freezer-safe plate. When stiffened, remove from freezer and drizzle cherry pie filling down the sides to represent lava. This refreshment will need time to refreeze and be served last.

Kid Songs

Let volunteers tell about a favorite Christian kids' song and why they like it. It could be a song from their childhood or a current song. Then sing the song together. You may want to do this team-builder while gathered around a piano, or ask a Leader to bring a guitar.

Personal Goals for VeBS®

Make copies of the background transparencies *(pages R.70-81)* on regular paper, and have colored pencils on hand. Give each staff member one copy, and encourage everyone to think through two goals for this VeBS®: (1) What they would like to see happen in the children's lives, and (2) How they would like to grow spiritually or personally. Some may find it helpful to color as they think and pray about choosing goals. Have everyone write their goals prominently on their page. Divide into small groups for prayer. Encourage the staff to display their goals at home as a prayer reminder.

Linked Together

Have everyone sit in a circle. Choose one person to begin as Link 1. This Link chooses a second player to come stand in the center with her and be Link 2. Link 1 asks questions to find one unique fact that she does not already know about Link 2. The fact could be anything big or small; for example, perhaps Link 2 once visited Guatemala or his favorite food is strawberries. Once a new fact is found, Link 1 questions seated players to find one who has something in common with this fact. *(For example, Link 1 may discover someone who studied Spanish in high school, which links because Spanish is spoken in Guatemala, or she may even find someone wearing red, which links because strawberries are red.)* The person with the common link stands by Link 2 and becomes Link 3. Then Link 2 questions Link 3 to discover one new fact and matches this to another seated player, who becomes Link 4. Continue until everyone has been "linked" to one another in some way. The last player needs to find a connection to the person who was Link 1.

Devotions

The devotions on the following pages provide an opportunity for you and the Leaders to learn about and experience the love of Jesus so that you can show that love to the precious children at your VBS. They can be easily used during a prayer time before each VBS session or in the training meeting before VBS begins. Whether you do these devotions as a group or as individuals in preparation for VBS, we encourage you to do them! Take the time to allow God to speak to your heart, to fill you with the hope that is in Jesus Christ so that hope may overflow to the children.

Be sensitive to the fact that there may be workers in your own group who have never developed a relationship with Christ or who, through this time working with the kids, realize their desire to recommit their lives to Him. If you sense that there may be someone like that in your staff, be sure to make some time to spend with that person alone, outside of VBS. God can use VBS to touch the lives of adults and children alike!

These devotional pages can be used as personal reflection and/or to facilitate group discussions. If you hold corporate devotions with all the volunteers, you will need to photocopy the devotions for volunteers.

Only One God

Commandments 1, 2

"Teach me, O Lord, the way of thy statutes; and I shall keep it unto the end. Give me understanding, and I shall keep thy law; yea, I shall observe it with my whole heart."
—Psalm 119:33-34

What opinions about God have you heard on TV lately? How many people have you encountered in the past year who follow a god or religion other than Jesus? Have you heard people speak of God and describe Him with characteristics that Scripture would not agree with?

The Bible commands us to worship only the one true God. But our society promotes many views of God, to the point where it's hard to know if our own beliefs are more influenced by the Bible or by our culture.

When God gave Moses the 10 Commandments for His people, they had just come from a country steeped in idol worship. The Israelites could not escape hearing about the many false gods that surrounded them and led most of Egyptian society. We find ourselves in a similar situation. We are surrounded by people and media who often proclaim the superiority of other belief systems.

In order to worship the one true God, we must know who He is—who He *really* is. And that is who He presents Himself to be in the Bible. Many people in our culture have ideas about "God." They say He is tolerant or judgmental or absent or many other things. Basically, people have invented their own idea of God, rather than understanding that God invented the idea of people. We cannot simply say that because we don't like a certain characteristic or truth about God we will therefore ignore that part of Him or say it couldn't possibly be true. God is who He is.

The Lord God of the Bible is the one true God, the Creator and our Savior. And He has given us the Bible to allow us to learn about Him. The Israelites did not have the privilege of picking up a Scripture scroll any time they wanted and reading it to learn about God. But we do have this privilege. As we try to avoid being influenced by the false ideas about God our culture offers, we can counter misplaced priorities and fears by immersing ourselves in Scripture. We can grow in hope and strength as we study and learn more about Him.

Just as the gods of the Egyptians competed with one another for attention, the different images of God in our culture complete for our allegiance. The only way to know we are accurate in our understanding of God is to study the Bible and to carefully evaluate what might be misrepresentations that we hear and see around us each day.

Personal Reflection

Pick favorite TV show or movie your family enjoys, and think about how that show presents God. Do the characters' statements about God agree with Scripture? Do the characters get along just fine without Jesus or the Bible in their lives? Reflect on how the entertainment industry influences your understanding of who God is.

NOTES

Worship the Lord

Commandments 3, 4

" . . . Present your bodies a living sacrifice, holy, acceptable unto God, which is your reasonable service." —**Romans 12:1**

Does your household or workplace have a problem with following the rules? How often do you stop and talk about the motivation behind those rules?

The 10 Commandments were fairly simply worded, yet the Jewish religious leaders developed a large body of rules around them. They tried hard to obey the 10 Commandments but ended up with a huge batch of complicated details that they could use to scrutinize their lives—and the lives of others. For example, in an effort to obey the command about avoiding work on the Sabbath, religious laws developed which stated how many footsteps a person could take on a Sabbath before a walk was considered "work." It ended up being a heavy load to carry!

Jesus and the New Testament writers made the laws both simpler and more challenging. Jesus dismissed the many little rules that had developed around keeping the Sabbath *(Mk. 7:8; Matt. 23)*. The laws about the Sabbath were referred to by the Apostle Paul as days that ended up getting more focus than the One the day was for *(Col. 2:16-17)*. That is a relief for all of us! But at the same time, the New Testament challenges us to keep the commandments about Sabbath and the worship of God as something to encompass our whole lives.

Worship is making our entire selves a "living sacrifice" *(Rom. 12:1)*. Worship is not reserved for the minutes or hours when we can sit and focus on God. Rather, it is to pour out of our entire lives, so that no matter where we are or what work we are doing, we are doing it as for the Lord *(Col. 3:23)*. Paul urges us to "pray without ceasing" *(1 Thess. 5:17)*. What a tremendous challenge! No wonder the Pharisees preferred the rules they could check off their list when completed.

We also can check off things that we do "for the Lord" each week. These efforts are good and can reflect our desire to obey the commandments to honor God and set aside time for Him. But as people who have been revolutionized by the events of the New Testament, we accept a challenge that can't be measured: worshiping God in all we do and are. Our very lives are transformed by His presence in us. We become like Him in our thoughts, feelings, and actions. Then we are freed from checklists and self-recrimination and measuring if we've done "enough."

Personal Reflection

Plan a way to remind yourself throughout the day to stop and reflect on God's presence. You might set your wristwatch to beep every hour as a reminder to stop and ask yourself how you're honoring God at that moment. Or you might take note of whenever you walk somewhere and ask yourself how you're walking with God at that moment. Make a plan, and go for it!

NOTES

Honor Your Father and Mother

Commandment 5

"Ye shall fear every man his mother, and his father . . . ." —**Leviticus 19:3**

Our most deeply connected relationships can be our most joyful—and our most frustrating! And even though we might assume that our closest relationships need no rules—because we love these people—God knew that we would have times when we need to be reminded of the basics. One of His rules is this: Even at times when we don't feel very close to or loving toward our parents, we still need to honor them.

"Honor" means different things in different cultures. In traditional Asian countries, honoring parents borders on not even questioning their decisions about our lives. In western cultures, honor and respect are attitudes that are seen to be "earned"—and too bad for the parent who doesn't "deserve" our respect.

In Bible times, honoring was more than an attitude. It was an action, an active expression of serving. In our day and time, we tend to focus on honor as an emotion, yet the Bible encourages us to make honoring our parents an action. Honor can be something that we feel, but it is especially something that we do.

One of the criticisms Jesus gave the Pharisees was for not honoring their parents *(Mark 7:9-13)*. It was the Pharisees' religious commitment that got in their way of obeying that command. They chose to give offerings to the temple rather than providing for their elderly parents. Jesus saw not only the heart of the matter, but pointed out that action is as important as attitude.

Not every adult has a close or loving relationship with his or her parents, and even those that do experience times of friction. But we can always keep our parents in our prayers. We begin by searching for things about our parents to thank the Lord for, both little and big.

Then we need to look for hands-on ways to honor our parents. Look at honor from *their* point of view. Would they consider it honor for you to spend time with them, communicate with them more, provide for some need, or do something special for them? Would they consider it honor if *they* could do the giving to *you* and have you graciously receive their help? Can you honor our parents by speaking *about* them respectfully when you mention them to others? Can you honor them by teaching your kids to give time and attention to their grandparents? Can you honor them by lovingly accepting not to argue over a differing viewpoint—even on an important issue?

God will guide you if you ask His help in finding ways to honor your father and your mother. Spend time thinking about your parents and their needs as you go throughout your day.

Personal Reflection

Write a prayer of thanks to God for your father and your mother. Then make a plan to incorporate actions of honor for your parents into your lifestyle.

NOTES

Don't Hurt Others

Commandments 6, 7, 8, 9

"But when he saw the multitudes, he was moved with compassion on them . . . ." —**Matthew 9:36**

Our lives are so busy, filled with good commitments and important priorities. The last thing we need is a guilt trip about not doing enough or the aggravation of unexpected interruptions.

Jesus experienced countless interruptions to His plans, and the crowds who relentlessly followed Him apparently thought that He wasn't doing enough, or that He could do more—for them. Since interruptions will happen to us, we can learn from Jesus how to handle them.

Jesus saw people not as interruptions but as opportunities. And this viewpoint sprang from His heart. Jesus approached all people—whether planned or accidental—with compassion.

When Jesus told the story of the good Samaritan, He was aware of the important items on the busy schedules of priests and Levites. But He made the point that compassion is more important.

Jesus didn't just tell stories; He lived out His own teachings. Luke 9:10-11 tells that Jesus took His disciples to a secluded place, where He planned to have some valuable teaching time. But the crowds found Him. Rather than sticking to His schedule, He had compassion on them and taught and healed them. Maybe this was part of the valuable lesson Jesus was trying to teach! Another time Jesus had gone off to pray alone *(Mark 1:35-36)*, but when He was found He again responded with compassion.

Jesus stopped to interact caringly with each one He healed. Mark 1:40-41 details that He reached out His hand to touch a man with leprosy. In truth, Jesus could have just stretched out His arms and performed a mass healing over any crowd. But His compassion for the individual made Him reach out in one-on-one love.

We can find strength to tackle our own interrupted schedules by leaning on Jesus' example. Our families, friends, and coworkers may sometimes need more than the effort or time we've allotted on a given day. To have a plan is a good starting point; Jesus made plans, too. But we can be so much more effective by pausing to look deeper and listen harder to see if there's a need we haven't noticed in these people. Then there are the other people—acquaintances and strangers—for whom God's compassion shining through us could make a world of difference.

Let the lesson of the good Samaritan serve as a reminder to keep our spiritual antennae tuned for people in need of a dose of compassion.

Personal Reflection

Make a list of every individual you come across today. If you don't know a name, list the person's job or capacity in which you saw them *(e.g. "grocery cashier this morning who wasn't helpful")*, but try to avoid lumping people as a group *(e.g. "all store clerks")*. Then pray for each person and for needs you're aware of. If the person is a stranger, pray that they will know God's compassionate love.

NOTES

Be Happy with What You Have

Commandment 10

"But let every man prove his own work, and then shall he have rejoicing in himself alone, and not in another."
—**Galatians 6:4**

Do a brief experiment. Stand up and walk around the room you're in. Look for any item that suggests that you *need* something or *want* something or *should* want something—ad flyers, commercials, magazines, newspapers, computer screen pop-ups, promos on existing products, and so on.

Just in the room you're in, you've probably found it hard to escape the barrage of "wants" our society instills in us. Our eyes are trained to compare ourselves with what others have. Our brains are conditioned to sense any feeling of unfulfillment. Our emotions are tuned to respond to material pleasures.

It's the emotional buy-in to materialism that the Bible warns us about. Scripture urges us to examine our emotional response to possessions and money and learn to be content (Phil. 4:12). So many Bible verses are directed not toward people who already have money, but toward Christians who *want* it.

1 Timothy 6:10 warns us against loving our money. Psalm 52:7 suggests that it's all too easy to feel financially secure *(or insecure)* because of what we own *(or don't own)*, rather than through God being our stronghold. Getting what we want, Mark 4:19 tells us, can actually choke our spiritual growth because of "the deceitfulness of riches."

Our feelings often lead our actions. But the Bible gives us encouragement for standing strong.

First, we can train our focus to be on God. "Set your affection on things above, not on things on the earth," advises Colossians 3:2, and Romans 13:14 urges us to not even think about how to gratify our desires. As we intentionally set goals for knowing and loving God more, we train ourselves to set our minds and hearts on Him.

Secondly, we can resist comparing ourselves to others

(Gal. 6:4) and avoid all temptation (Matt. 5:29). If looking at ads and watching commercials or even walking through stores tugs our hearts toward "wanting," then we need to take steps to avoid looking at ad flyers, sitting through commercials, or shopping without a specific purpose.

Thirdly, we can be thankful. We can thank God for each possession that we do have. We can thank Him for what we don't have. By not owning the things we want or even need, we are learning to be dependent on Him.

Always remember that the Lord loves you very much. His lack of new gifts for you is no indication of His affection for you or your "success" as a Christian. God's goal is to build your spirit and make you full of joy, without needing "things" to do so.

Personal Reflection

What are some things you found yourself wishing you had this past week? What types of possessions are generally a problem for you? Take time to thank God that you don't have these things. Jot down ways you can avoid involving your feelings in wanting what others have.

NOTES

Appreciate Your Staff!

VBS could never happen without all the volunteers. Let them know that they are appreciated and that the time and effort they put in is valued. Here are some ideas to get you started. There's no such thing as too much appreciation, so plan a number of ways to say thanks throughout VBS!

○ Arrange a full Saturday or an evening when high school kids babysit for Leaders' kids so the Leaders can have some free time.

○ Take your Leaders out for a team lunch.

○ Purchase small baskets and fill them with fruit and an encouraging note for each Leader.

○ Create a snack pack with chocolates, candies, and other treats.

○ Do something crazy, challenging, team-building, and adventurous with your team of leaders: Have your own game day where the Leaders take part. Play the games from the various Discovery Sites. This will bond the team and allow for more open and effective communication once the kids arrive.

○ Place a colorful plant or flower in each classroom to brighten the Leaders' day.

○ At the beginning of VBS, give each Leader a "survival kit" with notes of encouragement, treats, fun gifts, uplifting verses, and so on, that they can dive into anytime they need a lift during VBS.

○ Give out gift certificates from a favorite restaurant, ice-cream shop, or coffee house.

○ Have volunteers from the church cook and deliver dinner for each leader and his or her family one night during VBS.

○ Give each Leader an inexpensive fanny pack, backpack, or bag to carry their supplies to and from VBS.

○ Create a *Time-Stone Travelers*™ team of adults who, for some reason, can't be present at VBS but want to be part of it. Have this team be in charge of coordinating prayer partners, making encouraging phone calls, and writing notes of encouragement to the leaders and volunteers for your VBS.

○ Throughout VBS, have a rope that you bring to Leader meetings. Have a few minutes set aside where Leaders can share encouraging and exciting things that are happening in their groups of kids. Each time they tell a story, have them tie a knot in the rope. At the end of VBS, schedule a time when volunteers can stand up in church, show the rope, and tell one of the stories that is represented by the knots. Leaders will appreciate the opportunity to share how God worked as well as the opportunity to be recognized by the congregation.

○ Give a pack of candy with a verse to encourage Leaders to hang in there through the adventure.

○ Give a "night at the movies" with a package containing a movie rental gift certificate and a bag of microwave popcorn.

○ Acknowledge your Leaders in front of the entire church. Display in a prominent area pictures of each Leader with a quote from a child about how much that Leader meant to them during VBS.

○ Print the *Time-Stone Travelers*™ logo or a favorite Key Verse on a water bottle or coffee mug for each leader.

○ Print Ephesians 6:10 on some colorful paper and put it in an inexpensive frame for each Leader.

○ If you know each of your Leaders well, select different gifts, appropriate for each person (a favorite candy bar would work). The fact that you thought of each one individually will mean a lot to the Leaders.

Promote

Promoting your VBS is an important part of your planning. The ways that you choose to promote VBS will partly determine who and how many attend *Time-Stone Travelers*™. Before you decide on methods of promotion, you may want to meet with your committee and determine the goals you have. How many children do you want to attend? How much money is in the budget for promotion?

Do you want to reach kids in your church first, kids in other churches, kids throughout the community, or all of the above? Clarifying these things in the beginning will help promotion to run smoothly.

Included in the Reproducible Resources section is artwork for promotional posters. There is also a full-color poster available on the *Time-Stone Travelers*™ CD. Place these posters in prominent places in your church and community to let people know that the *Time-Stone Travelers*™ VBS will be taking place at your church. Be sure to fill in the details—dates of your VBS, the time VBS will be held each day, and the name and location of your church.

Use any of the ideas listed here and the resources in the Reproducible Resources section and the *Time-Stone Travelers*™ CD. Feel free to customize them to fit your VBS.

Involve the Kids...

Print copies of the full-color poster found on the *Time-Stone Travelers*™ CD, or the black and white Event Poster provided on page R.8. Allow children to take the posters with them and hang them somewhere in their neighborhood, school, store, and so on.

○ **Use the postcard design to send out invitations to children in the church and the community. You may want to have extra copies of the postcard available for members of the church who would like to take them and give them to parents of children in their neighborhoods. Be sure the postcard includes information about when and where parents can register their children. (See the postcard invitation on page R.10 or on the *Time-Stone Travelers*™ CD.) Point out that although a child is invited by a friend, the parent must still register their child for VBS. (See Registration Form on page R.4.)**

○ **The art images in the Reproducible Resources section, and the electronic clip art on the *Time-Stone Travelers*™ CD can be used in many different ways. Use it on water bottles, T-shirts, hats, and bookmarks to add fun to any of the promotional activities that you do!**

Involve the Church...

Designate a certain Sunday as VBS Sunday to introduce your program. Be sure to include the bulletin insert *(page R.40 or on the CD)*. This will launch the VBS for this year and get people familiar with the theme and excited about the outreach potential for VBS.

○ As soon as you launch VBS, be sure to have plenty of registration cards *(page R.4)* available for people to fill out.

○ Even as early as a couple of months before VBS, start including flyers and information in the bulletins at your church. You may want to start with the flyer encouraging people to pray for VBS. *(See page R.11.)*

○ As it gets closer to VBS, hand out the volunteer flyer *(see page R.11)* to encourage volunteers to sign up for all areas of VBS.

○ All flyers and bulletin inserts will be most effective if supplemented by an announcement or skit during the service.

○ Make magnets or bookmarks out of the prayer reminders *(page R.11)* and send them to each person who has agreed to be a prayer partner. You may also want to have them available at worship services so people can take them home.

○ If you want to save some money by having some of the supplies and props for VBS donated, distribute a flyer to let people know what you need. Be sure to include information about whom they can contact and where they can leave the supplies. You will want to do

this close enough to VBS that you do not have to store the materials for too long, but far enough in advance so you know what additional supplies need to be purchased. Use the complete supply lists on pages D.17-24 and P.4-11 as a guide.

○ Make T-shirts using the T-shirt pattern and sell them before VBS begins *(or as part of pre-registration)* so that the kids can wear them and share the news about VBS with their friends and neighbors. *(Use the transfer art on the CD, or use other art images to create your own T-shirt design.)*

○ Use art images provided on the CD to create other items (inexpensive plastic cups or water bottles, stickers, bookmarks, and so on) for the kids to take home from VBS as a reminder of what they have learned.

○ Hang a large banner inviting neighborhood children to *Time-Stone Travelers™* in a prominent place in your church or over the registration table. Be sure to fill in the correct information for the dates, time, and place on the poster.

Involve the Community...

Many radio stations provide air time for public service announcements or community events. Let your local radio stations know about the upcoming VBS at your church. Use the Press Release *(see page R.41)* to provide the necessary information. You may also want to ask station managers to let you call in and talk live on the radio about your VBS. If your church has audio production capabilities, you might record a short *(15-second)* radio spot to advertise VBS. Use the Press Release information as your guide.

○ Some cable TV companies offer free advertising for local groups in the form of scrolling ads during off-time. Check with your local cable company for what they offer and what they require from you.

○ Host a *Time-Stone Travelers*™ Day in a park or nearby public area. Use this day to attract attention to VBS and to provide registration for people in the community who are not regularly involved in the church.

More Promotional Ideas...

Hand out balloons at church one Sunday with a Postcard Invitation *(page R.10)* attached to the bottom of the balloon.

○ **Have a race or walk where members of the church without kids can contribute to VBS through this fund-raiser.**

○ **Create one of the VBS Discovery Sites in advance and have it set up in the church where people can get information about VBS and register their kids.**

○ **Make magnetic reminders by printing the *Time-Stone Travelers*™ logo pattern on colorful cardstock and add the dates and times of your VBS. Put a magnetic strip on the back. Give the magnets to kids along with an extra to give to a friend with an invitation. You may also want to give them as reminders for people to pray for VBS.**

○ **Instead of including all the flyers as bulletin inserts *(page R.40)*, have some of the kids dress up in Bible-time outfits and hand out the flyers at the worship services.**

○ **Sell raffle tickets and give the winners gifts. *(T-shirt, gift certificate, stuffed animal, mini-golf tickets, and so on.)***

○ **For one of your VBS announcement times, sing a song instead of speaking. You may want to use one of the songs from the VBS CD or put the information you need to communicate to a familiar tune.**

○ **Make a short video clip to show on Sunday morning to introduce VBS. One idea is to ask a number of kids in your church this question and videotape their response. What's the most exciting place you've ever visited?**

○ **If your VBS schedule is other than five consecutive sessions, do a mid-VBS report for the church. Be sure to include some kids!**

○ **Print copies of the full-color promotional poster found on the *Time-Stone Travelers*™ CD to display around your church and in legal public notice areas in your community. Be sure to fill in the correct information for the date, place, and time on the poster.**

○ **There are many excellent Bible resources on the Internet. You may want to use these in addition to the promotional aids available through our VBS site at www.cookvbs.com.**

Follow-up on Kids

Give each of your kids a Bible or New Testament so they can learn more on how to study and grow in their new life in Jesus.

○ Take your VBS kids to visit a children's hospital, or a nursing home and share with the people the love that they have found in Jesus. Sing some of the VBS songs.

○ Encourage the Helpers who went to each of the five Discovery Sites with their groups to sponsor an activity just for their kids. This will help to maintain the relationship that was established in VBS and may give visiting kids just the contact and the encouragement they need to start attending church regularly.

○ Find out if there are any sports competitions in your area and take the kids to see one.

Even an outing to a college or community sporting event will be fun for the kids. This will give you a chance to spend time with those kids who may need extra encouragement.

○ Make a list of the kids that attended VBS and send them a postcard one month after VBS ends, encouraging them to continue studying and growing in their Christian life as they finish out the summer and head back to school.

○ Make a *Time-Stone Travelers*™ certificate for each child using the certificate sample on page R.9, or the color version from the *Time-Stone Travelers*™ CD, or create your own original certificate.

Follow-up on Leaders

Put together a slide show of pictures or video taken during VBS. Host a fellowship gathering for your staff. Show your slides or video to let them see the wonderful job they did for the kids.

○ Make the time over the next six months to have lunch with your volunteers *(you may want to do it one on one or in small groups).* This will not only help them feel appreciated, it will keep you in touch with them for next year—and they will probably have great ideas and suggestions for VBS in the future.

○ Be sure you have accurate mailing and phone lists of all the Leaders so that you can contact them easily in the future. Encourage them to let you know if any of their information changes.

○ Have kids make thank-you notes for people who donated time, supplies, prayer, and so on.

Follow-up on Families

If possible, plan a reunion a few weeks after VBS is over so kids and families can play games, enjoy refreshments, and catch up with one another.

○ Invite families to take part in a day-long "field trip" together, such as a day hike, a bike ride, or a tour of a local establishment.

○ Arrange a time in a worship service where the kids from VBS can sing some VBS songs for the congregation. Be sure to have this arranged by the end of VBS so that you can let all the parents know. This will be an excellent way to get kids and parents who do not attend church to come visit.

○ You may want to arrange host families that you can match up with non-church kids and their families after VBS is over. This will encourage those families to come visit church, get answers to questions they have, and help them feel comfortable coming to church.

Follow-up on the Church

Let the church know how VBS went by showing a videotape of the highlights of *Time-Stone Travelers*™ .

○ Present the Project Timeless Truth mission project to the church. Let them know what the kids have learned and how they have given of their money to help provide *New Testament Picture Bibles* for children in South America, Africa, the Middle East, Asia, and India. Challenge the church body to match the amount that the kids gave.

○ Ask a few kids to tell their favorite things about VBS in front of the church.

○ Schedule a time when kids from VBS can sing the songs they learned during VBS.

○ Invite all those in the church who prayed for VBS or who participated in any way to be part of the intergenerational closing program.

○ Put together a video, a slide show, or a picture collage to present to the church to let them know all about the exciting things that happened during VBS.

TIMELESS TRUTH

Share God's eternal love with the children of Latin America

This year's VeBS kids will zoom back in history to Mayan jungles and medieval castles. On their way they will learn about obedience to God's Word and His commandments. But do they realize that children in Latin America in 2006 don't know Jesus and can't read about God's timeless truth? They have no Bibles.

The Message Is Eternal, the Need Is Now

Time-Stone Travelers tell children who lived long ago about Jesus. Your VeBS kids can share Jesus with children who live in Latin America today by giving them the *New Testament Picture Bible* in Spanish. The grinding poverty these children face in Latin America is much worse than we can imagine. The average family earns about $10 to $50 per month. For as little as $5, your VeBS kids can give four children a *New Testament Picture Bible*.

Cook Communications Ministries International (CCMI) has mission projects around the globe, so your VeBS kids can choose the children they want to bless—Iraq to India, China to Myanmar. Just by giving their nickels and dimes, children in remote Cuban villages will have Spanish Bibles to learn of God's love. Bible club teachers in India's slums can give children Bibles in their language to take home. Many are from Muslim families. Children in Iraq or China can find out about God in Arabic or Chinese.

CCMI will print, bind, and distribute these colorfully illustrated Bibles. Many of these children generously share the Good News they read about with family and friends. In Cuba, where over 250,000 have already been distributed, it is often the little ones who bring unsaved friends to church. CCMI has countless stories of fathers and mothers, grandparents and uncles coming to salvation because of the children.

Get Your Church Involved

Each opening assembly: Talk about **Project Timeless Truth**. Make copies of the flyer on the next page for kids to show their parents. Post flyers around your church. Use a world map to show kids where Brazil, Cuba, India, Asia, and the Middle East are located. During each opening assembly, collect an offering. Each *New Testament Picture Bible* costs only $1.25—about the price of a candy bar.

Coin drive: Kids may not think they have much to give, but they will be amazed at how quickly their pocket change adds up! Use a clear container with a Bible or a map of the world painted on it. Or, use a box painted to look like a treasure chest.

All-church challenge: After the VeBS kids raise money, have them present **Project Timeless Truth** to the rest of the church and ask members to match what the children have raised.

Get a FREE *New Testament Picture Bible* from CCMI

Use the *New Testament Picture Bible* to show how the pictures and words explain Jesus—even to kids who can barely read. Every penny of the contributions goes to **Project Timeless Truth**. Call 1-800-323-7543 to receive one *New Testament Picture Bible* (#69906 VEBS PNT OFFER-SPANISH; #103329 VEBS PNT OFFER-ENGLISH) per VeBS program. Please specify to the service representative that this is Special Offer VBS06 and provide the item number.

Where to Send Your Offering:

CCMI/**Project Timeless Truth**
4050 Lee Vance View
Colorado Springs, CO 80918

Please make checks payable to CCMI/**Project Timeless Truth**. An envelope is provided following this page for you to send your VeBS offering to CCMI.

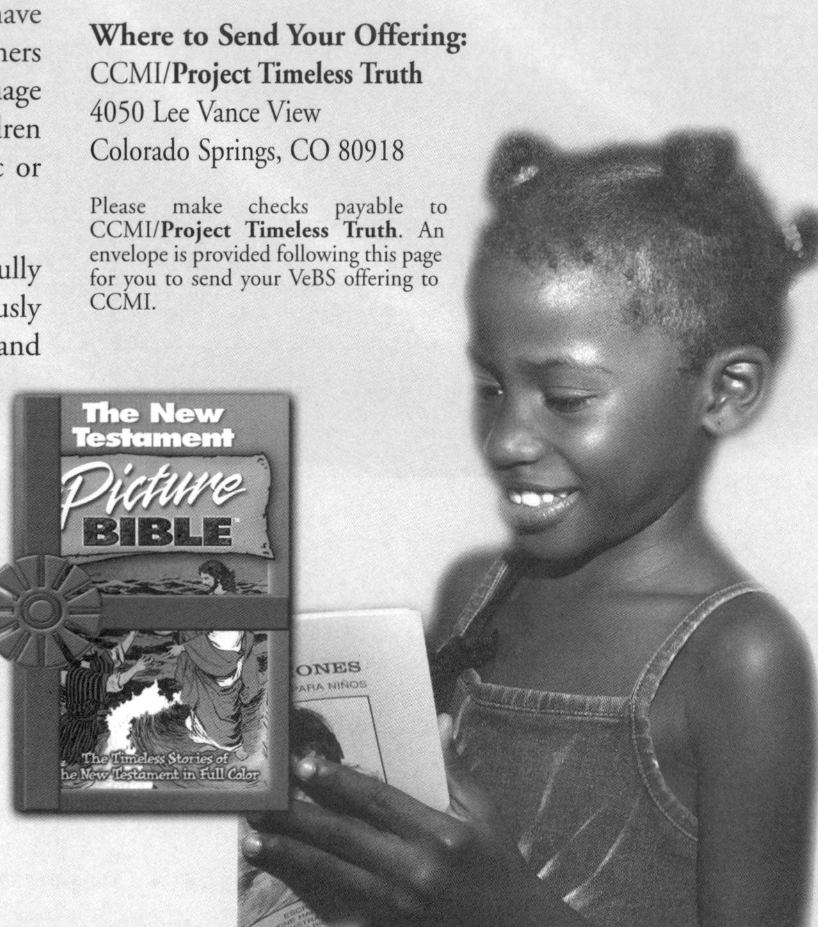

NOTES

E L E M E N T A R Y

Mayan Jungle

"My soul, wait thou only upon God; for my expectation is from him. He only is my rock and my salvation: he is my defence; I shall not be moved." — **Psalm 62:5-6**

INFO for the TRIP

Why Kids Need to Acknowledge that there Is Only One God

Everybody worships someone or something, whether they know or admit it. To worship means to make someone or something more important than anything else. The children you're working with have a tendency to "worship" other people, food, entertainment choices, possessions, or themselves. Because these other "gods" are so ingrained in our hearts, it can be quite difficult to even realize that they motivate and drive us. But God desires and mandates—from knowledge of what's best for us—that we have no other people or things above Him in our affections. And He expects us to demonstrate that He is our God by the way we worship and serve Him.

Most of the children will verbalize that they don't revere gods or idols. You'll need to assist them in recognizing which people and things do hold top place in their hearts by talking about and showing them the common gods that we all struggle against: our things, our bodies, other people, and ourselves. Ask them what they would do with a big amount of money. What do they think about when they're daydreaming or first wake up in the morning? How do they use their free time? These questions will help them uncover what they really hold dear. Then help the children to see that only the God who made them deserves to be at the center of their priorities and emotions.

Encourage the kids to get to know the one true God in Scripture and to worship that God, not the God they hear about in superficial songs or on secular TV shows. Use biblical word pictures to illustrate your teaching so the kids develop an accurate picture of God, whom they can safely and joyously worship.

FACTOID

The jungles where the Mayans lived spread from Mexico through Central America. In these lived exotic wildlife such as giant lizards that resembled small dragons, two-toed sloths, emerald tree boas, pink flamingoes, and the world's largest rodents, called capybaras. The Mayans used jungle materials, such as dried leaves to form their sleeping hammocks, tree poles to build homes, and stretchy vines that draped from treetops, almost like enormous rubber bands.

GETTING MORE FROM THE BIBLE STORY

Shadrach, Meshach, and Abednego were Daniel's peers, Jewish captives living in pagan Babylon. Daniel had already established himself as a credible ruler under King Nebuchadnezzar, who had previously recognized Daniel's devotion to God and honored it. But this time, the king was raging and furious (Dan. 3:13) at the men's refusal to obey the new law that compromised their faith. Nebuchadnezzar decided to make a public example of the them.

The furnace the three faced was industrial size, possibly used to make bricks or smelt metal, both activities that the Babylonians were involved with. God's protection was so all-encompassing that only the rope the men had been bound with was burned. God also sent a supernatural being—an angel or Christ himself—to stand with the three in their punishment.

The likely response of those watching was wonderment at the display of God's power in preserving the men. Help the children grasp that awe of the one true God. Our decision to worship only the true God has to be both in our actions and in our hearts.

Core Concept

Children will learn that there is only one God, that they should worship only Him, and that He should be the most important thing in their lives.

Key Bible Verse

Early Elementary

"[God] only is my rock and my salvation: he is my defence; I shall not be moved."

— **Psalm 62:6**

Upper Elementary

"My soul, wait thou only upon God; for my expectation is from him. He only is my rock and my salvation: he is my defence; I shall not be moved."

— **Psalm 62:5-6**

Puppet Option

A Leader can operate FINNEGAN to help lead the children to different areas and interact spontaneously with the teacher and children. *(See puppet pattern for FINNEGAN on pages R.53-57.)*

Bible Passage

**Daniel 3,
Exodus 20:3-4**
(Commandments 1, 2)

10 minutes: Introduction

15-20 minutes: Bible Story Time

10 minutes: Bible Memory Time

5 minutes: Music Time

20 minutes: Game Time

15 minutes: Snack Time

20 minutes: Craft Time

10 minutes: Application Time

10 minutes: Time-Stone Take Off

Setting the Scene

Use the transparency in the Resource section *(page R.70)* to create a South American jungle setting. Project the picture onto a length of mural paper hung on a wall, and trace the outlines. Use real or artificial bushy plants, palm trees, and vines that can be hung and draped, along with large tropical flowers in purples, yellows, and orange. Lay a green carpet, felt, or artificial turf on the ground. You might add stuffed monkeys swinging in the trees, a parrot perched on a branch, and a fake snake. Have the jungle sounds from the *Time-Stone Travelers*™ CD playing in the background.

Introduction

(A1) Supplies

- ○ Jungle sounds from *Time-Stone Travelers™* CD
- ○ CD or tape player
- ○ Large foam-core board "replica" of the 10 Commandments tablet with just the first two commandments clearly printed on it *(page R.45)*
- ○ Realistic looking, colorful, pretend snake
- ○ Soccer ball
- ○ Beautiful piece of girls' clothing
- ○ Video game

Advanced Preparation

COMMANDMENTS
1&2

1. Have craft samples prepared in advance to show Travelers. For each site, create a large foam-core board "replica" of the 10 Commandments tablet with the applicable commandments clearly printed on it.

2. Be sure all supplies are gathered and your site is ready each day for Travelers to arrive.

3. Post the Schedule of Activities where Leaders and Helpers can refer to it.

4. Address each other by site titles. Children should be referred to as Travelers.

5. After taking attendance, a Leader should tell those responsible for refreshments how many Travelers are present to be prepared for snack time.

6. You may wish to do some background research into the Bible story. Refer to Bible commentaries, encyclopedias, and dictionaries for additional information.

In Advance: Hide the snake, ball, clothing, and video game in the jungle set-up. Have jungle sound effects playing audibly as kids enter.

(Josh, Will, and Ellen should come to the front from behind the kids, talking about finding a snake.)

JOSH: *(Mad.)* **I told you not to leave the cage open, even a little!**

WILL: I know I didn't leave it open. I didn't!

ELLEN: Let's look around this part of the jungle.

(The three hunt for the snake and one finds it. Josh holds it.)

WILL: Phew. I'm SO glad we got this snake rounded up. *(Asks kids.)* **Aren't you?**

Leaders Profile

Josh, Will, Ellen
These three kid characters may wear kid-looking pajamas *(which is what they often wore when they time traveled in the stories)*, or they may wear summer vacation clothing.

This snake is something you'll for sure find in a place like a South American jungle. There are tiny snakes and huge ones, snakes that live in the water and some that climb in trees.

ELLEN: Today we're going explore life in the jungle. *(Looks at Josh and Will.)* **Should we see what these kids already know about jungles and rain forests?** *(They nod.)*

JOSH: Who knows something about what it's like in a rain forest or jungle? *(Call on kids to share what they know.)*

WILL: You already know lots! But we're going to find out even more cool things.

JOSH: But first, let's see what else we can find in our jungle. *(The three look around and bring out the soccer ball, girls' clothing, and video game.)*

ELLEN: Here's a real mystery for you. *(Looks around at the kids.)* **What do these three things—and the snake—all have in common?** *(The actors hold up each item and call on kids to offer ideas.)*

JOSH: Good ideas! First, let's see who likes these things. We'll each name one of these things. You decide which one you like the most. This ball stands for playing sports. Stand up if you like playing sports. *(Kids who like sports stand, then sit again.)*

ELLEN: How about cool, new clothes to wear? *(Kids who like that stand, then sit again.)*

Will: Do you like playing video games or computer games or things like that? *(Kids who like that stand, then sit again.)*

JOSH: This snake will have to stand for our pets. How many of you like pets? *(Kids who like them stand, then sit again.)*

WILL: Here's what these all have in common. People really, really like these things. For some people, these are the most important things to them. Sports or games or clothes or their pets are so important, nothing else matters as much.

ELLEN: It's okay to like the things you have or do. But God says nothing should be more important to us than He is. We can enjoy playing, having pets, buying clothes, and lots of other things. In God's 10 rules for life—in the second rule—He says we should never let anything or any person become more important to us than God.

WILL: The 10 rules. Hmm. I think I've heard about that before, but with a different name. Hmm. Guidelines? No. Um. The 10 best ideas? The 10 suggestions? I don't think that's it.

JOSH: Anyone out there know what God's 10 rules for living are called in the Bible? If you do, shout it out with us. *(Actors lead kids in shouting, "The 10 Commandments!")*

ELLEN: You're right. And what is the one we just pointed out? God says nothing should be more important to us than Him. *(Josh and Will bring out the 10 Commandments tablets on foam core board. One points to the second commandment and reads it.)*

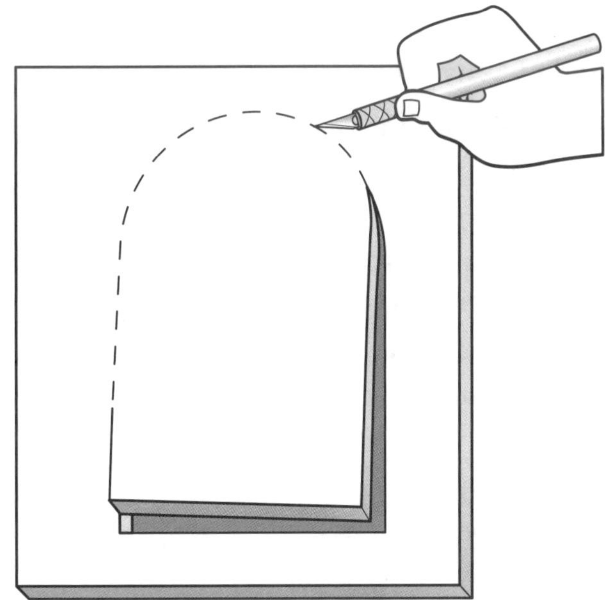

WILL: Should we tell them the other one for today? *(Actors huddle and whisper, build suspense).*

JOSH: Okay, we decided we'd tell you the other commandment we'll be finding out about today. It has to do with a snake! *(Holds out snake to audience.)* **The very first commandment in God's 10 rules for living is this: "Thou shalt have no other gods before me." That means we should love and obey only the one true God and not any other god.**

ELLEN: So how does a snake have anything to do with loving only God and not worshipping other gods?

WILL: Were any of the rest of you wondering that? *(Asks kids.)* **In some places around the world, people worship animals and things like the sun or moon. Some people believe there are lots of gods to worship. This snake stands for a god that people deep in the South American jungle believe is a powerful spirit. They're afraid of it and worship it because they think it is their god. But that goes against the true God's very first rule, which is . . . .** *(Motions to kids to shout out the answer: "Thou shalt have no other gods before me.")* **Yes, there is only one God and we are to obey and love only Him and not any other god.**

JOSH: Wow. That's a lot to remember already.

ELLEN: I know. How about listening to a really amazing story to help understand God's rules better?

JOSH: Sure. Stories are great! *(Three actors sit down among kids to listen.)*

# Bible Story Time

Daniel 3, Exodus 20:3-4

(A2) Supplies
- ○ Bible
- ○ Yellow, bigger-than-life statue *(Made of cardboard, foam, etc. Pattern found on p. R.46.)*
- ○ Bible-time clothes for King Nebuchadnezzar and three Hebrew men

- ○ Throne *(large, decorated chair)*
- ○ Toy instruments *(tambourines, horns, kazoos, bells, drums, etc.)*
- ○ Room divider or large appliance box *(to serve as fiery furnace)*
- ○ Something to make sound effects of crackling fire
- ○ Yellow and red lights *(can be flashlights with colored film over the lenses)*
- ○ Life-size cardboard shape of a person
- ○ Ropes or binding

In Advance: Recruit adults or teens to read the narration and to play the roles of:

- King Nebuchadnezzar
- Shadrach, Meshach, and Abednego
- A herald
- A few people to play various parts *(may double for each other)*—magistrates, astrologers, advisors, guards
- "Backstage" helpers

These actors may memorize their parts from the Bible or simply repeat what the Narrator reads.

Set up the story background in a different area from the jungle. The statue should be in a prominent side position. Put King Nebuchadnezzar's throne (large chair) near the middle of the setting and the "furnace" on the side opposite the statue. Have helpers hide inside or behind the furnace to shine the lights and make the fire sounds. *(You may wish to use a sound system to play the fire sounds.)*

Begin by showing the children the Book of Daniel in a Bible. **This story is from the book of Daniel in the Old Testament of the Bible. Some people are going to help me tell this story.**

Have Ellen, Josh, and Will hand out toy instruments to kids. Instruct kids to make noise with their instruments when the Bible story says the people hear the sound of the horns and other instruments.

The Narrator should stand off to the side to clearly and dramatically read the story from Daniel 3. King Nebuchadnezzar should be sitting on throne as the story begins. Other actors should be out of sight until their parts happen. The Narrator should pause whenever there is action for the actors to pantomime. The Narrator should also cue the children whenever it's time to play their instruments.

After the dramatization, thank the actors, and have Will come to the front to lead this discussion with the kids.

Who in the Bible story followed God's command that we worship only Him and no other gods? *(Shadrach, Meshach, and Abednego.)* **Who disobeyed this rule of God's?** *(The king and his people.)* **How did God show He was pleased with the men who did what He commanded and worshiped only Him?** *(He saved them from being hurt in the furnace and sent His angel to encourage them.)* **God always will stick close to you and give you strength when you choose to follow His commandments. He wants us to know that only He is the true God. He wants nothing to be more important than He is in your life.**

Have Leaders direct kids to the Bible Memory activity.

# Bible Memory Time

(A3) Supplies
- ○ **Yellow banana-shaped sheets of construction paper, each with a word of the verse on it**
- ○ **Key Bible Verse poster on an easel**
- ○ **Key Bible Verse cards** *(page R.58)*
- ○ **Traveler's Journals** *(page R.59-66)*
- ○ **Masking tape**
- ○ **Transparent tape**

In Advance: Cluster four to six of the bananas together *(out of order)*. Hang them on trees in the "jungle" setting or on a tree prop in the Bible memory area in a way that can be easily removed. If using the early elementary simplified verse, make a set of "bananas" for those words and hang in its own area of the jungle so early readers can be directed there.

Early Elementary
"[God] only is my rock and my salvation: he is my defence; I shall not be moved."
—Psalm 62:6

Upper Elementary
"My soul, wait thou only upon God; for my expectation is from him. He only is my rock and my salvation: he is my defence; I shall not be moved." **—Psalm 62:5-6**

Show the Key Bible Verse poster, and read the verse aloud to the kids, pointing to each word as you say it. Then have the group read the verse in unison with you.

Who should we trust to take care of us and help us? *(Only God.)* **What does this verse promise that God is or that He will do for us?** *(Be our expectation, hope, be strong for us like a rock or fortress, be our salvation, keep us from being "moved" or fearful.)* **How is God like a rock? How is He like a defense?** *(He is strong* *and sturdy, He is trustworthy and dependable.)*

Explain that the kids will practice learning the verse by picking bananas from the tree and re-creating the verse so the words are in the right order. The children may look at the verse poster as they work. Split the group into smaller groups, and let each group take a cluster of bananas and work on part of the verse. By the time the final group is finished, the whole verse will be in place.

Read the banana verse together aloud to be sure the verse is right. Take out a few bananas and ask if someone can still say the whole verse. Do this until all the kids have had a chance to try to say the verse. Affirm and encourage all the children as they memorize the verse.

Before leaving this activity, help the kids tape verse cards in their Traveler's Journals.

# Music Time

Only One God
(A4) Supplies
○ Copy of song lyrics for each child, or have the words on an overhead transparency *(page R.22)*
○ *Time-Stone Travelers*™ CD or tape copy of "Only One God" *(Track 2)*
○ CD or tape player
○ Overhead projector *(optional)*
○ FINNEGAN Puppet *(optional)*

Have the children listen to the song for this site, "Only One God." Play the song again and have the kids join in with the singing. Allow them to stand and move around if you have the space. If appropriate, project the lyrics onto a screen for the children to follow along as they sing. You may want to have FINNEGAN help teach the song.

# Game Time

Down with the Idol
(G1) Supplies
○ Empty boxes and cardboard containers, taped closed
○ Masking tape
○ Beanbags or small foam balls

Aim for groups of 5-7 to play this game. With large numbers of children, plan on two or more sets of supplies so groups can play simultaneously. Remind children what an idol is *(anything that becomes more important to us than God is)*. Explain that in some religions, people build or make statues or sculptures of the things they worship, such as animals, spirits, or even people. But an idol can also be something that has value to a person and keeps them from giving God their first love and worship.

To play the game, stack up the boxes into a large shape or sculpture. Use masking tape to mark a line on the floor a distance from the "idol." One by one, players take turns standing behind the line and tossing one or two bean bags or foam balls at the idol to knock it down. When the whole idol

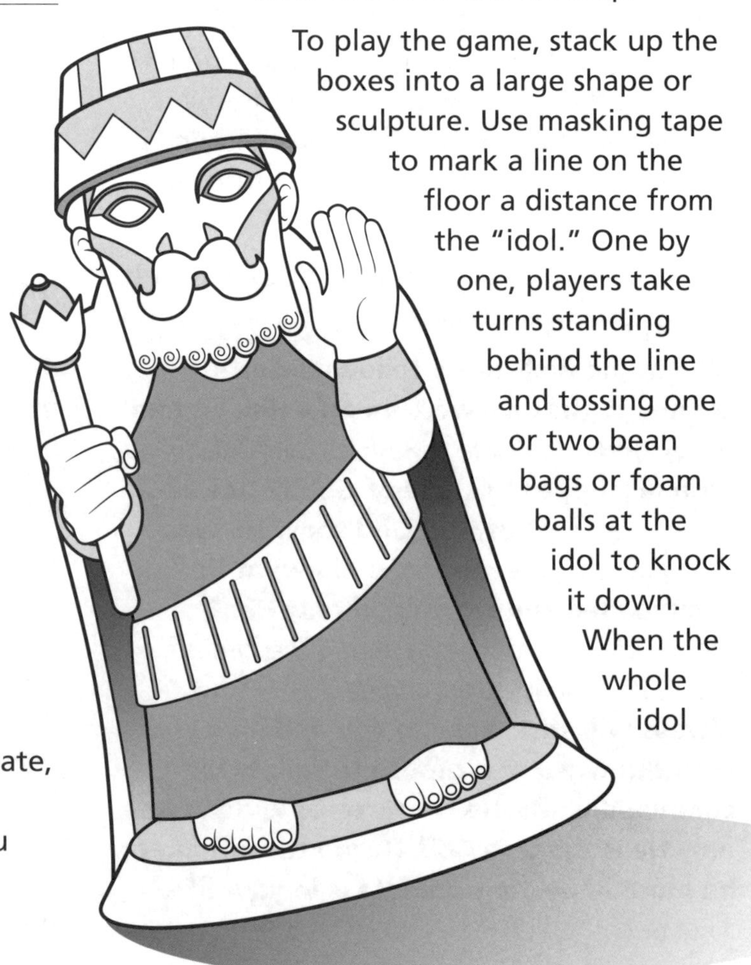

has fallen, the group celebrates by jumping up and down and shouting "There is only one God!"

To replay the game, have the kids cooperatively rebuild the idol and then take turns knocking it down again.

Jungle Snake Sneak

(G2) Supplies

- Numerous small toys and other items (*such as wooden blocks, miniature stuffed animals, etc.*)
- Blindfolds

This game needs a fairly large space where kids can lie on the floor or ground. Ask the children to describe some of the creatures that might live in a steamy South American jungle (*panthers, sloths, monkeys, parrots, tree frogs, toucans, orangutans, boa constrictors, pythons, etc.*)

This game challenges players to be small jungle creatures moving along on the jungle floor, finding food. The object is to collect as many of the small toys as possible without being caught by a large slithering jungle snake. Scatter the small items all over the floor of the playing area. Half the children will be snakes, blindfolded and lying randomly around the playing floor among the toys. The other half will be the creatures who are seeking food. As they move around the floor as silently and carefully as possible picking up the toys, the snakes try to tag them by listening to their movements. When a "snake" tags someone, he or she says, "Put God first!" The tagged player puts down his collected "food" and sits on the sideline until the game is over. Once a jungle creature has collected a load of items (*you may want to designate a set amount*), he carries them to the sideline, says, "Nothing is more important than God," and sits down. Play for a designated amount of time or until all the players are tagged or have collected all the food.

Snack Time

Bugs on a Log

(S1) Supplies

- Bananas (*cut in half*) or celery sticks
- Peanut butter or cream cheese
- Raisins
- Small paper plates
- Plastic knives
- Napkins

Help the kids spread one teaspoon of peanut butter on 1/2 banana. They may top their banana with 10-12 raisins.

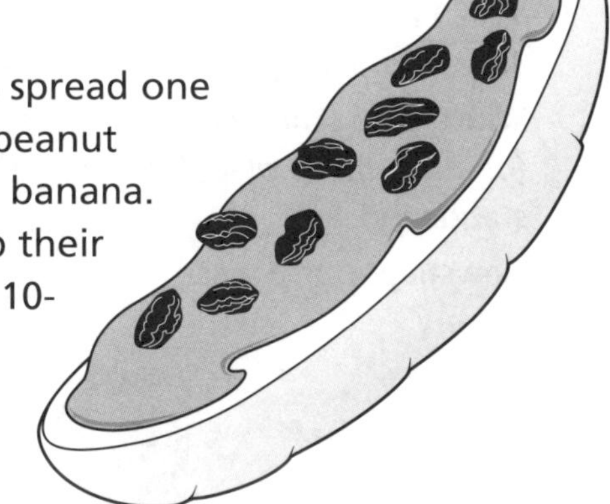

NOTE: Be aware of children with nut allergies, and have another option on hand. You may do this same snack using celery sticks, cream cheese, and raisins.

Dried Fruit

(S2) Supplies

- Banana chips
- Dried pineapple
- Dried apricots (*cut into small pieces*)
- Dried cranberries
- Napkins
- Small plastic cups

Mix together the ingredients. Place into small cups, 1/3 cup per child. Serve with a green napkin cut in a leaf shape.

Craft Time

Marbleized Stationery

(C1) Supplies

- ○ Blank stationery or card stock, cut and folded to fit into envelopes *(3 per child)*
- ○ Envelopes *(3 per child)*
- ○ Colored chalk
- ○ Water
- ○ 9" x 13" foil pans
- ○ 150 sand paper, cut into 2" squares
- ○ White card stock, cut into 3" heart shapes *(or a size that will look nice on your blank stationery)*
- ○ Newspaper or paper towels
- ○ Glue

Fill foil pans half full of clean water. Rub chalk on sandpaper above the water so the chalk dust falls onto the water surface. Let children repeat this with two other colors of chalk so dust is floating on the surface of the water. Help the

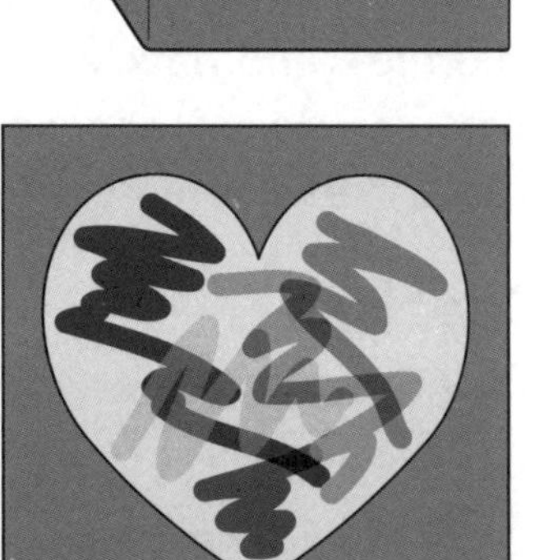

children dip a heart shape into the water and pull it back out. The colored dust will cling to the paper. Place marbleized hearts on newspaper or paper towels to dry. Once dry, glue the marbleized hearts onto blank stationery. Let the children repeat this two more times to marbleize three hearts each.

NOTE: To clean off chalk dust from water surface *(to prepare a fresh pan)*, drag a clean paper towel over the surface of the water to remove chalk particles.

Rain Stick

(C2) Supplies

- ○ Mailing tube 1 1/2" x 15" with end stoppers
- ○ Uncooked rice *(1/2 cup per rain stick)*
- ○ Nails 3/4" - 1" *(80-100 per rain stick)*
- ○ Brown, self-adhesive paper 15" x 6"
- ○ Funnel
- ○ Craft glue
- ○ Green construction paper *(two different shades)*
- ○ Hammer
- ○ Key Bible Verse printed on 6" x 2" paper
- ○ Yarn in a variety of colors *(optional)*

In Advance: Hammer nails into the mailing tube over the length of the tube about an inch apart. Glue the stopper into one end. Cover with brown, self-adhesive paper. Cut leaf shapes from green paper.

Let the children use a funnel to pour 1/2 cup of uncooked rice into the mailing tube. Glue the second stopper in the open end. Let a volunteer glue the Bible verse to the tube. Let the children all have a turn to glue a couple of paper leaves, overlapping, to mailing tube. The children may then glue lenths of yarn to the rain stick. You may wish to have the class make more than one.

Application Time

(A5) Supplies

- ○ Piece of artificial fruit
- ○ Pencils
- ○ Traveler's Journals *(found on R.59-66)*

Josh, Will, and Ellen bring the children together at the jungle scene for the final interaction of the day.

JOSH: Boy, this has been one cool day in the jungle! I haven't swung on so many vines or seen so many amazing animals in my whole life!

ELLEN: Yeah, if you swing on one more vine, you'll start howling like Tarzan or like one of those loud monkeys!

WILL: Life in the jungle is sure nothing like it is in *(name of your town or city)*. Everything is different—the food, the weather, even the sounds.

ELLEN: Well, almost everything. The first two of God's rules that we all learned today are true all around the world. No matter where you live, we need to know that He's the only one true God.

WILL: And because He's our God, we want to be careful that nothing becomes more important in our lives than He is. Let's play a short game. I'll toss this jungle fruit to someone out there. If you catch it, say something that you might be tempted to let become more important than God. We all are tempted to let things become idols and take God's place in our lives.

(Actors spend a couple of minutes tossing fruit to various individuals and affirming the kids' ideas. Other kids and Leaders can help think up what takes God's place in our lives. After each idea, the child tosses it back up to the actors.)

JOSH: God's first rule says we should love and obey Him first above all. We shouldn't let any person or thing get in the way of our love for God. I think there's a word for how we show our love and devotion to God. Hmm, what's that called?

WILL: I think it's worship.

ELLEN: Yes! That's it. We worship God because He's the one true God and He deserves our attention and love.

(Josh falls to his knees and fans his arms up and down in an exaggerated worship posture.)

ELLEN: That's not what God means by worship, Will.

JOSH: I don't think so either. But what does it mean to worship? See if you can guess.

(Actors take turns miming and acting out forms of worship: prayer, singing, Bible reading, and other forms appropriate to your faith community.)

ELLEN: Let's worship God together right now by singing *(name of a VBS song)*.

JOSH: Here's something else I bet you didn't know about worship. We can worship God by ourselves and at any time or place! At any time, we can be telling God we love Him.

ELLEN: Before you come back for tomorrow's *Time-Stone Traveler's*™ adventure, see if you can worship God in some way—on your own or with your family.

Have kids work on the jungle page of the Traveler's Journals *(pages R.59-66)* either alone or with a friend. Leaders should be available to help children read and follow the instructions or come up with ideas as needed. Be available to children who may want to ask questions about the day's

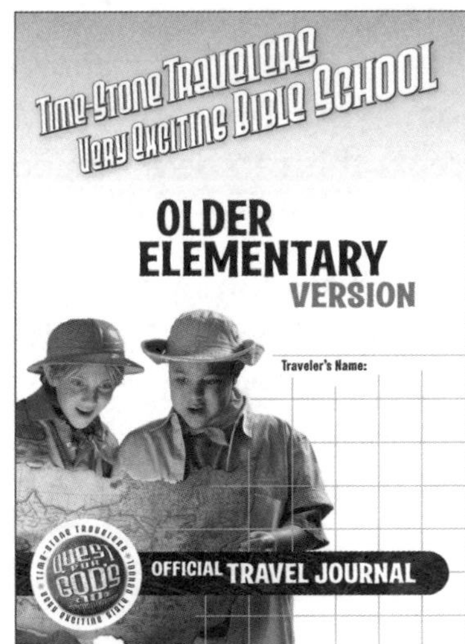

learning, talk, or pray about a personal concern.

Time-Stone Take Off

(A6) Supplies

- ○ Copies of symbols for Time Stones *(page R.67)*, *one set per child*
- ○ Clean stones for the Time Stones
- ○ "The Quest Continues" Take-Home Page *(one per child)*
- ○ Craft projects from the day

When the time is ended for work in the Travel Journals, get everyone's attention. **Today, we will be adding symbols to our Time Stones that represent the commandments we have studied today.** *(See the directions for making the Time Stones and adding the symbols in Resources on page R.67.)* **When you take home your Time Stone at the end of the week, this can be a reminder of the commandments that God has given to us.**

End the session by doing a huge cheer using the day's theme, "There is only one God!" Pray a short prayer of worship to God and blessing of the children in the name of the one true God.

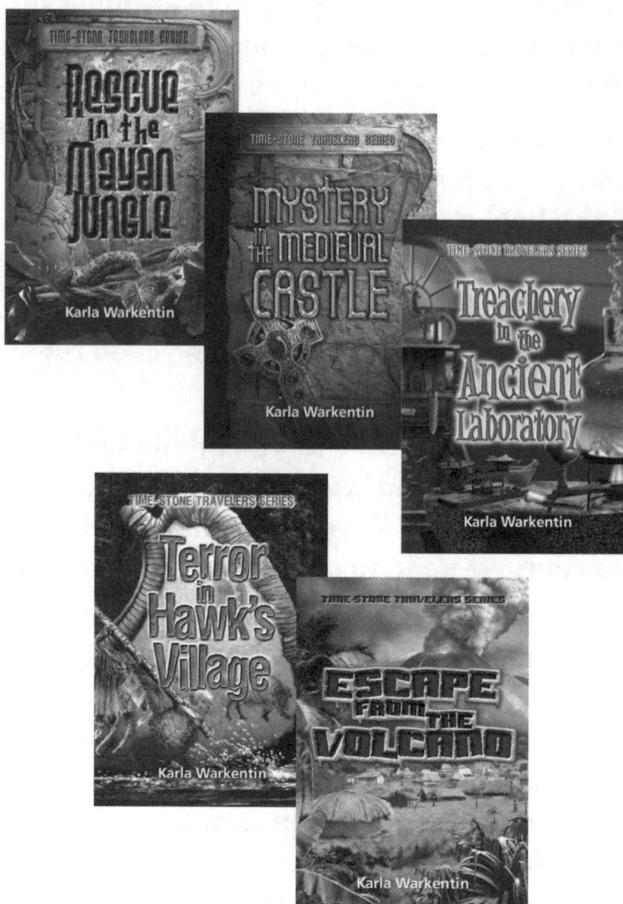

See all the *Time-Stone Travelers*™ books at
www.CookVBS.com

Site Supplies

GENERAL

- Mayan Jungle mural
- *Time-Stone Travelers*™ CD or tape copy
- CD player or cassette tape player
- Overhead transparency of lyrics and overhead projector
- Bible
- FINNEGAN Puppet
- Copy of "Traveler's Journal" for each child *(pages R.59-66)*. Note the two age levels and use accordingly.
- Copy of "The Quest Continues" student Take-Home Page *(pages E1.15-16)* for each child

SNACKS

- Bananas or celery sticks
- Peanut butter or cream cheese
- Raisins
- Banana chips
- Dried pineapple
- Dried apricots *(cut into small pieces)*
- Dried cranberries
- Small paper plates
- Plastic knives
- Napkins
- Small plastic cups

GAMES AND ACTIVITIES

- Large foam-core board "replica" of the 10 Commandments tablet with just the first two commandments clearly printed on it
- Realistic looking, colorful, pretend snake
- Soccer ball
- Beautiful piece of girls' clothing
- Video game
- Yellow, bigger-than-life statue *(of cardboard, foam, etc.)*
- Bible-time clothes for King Nebuchadnezzar and three Hebrew men
- Toy instruments *(tambourines, horns, kazoos, bells, drums, etc.)*
- Room divider or large appliance box *(to serve as fiery furnace)*
- Something to make sound effects of crackling fire
- Yellow and red lights *(can be flashlights with colored film over the lenses)*
- Life-size cardboard shape of a person
- Ropes or binding

- Yellow banana-shaped sheets of construction paper, each with a word of the verse on it
- Key Bible Verse poster on an easel
- Key Bible Verse cards *(page R.58)*
- Masking tape
- Transparent tape
- Empty boxes and cardboard containers, taped closed
- Beanbags or small foam balls
- Numerous small toys and other items *(such as wooden blocks, miniature stuffed animals, etc.)*
- Blindfolds
- Piece of artificial fruit
- Pencils
- Clean stones for the Time Stones
- Copies of symbols for Time Stones *(page R.67)*, one set per child

CRAFTS

- Blank stationery or card stock, cut and folded to fit into envelopes *(3 per child)*
- Envelopes *(3 per child)*
- Colored chalk
- Water
- 9" x 13" foil pans
- 150 sand paper, cut into 2" squares
- White card stock, cut into 3" heart shapes *(or a size that will look nice on your blank stationery)*
- Newspaper or paper towels
- Glue
- Mailing Tube 1 1/2" x 15" with end stoppers
- Uncooked rice *(1/2 cup per rain stick)*
- Nails 3/4" - 1" *(80-100 per rain stick)*
- Brown, self-adhesive paper 15" x 6"
- Funnel
- Craft glue
- Green construction paper *(two different shades)*
- Hammer
- Key Bible Verse printed on a 6" x 2" paper
- Yarn in various colors *(optional)*

Site 1 Notes

Today your child visited a mysterious and lively South American jungle to find out that God has given us 10 rules for living—the Ten Commandments. These rules say that there is only one God and that we should not allow anything to be more important to us than Him. These truths were illustrated through the Old Testament story of three men who refused to worship a false god *(Dan. 3)*. As a consequence of the men's choice to worship only the one true God instead of a man-made idol, they were thrown into a flaming hot furnace. However, an angel of God kept the men from being incinerated. In fact, they weren't even scorched.

Go online to **www.CookVBS.com** for more information about *Time-Stone Travelers™* VBS and what your child is experiencing each day.

FAMILY FUN ACTIVITY AND INSIGHT QUESTIONS ON BACK

SHARE WHAT YOU LEARNED TODAY WITH YOUR FAMILY!

COLOR YOUR OWN MURAL

SITE ONE ELEMENTARY

The **QUEST CONTINUES**

SITE ONE ELEMENTARY

💬 TALK IT OUT

- **What kinds of things can easily become so important to us that God becomes less important?**
- **What are ways we can worship God outside of church?**

👪 FAMILY STUFF

Treasure Box Activity

Point: Becoming aware of things that might become idols helps us avoid letting those things take the place of God in our lives.

Supplies

○ Treasure chest (*such as a picnic basket, decorated cardboard box, fancy hatbox, or other container*)

Activity: Explain that it's worthwhile to do a check-up on the things that are most valuable to us, noting whether they are becoming idols and taking first place in our lives instead of God.

Put the Treasure Box on a table where the family is gathered. Send everyone (*parents included!*) on a treasure hunt around your home (*and possibly yard*) to collect items that represent what each person values most. For example, a trading card could symbolize someone's interest in baseball, a dog toy could represent a special pet, a tool might stand for Dad's woodworking hobby.

Have each person add one or more items to the treasure box. Be creative!

Take turns pulling out items and having the one who chose it explain what it stands for and why it's valuable to them.

Discuss what is valued and what it shows about family members.

- **Do any of the things you value take God's place as most important in your life?**
- **How does this verse help us decide how much something means to us: "For where your treasure is, there will your heart be also" (*Matt. 6:21*)?**
- **As a family, how do we show God He is important to us?**

Consider making regular or occasional dates to worship as a family—singing, praying, praising God, or showing your devotion to Him through your use of time and resources.

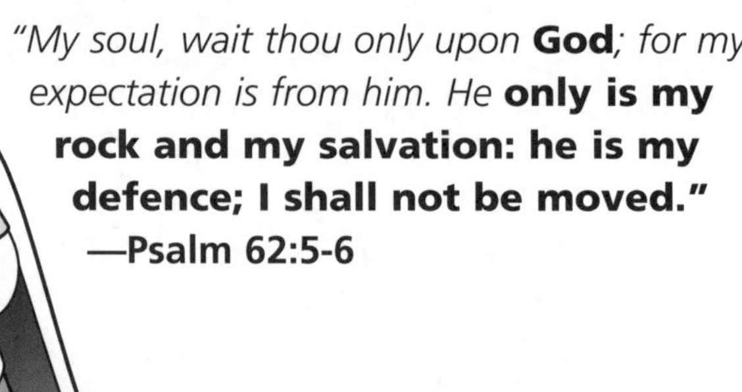

BIBLE VERSE

(*Early elementary verse in **bold** type.*)

*"My soul, wait thou only upon **God**; for my expectation is from him. He **only is my rock and my salvation: he is my defence; I shall not be moved.**"*
—Psalm 62:5-6

E L E M E N T A R Y

MEDIEVAL CASTLE

"There remaineth therefore a rest to the people of God . . ."
— **Hebrews 4:9-10**

INFO for the TRIP

Why Kids Need to Understand that God's Name Deserves Respect and that Sunday Should be Set Apart for Rest and Worship

The children you minister to in VBS need to realize that God's name is worthy of our utmost respect. People today often have a warped image of God. They gain their ideas of Him from media, distorted Scripture references, and offhand remarks that they can't put into context. They've heard Him spoken about in unworthy terms or in ways that misuse His name and authority. The names in Scripture that describe God give a broader understanding of who He is and why we must revere His very name; yet most kids are unaware of the astonishing list of names the Bible has for God. To help the children make sense of this commandment and the holiness of God's name, give them real-life, everyday examples of how we use people's names. Help the children remember how good it feels when someone uses their name sweetly or as a compliment.

As for keeping the Sabbath, you're likely to encounter children who think of Sunday primarily as a day off. Some connect it with church attendance, yet rarely grasp the essence of worship. Malls, restaurants, errands, and athletic events all call out to kids and families on Sunday, obscuring the purpose for which God instituted this rest. Help children recognize Sunday as a special treat from God, a day off from the usual routines but with a sacred purpose. Let the children creatively develop and imagine ways to worship God and keep His day separate from the other six. The more they invest in and strategize how to honor God on His day, the more likely they'll be to actually want to do so and prompt their families in that direction.

FACTOID

A knight's training began at age seven, when boys left home to serve as pages. Pages learned the use of small weapons and the code of behavior. At age 15, the page became a squire who acted as a personal servant to a knight while learning how to wage battles. After five years, the squire could be knighted by another knight. Before his knighting, the candidate spent time in solitude praying and pledging to use his weapons for sacred purposes.

GETTING MORE FROM THE BIBLE STORY

The Jewish Sabbath begins at sundown Friday and ends at sundown on Saturday, observing the seventh day of the week as the one God set aside for rest and worship. God's intent for this rest day included the chance to pause from one's daily work to be restored physically and to remember the Creator. Jewish leaders added to God's commandment from Exodus 20, stating that healing was work and therefore prohibited. Many other "manmade" rules sprang up around the Sabbath as well.

Jesus' healing of the crippled woman is one of seven biblical accounts of Christ restoring health to someone on the Sabbath. In this passage, the Jewish religious leaders were observing Him closely, waiting for Him to do something of which they could accuse Him. Their mindset demonstrated their preoccupation with the minute details of the law; their perspective obscured God's desire that mercy and compassion be given as a form of worship to our merciful, compassionate God.

Core Concept

Children will learn that God deserves their worship, which they can show by respecting His name and setting aside time for Him.

Key Bible Verses

Early Elementary

"For he that is entered into his rest, he also hath ceased from his own works, as God did from his." — **Hebrews 4:10**

Upper Elementary

"There remaineth therefore a rest to the people of God. For he that is entered into his rest, he also hath ceased from his own works, as God did from his." — **Hebrews 4:9-10**

Puppet Option

A Leader can operate FINNEGAN to help lead the children to different areas and interact spontaneously with the teacher and children *(See puppet pattern for FINNEGAN on pages R.53-57.)*

Bible Passage

Luke 13:10-17,
Exodus 20:7-8
(Commandments 3, 4)

Schedule of Activities

10 minutes: Introduction
15-20 minutes: Bible Story Time
10 minutes: Bible Memory Time
5 minutes: Music Time
20 minutes: Game Time

15 minutes: Snack Time
20 minutes: Craft Time
10 minutes: Application Time
10 minutes: Time-Stone Take Off

Setting the Scene

Use the transparency *(page R.71)* to create a medieval castle scene. Hang mural paper on the classroom wall, project the picture onto it, and trace the outlines. Paint or color it in, using gray or brown for stones and bright reds, golds, and blues for tapestries and décor. To create a 3-D effect, build tall cardboard towers or walls with stones drawn on; add an iron-looking gate. On another wall, hang a majestic fabric or banner and a paper coat of arms. If you can find a knight in armor *(life-size poster or actual)*, stand it in a corner.

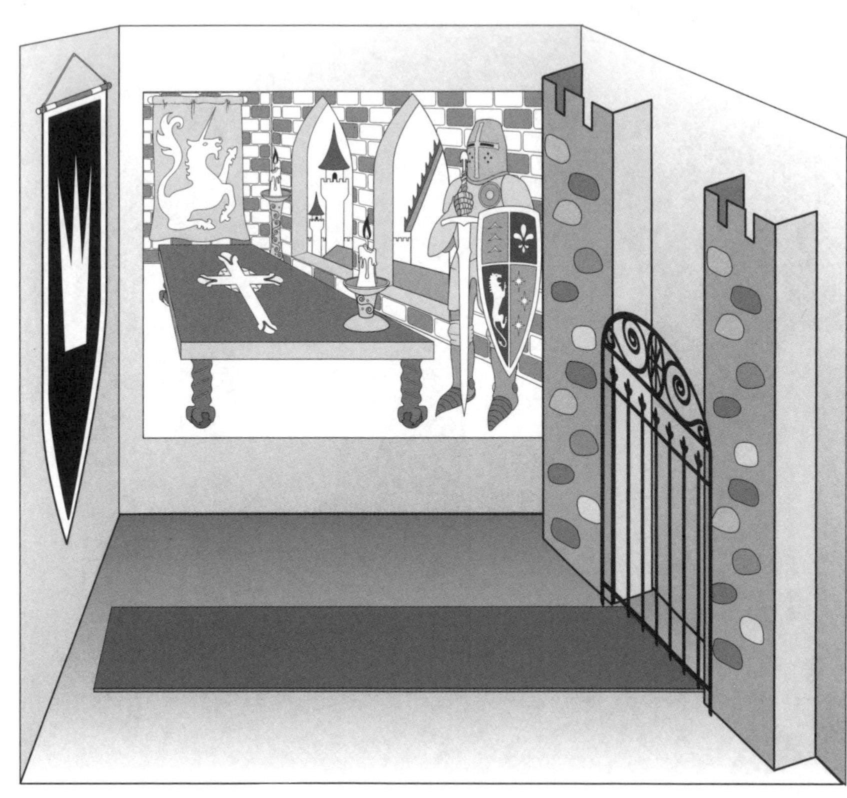

Introduction

(A7) Supplies

- ○ Toy swords and shields
- ○ A couple of pillows or cushions
- ○ A wall calendar, on the floor near the pillows
- ○ Large, foam-core board "replica" of the 10 Commandments tablet with commandments 3 and 4 clearly printed on it. *(page R.45) (Loosely attach a piece of paper over each commandment to cover it until needed.)*

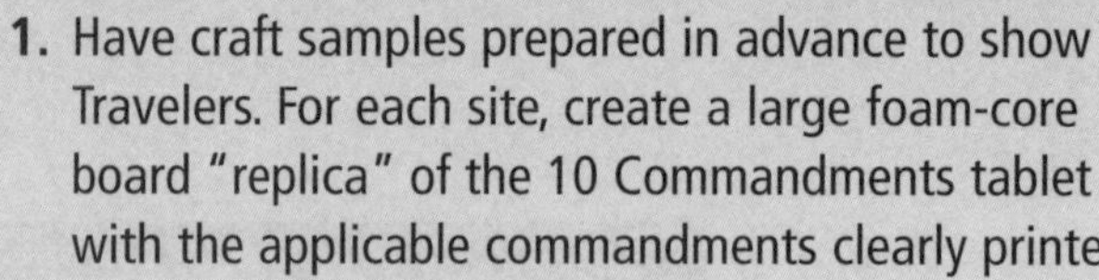

Advanced Preparation

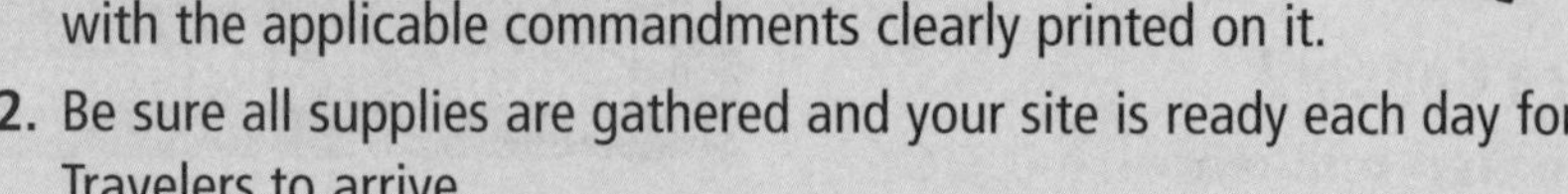

1. Have craft samples prepared in advance to show Travelers. For each site, create a large foam-core board "replica" of the 10 Commandments tablet with the applicable commandments clearly printed on it.

2. Be sure all supplies are gathered and your site is ready each day for Travelers to arrive.

3. Post the Schedule of Activities where Leaders and Helpers can refer to it.

4. Address each other by site titles. Children should be referred to as Travelers.

5. After taking attendance, a Leader should tell those responsible for refreshments how many Travelers are present to be prepared for snack time.

6. You may wish to do some background research into the Bible story. Refer to Bible commentaries, encyclopedias, and dictionaries for additional information.

In Advance: If toy swords and shields are not available for Will and Josh, make some out of cardboard and metallic paint. You can make knight's costumes by fashioning a breastplate from cardboard and a helmet from a paper grocery bag, all painted in metallic silver paint.

(Will and Josh are comparing their outfits and doing a little play sword fighting when Ellen walks in.)

ELLEN: Whoa, look at you guys! What are you dressed up for?

JOSH: We're going back in time today to a majestic castle of old times, so we decided we wanted to be knights. It would be so cool to really wear a knight's clothes and ride a royal horse.

ELLEN: I don't know. I thought the medieval days of knights and castles were pretty

Leaders Profile

Josh, Will, Ellen
Josh and Will wear clothing to resemble knight's armor; Ellen wears kid-like, summer vacation clothes.

dangerous. Lots of people died in battles, and there were awful sicknesses, and things like that.

WILL: I'm not worried about dying in battle. I'm William the Courageous. *(He brandishes his sword and thrusts out his chest proudly.)*

ELLEN: Okay, Sir William, since you're so impressive, tell us which of the 10 Commandments we get to explore today.

WILL: Certainly, my fair maiden. Today we will learn about why we need to respect God's name.

JOSH: What? I don't think so. Today we're finding out that God made one day a week just for worshiping Him and resting.

WILL: You're wrong! *(Begins sword fighting with Josh.)*

JOSH: No, you're wrong! *(They play fight briefly, until Ellen pipes us.)*

ELLEN: Hold on there, you two. Before you get your armor dented, you need to know that you're both wrong. And right.

(They stop and act confused, shaking their heads.)

ELLEN: Today we're going to get the scoop on BOTH of those commandments.

JOSH AND WILL: *(In unison.)* **Cool!**

ELLEN: Will, which of God's 10 rules of living were you going to introduce?

WILL: It's the one where God says we should respect Him and be careful how we speak about Him. *(Holds up the foam core tablet, removes the paper covering commandment 3, and reads it aloud.)* **That means that we talk about God with the right kinds of words and attitudes. Because He's our holy Lord and our loving heavenly Father, we need to be sure**

our words about God are respectful.

JOSH: Like, you mean people shouldn't use God's name when they goof up or are surprised?

WILL: That's part of it. Here's another way to see it. Remember when you got stuck at the back of the bus with those kids from school who made fun of your name? They called you—

JOSH: Yeah, I remember—"Josh, the squash." I was mad and then my feelings were hurt. They laughed and made jokes about me. I wished I could have become invisible so I could get out of there.

ELLEN: It's the same with God's name. There are lots of names for God in the Bible, and they describe some of the things He does and the way He is. When we treat His name like it's not special, we're being disrespectful. After all, God is the ruler of the universe. He deserves to be treated the best we can possibly treat Him.

JOSH: Can I tell everyone what commandment I was going to introduce?

ELLEN: Sure, what is it?

JOSH: Instead of telling you, I'm going to show you! *(He picks up a large wall calendar and then lies down on the floor cushions and looks like he's relaxing. Ellen and Will make guesses about what he's doing. Josh points to the Sundays on the calendar as a hint. Finally, he gives up and tells them.)*

JOSH: Didn't you see me pointing to a certain day on this calendar? And then I was resting.

ELLEN: Oh, now I get it. You're telling us

about God's commandment to keep Sunday special, as a day of rest and worship.

JOSH: Finally! *(Removes paper covering commandment 4 and reads it aloud.)*

WILL: Hey! If God says Sunday's a day of rest, I can sleep in, watch cartoons, and play video games all day—that's the best way for me to rest.

JOSH: Wrong! God wants us to rest—that's right. Even He rested after He made the world in six days. But His idea is that our rest day is also a special day for remembering God and giving Him the worship He deserves.

ELLEN: Like going to church to worship or to Sunday school. And doing things with your family so you can all enjoy what God has given you. But what about doing good work on Sunday? Does God say to do absolutely nothing once a week? No brushing your teeth or helping a neighbor or anything?

JOSH: The best way to answer that is from the Bible. Let's hear what Jesus taught about this. The story from Luke tells about something that happened on the Sabbath, which was like Sunday for the Jewish people. *(They sit with the kids.)*

# Bible Story Time

Luke 13:10-17, Exodus 20:7-8

(A8) Supplies
- ○ Bible
- ○ Simple Bible-time costumes

In Advance: Ask three Leaders to play the roles of Jesus, the Synagogue Ruler, and the Woman. If available, have a couple more Leaders or Helpers play Pharisees *(in non-speaking roles)*.

Invite the kids to imagine that they are in a Bible-time synagogue. **The synagogue leaders sat near the front in the important seats.** *(Have the Synagogue Leader and Pharisees enter from the back and walk proudly to the front row to be seated.)* **Today, the famous teacher named Jesus is visiting, and everyone is watching Him carefully.** *(The person playing Jesus should enter from the back, smiling and humble, and take a seat to the side, but in the front row so all the children can see him. The Synagogue Leader and Pharisees look over at him and scowl.)* **On this day, Jesus came up to the front to teach.** *(Jesus stands at the front and waits patiently.)*

(The woman should hobble slowly up to the story area, bent over, moving slowly and clearly in pain. Jesus sees the woman and his facial expression and body language show he feels compassion for her. He calls her over to himself. When she has slowly moved to stand in front of him, he speaks.)

JESUS: Woman, you are set free from your sickness.

(He puts his hands gently on her shoulders. As soon as he touches her, the woman straightens up, a surprised look on her face. She becomes exuberant.)

WOMAN: Praise God! I'm all better! Thank You, thank You! Oh, I can't believe I'm finally well. God, I thank You from the bottom of my heart!

(The Synagogue Leader and Pharisees stand up and move near Jesus, with frowns and angry body language. They point at the woman and Jesus, shaking their heads in disapproval.)

SYNAGOGUE LEADER: There are six days to do work like healing people. But no healing should be done on the Sabbath—the special day God gave us to rest.

JESUS: But that's not right. You know it's okay to untie your ox or donkey and take it to get a drink on the Sabbath. So why don't you think it's right that this woman, who has been sick for 18 years, should be given health on the Sabbath?

(The Synagogue Leader and Pharisees slink away in shame. Jesus and the woman walk out happily.) Josh stands up in front of the kids to reinforce the story.

JOSH: For the Jews, the Sabbath was their day of rest. They obeyed God's commandment to rest one day a week. But they didn't understand what it meant to honor God on that day. They made lots of extra rules about all the things they couldn't do on that day. But Jesus knew what the day of rest was all about. By healing the woman, Jesus showed love and care for her. She praised and worshiped God when she was healed. God says we need one day to rest each week, and that's the day for giving special attention to Him, too. In that woman's case and in our lives, God deserves our worship.

Have Leaders direct kids to the Bible memory activity. If desired, they can line up like castle guards and march in rhythm to the next activity.

Bible Memory Time

(A9) Supplies
- Key Bible Verse poster on an easel
- Key Bible Verse cards
  (found on page R.58 in Resources)
- Traveler's Journals
  (found on page R.59-66 in Resources)
- Transparent tape
- Card stock sheets, each with one word of the verse in block printing

Early Elementary

"For he that is entered into his rest, he also hath ceased from his own works, as God did from his." — **Hebrews 4:10**

Upper Elementary

"There remaineth therefore a rest to the people of God. For he that is entered into his rest, he also hath ceased from his own works, as God did from his." — **Hebrews 4:9-10**

Display the Key Bible Verse poster. Have the children read the verse with you as you point to the words. Explain that the Sabbath was the special day each week that God set aside for His people to rest.

Explain that the children are going to begin learning the verse by playing a game of Build the Castle Walls. Scramble the sheets containing the verse words, and hand them out to the kids. *(If you have fewer kids than words, give some kids two words that are together in the verse.)*

Have a Helper blow a pretend trumpet in a medieval way. At that signal, the kids line up side by side displaying the verse words they hold. Encourage them to use the verse poster for help at first. Have a leader walk along the "wall" of kids and read the verse. If it's not right, let the kids correct any mistakes. Then collect the cards and do it again. Challenge the kids to build their castle wall as quickly as possible with no mistakes. When done, let everyone trumpet their success using their hands as pretend trumpets.

Help the children tape a key verse card in their Traveler's Journals before moving on to the next activity.

Music Time

God's Name Is Powerful
(A10) Supplies
- Copy of song lyrics for each child, or have the words on an overhead transparency *(page R.23)*
- *Time-Stone Travelers*™ CD or tape copy of "God's Name Is Powerful" *(Track 3)*
- CD or tape player
- Overhead projector
- FINNEGAN Puppet *(optional)*

Have the children listen to the song for this site. Play the song again and have the kids join in with the singing. Allow them to stand

and move around if you have the space. If age appropriate, project the words of the song onto a screen for the children to follow along as they sing. You may want to have FINNEGAN help teach the song.

Game Time

Castle Wall Lob

(G3) Supplies

○ **Something to serve as a "castle wall"** *(large screen, blanket draped over a rope, plywood board securely propped up, stacked boxes, etc.)*

○ **Soft lobbing objects** *(foam balls, bean bags, etc.)* **in buckets or boxes**

○ **Beach towels, blankets, or burlap bags**

Set up the castle wall to divide the game area. If you have mostly upper elementary children, make it taller than the kids' heads so they can't see over it but can still throw over it. If you have mostly early elementary children, the divider may be lower so they can see the "boulders" coming toward them.

Divide the kids to stand on either side of the castle wall. Give one side the buckets of "boulders" and tell them they are outside the castle and will try to storm it by lobbing *(tossing)* over boulders. On each toss, the child calls out one word of what those on the other side should do on the Lord's Day, such as "rest," "worship," or "help." *(The children may choose their own words and may repeat words.)* Give the other group the towels and tell them they are inside the castle and must work as a team using the towels to catch the

boulders before they hit the floor. Demonstrate how several children hold the edges of one towel and move at the same time to catch a boulder with it. Let them practice catching a few balls that they can see coming.

If you have more kids than can play at once, rotate the catcher job by having groups of four kids with one towel play at a time. If you have more space, have three or four groups with towels playing. Have no more than two to three lobbers throwing for each group holding a blanket. Set the buckets of boulders at the back of the game area, and instruct the lobbers to run to the bucket, remove only one boulder, run to the castle wall to gently lob it over, and then run back for another boulder.

At your signal, let the castle storming begin. You may set a certain amount of time or you may play until all the boulders have been lobbed. Items caught in the towels can be tossed to the side. Those missed are left on the ground. When finished, have the children collect the boulders and change sides to play again.

Castle Defenders' Javelin Throw

(G4) Supplies

- ○ Colorful index cards with a name of God on each
- ○ Cotton swabs
- ○ Four boxes or other containers
- ○ Tape

In Advance: On index cards, clearly print names for God found in Scripture, one name per card. For example, Rock, Shield, Tower of Strength, Heavenly Father, Savior, Lamb of God, Light of the World, Living Water, Protector, Most High, and so on. For more examples, see the castle activities page in the Traveler's Journals *(R.59-66)*. Prepare at least one card for each child. Divide up the cards and place them in the four boxes.

Tell kids that they're going to be practicing their javelin throwing skills. Javelins are a type of spear; as castle defenders the kids need to be skillful in throwing them. Set out the four boxes at varying distances from the throwing line. Let the line up and take turns throwing a cotton swab "javelin." Whenever a javelin lands in a box, that child goes and takes one index card from the box and reads it aloud. Then that child goes and tapes the card to one of the stones on the castle wall backdrop. Have Helpers on hand to assist

with reading and taping as needed. The other children continue playing while cards are being taped. If you have a large group, set up two or three lines for children to play at the same time.

 # Snack Time

Castle Cubes

(S3) Supplies

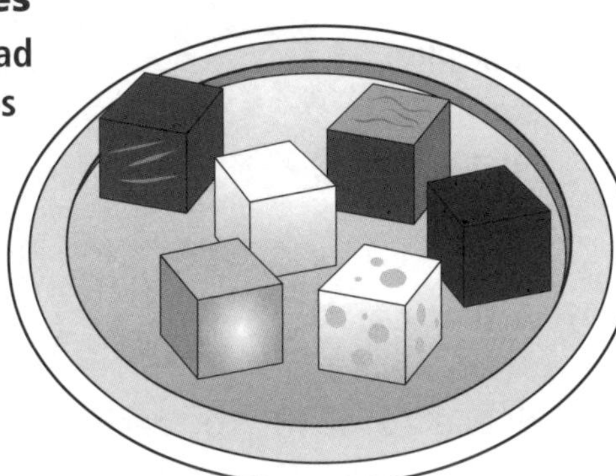

- ○ French bread cut in cubes
- ○ Cheese cubes
- ○ Pewter or wooden plates, goblets, and bowl
- ○ Tapestry table runner *(optional)*
- ○ Small disposable plates

Make a centerpiece of French bread in a display bowl with cheese cubes on pewter or wooden plates. Have a tapestry table runner with goblets surrounding the centerpiece. Serve French bread cubes and cheese cubes on a small paper plate. The children may stack their bread and cheese cubes like a castle wall before eating.

Fruit Fancies

(S4) Supplies

- ○ Apples, sliced
- ○ Pears, sliced
- ○ Plums, sliced
- ○ Seedless grapes
- ○ Small doilies
- ○ Small disposable plates

Cut apples, pears, and plums into slices. Place a slice of each with several grapes on a small doilie on a plate. Give each child a prepared plate.

Craft Time

Fleece Fringed Pillow

(C3) Supplies

- Two pieces of fleece *(16" x 18")* per child
- Straight pins
- Ruler
- Sliver of soap bar or chalk
- Scissors
- Fiberfill stuffing *(about 4-6 ounces per child)*

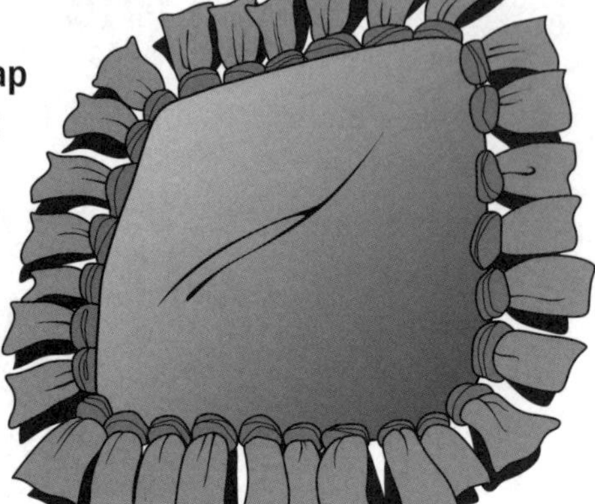

In Advance: Cut two pieces of fleece 16" x 18" for each child, and pin them together. Measure 4" in from the edges to make a rectangle 8" x 10"; mark this rectangle with a soap sliver or chalk. From the drawn rectangle to the outer edge, draw lines for 1" fringe. Cut on these lines to make fringe. Discard the four corner blocks. Remove the pins, but leave the pairs of fleece rectangles together.

Give each child a pair of prepared fleece rectangles, and show the class how to double knot the top fleece fringe to the bottom piece of fleece fringe. Continue around the rectangle double knotting the fringe. Have the children leave four fringe pieces untied to make an opening. Give each child fiberfill to stuff their pillow with. Double knot the remaining four fringe pieces to complete the pillow.

Jester Hats

(C4) Supplies

- Poster board *(various colors)*
- Scissors
- Clear packing tape
- Assortment of 1" pom-poms *(about 6 per child)*
- Glue

In Advance: Cut poster board into a 22" x 8" strip. Make a line 3" from the bottom of the poster board. On that line, mark a dot every 4" starting on the left side of the poster board. At the top of the poster board mark one dot 2" from the left side of the poster board. Mark a dot 4" from that dot. Start at the left side edge and make a line from the dot on the line to the top first dot. From that dot, draw a line to the lower dot forming a triangle. Continue connecting dots to form triangular shapes across the entire poster board. Cut out the tops of the triangles *(do not cut them off the base)*. Prepare one strip of triangles for each child.

Let the children select the color of triangle strip they want. Measure the strip to the child's head, cutting off excess (allow for a 1" overlay). Tape the two ends to form the hat. Then let the children adorn their jester hats with pom-poms by gluing them to the points of the triangles or wherever they wish. Children can curl the triangle shapes around their fingers or a pencil to make the triangles curve outward.

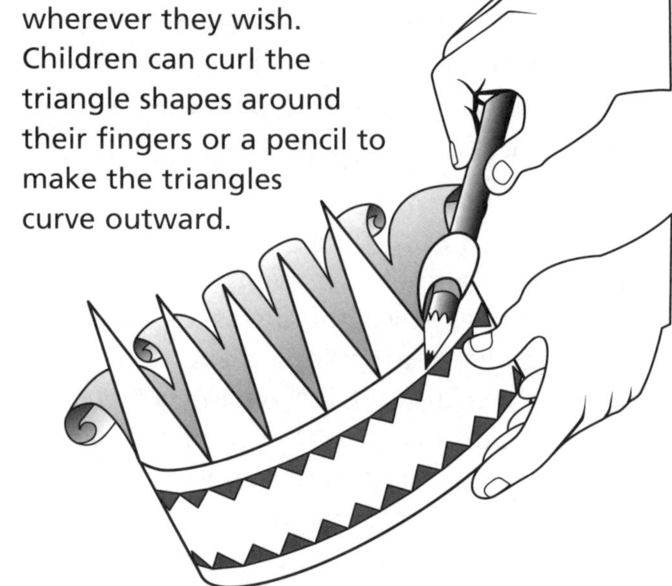

Application Time

(A11) Supplies

- Pillows *(may be towels stuffed in pillow cases),* on per child
- Traveler's Journals *(Found on pages R.59-66 in Resources.)*
- Pencils
- Markers or colored pencils

Gather the children together, and have the actors lead them in a closing discussion.

JOSH: Today we found out about two more of God's 10 rules for living. Who can remember these commandments? *(Call on volunteers to state one of the commandments. You may let several kids say them in their own words.)*

WILL: Right! We need to respect God's name by not misusing it. His name is powerful, and we want to treat it with respect and honor.

ELLEN: And God made one day of the week for us to rest and worship Him. After six days of work, we can relax and show our appreciation to God for what He's given us and done for us.

JOSH: Let's practice resting right now. Everyone find a comfortable spot and just relax for a few minutes. *(Pass out pillows and have kids stretch out on the floor and relax.)*

ELLEN: While we're relaxing, let's pray. The Bible gives us lots of names of God that help us understand more about Him, and we can pray to God using those names. Close your eyes right where you are, and let's pray.

WILL: God, we think You're great because You're our rock and our tower of strength. We can run and hide in You when we need help.

ELLEN: God, we praise You for being a shield around us. What a powerful king You are.

JOSH: Thank You, God, that You're our Father in heaven. You know everything little thing about us, and You hear us. In Jesus' name, amen.

WILL: Get into small groups with a Leader right now so you can praise God together. Also pray about keeping one day a week special for God and about respecting God's name.

Have Leaders and Helpers gather with small groups to lead them in prayer, allowing each child to pray using one of the names of God as given on the castle page of the Travel Journals. After worshiping God in prayer, the Leaders should close the prayer time thanking God for what has been

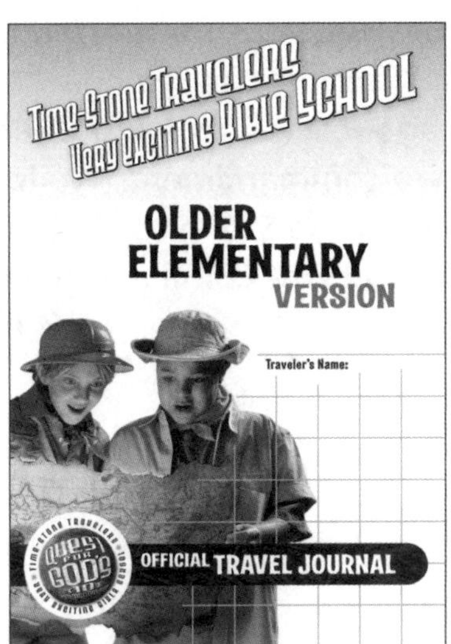

learned and helping the children to make it happen in their lives.

After the prayer time, have children complete the castle page in their Traveler's Journals. Help younger children understand the instructions, and give ideas and encouragement as needed.

Time Stone Take-Off

(A12) Supplies

- ○ Copies of symbols for Time Stones *(page R.67)*, *one set per child*
- ○ Clean stones for the Time Stones
- ○ "The Quest Continues" Take-Home Page, one per child
- ○ Craft projects from the day

Hand out the Time Stones, and briefly discuss the symbol for today's lesson. *(See the directions for making the Time Stones and adding the symbols in Resources on page R.67.)* **This symbol can remind us of the two commandments we learned today, and your Time Stone can help you remember all of God's 10 Commandments when you take it home at the end of the week.**

When finished working on the Time Stones, have everyone stand and sing the theme song, "Time-Stone Travelers." Conclude the session by praying that God will help each child learn His commandments and practice them today and each day forward. Dismiss the kids, handing out crafts and take-home papers as they leave.

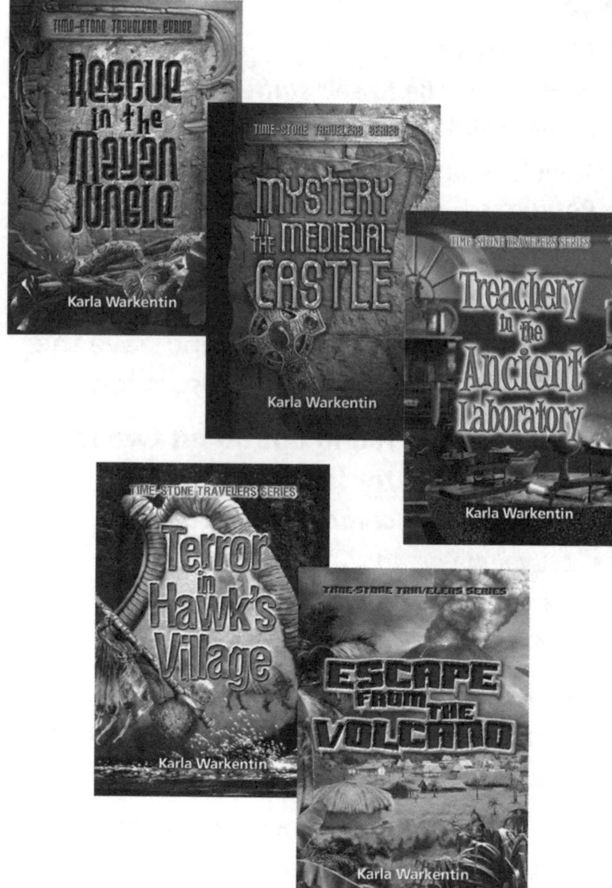

See all the *Time-Stone Travelers*™ books at
www.CookVBS.com

Site Supplies

GENERAL

- Medieval Castle mural
- *Time-Stone Travelers™* CD or tape copy
- CD player or cassette tape player
- Overhead transparency of lyrics and overhead projector
- Bible
- FINNEGAN Puppet
- Copy of "Traveler's Journal" for each child *(pages R.59-66)*. Note the two age levels and use accordingly.
- Copy of "The Quest Continues" student Take-Home Page *(pages E2.15-16)* for each child

SNACKS

- French bread cubes
- Cheese cubes
- Pewter or wooden plates, goblets, and bowl
- Tapestry table runner *(optional)*
- Apples, sliced
- Pears, sliced
- Plums, sliced
- Seedless grapes
- Small doilies
- Small disposable plates

GAMES AND ACTIVITIES

- Toy swords and shields
- A couple of pillows or cushions
- Wall calendar
- Large, foam-core board "replica" of the Ten Commandments tablet with commandments 3 and 4 clearly printed on it *(Loosely attach a piece of paper over each commandment to cover it.)*
- Simple Bible-time costumes
- Key Bible Verse poster on an easel
- Key Bible Verse cards *(found on page R.58 in Resources)*
- Transparent tape
- Card stock sheets, each with one word of the verse in block printing
- Something to serve as a "castle wall" *(large screen, blanket draped over a rope, plywood board securely propped up, stacked boxes, etc.)*
- Soft lobbing objects *(foam balls, bean bags, water balloons, etc.)* in buckets or boxes
- Beach towels, blankets, or burlap bags
- Colorful index cards with a name of God on each
- Cotton swabs
- Four boxes or other containers
- Pillows *(may be towels stuffed in pillow cases)*, one per child
- Pencils
- Markers or colored pencils
- Clean stones for the Time Stones
- Copies of symbols for Time Stones *(page R.67)*, one set per child

CRAFTS

- Two pieces of fleece *(16" x 18")* per child
- Straight pins
- Ruler
- Sliver of soap bar or chalk
- Scissors
- Fiberfill stuffing *(about 4-6 ounces per child)*
- Poster board *(various colors)*
- Clear packing tape
- Assortment of 1" pom-poms *(about 6 per child)*
- Glue

Site 2 Notes

TIME-STONE TRAVELERS™ VBS® TAKE-HOME PAGE

Today your child heard about commandments 3 and 4 of God's 10 Commandments: to respect God's name by using it with care, and to keep one day each week for rest and worship. The commandment to rest and worship was illustrated through an event recorded in Luke 13, where Jesus compassionately healed a woman who had been crippled for 18 years. He restored her health even though it was the Sabbath, the Jewish day of rest. Jesus used the day of rest to show love and do good for another. His action prompted the woman to worship God, which is what God desires us to do on our day of rest.

Go online to **www.CookVBS.com** for more information about *Time-Stone Travelers™* VBS and what your child is experiencing each day.

FAMILY FUN ACTIVITY AND INSIGHT QUESTIONS ON BACK
SHARE WHAT YOU LEARNED TODAY WITH YOUR FAMILY!

COLOR YOUR OWN MURAL

The QUEST CONTINUES

💬 TALK IT OUT

- **How can we honor God and His name with our words?**

- **In what new and different ways could we keep a day of rest and use that time to worship God?**

👥 FAMILY STUFF

Point: Becoming aware of how we honor God helps us plan ways to do so, both by taking a day of rest and by considering how we honor His name.

Activity: It wasn't that long ago that Sundays were different from the other days of the week in mainstream North America. People in today's older generation *(grandparents, senior citizens)* will likely recall how Sunday stood out from the rest of the week. As a family, choose one or more older people to interview about this topic. Ask them for examples of how they spent Sundays when they were young people and what things they did or didn't do on that day of the week.

After the interview(s), talk about how your Sundays are like and unlike those of the previous generations. Decide on one way to make Sundays more restful, worshipful, and loving. How will you honor God that day? Try out your idea for at least four weeks and then evaluate—what difference does it make?

BIBLE VERSE

*(Early elementary verse in **bold** type.)*

"There remaineth therefore a rest to the people of God. **For he that is entered into his rest, he also hath ceased from his own works, as God did from his."**
— Hebrews 4:9-10

ELEMENTARY

ANCIENT LABORATORY

"Children, obey your parents in the Lord: for this is right."
— **Ephesians 6:1**

INFO for the TRIP

Why Kids Need to Understand that God Wants Them to Honor Their Parents

No honest parent feels worthy of their child's total honor and respect. And most kids aren't inclined to give it, no matter how much their parents may deserve it. God's fifth rule for living isn't built on parents' worthiness or children's desires. It is a building block for the order and authority God desires for successful family-building.

God created the pattern for family life just as He wanted it. Parents function not just as caregivers for their offspring, but more importantly, as models of the God-human relationship. As a child learns to obey, honor, and respect mom and dad, he or she learns that God, also, is to be honored, obeyed, and respected. Parents don't earn this respect—it's due them because that's how God created the family.

Our current society brings legitimate struggles to understanding how to apply this fifth commandment. Your students may wonder about the role of step-parents and other legal guardians such as grandparents. Children may fear a command to obey abusive or neglectful parents, and as a result may learn to mistrust God. Reassure your students that God's command is one of love and care, and children should seek help when they are in a dangerous or unloving home situation.

The concept of honoring and respecting isn't well developed in our society. Offer tangible ideas for how kids can honor their parents. Kids will get the idea as they begin using your suggestions at home and see positive results.

FACTOID

Alchemists were on a lifelong quest for inner purity as they sought to recreate the most pure metal—gold—from other imperfect metals. An alchemist's efforts were a combination of scientific, spiritual, and philosophical thought. Many great philosophers and religious leaders dabbled in alchemy, including Roger Bacon, Thomas Aquinas, Pope John XXII, and Isaac Newton. Many alchemists were monks who worked toward the salvation of the natural world.

GETTING MORE FROM THE BIBLE STORY

This narrative takes place during the Jewish Passover celebration, which was in the spring and lasted a week. Families traveled together on foot to reduce their chances of being robbed along the way. On their way back to Nazareth after the Passover, Jesus' parents probably assumed that their son was elsewhere in the group. By the time they returned to the city, Jesus had been on His own for two days; then they searched for three days before they discovered Him.

As a Jewish, 12-year-old male, Jesus was nearly an adult. The temple school where He talked with the rabbis was the same seminary where Paul later studied (Acts 22). Because the Passover was such a significant gathering for the Jews, the most important and learned rabbis would have gathered at the temple where Jesus sat to listen and ask questions.

The end of the passage (Luke 2:49-50) is the first indication to us that Jesus knew He was God's Son. However, despite this declaration, He submitted to the authority of His earthly parents by obeying them. There's no other mention of Christ's youth or life until He commenced His ministry at age 30.

Core Concept

Children will discover that God expects us to respect, honor, and obey our parents, because God has given them the responsibility to take care of us.

Key Bible Verses

Early & Upper Elementary

"Children, obey your parents in the Lord: for this is right."
–Ephesians 6:1

Puppet Option

A Leader can operate FINNEGAN to help lead the children to different areas and interact spontaneously with the teacher and children. *(See puppet pattern for FINNEGAN on pages R.53-57.)*

Bible Passage

Luke 2:41-51,
Exodus 20:12
(Commandment 5)

Setting the Scene

Use the transparency *(page R.72)* to make a backdrop of a mysterious, old laboratory. Use an appliance box to make a furnace extend from the wall—filled with yellow

---

Schedule of Activities

10 minutes: Introduction	**15 minutes:** Snack Time
15-20 minutes: Bible Story Time	**20 minutes:** Craft Time
10 minutes: Bible Memory Time	**10 minutes:** Application Time
5 minutes: Music Time	**10 minutes:** Time-Stone Take Off
20 minutes: Game Time	

and orange paper for a glowing fire. Make replicas of a bellows and large fire tongs near the furnace. Set up a long wooden table, and fill it with non-breakable bottles, mortar and pestle, and ancient-looking books. Paint coffee cans black, and fill them or other metal or wooden containers with things like tree bark, colorful stones, oozing liquid, dried flowers and seeds, and so on. If possible, plug in a single burner; on top have a colored liquid bubbling in a heat-stable jar. On shelves, set out books, such as large dictionaries with handmade covers of dark paper with mysterious designs on them.

Introduction

(A13) Supplies

- ○ Non-breakable, clear beaker of colored fluid
- ○ Handful of dried plants still on the stems
- ○ Thick book covered in a brown paper jacket and darkened (*covered with powder to give the appearance of dust*)
- ○ Fountain pen and parchment paper on the table

Advanced Preparation

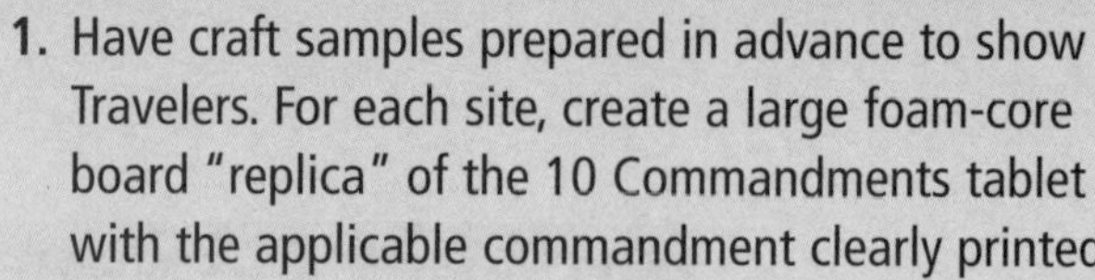

1. Have craft samples prepared in advance to show Travelers. For each site, create a large foam-core board "replica" of the 10 Commandments tablet with the applicable commandment clearly printed on it.
2. Be sure all supplies are gathered and your site is ready each day for Travelers to arrive.
3. Post the Schedule of Activities where Leaders and Helpers can refer to it.
4. Address each other by site titles. Children should be referred to as Travelers.
5. After taking attendance, a Leader should tell those responsible for refreshments how many Travelers are present to be prepared for snack time.
6. You may wish to do some background research into the Bible story. Refer to Bible commentaries, encyclopedias, and dictionaries for additional information.

(The three actors are searching through things in the lab. The alchemist is sleeping out of sight somewhere in the lab.)

JOSH: *(Blows dust off book and looks through it.)* **I don't understand how we'll ever figure out this mystery. I can't make any sense of these weird symbols and equations.**

ELLEN: I think you're right. How can we make anything out of these dried plants and this strange liquid?

WILL: But that's what I was told to do.

ELLEN: Who told you about using these things to figure out our question?

Leaders Profile

Josh, Will, Ellen, Alchemist (lab scientist)
The three kid characters will guide children through time at the laboratory. They may wear kid-like summer vacation clothes or simple, historic Eastern Europe clothing (*such as knickers and a white shirt for the males and a long plain dress for the female*). The Alchemist may also wear period clothing— such as trousers with a long overcoat— or may simply wear a lab coat.

WILL: It was some very wise man. He does these kinds of things all the time, and he knows lots about learning the answers to important questions.

JOSH: Did he give you some instruction sheet or a video or something? Otherwise, this is just impossible. *(Looks discouraged.)*

WILL: No, nothing like that. But he did tell me several times that this problem—when you figure it out and make it real—gives you something very special. Like a fortune or something. *(All three look very interested at that comment.)*

ELLEN: Why don't we try to get hold of this . . . er, what's he called?

WILL: Alchemist.

ELLEN: Yeah, this alchemist—scientist. He has to be able to help us know how to make sense of this puzzle.

(She bumps into something and that causes a loud noise, which awakens the alchemist with a snort. He makes all sorts of sounds as he's startled awake. He surprises the three kids as he gets up from behind the table, rubs his eyes, straightens out his messed up hair, and organizes himself. The three stare at him as he does this.)

JOSH: Who are you?

ALCHEMIST: Me? I assume you're speaking to me?

JOSH: Ah, yes, sir, I guess I was.

ALCHEMIST: Is there something I can help you with? *(Looks at the things they're carrying.)*

WILL: Uh, well, maybe.

ELLEN: We're trying to make sense of a big question, and we just can't figure it out.

(They put their things on the table. He inspects each one, mumbling to himself, appearing lost in thought, nodding, shaking his head, etc. The three watch him, look at each other and shrug, wait.)

JOSH: Well, what do you think?

ALCHEMIST: I'm working on it, young man. *(Rifles through some books, holds up a beaker to the light and looks at its contents, hunts for something. He keeps humming and mumbling to himself, pauses now and then to look deep in thought, nods and writes on a paper as if deciphering a complicated math problem.)*

ALCHEMIST: Yes. Uh, huh. Mmmm. Oh, yes.

(The three look expectant, crane their necks to see what he's writing.)

ALCHEMIST: Aha! *(His sudden exclamation startles them and they jump in surprise.)*

JOSH: Uh, do you know what the answer is?

ELLEN: Yes, what's the information we've been looking for?

ALCHEMIST: It's really quite simple. What you have here is very clear. It's the fifth of God's 10 Commandments. Do you know what that is? *(The three look at each other and aren't sure, but they're thinking hard.)*

ALCHEMIST: The fifth of the 10 Commandments is this: Honour thy father and thy mother. "Honour," you see, means to respect them. Treat them with politeness and caring. Take seriously what your father and mother say to you. Use what they teach you. Follow their instructions . . . .

WILL: That's the whole puzzle we've been trying to work out? It seems too easy.

JOSH: Easy? Honoring my parents—showing them love and respect—isn't always easy.

ALCHEMIST: No, young man, it isn't. But it's quite important, since God made it one of His 10 rules for living. You see, God has given your parents the responsibility of taking care of you. When you honor and love and obey them, you are accepting this family plan that God set up.

ELLEN: Hey, I remember a story from the New Testament that kind of goes with this commandment. Want to help me share it

with the kids? *(Looks at Will and Josh, who nod. The alchemist sits with the children to listen.)*

Transition the group to another part of the room so the lab scene is not dominant. If necessary, have FINNEGAN lead the kids in a few stretches and active moves before they're seated for the Bible story.

Bible Story Time

Luke 2:41-51; Exodus 20:12

(A14) Supplies

- ○ Bibles
- ○ Three copies of the story, cut to fit inside a Bible
- ○ Large foam-core board "replica" of the Ten Commandments tablet with Commandment 5 clearly printed on it *(Pattern on page R.45.)*

Will, Josh, and Ellen should read their story portions from the papers, but place the scripts in the Bibles so the children will understand that the story comes from God's Word.

ELLEN: Luke was a man who lived when Jesus lived. He wrote about Jesus' life. Here's one event he wrote about.

JOSH: Every year Jesus traveled to Jerusalem with His family, friends, and neighbors for a big festival called the Passover. It was a long walk that took several days.

WILL: His mother was Mary, who gave birth to

Him. Joseph was Mary's husband, and he was raising Jesus as he would raise his own son. Jesus also had brothers and sisters and aunts and uncles and cousins.

ELLEN: When Jesus was 12 years old, the whole family went to Jerusalem as usual. When the festival was over, the family, friends, and neighbors started traveling back home.

JOSH: But Jesus stayed behind in Jerusalem. His parents didn't know He had done that. They believed He was in another part of their group.

WILL: They walked for a day before they realized Jesus wasn't with them. They started to look for Him among the other people and their relatives.

ELLEN: But they didn't find Him, so they turned around and went back to Jerusalem. They searched for Him for one, two, and then three days.

JOSH: Finally, they found Jesus. He was at the temple, where people went to worship God. Jesus was sitting with the teachers, listening to them and asking them questions about God and the Scriptures.

WILL: Everyone who heard Jesus talk was amazed at His understanding and His answers. After all, He was only 12!

ELLEN: When His parents found Him they were relieved and also surprised. His mother said, "Son, what did You do this for? Your father and I have been searching for You! We were really worried about You."

JOSH: Jesus answered, "Why were you searching for Me? Didn't you know that I would be in My Father's house, the temple?"

WILL: But Mary and Joseph didn't understand. They didn't really know yet what it meant that Jesus was the Son of God.

ELLEN: Jesus left Jerusalem with them and went home to Nazareth. He kept on honoring His parents by obeying them. His mother remembered all about this as Jesus was growing up.

(Readers exit.)

ALCHEMIST: *(Stands in front of the group.)* **Even though Jesus seemed to be disobedient because He stayed back in Jerusalem, He was doing what His real Father—God in heaven—had wanted. When Jesus' parents came to find Him, He obediently followed them home and He honored them day after day. Jesus was obeying the fifth commandment.** *(Holds up the foam core tablet and reads commandment 5 aloud while pointing to each word.)* **Jesus is an example to us of how to honor the people God has given to take care of us.**

Have Leaders direct kids to the Bible memory activity.

Bible Memory Time

(A15) Supplies
- Two poster board puzzles of the verse
- Key Bible verse poster on an easel
- Key Bible verse cards *(found on page R.58)*
- Traveler's Journals *(found on pages R.59-66)*
- Transparent tape

In Advance: Make two identical poster board puzzles of the verse, and cut them into about 8-10 pieces each. Use two colors of marker to distinguish the puzzles from each other. *(One set should be purple, for instance, the other green).* Draw alchemy symbols on the backs of all the pieces. Hide

the pieces of both poster-puzzles in a large area.

Early and Upper Elementary Verse

"Children, obey your parents in the Lord: for this is right." –Ephesians 6:1

Divide the group into two teams. Explain that the groups will race to solve their puzzles. First they have to find a puzzle piece and then bring it to their team's "lab" to put together. Assign each group an area with a hard surface as their "lab." If you have enough players, make a rule that each player can find only one piece. If necessary, teammates can help one another find missing pieces. When a team completes their puzzle, they read it aloud together. If you want to play again, try having teams hide each other's pieces. Give extra points for teams whose members can say the verse from memory.

Tape the Key Verse Cards into each child's Traveler's Journal.

Music Time

Obey, Obey
(A16) Supplies
- Copy of song lyrics for each child, or have the words on an overhead transparency *(page R.24)*
- *Time-Stone Travelers™* CD or tape copy of "Obey, Obey" *(Track 4)*
- CD or tape player
- Overhead projector
- FINNEGAN Puppet *(optional)*

Have the children listen to the song for this site. Play the song again and have the kids join in with the singing. Allow them to stand and move around if you have the space. If age appropriate, project the words of the song onto a screen for the children to follow along as they sing. You may want to have FINNEGAN help teach the song.

Game Time

Alchemist Relay

(G5) Supplies *(for each team)*

- ○ Plastic jars half full of colored water
- ○ Cans of dried plant material *(leaves, twigs, etc.)*
- ○ Paper lunch bags of wood chips or pebbles
- ○ Fabric bags of dirt
- ○ Tongs
- ○ Stuffed critters *(snake, lizard, alligator, etc.)*
- ○ Laundry baskets or boxes

Divide into teams and have each team line up across from a table. The table should be several feet behind the last person in each line. Several feet in front of each team, place a laundry basket. Explain that in this relay race, teams try to be the first to make the "alchemist's potion." Explain that the laundry basket represents the furnace that an alchemist uses to heat and purify all his elements.

At the starting signal, the last person in line runs back to the table and grabs the first item and races back to his team. He passes it between his legs to the person in front of him, who does the same. The item travels up the line to the first person who runs to deposit it in the furnace *(basket)*. This teammate then runs to the table in the back and grabs the next item and passes it back up the line. The sequence continues until all the items have been deposited, one by one, in the basket. The team that finishes first wins.

Respect/Disrespect

(G6) Supplies

- ○ Signs that read RESPECT and DISRESPECT

Remind children of the Bible story and how Jesus honored His parents. To honor means to respect and value. The children can follow Jesus' example by respecting their parents. Explain that this game helps the children think about ways they can show respect and ways they should avoid because they are disrespectful and dishonoring.

Attach one sign at one end of the game area and the other at the opposite side. The kids gather in the middle. Read each of the following statements about how kids might behave or speak to their parents. The children quickly decide if the statement shows respect or disrespect and then run to that sign. Choose one player to explain why that particular action is or is not respectful of their parents. Affirm kids who make good decisions. *(Note: If any of the children in your group have a legal guardian other than their original parents, such as a grandparent, step-parent, or foster parent, reword some of the statements to reflect that and include those children.)*

Statements of Respect/Disrespect:

When your parents tell you dinner is ready, you wash your hands and come right to the table.

After your dad says no to something you want to do, you tell a friend what a terrible dad he is.

When your mom is talking on the phone, you interrupt her five times.

Your parents say to watch just one TV show a day; you do what they ask, even though you wish you could watch more.

After your dad fixes your bike, you tell him thank you and give him a hug.

You complain to your parents that you don't get enough allowance and other kids have more than you do.

Your forgot to make your mom a card for Mother's Day, so you tell her a dog ate it.

You forgot to make your mom a card for Mother's Day, so you tell her you're sorry and promise to help in the kitchen instead.

After your mom says no to something you want, you go ask dad and hope he says yes so you can get it.

Your parents ask you to do an extra chore every week. You hate chores, but you agree and do your best anyway.

Snack Time

Creative Concoctions
(S5) Supplies
- ○ Instant gelatin in various flavors (*1/2 cup per child*)
- ○ Whipped topping (*1/4 cup per student*)
- ○ Various cake decorating sprinkles in fun shapes
- ○ Clear plastic cups
- ○ Small disposable spoons

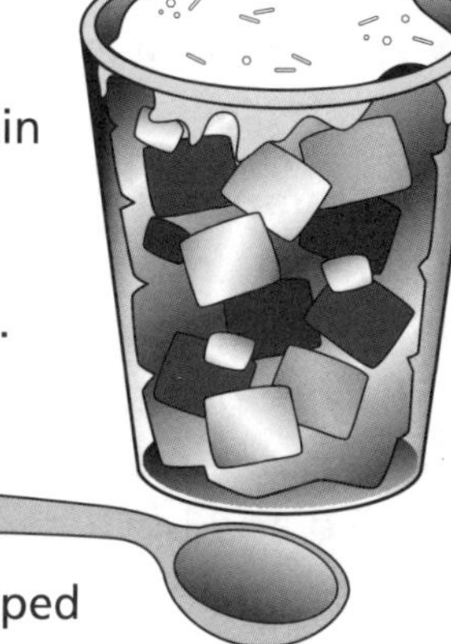

In Advance: Make gelatin as directed on package. Pour 1/2 cup into a clear plastic cup. Chill until set.

Let the children select a flavor of gelatin they would like and add whipped cream and sprinkles.

Flavor Experiments
(S6) Supplies
- ○ Animal cookies or other small shortbread or sugar cookies
- ○ A variety of creative dipping toppings (*yogurt, whipped cream, flavored sauces, melted butterscotch, etc.*)
- ○ Small disposable bowls
- ○ Small paper plates
- ○ Napkins

Set out each topping in its own bowl. Give each student a few cookies on a paper plate. Let the kids try dipping their cookies in the different sauces and toppings to try various flavor combinations.

Craft Time

Message Holders

(C5) Supplies

- Cardboard boxes with lids, about 4" x 5" x 1" *(one per child)*
- Scissors
- Poster paint or spray paint
- Felt rectangles, 1/4" smaller than the boxes
- Colorful paper, 1/2" smaller than the boxes
- Paint pens in assorted colors
- Craft glue

In Advance: Draw a line a third of the way from the end of each box lid. Cut on this line, and discard the two-thirds part of the lid. With poster paint or spray paint, paint the inside and outside of the box (including the lid and bottom of the box). Use spray paint only in a well-ventilated area!

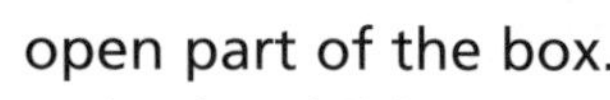

Have the children glue felt to the bottom of the inside of the box. Glue the one-third box lid to the open part of the box. Help the children use a paint pen to make their initials on the box lid. They may add decorative marks to embellish, if desired. Place paper in the box to use for messages.

Potpourri Jars

(C6) Supplies

- Potpourri ingredients *(dried rose pedals, dried orange slices, lemon peels, cloves, cinnamon sticks, dried straw flowers, etc.)*
- Disposable bowls
- Fragrant oil
- Paper plates
- Small jars with 3" diameter opening
- White netting, cut in 6" squares
- 1/4" ribbon, 22" long
- Rubber bands

In Advance: Put each potpourri ingredient in its own bowl. Add a couple of drops of fragrant oil to each bowl.

Let the children scoop a spoonful of each potpourri ingredient onto a paper plate and mix it up. Children pour their potpourri into a small jar. Show the children how to place netting over the top of a jar and secure it with a rubber band. The children may tie a ribbon around the jar to cover rubber band.

Application Time

(A16) Supplies
- Traveler's Journals *(pages R.59-66)*
- Pencils

Josh, Will, and Ellen bring the children together at the lab scene for the final interaction of the day.

ELLEN: Back in the old days scientists called alchemists did lots of experiments. They had to think hard, wait for things to happen, and keep trying. Sometimes things didn't go right and they were disappointed, but they didn't give up. How is following God's rule about honoring your parents like the work of the alchemists? *(Let children share ideas.)* **That's right. Honoring and obeying our parents is sometimes hard work and we have to keep trying. Sometimes no one might notice your hard work at honoring your parents. There are days when things don't go well, and we need to apologize. Then you can be thankful that God gives you more chances the next day!**

JOSH: How did Jesus show honor and respect for His mother and father in the Bible story we heard? *(Listens to children's responses.)*

WILL: Our parents have a big responsibility to raise us to know God, to help us make good choices and live the way God wants. They have a hard job—and one that takes lots of years! What is one way you will work your hardest this week to honor and respect your parents? *(Let volunteers answer. Encourage a variety of responses.)*

ELLEN: Right now we're going to divide up into smaller groups. In your small group, you'll be able to ask God for His help to honor your mom and dad or whoever it is that God has put in charge of you at home. God takes your prayers seriously and He will be helping you every day as you try your best to follow His commandments.

Have leaders divide the kids into small groups. Leaders should lead the children in prayer and help them pray individually about honoring their parents. If a child seems to have a need to pray or talk more, take him or her aside after the prayer time for one-on-one interaction.

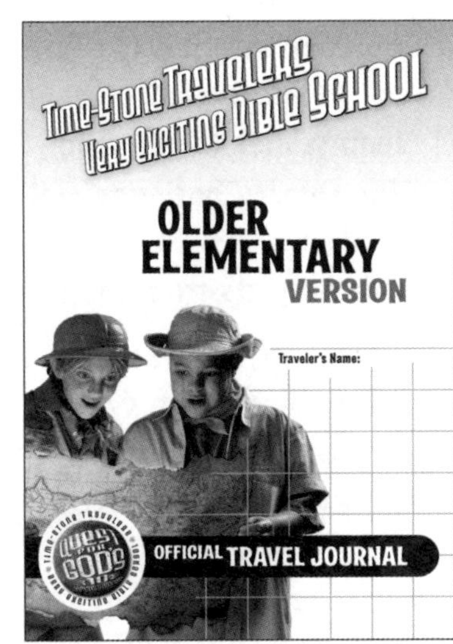

After prayer, have the children work on the laboratory page of their Traveler's Journals. Leaders should help the children understand the directions and work successfully on the page.

 # Time Stone Take-Off

(A17) Supplies

- ○ Copies of symbols for Time Stones *(page R.67)*, one set per child
- ○ Clean stones for the Time Stones
- ○ "The Quest Continues" Take-Home Page, one per child
- ○ Craft projects from the day

Give out the Time Stones, and invite the children to add the symbol for today's lesson. Remind the children that this can help them remember today's commandment. *(See the directions for making the Time Stones and adding the symbols in Resources on page R.67.)* **When you take home your Time Stone at the end of the week, this can remind you of the commandments that God has given us.**

Gather the children and sing together the theme song. Ask them to say the memory verse in unison, and repeat it louder and louder a few of times. Send the children out with joyful encouragement to do what God commands.

Hand out the "The Quest Continues" Take-Home Page and the projects the children made during the session.

See all the *Time-Stone Travelers*™ books at www.CookVBS.com

Site Supplies

GENERAL

- ○ Ancient Laboratory mural
- ○ *Time-Stone Travelers™* CD or tape copy
- ○ CD player or cassette tape player
- ○ Overhead transparency of lyrics and overhead projector
- ○ Bibles
- ○ FINNEGAN Puppet
- ○ Copy of "Traveler's Journal" for each child *(pages R.59-66).*
- ○ "The Quest Continues" student Take-Home Page *(pages E3.15-16)* for each child

SNACKS

- ○ Instant gelatin in various flavors *(1/2 cup per child)*
- ○ Whipped topping *(1/4 cup per student)*
- ○ Various cake-decorating sprinkles in fun shapes
- ○ Clear plastic cups
- ○ Small plastic spoons
- ○ Animal cookies or other small shortbread or sugar cookies
- ○ A variety of creative dipping toppings *(yogurt, whipped cream, flavored sauces, melted butterscotch chips, etc.)*
- ○ Small disposable bowls
- ○ Small paper plates
- ○ Napkins

GAMES AND ACTIVITIES

- ○ Non-breakable, clear beaker of colored fluid
- ○ Handful of dried plants still on the stems
- ○ Thick book covered in a brown paper jacket and darkened *(covered with powder to give the appearance of dust)*
- ○ Fountain pen and parchment paper
- ○ Large, foam-core "replica" of the 10 Commandments tablet with commandment 5 clearly printed on it
- ○ Three copies of the story, cut to fit inside a Bible
- ○ Two poster board puzzles of the verse
- ○ Key Bible verse poster on an easel
- ○ Key Bible verse cards *(found on page R.58 in Resources)*
- ○ Transparent tape
- ○ Plastic jars half full of colored water
- ○ Cans of dried plant material *(leaves, twigs, etc.)*
- ○ Paper lunch bags filled with wood chips or pebbles
- ○ Fabric bags of dirt
- ○ Tongs
- ○ Stuffed critters (snake, lizard, alligator, etc.)
- ○ Laundry baskets or boxes
- ○ Signs that read RESPECT and DISRESPECT
- ○ Pencils
- ○ Clean stones for the Time Stones
- ○ Copies of symbols for Time Stones *(page R.67)*, one set per child

CRAFTS

- ○ Cardboard boxes with lids, about 4" x 5" x 1" *(one per child)*
- ○ Scissors
- ○ Poster paint or spray paint
- ○ Felt rectangles, 1/4" smaller than the boxes
- ○ Colorful paper, 1/2" smaller than the boxes
- ○ Paint pens in assorted colors
- ○ Craft glue
- ○ Potpourri ingredients *(dried rose pedals, dried orange slices, lemon peels, cloves, cinnamon sticks, dried straw flowers, etc.)*
- ○ Fragrant oil
- ○ Paper plates
- ○ Small jars with 3" diameter opening
- ○ White netting, cut in 6" squares
- ○ 1/4" ribbon, 22" long
- ○ Rubber bands
- ○ Disposable bowls

Site 3 Notes

TIME-STONE TRAVELERS™ VBS® TAKE-HOME PAGE

Maybe you'll observe some delightful behaviors and attitudes in your child today, since the theme was God's fifth commandment for children to honor and respect their parents. In the Bible story, your child heard how Jesus, along with His mother Mary and her husband, Joseph, had traveled to Jerusalem for an annual festival. Joseph filled the role of an earthly father for Jesus, since Jesus was conceived by God's Spirit. Twelve-year-old Jesus remained behind in Jerusalem while His parents set out for home. When they discovered Him missing and returned to Jerusalem to look for Him, they found Him in the temple, listening and talking to teachers, astounding people with His knowledge and wisdom. Though Jesus recognized God as His Father, He still obediently returned home with Mary and Joseph and continued to honor them as His parents.

Go online to **www.CookVBS.com** for more information about *Time-Stone Travelers™* VBS and what your child is experiencing each day.

FAMILY FUN ACTIVITY AND INSIGHT QUESTIONS ON BACK
SHARE WHAT YOU LEARNED TODAY WITH YOUR FAMILY!

COLOR YOUR OWN MURAL

The QUEST CONTINUES

💬 TALK IT OUT

- **What examples of respect and honor have parents seen their children do that can encourage them to continue? What examples have children done that can encourage parents?**
- **Share one way each family member thinks parents could be respected and honored in a daily way.**

👪 FAMILY STUFF

Family Time Line Activity

Point: As children grow, their ways of honoring parents also change.

Supplies

- ◯ Length of butcher paper or 6-10 sheets of paper taped together end to end
- ◯ Tape
- ◯ Pens
- ◯ Markers or crayons
- ◯ Self-stick notes

Activity: Create a timeline of your family's life. Make a long banner-style sheet, and draw on it a horizontal line from one end to the other. Choose a family starting point, such as the date the parents married, and write it at the far left end. Then mark short vertical lines at equal distances along the horizontal line, one per year since that date. Have family members take turns writing their birthdates at the appropriate point on the line, and then other significant dates, such as moving to a new home, starting school or a new job, acquiring a pet, and so on.

Think together about ways the children have demonstrated honor and respect to the parents at various ages. Note them on the time line with a little drawing or a phrase. For the time beyond the current date on the timeline, have both parents and children use self-stick notes to jot or draw ideas on how the kids can grow in their honor and respect for mom and dad. Parents can offer their suggestions as well.

Talk about how showing honor and respect can change as people grow older. Parents might share their experiences with honoring their own parents. Join hands around the timeline to pray and ask God to teach the children how to live out the fifth commandment, along with the parents' desire and ability to obey the fifth commandment with their own parents. Have children pray sentence prayers of thanks and appreciation for each parent. End with a fun snack.

Post the timeline in a place where it can act as an occasional reminder. Or put it away, but note on the family calendar to take it out in six months to check the progress and suggestions on the self-stick notes.

BIBLE VERSE

"Children, obey your parents in the Lord: for this is right."
— **Ephesians 6:1**

ELEMENTARY

HAWK'S VILLAGE

*"Love the Lord thy God with all thy heart, . . .
and thy neighbour as thyself."* — **Luke 10:27**

INFO for the TRIP

Why Kids Need to Know That Kindness Is the Way to Treat Everyone

Kindness is not as easy as it sounds. Bullying has become a commonly discussed topic in communities, schools, and professional journals dealing with social issues. Some schools have adopted anti-bullying rules, hold special assemblies, and promote slogans to prepare kids to face bullying. What a statement this makes about how necessary it is for kids to learn that God commands us to treat one another with kindness.

Having been born sinners and with an innate sense of self-interest, each child needs to learn to tell the truth, control anger, maintain faithfulness in the covenant of marriage, and be honorable regarding the possessions of others. These commandments can be succinctly summarized as treating others kindly.

Some of the children at your VBS are growing up in situations not conducive to this mindset. Abuse and neglect may be hard to see, but they're widespread today. The only way the children will genuinely be able to learn to become like Jesus is to learn how to show kindness, not only to those whom they consider friends, but also to those to whom they have no relationship or allegiance. Your examples of kindness this week will be the starting point for some kids to "go and do likewise." Look for chances to go out of your way to show sincere kindness while the children are watching, not only to the kids, but also to other Leaders or any person.

FACTOID

The Ojibwa, also known as the Chippewa, were masters of the North American waterways. They excelled at building canoes from birch, white cedar, and spruce. Near the Great Lakes, just one birch tree could supply enough bark for a whole canoe. The bark was peeled off, or in winter, the tree was cut down and had boiling water poured on it to thaw the wood. Roots of conifer trees were used to fasten the various canoe parts together.

GETTING MORE FROM THE BIBLE STORY

Jesus told this parable about a kind Samaritan when a Jewish lawyer in the audience sought to test Jesus' knowledge of Judaic law. The lawyer's question about inheriting eternal life was based on Moses' law in Deuteronomy 6:5 and Leviticus 19:18. The lawyer himself became a part of the parable's truth because he considered his question as a point of law, while Jesus showed that care for the person is the central point.

Interestingly, Jesus, who was Jewish, told a parable featuring a Samaritan, someone strongly disliked by the Jews. The Samaritan was the "good guy" in the story, which would have rankled those listening to Jesus. The Samaritans were a race of people of mixed heritage who were the result of intermarriage after the Hebrew exile between the Jews from the northern kingdom and other people groups. The Jews scorned this group.

By telling this particular story, Jesus was emphasizing that only one attitude toward others is acceptable to God: kindness motivated by love.

Core Concept

Children will understand that God wants them to treat other people with kindness.

Key Bible Verses

Early Elementary

"Love the Lord thy God with all thy heart . . . and thy neighbour as thyself." — **Luke 10:27**

Upper Elementary

"Thou shalt love the Lord thy God with all thy heart, and with all thy soul, and with all thy strength, and with all thy mind; and thy neighbour as thyself." — **Luke 10:27**

Puppet Option

A Leader can operate FINNEGAN to help lead the children to different areas and interact spontaneously with the teacher and children *(See puppet pattern for FINNEGAN on pages R.53-57.)*

Bible Passage

Luke 10:25-37, Exodus 20:13-16 *(Commandment 6, 7, 8, 9)*

Setting the Scene

Create an Ojibwa Indian encampment in a forest setting. Use the

<table>
<tr><td colspan="2">Schedule of Activities</td></tr>
<tr><td>10 minutes: Introduction</td><td>15 minutes: Snack Time</td></tr>
<tr><td>15-20 minutes: Bible Story Time</td><td>20 minutes: Craft Time</td></tr>
<tr><td>10 minutes: Bible Memory Time</td><td>10 minutes: Application Time</td></tr>
<tr><td>5 minutes: Music Time</td><td>10 minutes: Time-Stone Take Off</td></tr>
<tr><td>20 minutes: Game Time</td><td></td></tr>
</table>

transparency *(page R.73)* to project the picture onto mural paper. Trace the outlines; then paint or color in the pictures. Hang the mural on a wall in the classroom. Make a rounded wigwam of sticks covered in what looks like birch bark *(use burlap or felt painted to resemble bark)*. Build a cooking fire by mounding up some sticks in a circle of stones; simulate fire with red and orange tissue paper, crumpled and molded to look like flames. Set some rustic, woven baskets near the wigwam. Some animal skins *(real, fake, or painted)* can be draped over a log or branch. If possible, paint or create a birch bark canoe *(all or just one end could be visible)* to set at the side of the scene.

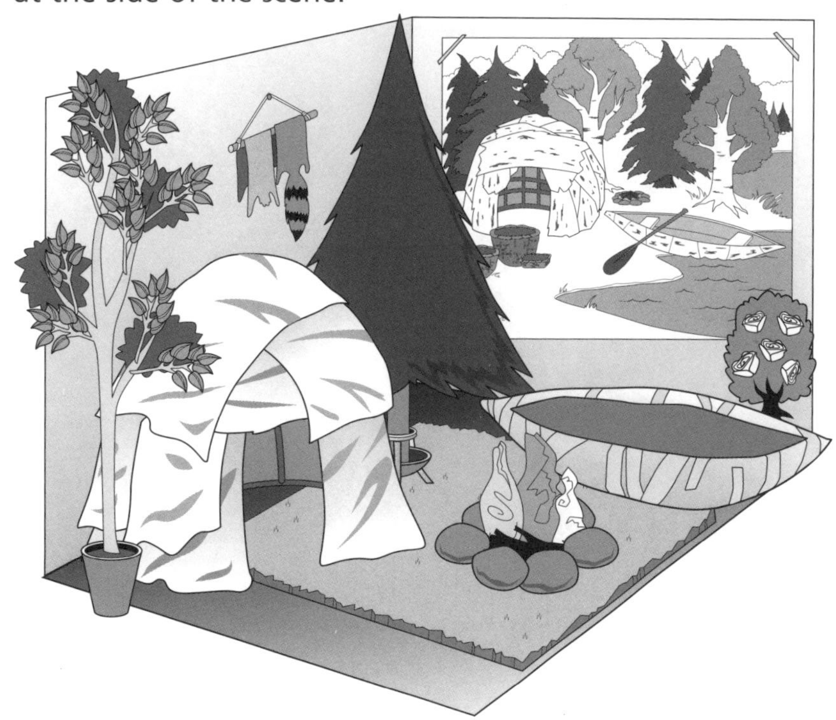

Introduction

(A18) Supplies
- ○ Rustic baskets
- ○ Wigwam

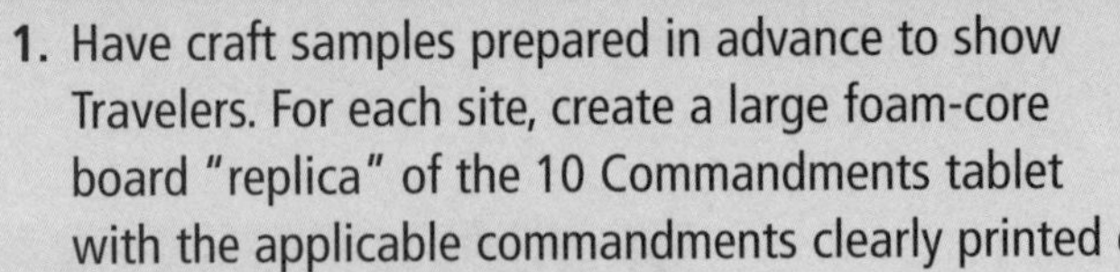

Advanced Preparation

1. Have craft samples prepared in advance to show Travelers. For each site, create a large foam-core board "replica" of the 10 Commandments tablet with the applicable commandments clearly printed on it.

2. Be sure all supplies are gathered and your site is ready each day for Travelers to arrive.

3. Post the Schedule of Activities where Leaders and Helpers can refer to it.

4. Address each other by site titles. Children should be referred to as Travelers.

5. After taking attendance, a Leader should tell those responsible for refreshments how many Travelers are present to be prepared for snack time.

6. You may wish to do some background research into the Bible story. Refer to Bible commentaries, encyclopedias, and dictionaries for additional information.

(The Ojibwa Indian waits in or behind the wigwam as the other three characters walk up to the scene.)

WILL: I've been looking forward to visiting the Ojibwa village. Finally we're here!

JOSH: What's an Ojibwa?

WILL: It's one of the Indian tribes that lived in Canada and the Midwestern part of the United States, around all the lakes. They were very good fishermen and made some unbelievably strong birch bark canoes. They were like the kings of the waterways. It would be so cool to live with their tribe for a while.

ELLEN: Were these the Indians that

Leaders Profile

Josh, Will, Ellen, Ojibwa Indian

The three kid characters wear kid-like summer vacation clothes or Indian costumes. Outfit the Indian actor in as authentic a costume as possible.

caught fish by tickling them?

JOSH: No way! How could anyone even get close enough to a fish to tickle it? Besides who knows if fish are even ticklish?

WILL: But it's true! *(Acts it out as he describes it.)* The Indians would get into the water and move really slowly. They would figure out where the fish were hiding on the sides of the river or stream. Then they would slowly stroke the fish's belly. Once the fish relaxed, then they could grab it.

JOSH: Sounds like a strange way to fish.

WILL: I think they might have also used spears to fish.

ELLEN: The Ojibwas were very smart and good craftsmen. They made all sorts of things with birch bark, like these baskets. *(They move to the baskets; Ellen examines one closely. They don't notice the Ojibwa enter.)* But living in an Ojibwa village wouldn't be my choice. It seems like Indians were always fighting other Indian tribes.

INDIAN: You are right. *(The three are startled and turn around, surprised seeing at the Indian.)*

WILL: Who are you?

INDIAN: I am an Ojibwa.

JOSH: Whoa! I think you're actually getting your wish to find out about this tribe, Will!

WILL: Yeah, I never thought I'd really meet an Ojibwa Indian, especially one from a village of hundreds of years ago.

INDIAN: Are you from a peaceful tribe?

(Ellen, Will, and Josh look at each other with puzzled expressions.)

ELLEN: We're not really a tribe. But sure, we're peaceful. *(Hesitates.)* Are you from a peaceful tribe?

(Indian looks at the three thoughtfully, walks around them, looking at them up and down, thinking.)

WILL: Ah, what does your tribe believe about treating visitors?

INDIAN: Ojibwa warriors protect our village. We believe that the spirits show us who is peaceful and who is not.

JOSH: We follow a Spirit, too. He's the God who created us.

INDIAN: What does your God say about how to treat visitors?

ELLEN: God has some pretty strong commandments about how we're supposed to treat people. He says we should treat others with kindness.

JOSH: And that's not just visitors. God says to be kind to people you know and those you don't know, those you like and those you don't like.

INDIAN: I see. Do your people have stories from your ancestors that teach you how to follow these rules?

WILL: *(To Ellen and Josh.)* I think the Bible would be our storybook, don't you think? *(They nod. Will turns back to Indian.)* Yes, we have a book of stories, things that really happened. This Book gives us all the information we need to know about God, ourselves, and other people. Would you like to hear one of our stories about how we should treat other people?

(The Indian nods and sits down at the front of the group of kids to wait for the Bible story.)

Bible Story Time

Luke 10:25-37, Exodus 20:13-16

(A19) Supplies

- ○ Bible
- ○ Cloth or bandanna
- ○ Two towels in different colors
- ○ Two strips of fabric or rope
- ○ A few coins

- ○ Small jug
- ○ Donkey or horse *(rocking horse, cardboard replica of a donkey, etc.)*
- ○ Large foam-core board "replica" of the Ten Commandments tablet with commandments 6, 7, 8, 9 clearly printed on it *(You may use an abbreviated form of the commandments.)*

Begin by showing the children where Luke 10 is found in a Bible. **In the Bible, we learn about many things Jesus taught. Sometimes He taught using stories. One day, a man who was like a lawyer was in the crowd. He stood up and asked Jesus a question. But the man didn't really want to know the answer. He really just wanted to show how smart he was. Boy, was he surprised at the answer Jesus gave him!**

Read Luke 10:25-29 aloud. Then ask the children: **What did Jesus say the man should do?** *(Love the Lord with all his heart, soul, mind, and strength, and love his neighbor as himself.)* **The lawyer wanted to know just who his neighbor was, so Jesus told this story.**

Ask for six volunteers to play parts in the Bible story: traveler, robber, Levite, priest, Samaritan, innkeeper. Bring them to the front, and explain that they will simply listen for what you read and act it out. For costumes, tie a cloth or bandanna around the lower face of the robber. Drape a towel over the head of the Levite and the priest. Tie a length of fabric like a belt around the Samaritan and the innkeeper. Give the jug and coins to the Samaritan. Have everyone all stand off to the side. If the donkey is too large or heavy to pull, place it near the center of the "stage."

Read Luke 10:30-35 slowly from the Bible. Pause whenever there is action for one of the actors to pantomime. Prompt the children as necessary. When finished, thank the actors and let them be seated.

When Jesus finished telling this story, He asked the lawyer a question. I'll ask it to you: "Which now of these three, thinkest thou,

was neighbour unto him that fell among the thieves?" *(The one who helped him, the Samaritan.)* **That's right, and that's the same answer the lawyer gave. It was a hard answer for him, though, because his people did not like the Samaritans. Jesus told the man that he should treat people in the loving way the Samaritan treated the hurt man. Jesus meant that we should even help people we don't get along with—because our neighbor is anyone we come in contact with.**

Explain that this is very much like commandments 6, 7, 8, and 9 of the 10 Commandments. Hold up the foam core commandments, and read them together with the children as you point to each word. Explain that these four commandments teach us not to murder, to be faithful in marriage, not to steal, and not to lie. If we love our neighbor as we love ourselves, we won't be breaking these commandments.

Have Leaders direct kids to the Bible memory activity.

Bible Memory Time

(A20) Supplies

- ○ Key Bible verse poster on an easel
- ○ Traveler's Journals *(found on pages R.59-66)*
- ○ Key Bible Verse cards *(found on page R.58)*
- ○ Four extra verse cards, written and underlined as described below
- ○ Transparent tape

In Advance: Divide the verse into four segments and clearly print each segment on an index card; underline the key words, like this:

Thou shalt <u>love</u> the <u>Lord thy God</u>

with <u>all</u> thy <u>heart,</u> and with <u>all</u> thy <u>soul,</u>

and with <u>all</u> thy <u>strength,</u> and with <u>all</u> thy <u>mind;</u>

and thy <u>neighbour</u> as <u>thyself</u>. **Luke 10:27**

Early (in bold) and Upper Elementary Verse

*"Thou shalt **love the Lord thy God with all thy heart**, and with all thy soul, and with all thy strength, and with all thy mind; **and thy neighbour as thyself.**"* — Luke 10:27

Display the Key Bible Verse poster, and lead the children in reading it together as you point to each word. Then divide the children into four groups. Give each group one of the prepared verse cards, and explain that as a group they are to make up actions that represent the underlined words, as well as memorize their verse part. After a sufficient time, gather everyone again and stand in a circle with groups remaining together *(side by side)*, in correct verse order. Have the first group say their segment and do the actions they've chosen. Do this with each group in succession. Go around the circle again, having everyone repeat the verse in unison with each group and do the actions. Continue a few times so the verse with actions becomes familiar.

What do you think it means to love God with all your heart, soul, strength, and mind? *(That we make loving God our top priority, that we are committed to Him and put effort into following Him, that we choose to think and do things that help our love for Him grow, etc.)* **How do we love others in the same ways we love ourselves?** *(By taking time to notice their needs, by putting effort into helping them, by thinking less self-centeredly and making others a priority, etc.)*

Before leaving this activity, help the children tape the verse cards in their Traveler's Journals.

Music Time

Show Others Love
(A21) Supplies

○ Copy of song lyrics for each child, or have the words on an overhead transparency *(page R.25)*
○ *Time-Stone Travelers*™ CD or tape copy of "Show Others Love" (Track 5)
○ CD or tape player
○ Overhead projector *(optional)*
○ FINNEGAN puppet *(optional)*

Have the children listen to the song for this site. Play the song a second time and have the kids join in with the singing. Allow them to stand and move around if you have the space. If age appropriate, project the words of the song onto a screen for the children to follow along as they sing. You may want to have FINNEGAN help teach the song.

Game Time

Ojibwa Fishing
(G7) Supplies

○ One or more playground balls

Divide the children into two equal groups. Have one group stand in a cluster while the other group creates a large circle around them. Explain that the kids on the perimeter of the circle are Ojibwa Indians and those inside are fish. The Ojibwa are going to try to catch the fish; they do this by tossing or rolling one or more balls across the circle. *(Choose how many balls to use based on the size of the group and their skill level.)* Any fish touched by the balls are "caught" and come out to join the Ojibwa and fish for more fish. Whenever a fish is caught and comes out of the circle, he or she must call out one of the four commandments for today: *Don't murder, don't steal, don't lie, or be faithful in marriage.* Play until all the fish are caught; then have the groups switch places and play again. Be sure to include safety rules that balls must be tossed gently and "Indians" must try to hit below the hip.

Neighborly Toss

(G8) Supplies

- ○ Bean bags
- ○ Bag of small treats *(such as individually wrapped candies, stickers, etc.)*
- ○ Construction paper sheets, each labeled in bold lettering spelling out a type of person: classmate, friend, little lost child, neighbor, teammate, kid on the playground, elderly person, teacher
- ○ Masking tape

Tell the children that this game gives them chances to think up ways to treat others with kindness. Explain that the groups of people written on the paper are all our neighbors—people whom we might see or run into in our daily lives. Lay the sheets randomly in a central part of the play area.

Have kids take turns standing behind a masking tape line and tossing a bean bag onto one of the sheets and naming the person written there. The child thinks up a realistic way he could treat that person with genuine kindness and tells the rest of the group his idea. Then the child gets to reach into the treat bag and pull out one item to enjoy.

 # Snack Time

Fishin'

(S7) Supplies

- ○ Fish crackers
- ○ Small, new fishnet *(the kind used for scooping aquarium fish)*
- ○ Large, clear glass or plastic bowl
- ○ Clear plastic cups

Place fish crackers in a big clear bowl to look like a fishbowl. Let the children use the fishnet to dip into bowl and scoop some fish crackers. Have the children empty their fish crackers into clear plastic cups *("mini fish bowls")* to eat from.

Blueberry Muffins

(S8) Supplies

- ○ Store-bought or homemade blueberry muffins
- ○ Fresh or frozen blueberries in a bowl
- ○ Small plates
- ○ Hand wipes for blueberry stains

Serve blueberry muffins. Let the children pick a few fresh or frozen blueberries from a bowl to pretend they are picking blueberries in the forest around Hawk's Village.

Craft Time

Ojibwa Sand Designs

(C7) Supplies

○ Sandpaper, 4 1/2" x 5 1/2"
○ Hole punch
○ Jute or leather lacing, 12" strips *(one per child)*
○ Newspaper
○ Examples of historic Native American artwork
○ Scrap paper
○ Pencils
○ Paintbrushes
○ Water
○ Glue
○ Colored craft sand in a variety of colors
○ Foil
○ Disposable cups

In Advance: In each piece of sandpaper, punch two holes 1/2" from the top edge and one hole 1/2" in on each side. Mix glue and water *(50/50)* into small cups for children to share. Cover tables with newspaper to protect them.

Let the children use scrap paper and pencils to try drawing designs that look like historic Native American artwork. They may look at the examples for ideas. Encourage the children to keep their sketches very simple. Then have the children lightly sketch their favorite design on sandpaper. With a paintbrush, the children paint the glue mixture on one the part of their design. They sprinkle one color of craft sand over this glued area. Help the children tap off excess sand onto squares of foil. *(This can be transferred back into the sand container.)* Then the children paint glue on another section of their picture and repeat this process with another color. *(Note: When finished, rinse the paintbrushes immediately in warm water to remove the glue.)* When sand designs are completely dry, tie the lacing to the holes on upper edge to make a hanger for the artwork.

Birdfeeder

(C8) Supplies

○ Clear, bowl-shaped plastic lids, 8"-10" diameter *(one per child) (These must be concave or bowl-shaped lids.)*
○ Clear, flat plastic lids, 4" diameter *(one per child)*
○ Hole punch
○ 12" long dowels or sticks smaller than 1/8" diameter *(12 per child)*
○ Jute, 2' long *(3 per child)*
○ Small zipper-closure plastic bags with birdseed

In Advance: Punch 12 holes evenly spaced around the sides of each large lid. *(Note: Lids of this type may be obtained from bakeries and carry-out containers.)*

Give each child 12 sticks, one large lid, and one small lid. Show the children how to poke one stick into any hole from the outside. Pull the stick across the inside of the lid and out the fourth hole over. Adjust the stick so it is evenly placed between the holes. Have the children place another stick in the next hole and out the fourth hole from it. Continue around the entire lid until all 12 sticks are used. Eventually each hole will have two sticks in it, forming an X.

Help the children tie three pieces of jute together in a double knot at one end. They tie the other ends to three evenly spaced sticks to hold the bird feeder balanced. Place a small lid in the center of each birdfeeder. Give each child a baggie of birdseed to put in their birdfeeder at home.

Application Time

***(A22)* Supplies**
- Traveler's Journals *(found on pages R.59-66)*
- Pencils

Gather the children in front of the Hawk's Village scene. Have the Ojibwa Indian who took part in the Introduction return to interact with the children.

OJIBWA: I have learned much about God today. But I have some questions. First, what does it mean to love your God with all your heart, soul, mind, and strength? *(Children raise their hands so the Indian can call on them to answer. Let as many children as want to respond.)*

OJIBWA: Also, I would like to know what God means when He talks about our neighbors. Who are our neighbors? *(Allow kids to volunteer answers.)*

OJIBWA: Now I want to understand why it is that you should treat others with such kindness. *(Allow kids to volunteer answers.)*

OJIBWA: You are very wise children to have learned so much about what God says. I think you would make good Ojibwa people. The Ojibwa make plans so we can do the things we know must be done. We plan to go on hunts to get meat to dry for the winter. We plan for the seasons that bring us wild berries and nuts. We plan to make our wigwams and canoes when the birch bark is best. Now you will plan. You will find a partner and make a plan. Your plan is about how you will show kindness soon to someone. Make a plan and share it with your partner.

Allow a few minutes for kids to pair up and share a plan with their friend. The Indian quietly departs while the kids are talking in pairs.

Leaders should gather pairs together to make small groups and lead them in prayer. Pray that each child will have eyes to see who needs them to show kindness and that the children will

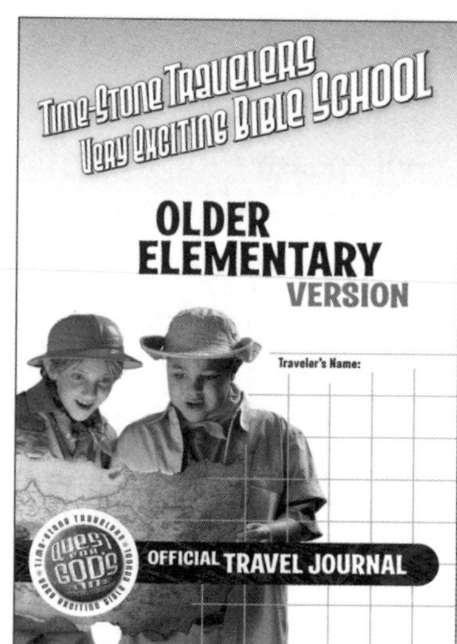

choose to be kind to each person they are with. Pray the memory verse as part of the prayer.

Hand out the Traveler's Journals so children can work on the Indian village page. Circulate among the kids to help younger ones read and understand directions and to answer questions as needed.

Time Stone Take-Off

(A23) Supplies

- ○ Copies of symbols for Time Stones *(page R.67)*, one set per child
- ○ Clean stones for the Time Stones
- ○ "The Quest Continues" Take-Home Page, one per child
- ○ Craft projects from the day

When the children are finished their Traveler's Journal page, get everyone's attention.

Today, we will be adding symbols to our Time Stones that represent the commandments we have studied today. *(See the directions for making the Time Stones and adding the symbols in Resources on page R.67.)* **When you take home your Time Stone at the end of the week, this can be a reminder of the 10 Commandments.**

Bring out the Key Verse Poster and have the children recite the verse using the actions they all helped develop. Sing the theme song and dismiss the group.

See all the *Time-Stone Travelers™* books at
www.CookVBS.com

SITE FOUR ELEMENTARY

GENERAL

- ○ Hawk's Village mural
- ○ *Time-Stone Travelers*™ CD or tape copy
- ○ CD player or cassette tape player
- ○ Overhead transparency of lyrics and overhead projector
- ○ Bible
- ○ FINNEGAN Puppet
- ○ Copy of "Traveler's Journal" for each child *(pages R.59-66)*. Note the two age levels and use accordingly.
- ○ Copy of "The Quest Continues" student Take-Home Page *(pages E4.13-14)* for each child

SNACKS

- ○ Fish crackers
- ○ Small, new fishnet *(the kind used for scooping aquarium fish)*
- ○ Large, clear glass or plastic bowl
- ○ Clear plastic cups
- ○ Store-bought or homemade blueberry muffins
- ○ Fresh or frozen blueberries in a bowl
- ○ Small plates
- ○ Hand wipes

GAMES AND ACTIVITIES

- ○ Rustic baskets
- ○ Wigwam
- ○ Cloth or bandanna
- ○ Two towels in different colors
- ○ Two strips of fabric or rope
- ○ A few coins
- ○ Small jug
- ○ Donkey or horse *(rocking horse, cardboard replica of a donkey, etc.)*
- ○ Large foam-core board "replica" of the Ten Commandments tablet with commandments 6, 7, 8, 9 clearly printed on it. *(You may use an abbreviated form of the commandments.)*
- ○ Key Bible verse poster on an easel
- ○ Key Bible Verse cards *(found on page R.58 in Resources)*
- ○ Four extra verse cards, written and underlined as described below
- ○ Transparent tape

- ○ One or more playground balls
- ○ Bean bags
- ○ Bag of small treats *(such as individually wrapped candies, stickers, etc.)*
- ○ Construction paper sheets, each labeled in bold lettering spelling out a type of person: classmate, friend, little lost child, neighbor, teammate, kid on the playground, elderly person, teacher
- ○ Masking tape
- ○ Pencils
- ○ Clean stones for the Time Stones
- ○ Copies of symbols for Time Stones *(page R.67)*, one set per child

CRAFTS

- ○ Sandpaper, 4 1/2" x 5 1/2"
- ○ Hole punch
- ○ Jute or leather lacing, 12" strips (one per child)
- ○ Newspaper
- ○ Examples of historic Native American artwork
- ○ Scrap paper
- ○ Pencils

- ○ Paintbrushes
- ○ Water

- ○ Glue
- ○ Colored craft sand in a variety of colors
- ○ Foil
- ○ Disposable cups
- ○ Clear, bowl-shaped plastic lids, 8"-10" in diameter *(one per child)* *(These must be concave or bowl-shaped lids.)*
- ○ Clear, flat plastic lids, 4" in diameter *(one per child)*
- ○ Holepunch
- ○ 12" long dowels or sticks, smaller than 1/8" in diameter *(12 per child)*
- ○ Jute, 2' long *(3 per child)*
- ○ Small zipper-closure plastic bags filled with birdseed

The QUEST CONTINUES

TIME-STONE TRAVELERS™ VBS® TAKE-HOME PAGE

Today your child was transported to an ancient Ojibwa Indian village and grew in understanding of four of the 10 commandments that direct us to not hurt others. These four commandments include not lying, stealing, or murdering, along with being faithful to one's spouse. The Bible story about the Good Samaritan in Luke 10 was the basis for finding out how to be kind to those around us and who a "neighbor" really is *(anyone we come in contact with)*.

Go online to **www.CookVBS.com** for more information about *Time-Stone Travelers™* VBS and what your child is experiencing each day.

FAMILY FUN ACTIVITY AND INSIGHT QUESTIONS ON BACK

SHARE WHAT YOU LEARNED TODAY WITH YOUR FAMILY!

COLOR YOUR OWN MURAL

The QUEST CONTINUES

💬 TALK IT OUT

- **As a family, who are "neighbors" (aside from those who live near you) to whom you can show kindness?**
- **How can each of us become more intentional in the ways we demonstrate kindness to those around us, both in and outside our home?**

👫 FAMILY STUFF

WWYD Activity

Point: Making a family motto about being kind to others prompts intentional acts of kindness in the name of Christ.

Supplies:
- ○ Paper
- ○ Art supplies, such as markers and colored pencils
- ○ Magnetic tape
- ○ Shrinkable plastic *(optional)*

Activity: Remember the WWJD *(What Would Jesus Do?)* slogan that spawned bumper stickers, books, music, and jewelry? Take that concept and tweak it a little—making it WWYD or "What Would You Do?" Decide on a family motto related to being kind to those around us, and spread the motto around your home as a frequent reminder.

First, have a family brainstorming session to dream up a catchy sentence or phrase or acrostic that succinctly states your desire to show kindness to others as God wants.

Next, create memory prompts to keep the idea alive in your home. Family members might make bumper stickers, a poster, wearable pins with shrinkable plastic, refrigerator magnets, locker stickers—whatever comes to mind. Use these tools to help you all be more intentional in showing kindness in the same way the Samaritan traveler showed kindness when he happened upon someone in need.

Finally, make a note on the family calendar for a date a week or a month away. On that day, meet again and see how your family motto has been expressed in actions since this meeting.

BIBLE VERSE

*(Early elementary verse in **bold** type.)*

*"Thou shalt **love the Lord thy God with all thy heart**, and with all thy soul, and with all thy strength, and with all thy mind; **and thy neighbour as thyself."** — Luke 10:27*

E L E M E N T A R Y

HAWAIIAN VOLCANO

"Take no thought for your life . . . . The life is more than meat, and the body is more than raiment." — **Luke 12:22-23**

INFO for the TRIP

Why Children Need to Learn to Be Happy with What They Have

What child—or adult—hasn't felt a sag in their hearts when they see another person with something they wish was theirs? Coveting—having a strong desire to possess what belongs to someone else—is a sin everyone can relate to. God made this one of His 10 Commandments so that His people could attain spiritually glorifying and satisfying lives.

The human character, without God, can never be content. Some kids may be in a persistent state of "I wish I had" because the acquisition of possessions is so prevalent in North American culture. Don't heap guilt on the children for wanting what others have. Just help them see that this thought process or behavior isn't what God wants. Instead, He desires to fill them with love and security because He is their provider. Try turning kids' thoughts in the positive direction of being thankful for what they do have. Encourage them in learning to turn on their "coveting antennae," noticing when they're in the coveting mode instead of the thankful mode.

Coveting begins in the heart, so kids need to learn to recognize coveting in their thoughts so they can halt it before they act on their desires. Children who lack a nurturing family life, who are low in self-esteem, or who are part of a family culture that prizes possessions are some who might struggle more with big-time coveting troubles. All children can begin to quench their thirst for contentment by knowing God in a deeper, more fulfilling way.

FACTOID

Volcanic eruptions cause lava, ash, and gas to spew from volcanoes, ruining forests, filling lakes, and destroying cities. Seemingly simple ash, if erupting in large quantities, can create heavy rainfalls and even boiling mudflows that can move 60 miles per hour. However, mild ash falling can provide farmers with nutrient-rich fertilizer, and hardened lava forms rocks such as pumice that is used to grind and polish metal.

GETTING MORE FROM THE BIBLE STORY

Ahab, the seventh king of the northern kingdom of Israel, was a contemporary of the prophet Elijah. Ahab ruled over Israel in Samaria for 22 years beginning in 874 B.C. 1 Kings 16:30 describes him as the most evil of all of Israel's kings. He chose to marry Jezebel, a foreigner who worshiped false gods and who led Ahab farther from God.

This story takes place after Elijah proves God's power to Ahab by calling down fire on God's altar after the prophets of Baal failed to elicit a response from their gods. Ahab's pouting when he couldn't get Naboth to give him the vineyard was one of his trademarks; he showed the same immature reaction in the previous chapter.

Naboth's refusal to give up the property was in accordance with Israel's laws. It was a duty in that time and Mosaic law (Num. 27) to keep one's ancestral lands and pass them on to one's descendents. Ahab's covetousness was great enough to cause him to disregard the law and then to kill Naboth, at Jezebel's suggestion, just to get his hands on that piece of property. Elijah's prophecy of God's judgments on Ahab and Jezebel came true, as recorded in 1 Kings 22:38 and 2 Kings 9:33.

Core Concept

Children will discover that God wants them to be happy with what He has given them and not want the things that others have.

Key Bible Verse

Early Elementary

"Take no thought for your life . . . . The life is more than meat, and the body is more than raiment."
— **Luke 12:22-23**

Upper Elementary

"Therefore I say unto you, Take no thought for your life, what ye shall eat; neither for the body, what ye shall put on. The life is more than meat, and the body is more than raiment."
— **Luke 12:22-23**

Puppet Option

A Leader can operate FINNEGAN to help lead the children to different areas and interact spontaneously with the teacher and children. *(See puppet pattern for FINNEGAN on pages R.53-57.)*

Bible Passage

**1 Kings 21,
Exodus 20:17**

Schedule of Activities

10 minutes: Introduction
15-20 minutes: Bible Story Time
10 minutes: Bible Memory Time
5 minutes: Music Time
20 minutes: Game Time

15 minutes: Snack Time
20 minutes: Craft Time
10 minutes: Application Time
10 minutes: Time-Stone Take Off

Setting the Scene

Use the transparency *(page R.74)* to create a background scene with a volcano as the prominent feature. If possible, use some red lights poking through from the back that glow like lava in a few spots down the side of the crater. Another captivating effect would be to have something emitting steam or smoke that can be directed through a hole where the crater is *(vaporizer, dry ice, etc.)* On the floor of the scene, set large and medium size bumpy black rocks *(volcanic rock)*. Foliage around the edges can be tropical plants, shrubs, and orchids—real or artificial.

Introduction

(A24) Supplies
- ○ Binoculars
- ○ Cell phone

In Advance: Plan to have someone call the cell phone at the proper time.

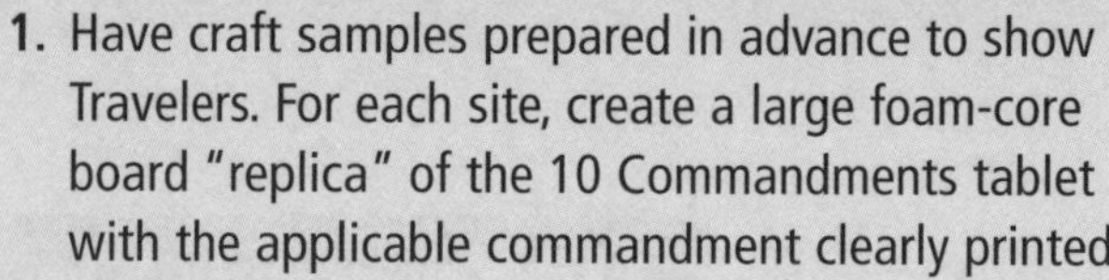

Advanced Preparation

1. Have craft samples prepared in advance to show Travelers. For each site, create a large foam-core board "replica" of the 10 Commandments tablet with the applicable commandment clearly printed on it.
2. Be sure all supplies are gathered and your site is ready each day for Travelers to arrive.
3. Post the Schedule of Activities where Leaders and Helpers can refer to it.
4. Address each other by site titles. Children should be referred to as Travelers.
5. After taking attendance, a Leader should tell those responsible for refreshments how many Travelers are present to be prepared for snack time.
6. You may wish to do some background research into the Bible story. Refer to Bible commentaries, encyclopedias, and dictionaries for additional information.

(Will, Ellen, and Josh trudge onto the setting with glum expressions, shuffling their feet, obviously in low spirits. Josh wears binoculars and a cell phone.)

WILL: What a waste of a vacation. I thought this would be the best summer trip we ever took. But it sure hasn't turned out that way.

ELLEN: I was expecting to go swimming every day and get some beautiful new clothes. But that sure isn't going to happen.

JOSH: I thought I would get to learn to surf. That's all I wanted to do on this vacation.

WILL: So why did Mom and Dad make us come on this trip, if they knew what we really wanted? All they're doing is working, and we can't do anything we want to. We should have just stayed home.

JOSH: Yeah. So what if we get to hike through a rainforest?

ELLEN: Or swim in two pools at the hotel.

Leaders Profile

Josh, Will, Ellen

These three kid characters may wear kid-like tropical vacation clothing.

JOSH: With a slide and a diving board.

ELLEN: Even the luau wasn't that special.

JOSH: I wish we could have climbed that volcano. *(Looks at it with the binoculars.)* **That would have made this vacation something to tell my friends about. One of my friends went to Disneyland this summer. Wish I could have done that.**

WILL: What about Taylor? He got to go to a science camp. That would have been so much fun.

ELLEN: My friend Brooke is going to New York City. She gets to see plays and go shopping and eat out. She's so lucky. I wish I was in her family.

(Cell phone rings; Josh pulls it out and answers it.)

JOSH: Hello? Oh, hi, Dad. Yeah, we're just hanging out at the beach . . . again. *(Listens.)* **What?** *(Turns to look at volcano.)* **It is?** *(Eyes are wide with surprise.)* **Oh, wow! Okay, I'll tell them. Bye.** *(Trains the binoculars on the volcano and looks.)*

WILL: What did Dad say?

ELLEN: What are you looking at, Josh?

JOSH: Dad said there's a level 4 volcanic alert on that island over there. Scientists have been watching it, and they think it's going to erupt real soon.

WILL: I wish we could be there so we could see it happen, close up.

JOSH: You don't get it! All the people who live there and the people who are there on vacation have to evacuate. If the volcano blows up, all their houses and everything will be destroyed.

(The three look at one other with concern.)

ELLEN: And here we were wishing we had a better vacation. We were really just thinking of ourselves. I mean, here we are on a Hawaiian island. How many of our friends get to go to a place like this ever?

WILL: I guess you're right. I feel really selfish. Especially after learning the 10 Commandments. I mean, remember the last one?

JOSH: Oh, yeah, you're right! Boy, have we gotten things turned around. God says in the tenth commandment that we shouldn't want what other people have. All I've been thinking of is my friend riding all those cool rides at Disneyland. I was wishing I had his mom and dad instead of ours.

ELLEN: Same here. I was wishing I could bring home a suitcase of new clothes like Brooke. She always has the best clothes. I wasn't thinking about the kids I know who don't get any new clothes for school. I always get nice things, even if they're not from New York.

WILL: The last commandment God gave us in the 10 Commandments says to be happy with what we have. We shouldn't wish to have someone else's home or their things or their clothes or their vacations or their brother or sister or their pets. Instead of wanting what other people have, God wants us to learn to be happy with what we have right now.

JOSH: I know just the story to help the kids learn more about this commandment. Here come the people who are going to tell us the story.

(The three actors sit down to listen as Naboth and Ahab come forward.)

S I T E   F I V E   E L E M E N T A R Y

Bible Story Time

1 Kings 21, Exodus 20:17

(A25) Supplies

- ○ Bible
- ○ Bible-time costumes for Naboth, Elijah, and Ahab—simple for Naboth and Elijah, royal for Ahab
- ○ Bunch of fake grapes with a few leaves
- ○ A piece of burlap or torn cloth onstage where Ahab can grab it
- ○ Large foam-core board "replica" of the Ten Commandments tablet with just the tenth commandment clearly printed on it

In Advance: Recruit three teens or adults to play the roles of Ahab, Naboth, and Elijah.

The principal characters of the Bible narrative will retell the story from their own perspectives. Naboth and Ahab should come up to the story area from opposite sides and stand in the front, several feet apart. Elijah comes on later.

Begin by showing the children the Book of 1 Kings in a Bible and explaining that today's story comes from there.

NABOTH: Hi! My name is Naboth. I lived during the Old Testament times of the Israelites. I owned a vineyard, where I raised grapes. *(Holds out grapes.)* My grapes made excellent wine. My vineyard was right next to the palace of the King of Samaria. His name was Ahab.

AHAB: I'm Ahab. I was the powerful king who ruled Samaria. *(Makes a grand sweeping motion with arm, looks proud.)* Naboth had a very nice vineyard. One day I decided that I liked Naboth's vineyard so much that I wanted to have it for myself. I told Naboth that I wanted to plant a vegetable garden there.

NABOTH: King Ahab told me he would give me another vineyard or some money so he could have my vineyard. But I said no. You see, this vineyard was given to me by my father, and his father had given it to him. It had been in my family for a long time, so it was very special to me. I didn't want to sell it or trade it. But Ahab didn't like that. Not one bit.

AHAB: I was really upset at Naboth. I wanted that vineyard for myself! *(Stomps feet and pouts.)* So what if it belonged to his family for a long time? Naboth should have given me that vineyard because I really wanted it. I went home and pouted. I lay on my bed and wouldn't talk or eat. My wife, Jezebel, wanted to know what was wrong. I told her about Naboth not giving me the vineyard that I wanted. It made me unhappy all over again just thinking about it. *(Sighs.)* But then Jezebel had a great idea. She said she would fix it so I could get Naboth's vineyard. *(Rubs hands together.)* Heh, heh, heh!

NABOTH: It's hard to think of someone wanting my vineyard so badly. Jezebel wrote letters to the city leaders where I lived. She told them to have a city meeting and put me in the front chair. Then she said the leaders should get two bad men to sit on either side of me and say that I had done wrong things. *(Looks scared, holds out hands.)* But I hadn't done those things at all!

AHAB: And you know what? I agreed to Jezebel's plan—because I wanted the vineyard so badly I didn't care who got hurt! So the men lied, and that got rid of Naboth. *(Crosses arms, looks satisfied.)*

(Naboth drops grapes and sadly leaves the stage.)

AHAB: As soon as Jezebel told me Naboth was gone, I ran down to the vineyard. It was all mine! Yea! *(Pretends to run in place, picks up grapes and hugs them; looks shocked when Elijah enters.)*

ELIJAH: *(Strides up to the story area and faces the kids, speaks dramatically.)* I am Elijah, a prophet of God! My job in the Old Testament was to listen to God and give His messages to people. God gave me a message for Ahab, so I went to see him. Whoa! What bad news he was about to hear! *(Turns to Ahab.)* God wants to know what you have done to Naboth! *(Points finger in Ahab's face.)* Why have you taken his vineyard?

AHAB: *(Looks ashamed, cowers.)* Uh, um.

ELIJAH: God said that since you weren't happy with what you had in your own palace, He is going to punish you for taking Naboth's life and his vineyard. What you did was wrong! God is very angry that you weren't happy with what you already had. He is angry that you took what someone else had. So God is going to punish you.

AHAB: I was so upset at this news that I wanted to apologize to God. *(Drops grapes. Wraps the torn cloth around his shoulders.)* I put on my oldest, saddest clothes—to show I didn't deserve any better—and I didn't eat for days. I wanted God to see I was sorry for the terrible things I had done. *(Walks off sadly.)*

ELIJAH: *(To kids.)* God wants each of us to be happy with what we have. Everyone has different things. Some people have more than others. Some people have nicer and newer things than we have. But God expects the same thing from every one of us—He wants us to be happy with just what we have. Wanting the things that others have only leads us to wrong choices, to sin, and to hurting ourselves and others. *(Exits.)*

WILL: *(Comes to the front.)* That's the commandment that we're learning about today. It's the last one of the 10 Commandments, but it's still as important as the others. God says we should be happy with what we have. Let's say it together. *(Holds up the foam tablets and leads kids in reading it in unison).*

Have Leaders direct kids to the Bible memory activity.

Bible Memory Time

(A26) Supplies
- ○ Key Bible Verse poster on an easel
- ○ Key Bible Verse cards *(found on page R.58)*
- ○ Traveler's Journals *(found on page R.59-66)*
- ○ Transparent tape

Early Elementary
"Take no thought for your life . . . . The life is more than meat, and the body is more than raiment." — Luke 12:22-23

Upper Elementary
"Therefore I say unto you, Take no thought for your life, what ye shall eat; neither for the body, what ye shall put on. The life is more than meat, and the body is more than raiment."
— Luke 12:22-23

Explain that the kids will practice memorizing the verse similar to the way a volcano erupts. It starts with small noises and little puffs of steam. The noises and steam grow in amount and sound until the eruption just bursts out of the mountain.

Gather the kids in a tight circle. Whisper the verse in segments, which the kids will echo in a whisper. Then do it again a bit louder. Continue getting louder until the final time when you have the kids squat and shout the verse and then leap up and throw their hands in the air to simulate a volcanic eruption.

Divide into small groups and have the children say the verse to you from memory as much as they can. Then help them tape the verse cards into their Traveler's Journals.

Music Time

Happy with What You Have

(A27) Supplies

- Copy of song lyrics for each child, or have the words on an overhead transparency *(page R.26)*
- *Time-Stone Travelers*™ CD or tape copy of "Happy with What You Have" *(Track 6)*
- CD or tape player
- Overhead projector *(optional)*
- Puppet *(optional)*

Have the children listen to the song for this site. Play the song again and have the kids join in with the singing. Allow them to stand and move around if you have the space. If age appropriate, project the words of the song onto a screen for the children to follow along as they sing. You may want to have FINNEGAN help teach the song.

Game Time

Eruption Clean-up Race

(G9) Supplies

- Crumpled-up newspaper balls
- Large container *(such as a garbage can)* covered in shelf paper to look like a volcano
- Timer

- Wet/dry shop vacuum, leaf blower, or air compressor
- Baskets *(laundry, wicker, etc.)*

Fill up the "volcano" with heaps of wadded-up paper to represent lava. Scatter lots of paper wads all over the game area. Set a timer for a short time, such as two minutes. When ready to begin the game, use the blower equipment to blow out the "lava" all over the room. Give kids a signal to start collecting all the cooled "lava" and deposit it in the baskets around the edges of the play area. Challenge kids to try to clean up all the lava before the volcano erupts again. While they're collecting, add some of the paper wads from a basket back into the "volcano" so that when the timer goes off, you can cause another eruption.

Naboth's Grape Stomp

(G10) Supplies

- Inflated purple and green balloons

Explain that the kids will be stomping grapes the old-fashioned way. Scatter the "grapes" *(inflated balloons)* around the play area. Divide the kids into two teams and assign each team one color. That team tries to pop only the balloons of their assigned color.

The two teams race to see which can pop all their "grapes" by stomping on them. To reinforce the Bible story teaching, instruct the kids to call out on each stomp something they can choose to be happy with rather than envying *(clothes, toys, videos, pets, vacations, etc.)*.

Complete the game by having the teams race to pick up their broken balloon pieces and put them in a garbage receptacle.

 Snack Time

Dippin' Grapes
(S9) Supplies
○ Grapes
○ Chilled fruit dip: 1 cup vanilla yogurt, 1 cup whipped topping, 1 teaspoon almond flavoring, 1/2 teaspoon lemon juice *(Makes about 32 tablespoons.)*
○ Small plates
○ Napkins

Give each child a small bunch of grapes with a tablespoon of fruit dip on a small plate. If you have kids with nut allergies, replace the almond flavoring with another flavor.

Shish Kabobs
(S10) Supplies
○ Pineapple chunks *(fresh or canned)*
○ Grapes *(red and green)*
○ Skewers, kabob sticks, or 4" toothpicks
○ Disposable plates

Have the children thread a chuck of pineapple, a red grape, and a green grape on a skewer, repeating the pattern until the stick is full to make "shish-kabobs."

Craft Time

Honeycreeper Parking Stopper
(C9) Supplies
○ Yellow tennis balls
○ Screw eyes
○ Yellow feathers *(3 per child)*
○ Craft glue
○ 1/4" movable eyes
○ Orange felt cut into 1/2" squares
○ String cut into 6' lengths

In Advance: Push a screw eye into each tennis ball. Tie string to the screw eyes.

Explain to the children that Honeycreepers are yellow birds found in Hawaii. Also explain that a "parking stopper" is something that hangs from the ceiling in a garage to alert the driver to how far forward to pull when parking. This is just one creative use for this bird craft. As the kids work, brainstorm more ways this Honeycreeper could be used at their home.

(For example, it could be tied to the top of a swing set and hang down as a decoration. Or with a much shorter (4") string, the honeycreeper could be tied to the handlebar of their bike or scooter as a decoration.)

Give out the prepared tennis balls, and help the children follow these directions: Glue three yellow feathers around the screw eye. This is the top of the head. Glue eyes to the middle of the tennis ball. Fold felt from corner to corner to make a triangular shaped beak. Glue felt beak below eyes. If being used as a parking stopper, attach a length of string to the screw eye.

Seashell Framed Mirror

(C10) Supplies

- White matt boards *(5" x 7")*
- Small mirrors *(4" x 6" or smaller)*
- Craft glue
- Small seashells
- Faux pearls

Help the children each glue a mirror to the center of a matt board. Then the children

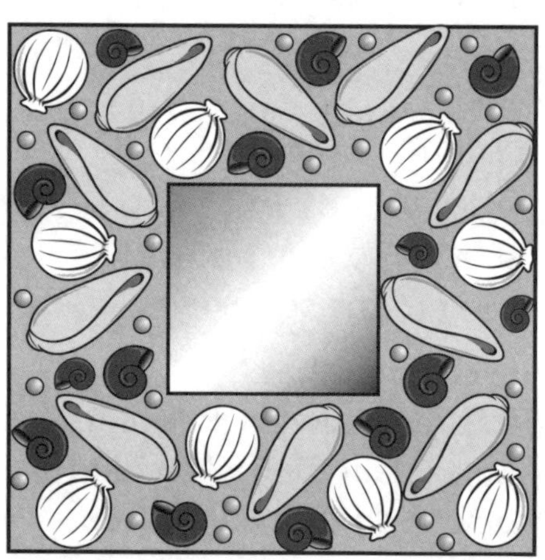

may glue seashells around the border, starting with larger shells first and filling in with smaller shells. The children may finish by gluing a few pearls here and there to add a bit of sparkle.

Application Time

(A28) Supplies

- Three small suitcases or carry-on bags
- Vacation photos
- Tropical or island postcards
- A glass jar partially filled with sand
- Traveler's Journals *(pages R.59-66)*

Will, Josh, and Ellen return to the volcanic setting. Each has a small suitcase or carry-on bag. Josh's contains photos, Will's contains postcards, and Ellen's contains the jar of sand.

ELLEN: This wasn't the vacation I thought it would be. But it was a pretty interesting trip anyway.

JOSH: It didn't turn out the way I was hoping, either. I know some of my friends got to go to such great places and do cool things.

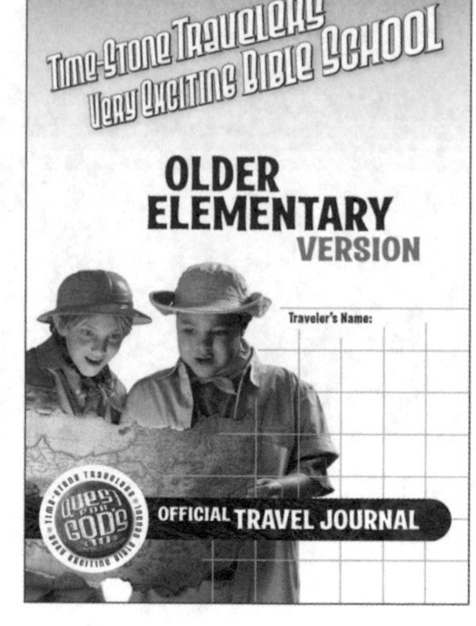

WILL: Yeah, like Disney World, shopping in New York, and science camp.

ELLEN: There's one thing I did learn from this vacation, though. I'm going to think about being happy with what I have. Other people have things I wish I had, or they do things I wish I could do.

WILL: You're right about that. Being happy with this vacation will make lots of better memories than being unhappy and wishing for something different.

JOSH: *(To the children.)* **Do you want to see what I'm taking home from our island vacation?** *(Opens his bag and pulls out the photos.)* **I'm taking home some pictures of the volcano and the beautiful beach. Maybe I can use one to make a mouse pad for my computer at home.**

WILL: *(Pulls out postcards.)* **I bought some postcards that have neat scenes of the island on them. I can put them on the wall in my room. What are you taking home, Ellen?**

ELLEN: I decided to take some sand from the beach. It will remind me of how warm it was here and how much fun we had swimming at

the beach. I think having something to remember our vacation will help us remember to be happy with what we have when other kids have things we wish we could have.

JOSH: What can you kids do to remember that God wants you to be happy with what you have? *(Calls on volunteers and affirms their ideas).*

Divide into small groups. Hand out the Traveler's Journals so kids can work on their island pages. When finished, use the small group time to pray with each child, asking God's help for them to be happy with what they have each day. Encourage the kids to thank God for what they own and opportunities they have.

See all the *Time-Stone Travelers*™ books at www.CookVBS.com

# Time Stone Take-Off

(A29) Supplies

○ Copies of symbols for Time Stones *(page R.67)*, one set per child
○ Clean stones for the Time Stones
○ "The Quest Continues" Take-Home Page, one per child
○ Craft projects from the day

When the kids are finished with their Travel Journals, hand out the Time Stones. **Let's add a symbol to our Time Stones to help us remember the commandment we have learned about today.** *(See the directions for making the Time Stones and adding the symbols in Resources on page R.67.)* **When you take home your Time Stone at the end of the week, set it somewhere to remind you of the commandments that God has given to us.**

Have the three actors review with the children the commandments they've learned so far this week. Divide the children into small groups, and see how many commandments they can remember.

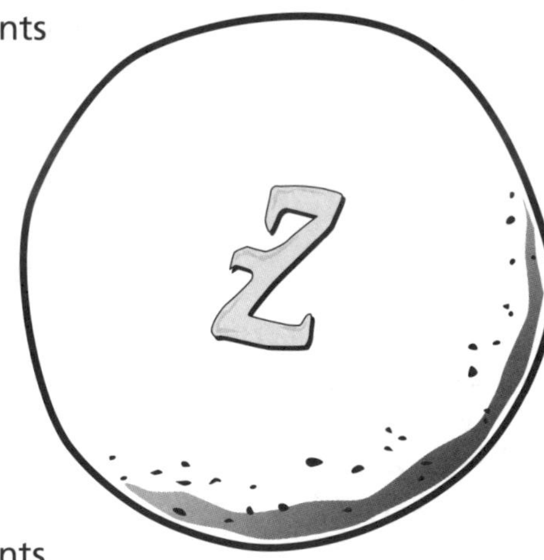

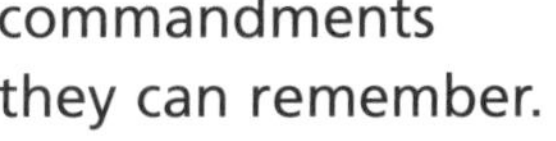

Sing the VBS Theme song, "Time-Stone Travelers," and end with prayer, requesting that God encourage each child as he or she seeks to live by His commandments.

S I T E F I V E E L E M E N T A R Y

GENERAL

- ○ Hawaiian volcano mural
- ○ *Time-Stone Travelers™* CD or tape copy
- ○ CD player or cassette tape player
- ○ Overhead transparency of lyrics and overhead projector
- ○ Bible
- ○ FINNEGAN Puppet
- ○ Copy of "Traveler's Journal" for each child *(pages R.59-66)*. Note the two age levels and use accordingly.
- ○ Copy of "The Quest Continues" student Take-Home Page *(pages E5.13-14)* for each child

SNACKS

- ○ Grapes
- ○ Chilled fruit dip *(1 cup vanilla yogurt, 1 cup whipped topping, 1 teaspoon almond flavoring, 1/2 teaspoon lemon juice)*
- ○ Pineapple chunks *(fresh or canned)*
- ○ Grapes *(red and green)*
- ○ Skewers, kabobs or 4" toothpicks
- ○ Napkins
- ○ Disposable plates

GAMES AND ACTIVITIES

- ○ Binoculars
- ○ Cell phone
- ○ Bible-time costumes for Naboth, Elijah, and Ahab—simple for Naboth and Elijah, royal for Ahab
- ○ Bunch of fake grapes with a few leaves
- ○ A piece of burlap or torn cloth
- ○ Large foam-core board "replica" of the 10 Commandments tablet with just the tenth commandment clearly printed on it
- ○ Key Bible Verse poster on an easel
- ○ Key Bible Verse cards *(page R.58)*
- ○ Transparent tape

- ○ Crumpled-up newspaper balls
- ○ Large container *(such as a garbage can)* covered in shelf paper to look like a volcano
- ○ Timer
- ○ Wet/dry shop vacuum, leaf blower, or air compressor
- ○ Baskets *(laundry, wicker, etc.)*
- ○ Inflated purple and green balloons
- ○ Three small suitcases or carry-on bags
- ○ Vacation photos
- ○ Tropical or island postcards
- ○ A glass jar partially filled with sand
- ○ Clean stones for the Time Stones
- ○ Copies of symbols for Time Stones *(page R.67)*, one set per child

CRAFTS

- ○ Yellow tennis balls
- ○ Screw eyes
- ○ Yellow feathers *(3 per child)*
- ○ Craft glue
- ○ 1/4" movable eyes
- ○ Orange felt cut into 1/2" squares
- ○ String cut into 6' lengths
- ○ White matt boards *(5" x 7")*
- ○ Small mirrors *(4" x 6" or smaller)*
- ○ Small seashells
- ○ Faux pearls

TIME-STONE TRAVELERS™ VBS® TAKE-HOME PAGE

Today your child encountered the tenth of God's 10 commandments: Be happy with what you have. The Old Testament story of Naboth and King Ahab in 1 Kings 21 illustrates how wanting what others have leads to hurt, sin, and further discontent. Naboth owned a vineyard that had been in his family for generations, but Ahab decided he wanted it. Seeing Ahab's discontent, his wife Jezebel schemed to do away with Naboth so Ahab could have the vineyard. But once Ahab had acquired Naboth's vineyard and had Naboth killed, the prophet Elijah told him that God would judge Ahab and Jezebel severely for their actions. Those prophecies later came true.

Go online to **www.CookVBS.com** for more information about *Time-Stone Travelers™* VBS and what your child is experiencing each day.

FAMILY FUN ACTIVITY AND INSIGHT QUESTIONS ON BACK
SHARE WHAT YOU LEARNED TODAY WITH YOUR FAMILY!

COLOR YOUR OWN MURAL

The QUEST CONTINUES

💬 TALK IT OUT

- **It's easy to look at what others have and wish we had it. What things do each of us have already that we can more deeply appreciate and be thankful for?**
- **How does being unhappy with what we have cause problems for us individually and for our family?**

👪 FAMILY STUFF

Sugar Cookie Smiles Activity

Point: Being happy with what you have is a choice; making the choice and sticking with it brings sweet rewards.

Supplies

- ○ Homemade or store-bought sugar cookies (*undecorated*)
- ○ Icing in tubes, frosting, sprinkles
- ○ Plastic knives

One thing many families don't have—and kids usually take for granted—is time together. Enlighten your kids with a reminder that they have something precious—their family. Enjoy each other by getting gooey and sticky with some sugar cookie decorating. Plan on each family member decorating several cookies, at least one of which should be decorated as a big smiley face. Ask each

person to decorate another cookie with a picture, word, or symbol that describes something they have that makes them happy. Let each person share what their cookie is about.

Tell some fun stories of earlier family experiences such as "the first time" and "the funniest time." Get different people's perspectives on these occasions. As you share, enjoy some of the cookies with milk.

Have each person choose another family member whom they will encourage in the next week or so by reminding them of all they have and can be happy with.

BIBLE VERSE

(*Early elementary verse in* **bold** *type.*)

"Therefore I say unto you, **Take no thought for your life,** *what ye shall eat; neither for the body, what ye shall put on.* **The life is more than meat, and the body is more than raiment."** — Luke 12:22-23

Preschool Introduction

This guide helps you adapt the *Time-Stone Travelers*™ program for preschoolers. Included are suggested schedules, descriptions of learning centers, stories, and activities suitable for three- to five-year olds.

Before reading, you may want to scan the Director's Guide for *Time-Stone Travelers*™ VeBS®. There you'll see that older children go to a different Discovery Site each day. Preschoolers do not; they remain in the same area. Use the suggestions in this manual to make the area a little different each day to fit with each area.

Very **e**xciting **B**ible **S**chool's® learning center approach is ideal for young children because they learn best by doing, seeing, hearing, touching, smelling, and even tasting. Learning centers also help children grow socially. The activities help them think about the theme of each session. Because young children learn so much through play, we include suggestions for guided playtimes. But be sure to allow unstructured playtimes as well.

Another important aspect of VBS for preschoolers is relationships. It is important for them to connect with and trust their leaders. The learning centers and activities in VBS are designed to help those relationships develop. Children will learn best if all the leaders are familiar with each day's Bible story, Key Verse, and theme found in **Site Mission** and are looking for teachable moments during the day to reinforce what is being taught. Leaders can then focus on kids and reinforce the process of discovery.

During **Hands-on Exploration**, some children may enjoy moving through all activities. However, because others will finish in your planned centers before time to move to the next activity, you might want to make available:

○ **Preschool books and puzzles relating to the specific Bible stories for this week. These can be placed in a Quiet Corner for children to enjoy without supervision.**

○ **An ample supply of art materials** (*washable markers, glue sticks, large confetti, stickers, magazine pictures, etc.*) **for children to use in adding to your daily theme murals.**

Remember, preschoolers are more process-than result-oriented, so enjoy each step with them without worrying too much about the final product. Your attention and approval are more important than a perfectly-made craft.

Staff needed: Two Leaders and enough Helpers to provide one adult or teen for every four to six children.

Large group option: If you have a very large group of preschoolers (*more than 20 children*) you may want to use more than one area and set up a different theme or room in each area. Divide your group so that every small group gets to visit each site during VBS.

The **Music Time** activities include singing. You can enhance this time by using rhythm instruments, singing song phrases antiphonally, clapping, or using motions to indicate specific words in the song. Be creative!

Daily assemblies: For the first and last 15 minutes of each day, you may want to provide separate activities for preschoolers while older children are in the large group assemblies. You might read books, listen to music, or use puppets. A review of finger plays and songs learned earlier might be fun too.

Backdrops and props: Use **Setting the Scene** sections in each of the Preschool Sites for suggestions. When setting up your room, try to create a central area for story time that is decorated to look like the theme for the day. Then arrange activity areas that fit with each day's theme around this central setting.

The storyteller may want to put on a different costume each day to help the children imagine the characters in the stories. Simple props will spark interest and hold attention.

Preparing for children: Each day before children arrive, make sure your area is well stocked. You'll want plenty of construction paper, glue sticks, safety scissors, crayons, and washable markers. You might also want music CDs or tapes and a CD or tape player to provide background music. For outdoor play, beanbags and large, soft, playground balls provide lots of fun for preschoolers. Be sure that any "in advance" tasks in the lessons are taken care of so that you and the Leaders can focus all of your attention on the children. If you know your children's names, it is very helpful to write their names on the crafts or activities in advance of the activity time. **Because snacks will be offered, be sure to check with parents on the first day of VBS regarding food allergies.** An attendance chart is provided in the Reproducible Resources section, page R.5. Name tags can be found in the Reproducible Resources section, page R.6 or on the *Time-Stone Travelers*™ CD.

Included in the *Time-Stone Travelers*™ kit is a CD containing original music and electronic clip art. Check with your VBS director concerning the use of these resources.

Colored name tags: If you have more than eight children in your group, divide into smaller teams by putting a colored dot or mark on the name tags and assigning an equal number of children to each color. If you have more than 14 children, consider using three colors on the name tags. That way, when you need to do activities in smaller groups, you can simply ask for each color group to go where you need them to go. It will also help if you assign an adult helper to each color, and give that adult a name tag with that color dot or mark.

Leader's tips: If you did not receive the Preschool Characteristics chart during staff training, ask your VBS director for this sheet. *(Reproducible Resources, pages R.16-20.)* Here are some other important points to remember when working with preschoolers:

- **Try to find time during the day to talk with each child.**
- **Look for "teachable moments."**
- **Try not to rush through activities.**
- **Allow plenty of time for children's questions and conversation with children.**
- **Experience the process with them— preschoolers care more about the process than the results.**
- **Enjoy yourself!**

Overview Chart

SITE	Mayan Jungle	Medieval Castle	Ancient Laboratory	Hawk's Village	Hawaiian Volcano
BIBLE STORY	Worship Only God Fiery Furnace (Dan. 3); Commandments 1, 2 (Ex. 20:3-4)	Honor God A Crippled Woman Healed on the Sabbath (Luke 13); Commandments 3, 4 (Ex. 20:7-8)	Honor Your Father and Mother Boy Jesus at the Temple (Luke 2:41-51); Commandment 5. (Ex. 20:12)	Don't Hurt Others The Good Samaritan (Luke 10:25-37); Commandments 6, 7, 8, 9 (Ex. 20:13-16)	Be Happy with What You Have Do Not Worry (Matt. 6:25-33); Commandment 10 (Ex. 20:17)
KEY VERSE	*"My expectation is from [God.]"* –Psalm 62:5	*"Worship the LORD."* –1 Chronicles 16:29	*"Obey your parents."* –Ephesians 6:1	*"Love . . . thy neighbour."* –Luke 10:27	*"Take no thought for your life."* –Luke 12:22
CONCEPT	I will worship the one true God.	I will worship God.	I will respect and obey my father and mother.	I will be kind to others.	I will be happy with what I have.
RESPONSE	The children will be able to state that there is only one God.	The children will be able to demonstrate that God deserves their worship.	Honor and obey your father and mother as God has commanded.	God wants us to treat others with kindness.	God wants us to be happy with what He has given us.

Supplies

The following comprehensive supply list can be combined with the Elementary supply list *(pages D.17-24)* to make planning easier.

Each activity, craft, game, and snack in this Preschool program has a corresponding list of supplies and are referenced in the PG *(page #)* column in the compiled list below. You may want to "✓" off the items you already have on hand, and pencil in the quantities you need of each item based on the estimated number of children attending your program.

CATEGORY & ITEM	PG	QTY	/UNIT	TOT	HAVE	NEED	✓
Common Supplies needed at each site							
Bibles							
Time-Stone Travelers™ CD (Duplicate CDs or cassettes)							
FINNEGAN puppet							
Scissors, pens or pencils, crayons, markers							
Glue, tape (clear and masking), hole punch, stapler							
Flannel board							
Paper plates, cups, napkins, and utensil for snacks							
Newspapers and paper towels for table protection and clean up							
Hand wipes for crafts and snacks							
Preschool murals and cutout transparencies							

CATEGORY & ITEM	PG	QTY	/UNIT	TOT	HAVE	NEED	✓
SITE 1: MAYAN JUNGLE Preschool Supplies							
Mayan Jungle mural	R.77	1	/site				
Copy of "The Quest Continues" (preschool version) student Take-Home Page *(pages P1.14-15)*	P1.12	1	each/child				
(PA1) 1-gallon plastic terrarium	P1.4		each/site				
(PA1) Stuffed or plastic lizard to fit inside terrarium	P1.4	1	each/site				
(PA1) Basketball	P1.4	1	each/site				
(PA1) Dictionary	P1.4	1	each/site				
(PA2) Sand table *(or playground sand in a hard-sided wading pool or in dishpans)*	P1.5	1	each/site				
(PA2) Small sand pails	P1.5	several	each/site				
(PA2) Sand shovels	P1.5	several	each/site				
(PA2) Large shells	P1.5	several	each/site				
(PA3) Table	P1.5	1	each/site				
(PA3) 6" flour tortillas	P1.5	1/2	each/child				
(PA3) Soft cream cheese or margarine spread	P1.5	1	each/site				
(PA3) Cinnamon sugar in a shaker jar	P1.5	1	each/site				
(PA3) Large craft sticks	P1.5	1	several/site				
(PA4) Hammocks on stands	P1.6	1-2	each/site				
(PA4) Pillows or mats to put under the hammocks	P1.6	4-6	each/site				
(PA5) Tissue paper-petals—bright pink, turquoise, yellow, orange	P1.6	8-10	each/child				
(PA5) 2" squares of cardstock	P1.6	1	each/child				
(PA5) Plastic tablecloth	P1.6	1	each/site				
(PA6) Large yellow cutout of statue (R.46)	P1.6	1	each/site				
(PA6) Flannel figures (R.46-47)	P1*6	1	set/site				
(PA7) Flannel figures (R.46-47)	P1.9	1	set/site				
(PA8) Maracas or shakers	P1.9	1	each/child				
(PS1) Bananas (cut in half) or celery sticks	P1.10	1	each/child				
(PS1) Peanut butter or cream cheese	P1.10	1	Tbsp/child				
(PS1) Raisins	P1.10	4-6	each/child				
(PS2) Banana chips	P1.10	1	tsp/child				
(PS2) Dried pineapple	P1.10	1	tsp/child				
(PS2) Dried cranberries	P1.10	1	tsp/child				
(PG1) Large green ropes or garden hoses in 8' lengths	P1.10	4-6	each/site				
(PC1) Plain white pillowcases	P1.11	1	each/child				
(PC1) Fine point, black permanent marker	P1.11	1	each/site				

INTRODUCTION PRESCHOOL

CATEGORY & ITEM	PG	QTY	/UNIT	TOT	HAVE	NEED	✓
SITE 1: MAYAN JUNGLE Preschool Supplies *(continued)*							
(PC1) Bright fabric paints	P1.11	1	assortment/site				
(PC1) Foam meat trays	P1.11	1	several/site				
(PC1) Paint shirts	P1.11	1	each/child				
(PC2) Copies of parrot pattern (R.48) on cardstock	P1.11	1	each/child				
(PC2) Spring clothespins	P1.11	1	each/child				
(PC2) Clear, self-adhesive plastic	P1.11	1	each/child				
(PA9) Large Time Stone (from the site)	P1.12	1	each/site				
(PA10) Clean stones	P1.12	1	each/child				
(PA10) Copies of the symbol for Site 1 (R.67)	P1.12	1	each/child				
(PA10) Permanent marker	P1.12	1	each/site				
SITE 2: MEDIEVAL CASTLE Preschool Supplies							
Medieval Castle mural	R.78	1	/site				
Copy of "The Quest Continues—Preschool" student Take-Home Page (pages P2.13-14)	P2.11	1	each/child				
(PA11) Large silver shields	P2.4	2	each/site				
(PA11) Cloths	P2.4	2	each/site				
(PA11) Piece of white cloth in an embroidery hoop	P2.4	1	each/site				
(PA12) Rocking horses	P2.5	1-2	each/site				
(PA12) Hobby horses	P2.5	1-2	each/site				
(PA12) Saw horses with thick blankets	P2.5	1-2	each/site				
(PA12) Step stools	P2.5	1	each/horse				
(PA13) Garlands	P2.5	2-3	each/site				
(PA13) Simple floor length shifts	P2.5	2-3	each/site				
(PA13) Simple tunics	P2.5	2-3	each/site				
(PA13) Capes	P2.5	2-3	each/site				
(PA13) Medieval costumes and hats	P2.5	2-3	each/site				
(PA13) Costume chains and necklaces	P2.5	6-8	each/site				
(PA13) Cloth purses	P2.5	2-3	each/site				
(PA14) Cardstock trumpet shapes	P2.6	1	each/child				
(PA14) Kazoos	P2.6	1	each/child				
(PA14) Red or purple chiffon fabric squares	P2.6	1	each/child				
(PA15) Bible-time costumes	P2.6	1	each/actor				
(PA15) Step stool	P2.6	1	each/site				
(PA16) Trumpet kazoos (from Herald Trumpet Center)	P2.8	1	each/child				
(PS3) French bread cubes	P2.8	3-4	each/child				
(PS3) Cheese cubes	P2.8	2-3	each/child				

CATEGORY & ITEM	PG	QTY	/UNIT	TOT	HAVE	NEED	✓

SITE 2: MEDIEVAL CASTLE Preschool Supplies *(continued)*

CATEGORY & ITEM	PG	QTY	/UNIT	TOT	HAVE	NEED	✓
(PS3) Pewter or wooden plates and bowl	P2.8	1	set/site				
(PS3) Tapestry table runner with pewter or wooden goblets *(optional)*	P2.8	1	each/site				
(PS4) Apples, sliced	P2.9	1	each/child				
(PS4) Pears, sliced	P2.9	1	each/child				
(PS4) Plums, sliced	P2.9	1	each/child				
(PS4) Seedless grapes, halved	P2.9	1	each/child				
(PS4) Small doilies	P2.9	1	each/child				
(PG3) 18" dowels	P2.9	2	each/site				
(PG3) Funnels to fit over the dowels	P2.9	2	each/site				
(PG3) Duct tape	P2.9	2	each/site				
(PG3) Small paper plates	P2.9	2	each/site				
(PC3) Poster board	P2.10	1	each/child				
(PC3) Shield pattern (R.48)	P2.10	1	each/site				
(PC3) Washable tempera paints	P2.10	variety	each/child				
(PC3) Paint brushes	P2.10	1	each/child				
(PC3) Paint shirts	P2.10	1	each/child				
(PC4) Copies of stained glass window pattern *(R.49)*	P2.10	1	each/child				
(PC4) Clear vinyl *(from fabric store)*	P2.10	1	each/child				
(PC4) Black permanent marker	P2.10	1	each/site				
(PC4) Paint pens or permanent markers	P2.10	1-2	set/site				
(PA18) "Time Stone" with symbols on it *(from the site)*	P2.11	1	each/site				
(PA19) Clean stones	P2.11	1	each/child				
(PA19) Copies of the symbol for Site 2 (R.67)	P2.11		each/child				

SITE 3: ANCIENT LABORATORY Preschool Supplies

CATEGORY & ITEM	PG	QTY	/UNIT	TOT	HAVE	NEED	✓
Ancient Laboratory mural	R.79	1	/site				
Copy of "The Quest Continues—Preschool" student Take-Home Page *(pages P3.15-16)*	P3.12	1	each/child				
(PA20) Mortar and pestle sets	P3.4	3	each/site				
(PA20) Stools	P3.4	3	each/site				
(PA21) Kitchen-size plastic trash bags (to make lab coats)	P3.5	1	each/child				
(PA21) Different sizes and shapes of plastic containers	P3.5	6-8	each/site				
(PA21) Large plastic tubs or basins	P3.5	3	each/site				
(PA21) Water for each tub	P3.5	few in.	each/tub				
(PA21) Liquid food coloring	P3.5	2-3 drops	each/container				
(PA21) Old towels	P3.5	3	each/site				
(PA22) Plastic tablecloth	P3..6	1	each/site				

CATEGORY & ITEM	PG	QTY	/UNIT	TOT	HAVE	NEED	✓
SITE 3: ANCIENT LABORATORY Preschool Supplies *(continued)*							
(PA22) Plastic container lids	P3.6	1	each/child				
(PA22) Small plastic containers (cleaned)	P3.6	1	each/child				
(PA22) Empty film canisters (cleaned)	P3.6	1	each/child				
(PA22) Baking soda	P3.6	1	Tbsp/child				
(PA22) White vinegar	P3.6	1	1/4 cup/child				
(PA22) Craft sticks	P3.6	1	each/child				
(PA22) Dishpan for used materials	P3.6	1-2	each/site				
(PA22) Plastic bag lab coats *(see instructions in Laboratory Center 1)*	P3.6	1	each/child				
(PA23) Paper or silk flowers of different colors	P3.6	4-5	each/child				
(PA23) Baskets	P3.6	1	each/child				
(PA23) Bundle of firewood	P3.6	1	each/site				
(PA24) Poster of the temple (R.50)	P3.6	1	each/site				
(PA25) Paper footprints	P3.9	1	set/site				
(PA26) Plastic containers and spoons	P3.9	1	set/child				
(PS5) Instant gelatin (various flavors)	P3.9	1	1/3 cup/child				
(PS5) Whipped topping	P3.9	1	Tbsp/child				
(PS5) Various cake decorating sprinkles in fun shapes	P3.9	1-2	each/child				
(PS6) Animal cookies or other small shortbread or sugar cookies	P3.9	3-4	each /child				
(PS6) A variety of creative dipping toppings *(yogurt, whipped cream, flavored sauces, melted butterscotch chips, etc.)*	P3.9	3-4	each/site				
(PG5) Plastic tape or paper streamers	P3.10	2	rolls/site				
(PG5) Small copy of the Ancient Laboratory mural (R.79)	P3.10	1	each/site				
(PC5) Small water vials from a florist	P3.11	1	each/child				
(PC5) Silk flowers	P3.11	1	each/child				
(PC5) Chenille stems of various colors	P3.11	1	each/child				
(PC5) Iridescent pony beads	P3.11	3-4	each/child				
(PC5) Small suction cups with hooks	P3.11	1	each/child				
(PC5) Sandwich-size zipper-closure bags	P3.11	1	each/child				
(PC6) Suspension clay *(see recipe)*	P3.11	1	recipe/6 children				
(PC6) Liquid food coloring	P3.11	2-3	drops/child				
(PC6) Black permanent marker	P3.11	1	each/site				
(PC6) Quart-size zipper-closure freezer bag	P3.11	1	each/child				
(PC6) Duct tape	P3.11	1	each/site				
(PA27) "Time Stone" with symbols on it *(from the site)*	P3.11	1	each/site				
(PA28) Clean stones	P3.12	1	each/child				
(PA28) Copies of the symbol for Site 3 (R.67)	P3.12	1	each/child				

CATEGORY & ITEM	PG	QTY	/UNIT	TOT	HAVE	NEED	✓

SITE 4: HAWK'S VILLAGE Preschool Supplies

CATEGORY & ITEM	PG	QTY	/UNIT	TOT	HAVE	NEED	✓
Hawk's Village mural	R.80	1	/site				
Copy of "The Quest Continues—Preschool" student Take-Home Page *(pages P4.13-14)*	P4.11	1	each/child				
(PA29) "Stone" arrowhead *(made from foam and painted)* tied onto a wood pole as a spear	P4.4	1	each/site				
(PA29) Fishing net	P4.4	1	each/site				
(PA30) Black or gray craft foam	P4.5	3-4	each/site				
(PA30) 1" thick dowels	P4.5	3-4	each/site				
(PA30) Duct tape	P4.5	1	each/site				
(PA30) Magnetic tape cut in 1" strips	P4.5	10-12	each/site				
(PA30) 2 yards of brown netting fabric	P4.5	1	each/site				
(PA30) Sheets of craft foam	P4.5	4-5	each/site				
(PA30) Paper clips	P4.5	15-20	each/site				
(PA30) Blue or green tarp	P4.5	1	each/site				
(PA31) Fist-sized stones	P4.5	8-10	each/site				
(PA31) Large baskets *(not flat)*	P4.5	4-5	each/site				
(PA31) Sticks for stirring	P4.5	4-5	each/site				
(PA31) Play vegetables	P4.5	variety	each/site				
(PA31) "Animal hides" *(from the site)*	P4.5	2-3	each/site				
(PA32) Long sticks from trees, about 1/2" in diameter and 3' long	P4.6	2	each/site				
(PA32) Twine cut into 3' lengths	P4.6	several	each/site				
(PA32) Large baskets	P4.6	2	each/site				
(PA32) Weaving materials—thin strips of fleece or felt, bark, rushes, leather, etc.—each 2' long	P4.6	3-4	each/child				
(PA33) Large, stand-up figures *(R.49, 51-52)*	P4..6	1	set/site				
(PA35) Different-sized drums or containers turned upside down that produce a good sound	P4.8	1	each/child				
(PS7) Fish crackers	P4.8	1	1/4 cup/child				
(PS7) Small, new fishnet *(the kind used for scooping aquarium fish)*	P4.8	1	each/site				
(PS7) Large, clear glass or plastic bowl	P4.8	1	each/site				
(PS7) Clear plastic cups	P4.8	1	each/child				
(PS8) Store-bought or homemade blueberry muffins	P4.9	1	each/child				
(PS8) Fresh or frozen blueberries in a bowl	P4.9	4-6	each/child				
(PG7) 36" cardboard canoe paddles	P4.9	4	each/site				
(PG7) Paper canoe shapes	P4.9	8	each/site				
(PG8) Trees *(from the site)*	P4.9	3-4	each/site				
(PC7) Pouches	P4.10	1	each/child				

CATEGORY & ITEM	PG	QTY	/UNIT	TOT	HAVE	NEED	✓
SITE 4: HAWK'S VILLAGE Preschool Supplies (continued)							
(PC7) Fabric markers	P4.9	1-2	set/site				
(PC7) Foam or wood shapes: cross, heart, Bible	P4.9	3	each/child				
(PC7) Paint shirts	P4.9	1	each/child				
(PC8) 3" x 5" foam core rectangles	P4.10	1	each/child				
(PC8) Fine-point permanent marker	P4.10	1	each/site				
(PC8) Small adhesive bandages	P4.10	8-10	each/child				
(PC8) Adhesive magnetic tape, cut into 2" strips	P4.10	2	each/child				
(PA36) "Time Stone" with symbols on it (from the site)	P4.10	1	each/site				
(PA37) Clean stones	P4.11	1	each/child				
(PA37) Copies of the symbol for Site 4 (R.67)	P4.11	1	each/child				
(PA37) Copies of stand-up figures	R.49, 51-52	1	set/child				
SITE 5: HAWAIIAN VILLAGE Preschool Supplies							
Hawaiian Volcano mural	R.81	1	/site				
Copy of "The Quest Continues—Preschool" Take-Home Page (*pages P5.13-14*)	P5.12	1	each/child				
(PA38) Small basket	P5.4	1	each/site				
(PA39) Foam core boards	P5.5	4	each/site				
(PA39) Various colors of electrical tape	P5.5	assortment	each/site				
(PA39) Wood strips 2" wide and 1" deep, cut in 3' lengths	P5.5	4	each/site				
(PA39) Duct tape	P5.5	1	each/site				
(PA40) Low table	P5.5	1	each/site				
(PA40) Small, green, paper plates	P5.6	1	each/child				
(PA40) Pineapple chunks	P5.5	1-2	each/child				
(PA40) Fresh coconut	P5.5	1	Tbsp/child				
(PA40) Honey ham cut in small bit-size pieces	P5.5	1-2	each/child				
(PA40) Rice pudding in bowls	P5.5	1	each/child				
(PA41) Wood or particle board base	P5.6	1	each/site				
(PA41) Film canister filled with baking soda	P5.6	1	each/site				
(PA41) Paper towel tube	P5.6	1	each/site				
(PA41) Wadded paper	P5.6		quantity/site				
(PA41) Window screening	P5.6	1-2	each/site				
(PA41) Two batches of dough, one green and one red	P5.6	1	set/site				
(PA41) 1 cup vinegar tinted with red food coloring	P5.6	1	each/site				
(PA40) Plastic leis	P5.8	4	each/site				
(PS9) Fruit wedges or grapes, cut in small pieces	P5.8	3-4	each/child				
(PS9) Chilled fruit dip (*see recipe*)	P5.8	1	Tbsp/child				

SITE 5: HAWAIIAN VILLAGE Preschool Supplies *(continued)*

CATEGORY & ITEM	PG	QTY	/UNIT	TOT	HAVE	NEED	✓
(PS10) Pineapple chunks *(fresh or canned)*	P5.9	1-2	each/child				
(PS10) Grapes *(red and green)*, cut in half	P5.9	2-4	each/child				
(PS10) Skewers, K-bob sticks, or 4" toothpicks	P5.9	1	each/child				
(PG9) Large cardboard boxes	P5.9	several	each/site				
(PG9) Duct tape	P5.9	1	each/site				
(PG10) Pictures of starfish, coral, and other coral reef creatures	P5.9	assortment	each/site				
(PG10) 1' x 1' squares of plywood or foam	P5.9	6-8	each/site				
(PC9) Precut craft foam flowers	P5.10	10	each/child				
(PC9) Large upholstery needle	P5.10	1	each/site				
(PC9) Uncooked rigatoni pasta	P5.10	11	each/child				
(PC9) Rubbing alcohol	P5.10	1	each/site				
(PC9) Food coloring	P5.10	assortment	each/site				
(PC9) 27" round shoelaces with plastic tips	P5.10	1	each/child				
(PC10) 9" x 12" sheets of white construction paper	P5.10	1	each/child				
(PC10) Washable tempera paints	P5.10	1	set/site				
(PC10) Marbles	P5.10	3-4	each/pan				
(PC10) Plastic dishpans or foil baking pans	P5.10	1	each/child				
(PC10) Paint shirts	P5.10	1	each/child				
(PA45) "Time Stone" with symbols on it *(from the site)*	P5.11	1	each/child				
(PA46) Clean stones	P5.11	1	each/child				
(PA46) Copies of the symbol for Site 5 *(R.67)*	P5.11	1	each/child				

INTRODUCTION PRESCHOOL

Mayan Jungle

"My expectation is from God." — **Psalm 62:5**

INFO for the TRIP

Why Kids Need to Acknowledge that there Is Only One God

Everybody worships someone or something, whether they know or admit it. To worship means to make someone or something more important than anything else. The children you're working with have a tendency to "worship" other people, food, entertainment choices, possessions, or themselves. Because these other "gods" are so ingrained in our hearts, it can be quite difficult to even realize that they motivate and drive us. But God desires and mandates—from knowledge of what's best for us—that we have no other people or things above Him in our affections. And He expects us to demonstrate that He is our God by the way we worship and serve Him.

Most of the children will verbalize that they don't revere gods or idols. You'll need to assist them in recognizing which people and things do hold top place in their hearts by talking about and showing them the common gods that we all struggle against: our things, our bodies, other people, and ourselves. Ask them what they would do with a big amount of money. What do they think about when they're daydreaming or first wake up in the morning? How do they use their free time? These questions will help them uncover what they really hold dear. Then help the children to see that only the God who made them deserves to be at the center of their priorities and emotions.

Encourage the kids to get to know the one true God in Scripture and to worship that God, not the God they hear about in superficial songs or on secular TV shows. Use biblical word pictures to illustrate your teaching so the kids develop an accurate picture of God, whom they can safely and joyously worship.

FACTOID

The jungles where the Mayans lived spread from Mexico through Central America. In these lived exotic wildlife such as giant lizards that resembled small dragons, two-toed sloths, emerald tree boas, pink flamingoes, and the world's largest rodents, called capybaras. The Mayans used jungle materials, such as dried leaves to form their sleeping hammocks, tree poles to build homes, and stretchy vines that draped from treetops, almost like enormous rubber bands.

GETTING MORE FROM THE BIBLE STORY

Shadrach, Meshach, and Abednego were Daniel's peers, Jewish captives living in pagan Babylon. Daniel had already established himself as a credible ruler under King Nebuchadnezzar, who had previously recognized Daniel's devotion to God and honored it. But this time, the king was raging and furious (Dan. 3:13) at the men's refusal to obey the new law that compromised their faith. Nebuchadnezzar decided to make a public example of the three Jews.

The furnace the three faced was industrial size, possibly used to make bricks or smelt metal, both activities that the Babylonians were involved with. God's protection was so all-encompassing that only the rope the men had been bound with was burned. God also sent a supernatural being—an angel or Christ Himself—to stand with the three in their punishment.

The likely response of those watching was wonderment at the display of God's power. Help the children grasp that awe of the one true God. Our decision to worship only Him has to be both in our actions and inside our hearts.

Core Concept

Children will be able to state that there is only one God.

Key Bible Verse

"My expectation is from God."
— **Psalm 62:5**

Puppet Option

A Leader can operate FINNEGAN to help lead the children to different areas and interact spontaneously with the teacher and children. *(See puppet pattern for FINNEGAN on pages R.53-57.)*

Bible Passage

Daniel 3 *(The Fiery Furnace);*
Exodus 20:3-4
(Commandments 1, 2)

Setting the Scene

Create a South American jungle setting. On mural paper on one wall, sketch a beach and water scene. On another wall, draw a simple Mayan temple. *(You may utilize the transparency on Resource page R.77 to create a backdrop.)* You will need a flannel board near the temple. As much as possible, fill the site with real or artificial bushy plants, palm trees, vines or garlands that can be hung

Schedule of Activities

5 minutes: Introduction	**10 minutes:** Snack Time
20 minutes: Hands-on Exploration	**15-20 minutes:** Game Time
10 minutes: Bible Story Time	**20 minutes:** Craft Time
10 minutes: Bible Memory Time	**5 minutes:** Application Time
10 minutes: Music Time	**10 minutes:** Time-Stone Take Off

and draped, and large paper flowers in purples, pinks, yellows, and orange. Lay a green carpet, felt, blanket, or artificial turf on the ground to serve as grass. Include some rain forest animals—stuffed or drawn—such as monkeys, a parrot or two in a tree, flamingos near the beach, and a lizard. Be sure to include a large "Time Stone" painted with the symbols from the reference section *(page R.67)*. You may also play the jungle sound effects from the CD.

Introduction

(PA1) Supplies:

- Jungle sounds from *Time-Stone Travelers*™ CD
- CD or tape player
- 1-gallon plastic terrarium
- Stuffed or plastic lizard to fit inside terrarium
- Bible
- Basketball
- Dictionary

Advanced Preparation

COMMANDMENTS **1&2**

1. Have craft samples prepared in advance to show Travelers.
2. Be sure all supplies are gathered and your site is ready each day for Travelers to arrive.
3. Post the Schedule of Activities where Leaders and helpers can refer to it.
4. Address each other by site titles. Children should be referred to as Travelers.
5. After taking attendance, a Leader should tell those responsible for refreshments how many Travelers are present to be prepared for snack time.
6. You may wish to do some background research into the Bible story. Refer to Bible commentaries, encyclopedias, and dictionaries for additional information.

Have the jungle sounds playing as the children enter and are seated on the floor.

(Josh, Ellen, and Will come to the front of the children, talking and pointing out different things in the jungle. Josh should bring in the basketball and set it down. Will carries the dictionary, and Ellen carries the Bible.)

JOSH: **Hi! I'm Josh. This is my brother, Will, and my sister, Ellen. One day we traveled to a jungle kind of like this one. It had a lot of trees, vines, and stuff like that.**

WILL: *(In a mock teacher voice.)* **Actually, a jungle is a special place. Only certain types of animals and bugs live in jungles. Take a look at the monkeys.** *(Points to a monkey in the scene.)* **They don't live in places where it gets cold in the winter. Let's look at some other creatures in the jungle . . .**

Leaders Profile

Josh, Will, Ellen, and Puma

The three boys should be wearing khaki shorts and T-shirts. Ellen should wear a long colorful dress.

ELLEN: (*Quickly interrupts Will.*) **Okay, Will. These kids need to hear more about our adventure than about the jungle.** (*To kids.*) **When we got to the jungle we didn't know where we were or why we were there. We didn't even know anyone in the jungle. But we did know a couple of things.**

JOSH: (*Picks up a basketball and starts dribbling.*) **I knew I was a good basketball player. That was really important to me.**

WILL: (*Opens dictionary and leafs through the pages.*) **I know that I'm really good at school. I know a lot of things. It used to be important to me that people would think I was smart.**

ELLEN: (*Holds up the Bible.*) **I knew to trust God. And I also knew there was something wrong about where we were. It didn't feel like a safe place to me. But I wanted to find out more about this jungle.**

(*Puma enters, looking around and carrying the plastic terrarium.*)

JOSH, WILL, ELLEN: Hi, Puma!

JOSH: This is our friend, Puma. He lives in the jungle. He helped us learn why we were in the jungle. Puma, we have some children here to learn all about the jungle. But we also want to tell them about the one true God.

PUMA: I'm glad to see you. Have any of you seen my pet lizard? (*Let the children look for the artificial lizard and help Puma put it in the terrarium.*) **Now that I have my pet back, I'd like you to learn more about the jungle.**

 Hands-on Exploration Centers

Have Leaders demonstrate the centers.

Sand Table
(PA2) Supplies:

○ Sand table (*or playground sand in a hard-sided wading pool or in dishpans*)
○ Small sand pails
○ Sand shovels
○ Large shells

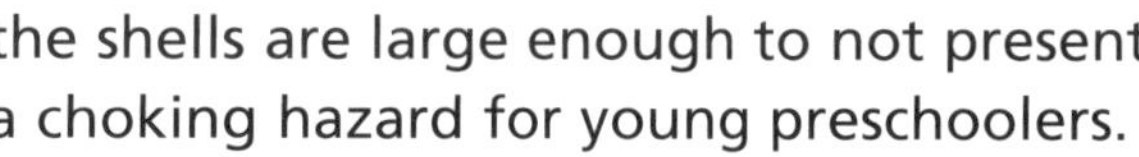

In Advance: Set out a sand table near the beach scene. Add small pails, shovels, and large shells to the sand table. Be sure that the shells are large enough to not present a choking hazard for young preschoolers.

Center Time: Talk about how Puma's home was close to a beach. Also talk about how sand and shells are found on a beach. Encourage the children to play in the sand with pails, shovels, and shells.

Cooking Center
(PA3) Supplies:

○ Table
○ 6" flour tortillas, cut in half
○ Soft cream cheese or margarine spread
○ Cinnamon sugar in a shaker jar
○ Large craft sticks
○ Hand wipes
○ Small paper plates
○ Napkins or paper towels

In Advance: Cut the tortillas in half. If you have children visiting this center with a dairy allergy or milk intolerance, have them use margarine instead of cream cheese. This center should be set up at a table.

Center Time: *The people in Puma's village often ate tortillas as part of a meal. To learn more about the people in the jungle, let's make a tortilla snack.*

After all the children have washed their hands, give each a paper plate with a tortilla half. Have the children use craft sticks to spread the cream cheese or margarine on the tortillas and then sprinkle with cinnamon sugar. The children can roll up the tortillas and enjoy!

Home Living Center

(PA4) Supplies:
○ One or two hammocks on stands
○ Pillows or mats to put under the hammocks

In Advance: Set the hammocks in a place away from the other centers. Place pillows or mats under the hammocks. Arrange your site staff so that this center is always supervised.

Center Time: *Puma and his family didn't sleep in beds as you and I do. They slept in beds called hammocks. Puma's hammock would have been made of leaves. This one is fabric. Try to climb into the hammock and pretend to rest.*

Help each child climb into the hammock and lie down. Be sure to hold the hammock steady so that it doesn't flip over. After a minute, help the child out of the hammock, and give another child a turn.

Art Center

(PA5) Supplies:
○ Tissue paper petals—bright pink, turquoise, yellow, orange
○ 2" squares of cardstock
○ Glue sticks
○ Hand wipes
○ Plastic tablecloth

In Advance: Cut out a variety of petal shapes from the tissue paper, no shorter than 2" long. Set the plastic tablecloth on the floor near one of your trees. Put the craft supplies in the middle of the tablecloth.

Center time: Invite the children to sit on the edges of the tablecloth. Point out the different plants in the jungle. Have the children create simple tropical flowers by gluing petals onto a cardstock square. You may need to show the children how to apply the glue to the paper and then stick another paper on top. Allow the children to create their own free-form flowers. Use the wipes to clean sticky fingers after the flowers are made.

Bible Story Time

Daniel 3 *(The Fiery Furnace);* **Exodus 20:3-4** *(Commandments 1, 2)*

(PA6) Supplies:
○ Bible
○ Flannel board
○ Large yellow cutout of statue *(page R.46)*
○ Flannel figures *(page R.47)*
○ Large brown cross

In Advance: Make a large yellow cutout of a statue using the pattern on page R.47. Copy, color, and cut out the figures for Preschool Site 1 on pages R.47. Glue a strip of flannel or felt to the back of each figure. Have a large brown cross ready to put up at the end of the story. Put the statue in front of the Mayan temple. Place the flannel board to one side of the statue where all the children can see it.

Gather the children together from the centers. Have the children be seated in the temple area. There are two options for the story, one for older preschoolers and one for younger. Use the option that best fits the children in your site each day.

Puma enters and speak to the kids: **You just learned a little bit about what my life was like in the jungle. But there was something else. Do you see this building? It's like your church building. We called it a temple. We didn't worship the one true God there. We worshiped a god that we made up. It was wrong but we didn't know it. Let's hear a story in the Bible about that.** The Bible storyteller continues telling the story.

Bible Story Option for Older Preschoolers:

Our Bible story today comes from the part, or book, of the Bible called Daniel. (*Show the children where Daniel is in the Bible, and keep it open as you tell the story.*)

The Bible tells us about a king named King Nebuchadnezzar. (*Put the figure of King Nebuchadnezzar on the flannel board.*) **King Nebuchadnezzar thought he was a very special king. He could order people to do anything he wanted.**

One day King Nebuchadnezzar put up a tall, gold statue. (*Point to the statue at the front of the temple.*) **He told all the people that when they heard the sound of the trumpets and horns and all kinds of music, they had to bow down and pray to the tall, gold statue. If anyone didn't bow down and worship the tall, gold statue, that person would be thrown into a very hot fire.**

Now there were three men who lived in King Nebuchadnezzar's kingdom whose names were Shadrach, Meshach, and Abednego. (*Add the figures of Shadrach, Meshach, and Abednego to the flannel board.*) **Shadrach, Meshach, and Abednego didn't worship tall, gold statues. They worshiped the one true God. They knew that there is only one God.** (*Hold up one finger.*) **They would not pray to the statue if they heard the special music.**

One day there was the sound of trumpets and horns and all kinds of music. Shadrach, Meshach, and Abednego did not bow down and worship the tall, gold statue.

King Nebuchadnezzar called Shadrach, Meshach, and Abednego. "Why didn't you bow down and pray to the tall, gold statue when you heard the sound of trumpets and horns and all kinds of music?" he asked them. "When you hear the music, all you have to do is bow down and worship the statue. If you don't, I'll have you thrown into the very hot fire. No god can save you from my fire!"

"King Nebuchadnezzar," they said, "there is only one God. (*Hold up one finger.*) **We pray only to Him. Even if you throw us into the very hot fire, our God can save us."**

This made King Nebuchadnezzar very, very mad. "Make the fire as hot as it can get!" he yelled. "Then throw Shadrach, Meshach, and Abednego into the fire."

So soldiers tied up the three men, and threw them into the very hot fire. (*Put the figure of* *the fiery furnace on top of the figures of Shadrach, Meshach, and Abednego.)*

King Nebuchadnezzar looked into the very hot fire to see what was happening. He couldn't believe his eyes! There were four men walking around in the fire. No one was tied up. *(Slide the figure of the angel behind the figure of the fiery furnace.)* **One of the men looked like the Son of God. And none of them were burning! The king asked the soldiers, "Weren't there three men tied up and thrown into the very hot fire?"**

"Yes, O king," the soldiers said.

King Nebuchadnezzar moved in front of the very hot fire. "Shadrach, Meshach, and Abednego!" he shouted. "Come out of the very hot fire!" *(Remove the figures of the angel and the fiery furnace.)* **Shadrach, Meshach, and Abednego came out of the very hot fire. They weren't burned or hurt. They didn't smell like they had been in fire.**

"Praise the one true God," said King Nebuchadnezzar. "He saved Shadrach, Meshach, and Abednego."

King Nebuchadnezzar learned that he didn't need to pray to tall, gold statues. He only needed to worship the one true God. *(Remove the gold statue. Replace it with the brown cross.)* **Shadrach, Meshach, and Abednego knew that there is only one God.** *(Hold up one finger.)* **We know there is only one God.** *(Ask the children to repeat after you, "There is only one God," while holding up one finger.)*

Bible Story Option for Younger Preschoolers:

Our Bible story today comes from a part of the Bible called Daniel. *(Show the children where Daniel is in the Bible, keeping it open as you tell the story.)*

The Bible tells us about a king named King Nebuchadnezzar. *(Put the figure of King Nebuchadnezzar on the flannel board.)* **He could tell people to do anything he wanted. One day King Nebuchadnezzar put up a tall, gold statue.** *(Point to the idol figure at the front of the temple.)* **He told all the people that when they heard the sound of loud music, they had to bow down and worship the tall, gold statue. They had to pray to it like it was God. Anyone who didn't would be thrown into a very hot fire.**

Shadrach, Meshach, and Abednego lived in King Nebuchadnezzar's kingdom. *(Add the figure of Shadrach, Meshach, and Abednego to the flannel board.)* **Shadrach, Meshach, and Abednego did not worship tall, gold statues. They worshiped the one true God. They knew that there is only one God.** *(Hold up one finger.)* **They would not bow down and pray to the statue if they heard the special music.**

King Nebuchadnezzar called Shadrach, Meshach, and Abednego. "Why didn't you bow down and worship the tall, gold statue?" he asked them. "When you hear the music, pray to the statue! If you don't, I'll have you thrown into the hot fire. No god can save you!"

But the men said, "There is only one God. *(Hold up one finger.)* **We pray**

only to Him. Even if you throw us into the very hot fire, our God can save us."

This made King Nebuchadnezzar very, very mad. "Throw Shadrach, Meshach, and Abednego into the fire," he yelled. So soldiers tied up the three men and threw them into the very hot fire. *(Put the figure of the fiery furnace on top of the figures of Shadrach, Meshach, and Abednego.)*

King Nebuchadnezzar looked to see what was happening. He couldn't believe his eyes! There were four men walking around in the very hot fire. *(Slide the figure of the angel behind the figure of the fiery furnace.)* **One looked like an angel.**

King Nebuchadnezzar moved closer to the very hot fire. "Come out!" he shouted. *(Remove the figures of the angel and the fiery furnace.)* **Shadrach, Meshach, and Abednego came out of the very hot fire. They were not hurt at all.**

"Praise the one true God," said King Nebuchadnezzar. "He saved Shadrach, Meshach, and Abednego."

King Nebuchadnezzar learned that he didn't need to pray to tall, gold statues. He only needed to worship the one true God. *(Remove the gold statue. Replace it with the brown cross.)* **Shadrach, Meshach, and Abednego knew that there is only one God.** *(Hold up one finger.)* **We know there is only one God.** *(Ask the children to repeat after you, "There is only one God," while holding up one finger.)*

 Bible Memory Time

(PA7) Supplies:
- ○ Flannel figures *(from Bible Story Time)*
- ○ Flannel board

Key Bible Verse

"My expectation is from God." — Psalm 62:5

Today we learned that Shadrach, Meshach, and Abednego knew there is only one God. Our words from the Bible tell us about our one God.

Say the verse slowly with the children. **Let's say the verse again with Shadrach.** Put the flannel figure of Shadrach on the board and say the verse slowly with the children. Repeat for both the Meshach and Abednego figures.

 Music Time

Only One God

(PA8) Supplies:
- ○ *Time-Stone Travelers*™ CD or tape copy of "Only One God" *(Track 2)*
- ○ CD or tape player
- ○ Maraca or shakers, one per child
- ○ FINNEGAN puppet *(optional)*

In Advance: If you do not have shakers or maracas, shakers can be made by putting dried beans or uncooked rice into plastic eggs. Seal the eggs by putting electrical tape around the seams.

One line at a time, say the words to the song for the jungle site, having the children repeat them after you. Then play the song for the children and let them listen.

Puma and his family may have used special instruments like these shakers when they sang. Let's play our instruments while we sing our song. Play the song a second time with the children playing the shakers. There is no right way for the shakers to be played. Younger preschoolers will either play the shaker or sing.

# Snack Time

Bugs on a Log

(PS1) Supplies

- Bananas *(cut in half)* or celery sticks
- Peanut butter or cream cheese
- Raisins
- Small paper plates
- Plastic knives

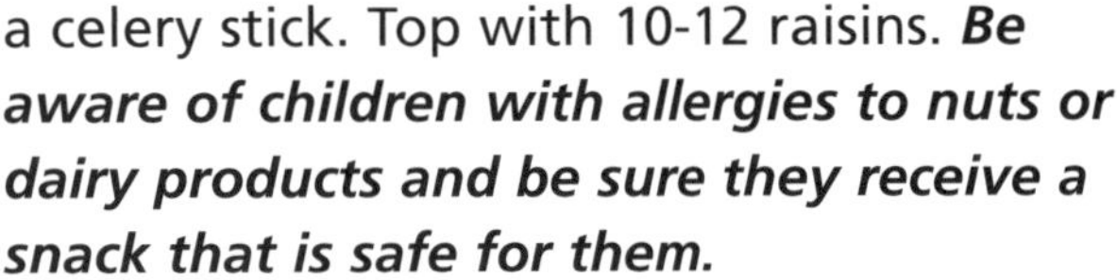

In Advance: Spread one teaspoon of peanut butter on a banana half or 1/2 teaspoon of cream cheese on a celery stick. Top with 10-12 raisins. *Be aware of children with allergies to nuts or dairy products and be sure they receive a snack that is safe for them.*

When serving the snack, ask the children to use their imaginations to pretend that the raisins are ants on a log. Some preschoolers are squeamish about bugs so don't over-dramatize this game.

Dried Fruit

(PS2) Supplies:

- Banana chips
- Dried pineapple
- Dried apricots *(cut into small pieces)*
- Dried cranberries
- Small disposable cups

Mix together the ingredients. Place into small cups, 1/3 cup per child. Serve with a green napkin cut in a leaf shape.

# Game Time

Use these games to give your preschoolers a chance to use some energy while still learning. Choose one or both options given, depending on your time and space.

Vine Climb

(PG1) Supplies:

- Large green ropes or garden hoses in 8' lengths

In Advance: Set the ropes or hoses next to one another, leaving a one-foot space between each rope.

Josh and Will had to climb vines while they were in the jungle. Let's pretend that our ropes are green vines hanging down from trees. Let's see if we can climb from vine to vine to get from one side to another. With the children lying on the floor, have them "climb" horizontally from one vine to the other to get across the vines.

Jungle Tag

(PG2) Supplies: None needed

Talk about two animals in the jungle: the two-toed sloth and the spider monkey. Explain that while both live in the trees, the sloth moves slowly and the spider monkey moves very fast.

One child will be a spider monkey while the rest of the children will be two-toed sloths. The monkey will move quickly and try to tag the slow-moving sloths. When a sloth is tagged, he or she should sit down. A tagged sloth can't get up and continue playing unless another sloth tags him or her. Change monkeys often.

Older preschool option: When a sloth "frees" another sloth, the freed sloth says the response for the day, "There is only one God."

 Craft Time

Pillowcases

(PC1) Supplies:

- Plain white pillowcase for each child
- Newspaper
- Fine point, black permanent marker
- Bright fabric paints
- Foam meat trays
- Paper towels
- Paint shirts
- Wipes

In Advance:
Line each pillowcase with a section of newspaper. On each pillowcase, neatly print the Key Bible Verse: "My expectation is from God. Psalm 62:5." Leave the newspaper in the pillowcase. Create large inkpads by laying a thick layer of paper towels inside each meat tray. Pour a different color of fabric paint into each tray. Set the ink pads at one end of the table, and lay the pillowcases flat around the edges.

Have each child put on a paint shirt. Review the Key Bible Verse by "reading" together one of the pillowcases. **We can remember both our verse and Puma's jungle with our pillowcases. There are many butterflies in the jungle. Let's decorate our pillowcases with butterflies made from handprints.**

Working with one child at a time, have each child choose one or two colors for his or her butterfly. Pressing one hand at a time, help the child "ink" both hands and then stamp the pillowcase. The bottom half of the butterfly is made by turning the pillowcase upside down and pressing both hands down with thumbs together. Turn the pillowcase right side up and press both hands at the tops of the butterfly, again with thumbs together. Draw antennae with the black marker. Help all the children sign their pillowcase creations. Wait until the fabric paint has dried before removing the newspaper and sending the pillowcases home.

Parrot Plant Watcher

(PC2) Supplies:

- Copies of parrot pattern *(page R.48)* on cardstock
- Washable markers
- Spring clothespins
- Craft glue
- Scissors for teacher
- Clear, self-adhesive plastic

In Advance: Make copies of the parrot pattern on cardstock, and cut them out. Precut pieces of the clear, self-adhesive plastic large enough to cover both sides of a parrot.

Josh, Will, and Ellen found many parrots sitting in the trees when they visited the jungle. We're going to make parrots that you can take home and put on plants.

Give each child a parrot to color. When finished, cover both sides with clear, self-adhesive plastic. Trim the plastic around the parrot leaving a 1/4" border of plastic. Help each child glue a clothespin to the back of his or her parrot.

Application Time

(PA9) Supplies:
- ○ Jungle sounds from *Time-Stone Travelers*™ CD
- ○ CD player
- ○ "Time Stone" with symbols on it *(from the site)*

Play the jungle sounds track from the CD to gather the children back together in a group.

JOSH: We've had a lot of fun and adventure in the jungle. I've had fun becoming friends with Puma. And we told everyone that there is only one God.

ELLEN: Remember Shadrach, Meshach, and Abednego? King Nebuchadnezzar wanted those three men to bow down and worship the tall, gold statue. When Shadrach, Meshach, and Abednego wouldn't do that, the king threw them into a very hot fire. But God saved them because they knew there is only one God.

JOSH: We can get busy playing and doing things. But the most important thing is remembering there is only one God.

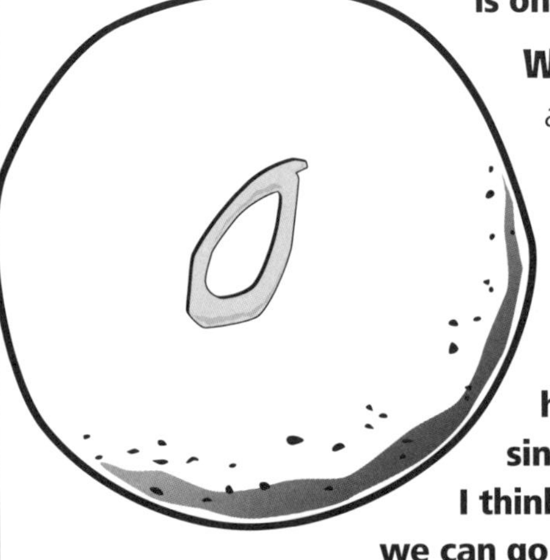

WILL: *(Wandering around and then tripping over the Time Stone.)* Hey, there's our Time Stone! We haven't seen it since we got here. I think this means we can go home now.

JOSH: But look at the Time Stone! See the symbol on it? That will help me remember to worship the one, true God.

WILL, ELLEN, JOSH: Something feels kind of strange. It feels like the world is starting to turn. It must be time to go! *(Exit.)*

Time-Stone Take Off

(PA10) Supplies:
- ○ Clean stone for each child
- ○ Copies of the symbol for Site 1 *(page R.67)*
- ○ Craft glue
- ○ Masking tape
- ○ Permanent marker
- ○ The Quest Continues

Josh, Will, and Ellen's Time Stone had a symbol on it that looked like a circle. It helped them remember there is only one God. Hold up one finger. **We're going to put the same symbol on our own stones.**

Gather the children around a table, and help them all glue a Site 1 symbol on their stones. If this is the first time the Time Stones have been used, write each child's name on a piece of masking tape and put it on the bottom of their stone. These stones will be added to at other sites during vacation Bible school. Have a Helper bring the stones to the next site when the glue is dry.

Be sure to send home "The Quest Continues—Preschool" Take-Home Page and craft projects from the day. Go to www.CookVBS.com to find these additional materials.

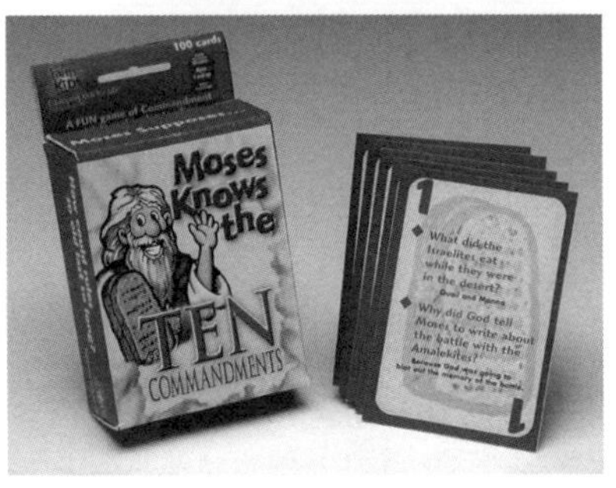

Site Supplies

GENERAL

- ☐ Mayan Jungle mural—Preschool version
- ☐ *Time-Stone Travelers™* CD or tape copy
- ☐ CD player or cassette tape player
- ☐ FINNEGAN Puppet
- ☐ Copy of "The Quest Continues—Preschool" student Take-Home Page *(pages P1.15-16)* for each child
- ☐ Bible

GAMES AND ACTIVITIES

- ☐ 1-gallon plastic terrarium
- ☐ Stuffed or plastic lizard to fit inside terrarium
- ☐ Basketball
- ☐ Dictionary
- ☐ Sand table *(or playground sand in a hard-sided wading pool or in dishpans)*
- ☐ Small sand pails
- ☐ Sand shovels
- ☐ Large shells
- ☐ Table
- ☐ 6" flour tortillas, cut in half
- ☐ Soft cream cheese or margarine spread
- ☐ Cinnamon sugar in a shaker jar
- ☐ Large craft sticks
- ☐ Hand wipes
- ☐ Small paper plates
- ☐ Napkins or paper towels
- ☐ One or two hammocks on stands
- ☐ Pillows or mats to put under the hammocks
- ☐ Tissue paper petals—bright pink, turquoise, yellow, orange
- ☐ 2" squares of cardstock
- ☐ Glue sticks
- ☐ Plastic tablecloth
- ☐ Flannel board
- ☐ Large yellow cutout of statue *(page R.46)*
- ☐ Flannel figures *(R.47)*
- ☐ Large brown cross
- ☐ Maracas or shakers
- ☐ Large green ropes or garden hoses in 8' lengths
- ☐ Large Time Stone *(from the site)*
- ☐ Clean stone for each child
- ☐ Copies of the symbol for Site 1 *(page R.67)*
- ☐ Craft glue
- ☐ Masking tape
- ☐ Permanent marker

SNACKS

- ☐ Bananas *(cut in half)* or celery sticks
- ☐ Peanut butter or cream cheese
- ☐ Raisins
- ☐ Small paper plates
- ☐ Plastic knives
- ☐ Banana chips
- ☐ Dried pineapple
- ☐ Dried apricots *(cut into small pieces)*
- ☐ Dried cranberries
- ☐ Small disposable cups

CRAFTS

- ☐ Plain white pillowcase for each child
- ☐ Newspaper
- ☐ Fine point, black permanent marker
- ☐ Bright fabric paints
- ☐ Foam meat trays
- ☐ Paper towels
- ☐ Paint shirts
- ☐ Wipes
- ☐ Copies of parrot pattern *(page R.48)* on cardstock
- ☐ Washable markers
- ☐ Spring clothespins
- ☐ Craft glue
- ☐ Scissors for teacher
- ☐ Clear, self-adhesive plastic

Site 1 Notes

TIME-STONE TRAVELERS™ VBS® TAKE-HOME PAGE

Today your child visited a Mayan ruin in a jungle and heard the story of Daniel's friends and the fiery furnace from Daniel 3. Your child learned that there is only one God.

Go online to **www.CookVBS.com** for more information about *Time-Stone Travelers*™ VBS and what your child is experiencing each day.

FAMILY ACTIVITY AND CREATIVE BIBLE STORY ON BACK

SHARE WHAT YOU LEARNED TODAY WITH YOUR FAMILY!

"MY EXPECTATION IS FROM GOD." PSALM 62:5

COLOR YOUR OWN MURAL

SITE ONE PRESCHOOL

The QUEST CONTINUES

Core Concept

There is only one God.

Child Response

Be able to state that there is only one God.

Key Bible Verse

"My expectation is from God." — **Psalm 62:5**

Bible Passage

Daniel 3 *(The Fiery Furnace)*;

Exodus 20:3-4 *(Commandments 1, 2)*

Bible Story from Daniel 3

Tell the story with your child at home. Let your child add appropriate sound effects.

One day King Nebuchadnezzar put up a tall, gold statue. He told all the people they had to bow down and worship the tall, gold statue. Anyone who didn't pray to the statue would be thrown into a very hot fire.

Shadrach, Meshach, and Abednego didn't worship tall, gold statues. They knew there was only one God. They worshiped only Him.

"Why didn't you bow down and worship the tall, gold statue?" King Nebuchadnezzar asked Shadrach, Meshach, and Abednego. "If you don't, I'll have you thrown into the hot fire. No god can save you!"

"We pray to only the one true God." they answered. "Even if you throw us into the hot fire, our God can save us."

This made King Nebuchadnezzar very, very mad. "Throw Shadrach, Meshach, and Abednego into the fire," he yelled. So soldiers tied up the three men and threw them into the very hot fire.

King Nebuchadnezzar looked to see what was happening. He couldn't believe his eyes! There were four men walking around in the very hot fire. One of the men looked like an angel.

King Nebuchadnezzar moved closer to the very hot fire. "Come out!" he called. Shadrach, Meshach, and Abednego came out of the very hot fire. They were not hurt at all!

"Praise the one true God," said King Nebuchadnezzar. "He saved these men who would worship only Him."

Shadrach, Meshach, and Abednego knew there is only one God. We can know there is only one God.

Family Activity

Color and Explore

As your child colors the jungle picture, help him or her explore the different things found in the jungle.

MEDIEVAL CASTLE

"Worship the LORD." — **1 Chronicles 16:29**

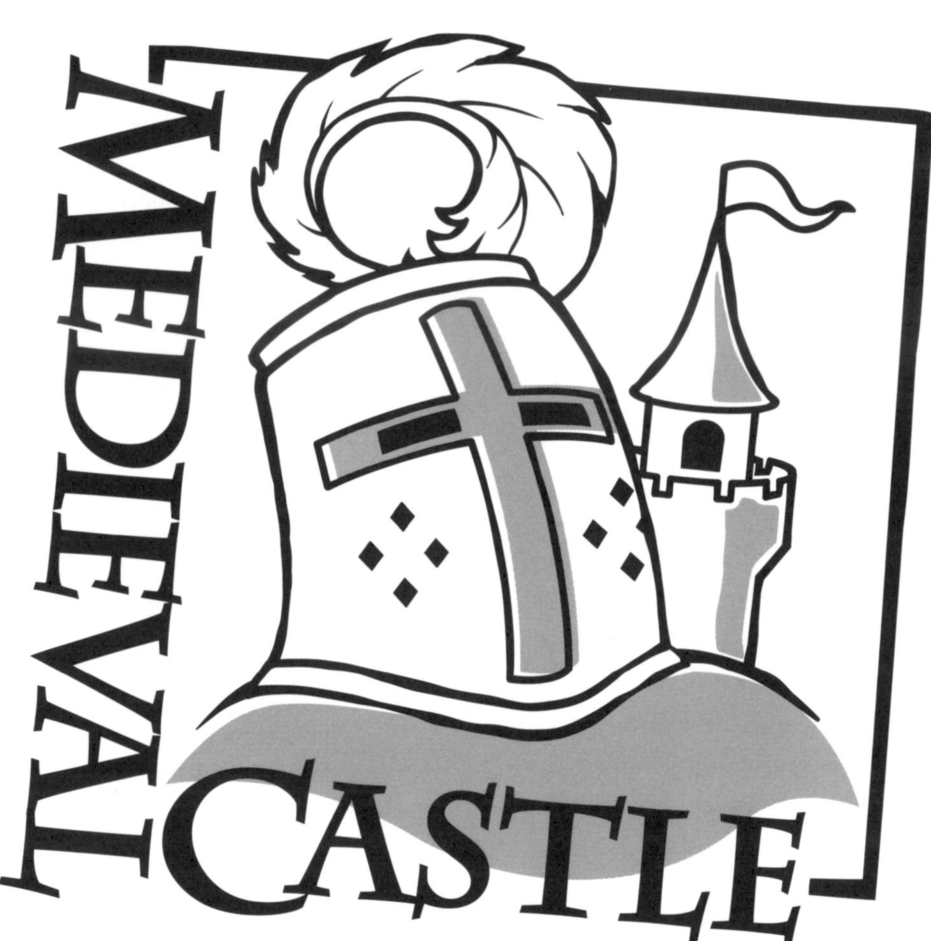

INFO for the TRIP

Why Kids Need to Understand that God's Name Deserves Respect and that Sundays Should be Set Apart for Rest and Worship

The children you minister to in VBS need to realize that God's name is worthy of our utmost respect. People today often have a warped image of God. They gain their ideas of Him from media, distorted Scripture references, and offhand remarks that they can't put into context. They've heard Him spoken about in unworthy terms or in ways that misuse His name and authority. The names in Scripture that describe God give a broader understanding of who He is and why we must revere His very name; yet most kids are unaware of the astonishing list of names the Bible has for God. To help the children make sense of this commandment and the holiness of God's name, give them real-life, everyday examples of how we use people's names. Help the children remember how good it feels when someone uses their name sweetly or as a compliment.

As for keeping the Sabbath, you're likely to encounter children who think of Sunday primarily as a day off. Some connect it with church attendance, yet rarely grasp the essence of worship. Malls, restaurants, errands, and athletic events all call out to kids and families on Sunday, obscuring the purpose for which God instituted this rest. Help children recognize Sunday as a special treat from God, a day off from the usual routines but with a sacred purpose. Let the children creatively develop and imagine ways to worship God and keep His day separate from the other six. The more they invest in and strategize how to honor God on the Sabbath, the more likely they'll be to actually want to do so and prompt their families in that direction.

FACTOID

A knight's training began at age seven, when boys left home to serve as pages. Pages learned the use of small weapons and the code of behavior. At age 15, the page became a squire who acted as a personal servant to a knight while learning how to wage battles. After five years, the squire could be knighted by another knight. Before his knighting, the candidate spent time in solitude praying and pledging to use his weapons for sacred purposes.

GETTING MORE FROM THE BIBLE STORY

The Jewish Sabbath begins at sundown Friday and ends at sundown on Saturday, observing the seventh day of the week as the one God set aside for rest and worship. God's intent for this rest day included the chance to pause from one's daily work to be restored physically and to remember the Creator. Jewish leaders added to God's commandment from Exodus 20, stating that healing was work and therefore prohibited. Many other "manmade" rules sprang up around the Sabbath as well.

Jesus' healing of the crippled woman is one of seven biblical accounts of Christ restoring health to someone on the Sabbath. In this passage, the Jewish religious leaders were observing Him closely, waiting for Him to do something of which they could accuse Him. Their mindset demonstrated their preoccupation with the minute details of the law; their perspective obscured God's desire that mercy and compassion be given as a form of worship to our merciful, compassionate God.

Core Concept

The children will be able to demonstrate that God deserves their worship.

Key Bible Verse

*"Worship the L*ORD*."*
— **1 Chronicles 16:29**

Puppet Option

A Leader can operate FINNEGAN to help lead the children to different areas and interact spontaneously with the teacher and children. *(See puppet pattern for FINNEGAN on pages R.53-57.)*

Bible Passage

Luke 13:10-17 *(Jesus Heals on the Sabbath);*

Exodus 20:7-8
(Commandments 3, 4)

Setting the Scene

Create a castle setting. On one wall, draw a castle scene using the transparency on page R.78. In front of the castle mural, build a low wall out of large blocks. *(You can make simple, lightweight blocks by stuffing newspaper inside paper lunch bags and taping them shut.)* Leave a break in the wall as a doorway. Create a moat around the wall by using blue paper or foil. Lay four

Schedule of Activities

5 minutes: Introduction	**10 minutes:** Snack Time
20 minutes: Hands-on Exploration	**15-20 minutes:** Game Time
10 minutes: Bible Story Time	**20 minutes:** Craft Time
10 minutes: Bible Memory Time	**5 minutes:** Application Time
10 minutes: Music Time	**10 minutes:** Time-Stone Take Off

or five 2" x 4" strips of wood over the moat and through the break in the wall as a bridge. If possible, lay green carpet, felt, blanket, or artificial turf all over the room to serve as grass. You may want to paint trees on the other walls of your area. Use real or artificial bushy plants and flowers to create a pleasant outdoor scene. You may add a couple of cutouts of knights in armor between the castle and the wall. Be sure to include a large stone painted with the symbols from Resources *(page R.67)*. Play the castle sound effects from the CD.

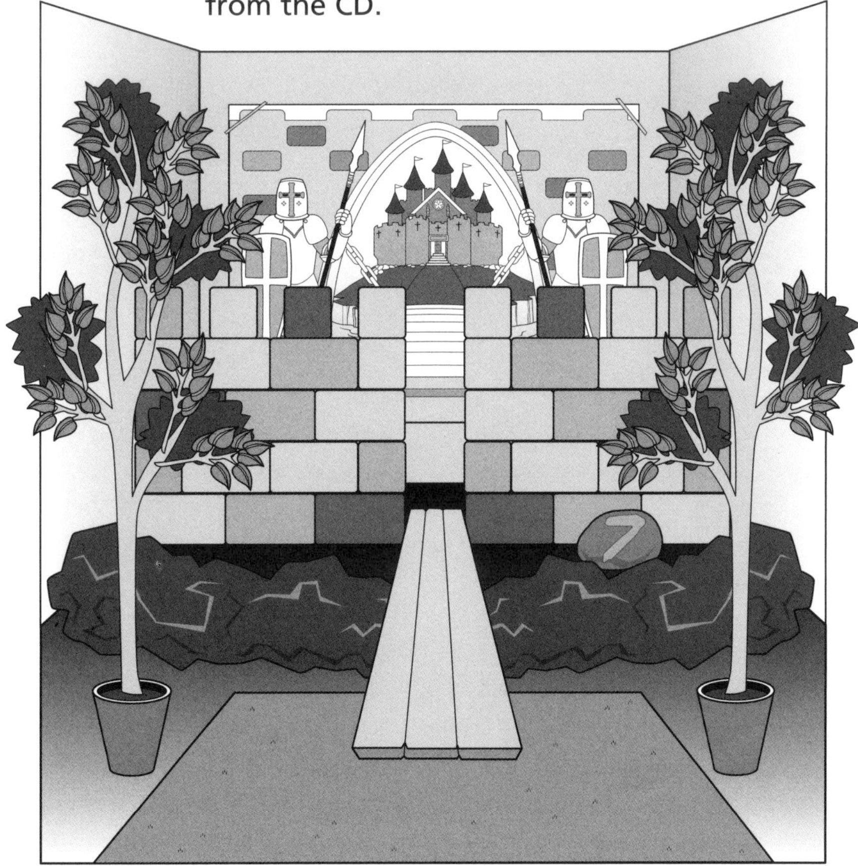

Introduction

(PA11) Supplies:

- ○ Castle sounds from *Time-Stone Travelers*™ CD
- ○ CD or tape player
- ○ Two large silver shields
- ○ Two cloths
- ○ Piece of white cloth in an embroidery hoop

Advanced Preparation

COMMANDMENTS 3&4

1. Have craft samples prepared in advance to show Travelers.
2. Be sure all supplies are gathered and your site is ready each day for Travelers to arrive.
3. Post the Schedule of Activities where Leaders and helpers can refer to it.
4. Address each other by site titles. Children should be referred to as Travelers.
5. After taking attendance, a Leader should tell those responsible for refreshments how many Travelers are present to be prepared for snack time.
6. You may wish to do some background research into the Bible story. Refer to Bible commentaries, encyclopedias, and dictionaries for additional information.

Have the castle sounds playing as the children enter are seated on the green in front of the moat.

(Josh, Ellen, and Will begin between the block wall and the castle. Josh and Will each hold a shield and a cloth. Ellen holds the embroidery hoop. When it's time to begin, the three enter from the castle and cross the bridge.)

JOSH: *(Bows to the children.)* **God speed, my lads and lasses. This is my brother, Will.**

WILL: *(Bows.)* **Good day to you all.**

JOSH: This is my sister, Ellen.

ELLEN: *(Curtsies to the children.)* **Good day to you all.**

JOSH: One day we traveled to a castle kind of like this one. It was exciting to see the knights and horses. In fact, Will and I got to be part of the squires' program.

Leaders Profile

Josh, Will, Ellen, Isabel

Josh and Will should wear shorts and T-shirts with a belted knee-length tunic over them and a long cape over the tunic. Ellen and Isabel should wear long medieval style dresses, with Isabel's dress fancier.

WILL: Squires were helpers for the knights. A knight was kind of like a soldier. Now Josh and I have to get busy cleaning these shields. *(Will and Josh start polishing the shields with the cloths.)*

ELLEN: While Josh and Will were learning how to take care of horses, armor, and their knights, I was to be a friend to a girl named Isabel. We sat and talked and embroidered and other things. Embroidering is a kind of sewing. *(Sits and starts to embroider.)*

JOSH: *(Stops polishing shield.)* Sometimes people at home say words like God and Jesus. But at the castle no one talked like that. They did say some funky things like "God speed" instead of "hi."

WILL: I also liked the chapel, or church building. It was really important to the people at the castle, especially Isabel's mom.

ELLEN: *(Stops embroidering.)* The castle was a very busy place. It was very different than what we saw at home. We'd like you to learn more about the castle.

Hands-on Exploration Centers

Demonstrate the exploration centers.

Stable Area
(PA12) Supplies:
- ○ Rocking horses
- ○ Hobby horses
- ○ Saw horses with thick blankets *(Pattern on page R.45)*
- ○ Step stools

In Advance: Set up a stable area off to one side of the castle. Try to provide three types of horses: rocking horses, hobby horses, and saw-horse horses. To make these, tape a paper horse head to one end of the saw horse and a tail to the other end. *(See pattern on page R.45.)* Lay a blanket over the crossbeam of the saw horse as a pretend saddle. Set a step stool on the horse's left side for children to use to "mount" the horse. Arrange your site staff so that this center is always supervised.

Center Time: Talk about how people at the castle rode horses because there weren't any cars, trucks, buses, or planes. Explain that a place where horses are kept is called a stable. Encourage the children to try "riding" the different horses in the stable.

Dress-up Center
(PA13) Supplies:
- ○ Garlands
- ○ Simple floor length shifts
- ○ Simple tunics
- ○ Capes
- ○ Medieval costumes and hats
- ○ Costume chains and necklaces
- ○ Cloth purses

In Advance: Sort the different costume pieces into various bins. Set the bins on the opposite side of the castle from the "stable."

Center Time: The people in the castle dressed in different clothes than we do. Let's pretend to be people living in the castle a long time ago. What would you wear?

Encourage the children to try on various dress-up clothes from medieval times. To add to their fun, refer to them as "Sir" and "Lady."

Herald Trumpets

***(PA14)* Supplies:**
- ○ Cardstock trumpet shapes
- ○ One kazoo per child
- ○ Transparent tape
- ○ Red or purple chiffon fabric squares
- ○ Disinfectant wipes

In Advance:
Make copies of the herald trumpet pattern *(page R.45)* on cardstock, and cut them out. Tape a trumpet to one side of each kazoo. Tape a chiffon square to the bottom of the trumpet as a flag. Set all the trumpets behind the block wall on either side of the drawbridge.

Center time: Josh, Will, and Ellen often heard the sound of trumpets at the castle. When an important announcement had to be made, trumpets were blown to get the people to listen. Let's pretend to be the people playing the trumpets at the castle.

Invite the children to blow and hum through the kazoo trumpets.

Be sure to disinfect each kazoo after a child is done playing on it if the kazoos will be shared. It is important that the kazoo isn't immersed. The paper in the kazoo has to stay dry to vibrate and make sounds.

Bible Story Time

Luke 13:10-17 *(Jesus Heals on the Sabbath);*
Exodus 20:7-8 *(Commandments 3, 4)*
***(PA15)* Supplies:**
- ○ Bible
- ○ Bible-time costumes
- ○ Step stool

In Advance: Set the stool in the middle of the drawbridge. Ask three teens or adults to play the non-speaking roles of Jesus, the crippled woman, and the synagogue ruler, all dressed in Bible-time clothes.

Gather the children together from the Hands-on Exploration Centers. Have them sit in a semicircle around the drawbridge. There are two options for the story—for older and younger preschoolers. Use the option that best fits the children in your site each day.

Isabel stands on the drawbridge in front of the stool and speaks to the kids: **You just learned a little bit about what life was like in a castle. We did not have TV or movies, and even books were hard to find. To hear stories, we often had people come to the castle to put on plays. Today some traveling storytellers have a story about worshiping God. Let's hear what they have to say.** The Bible storyteller should take over telling the story.

Bible Story Option for Older Preschoolers:

Our Bible story today comes from the part, or book, of the Bible called Luke. Show the children where Luke is in the Bible, and keep it open as you tell the story.

The Bible tells us about Jesus. *(The person portraying Jesus should come and sit on the stool.)* **One day Jesus was at a church building called a synagogue. It was a special worship day called the Sabbath. Every week on this day people were supposed to stop working and worship God.**

Jesus was telling the people about God. One of the people listening was a woman. She was bent over and couldn't stand up straight and tall. *(The crippled woman should come and stand at the end of the drawbridge, making sure to be bent over from the waist.)* **It must have hurt**

the woman to not be able to stand up. She had been like that for 1-2-3-4-5-6-7-8-9-10-11-12-13-14-15-16-17-18 years. *(Count on your fingers as you name the years.)* **That's a long time to not be able to stand up!**

When Jesus saw the woman, He asked her to stand in front of Him. *(The woman should stand in front of Jesus.)* **"Woman," He said, "I'm going to make you better. You can stand up straight now." Then Jesus put His hands on the woman. Right away, she stood up and praised God.** *(Jesus should put hands on the woman's shoulders. She should then stand up straight and put her hands up in the air. Then the woman should stand at the side of the stool.)*

What a wonderful thing Jesus did for the woman! But not everyone thought it was wonderful.

There was a man there who was in charge of the synagogue. *(The synagogue ruler should stand on the other side of Jesus.)* **He wasn't happy that Jesus had helped the woman. "There are 1-2-3-4-5-6 days for working,"** **said the man.** *(He should count on his fingers as the narrator says the numbers.)* **"People can come get healed on those days, not on our special worship day."**

Jesus turned to the man. *(Jesus should face the ruler, shaking his finger as if scolding.)* **"You know better than that. You give your animals food and water on our special worship day. Why shouldn't I help this woman? She has been bent over for so many years."**

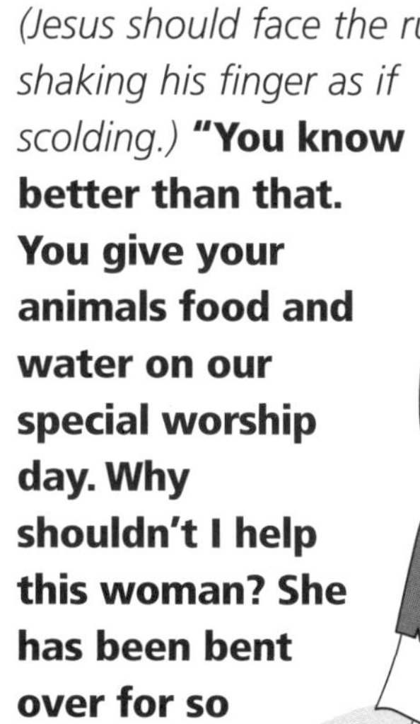

The man saw that he had been wrong. *(The ruler should hang his head down.)* **The woman was able to worship God.** *(The woman should fold her hands as if praying.)* **And the people were happy with all the things Jesus was doing.**

The woman and the people knew they should worship God. We can worship God.

Bible Story Option for Younger Preschoolers:
Our Bible story today comes from the part of the Bible called Luke. Show the children where Luke is in the Bible and keep it open to as you tell the story.

One day Jesus was at a church building called a synagogue. *(The person portraying Jesus should come and sit on the stool.)* **It was a special worship day. Every week the people were to stop working and worship God on the special day.**

Jesus was teaching about God. One of the people listening was a woman. She was bent over and couldn't stand up straight and tall. *(The crippled woman should come and stand at the end of the drawbridge, making sure to be bent over from the waist.)* **It must have hurt the woman to not be able to stand up. She had been like that many years.**

When Jesus saw the woman, He asked her to stand by Him. *(The woman should stand in front of Jesus.)* **He said, "I'm going to make you better. You can stand up straight now." Jesus put His hands on the woman. Right away, she stood up and praised God.** *(Jesus should put his hands on her shoulders. The woman should then stand up straight and tall and put her hands up in the air. Then the woman should stand at the side of the stool.)*

What a wonderful thing Jesus did for the woman! But not everyone thought it was wonderful.

There was a man in charge. *(The synagogue ruler should stand on the other side of Jesus.)* **He wasn't happy that Jesus had helped the woman. "There are 1-2-3-4-5-6 days for working," said the man.** *(He should shake his finger.)* **"But you should not help someone on God's special day."**

Jesus turned to the man. *(Jesus should face the ruler.)* **"You know better than that. You give your animals food and water on God's special day. Why shouldn't I help this woman?"**

The man saw that he had been wrong. *(The ruler should hang his head down.)* **The woman could worship God.** *(The woman should fold her hands.)* **And the people were happy with what Jesus did.**

The woman and the people knew they should worship God. We can worship God.

# Bible Memory Time

(PA16) Supplies:
○ Trumpet kazoos from Herald Trumpet Center

Key Bible Verse

"Worship the LORD." — **1 Chronicles 16:29**

Today we learned that the woman worshiped God. We can worship God. Our Bible words say, "Worship the LORD. 1 Chronicles 16:29."

Say the verse slowly with the children. **At the castle, trumpets played before important things were said. Let's stand and play our trumpets, then say our Bible words, because they are important.** Play the kazoos and then say the verse together as a class. Move to the drawbridge and have the children take turns being herald trumpeters. After each group of trumpeters, say the verse together as a class.

# Music Time

God's Name Is Powerful

(PA17) Supplies:
○ *Time-Stone Travelers™* CD or tape copy of "God's Name Is Powerful" *(Track 3)*
○ CD or tape player
○ FINNEGAN puppet *(optional)*

With the children in a group, say the words to the song for the castle site, one line at a time. Have the children say the words back to you. Then play the song for the children.

Isabel and her family may have danced to the music when special visitors came to sing songs. Let's move to the music while we sing our song. Play the song a second time with the children moving to the music. Encourage the children to move to the beat. You could encourage older preschoolers to work with a partner.

# Snack Time

Castle Cubes

(PS3) Supplies:
○ French bread cut in cubes
○ Cheese cubes
○ Pewter or wooden plates and bowl
○ Tapestry table runner with pewter or wooden goblets *(optional)*
○ Small paper plates

Make a centerpiece of French bread in a display bowl with cheese cubes on pewter or wooden plates. Have a tapestry table runner with goblets surrounding the centerpiece. Serve French bread cubes and cheese cubes on a small paper plate. The children may stack their bread and cheese cubes like a castle wall before eating.

Fruit Fancies

(PS4) Supplies:
- Apples
- Pears
- Plums
- Seedless grapes
- Small doilies
- Small disposable plates

Cut apples, pears, and plums into thin slices. Cut the grapes in half. Place a slice of each with a few grape halves on a small doily on a plate.

Game Time

Use these games as a time for your preschoolers to use some energy while still learning. Choose one or both options given, depending on your time and space.

Tournament for Knights

(PG3) Supplies:
- Two 18" dowels
- Two funnels that fit over the dowels
- Duct tape
- Small paper plates

In Advance: To make a jousting spear, slide a funnel onto a dowel leaving 4" of wood showing below the stem of the funnel to serve as a handle. Tape in place. Make two. Make rings for the tournament by cutting out the centers of the paper plates. You will need two Helpers to stand at the far end of your area holding the rings.

Have Isabel give the directions: **The knights in our castle would have games called tournaments. They would test their skills. Today we're going to have a tournament. Each of you will be a knight. You are to hold your jousting spear in one hand and skip or march down to a Helper. They will put a ring on your spear and you come back.** Let the children take turns skipping or marching down to the helper, getting a ring, and returning. For older preschoolers, you could have them try to catch the ring on the spear.

Lady, Lady, Knight

(PG4) Supplies: **None needed**

This game is a variation of "Duck, Duck, Goose." Choose one child to be "it" first. The rest of the children should sit in a circle. The child who is "it" walks around the outside of the circle, tapping each child on the shoulder. As a shoulder is tapped, "it" names either Lady or Knight. When a child is named "Knight," he or she jumps up and runs around the circle chasing the child who is "it." The first child who reaches the empty spot in the circle first sits down. The other child becomes the new "it."

Craft Time

Coat of Arms

(PC3) Supplies:

- Poster board
- Shield pattern *(R.48)*
- Washable tempera paints
- Paint brushes
- Newspapers
- Paint shirts
- Wipes
- Masking tape

In Advance:

Using the shield pattern on page R.48, trace and cut out a shield for each child. Make a handle on the back of each shield using two pieces of masking tape—one 8" long and the other 12" long. Lay the 12" long piece of tape on a table, sticky side up. Center the 8" piece of tape on top of the longer piece. Attach the sticky ends of the long piece to the back of a shield, leaving enough space for a child's hand to slide between the tape and the shield. Cover the table with newspapers. Pour small amounts of paint into containers for the children to share. Set the shields around the edge of the table.

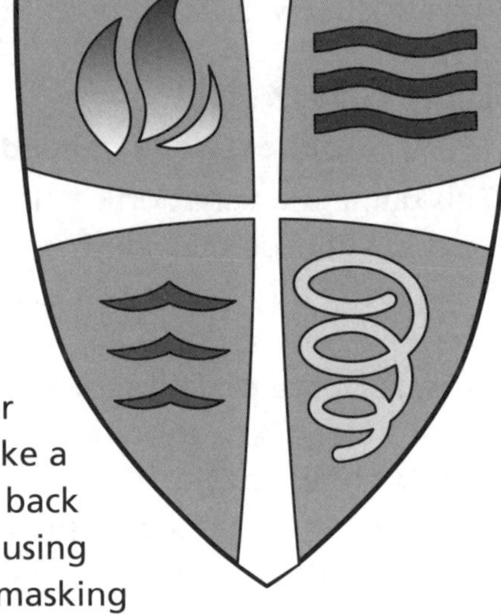

Have the children wear paint shirts. **Knights used to carry shields. Each shield would have a design on it to tell who it belonged to. Let's create a shield to help us remember that we belong to God and we should worship Him.** Encourage the children to decorate their shields with symbols that tell about themselves. Encourage each child to put a cross on a shield to remember that they should worship God. Use the wipes for a quick clean up. Send the shields home after the paint has dried.

Stained Glass Window Clings

(PC4) Supplies:

- Copies of stained glass window pattern *(R.49)*
- Clear vinyl *(from fabric store)*
- Black permanent marker
- Crayons or colored pencils
- Paint pens or permanent markers
- Paint shirts

In Advance: This craft should be done in a well ventilated area. Make copies of the stained glass window pattern *(R.49)*. Lay a piece of vinyl on top of each pattern. Trace the lines with the black marker. You will need a vinyl window for each child.

At the castle, the windows in the church building were made of colored glass. Let's make our own windows to help us remember our Bible words, "Worship the Lord."

After putting on paint shirts, let each child first color a paper window with crayons. Then lay the clear vinyl window

outlines on top of the papers so the children can copy their colors onto the vinyl windows using the markers or paint pens. Talk about the Bible words on the window.

 # Application Time

○ Castle sounds from *Time-Stone Travelers*™ CD
○ CD player
○ "Time Stone" with symbols on it *(from the site)*

Play the track of castle sounds from the CD to gather the children back together in a group.

ELLEN: We've seen many amazing things at the castle. Isabel and I have become good friends. And we told everyone that they can worship God. We can worship God, too.

JOSH: Remember the woman who couldn't stand up? Jesus made her better so she could stand straight again. But because it was the special worship day, the man in charge wasn't happy. He learned that part of worshiping God is loving people and caring for them.

ELLEN: Today we've learned and made things that will help us remember to worship God.

WILL: *(Wandering around and then tripping over the rock with the symbols.)* **Look what I found! It's the Time Stone! I've had a good time learning to be a squire, but it's time to go home.**

JOSH: But look at the Time Stone! See the symbol? That will help me remember that I will worship God.

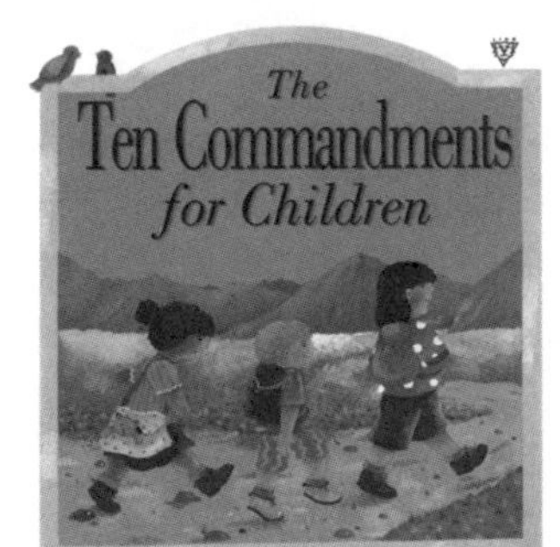

WILL, ELLEN, JOSH: Something feels kind of strange. It feels like the world is starting to turn. It must be time to go! *(Exit.)*

 # Time-Stone Take Off

○ Clean stone for each child
○ Copies of the symbol for Site 2 *(page R.67)*
○ Craft glue
○ Masking tape
○ Permanent marker
○ The Quest Continues

Josh, Will, and Ellen's rock had a symbol on it that looked like a seven. It helped them remember that they should worship God. We're going to put the same symbol on our own rocks.

Gather the children around a table, and help them all glue a Site 2 symbol on their stones. If this is the first day the stones have been used, write each child's name on a piece of masking tape and put it on the bottom of the stone.

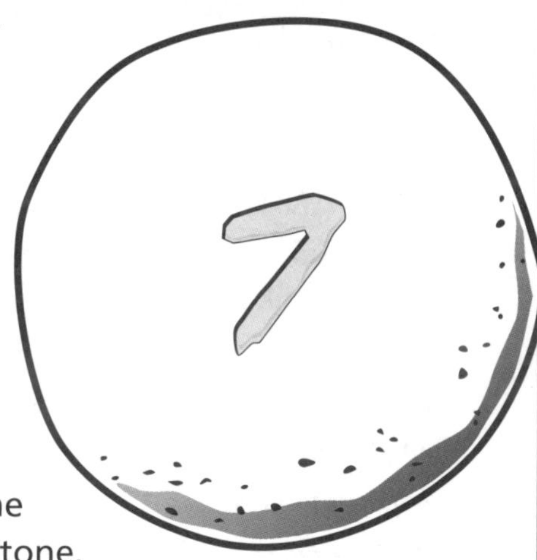

These stones will be added to at other sites during vacation Bible school. Have a Helper bring the stones to the next site when the glue is dry.

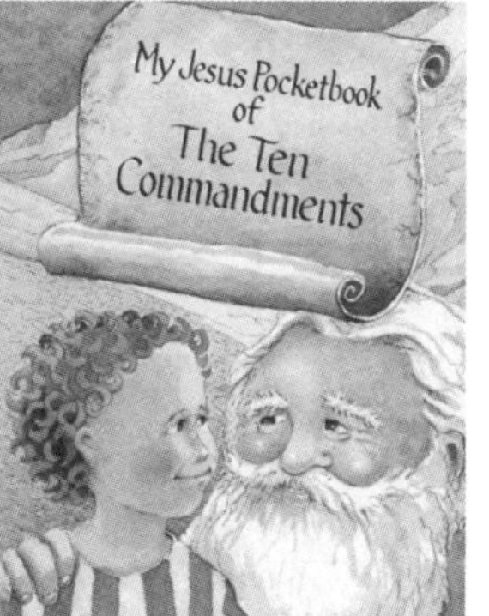

Be sure to send home "The Quest Continues— Preschool" Take-Home Page and craft projects from the day. Go to www.CookVBS.com to find these additional materials.

GENERAL

- ○ Medieval castle mural—Preschool version
- ○ *Time-Stone Travelers*™ CD or tape copy
- ○ CD player or cassette tape player
- ○ FINNEGAN Puppet
- ○ Copy of "The Quest Continues—Preschool" student Take-Home Page *(pages P2.13-14)* for each child
- ○ Bible

GAMES AND ACTIVITIES

- ○ Two large silver shields
- ○ Two cloths
- ○ Piece of white cloth in an embroidery hoop
- ○ Rocking horses
- ○ Hobby horses
- ○ Saw horses with thick blankets
- ○ Step stools
- ○ Garlands
- ○ Simple floor length shifts
- ○ Simple tunics
- ○ Capes
- ○ Medieval costumes and hats
- ○ Costume chains and necklaces
- ○ Cloth purses
- ○ Cardstock trumpet shapes
- ○ One kazoo per child
- ○ Transparent tape
- ○ Red or purple chiffon fabric squares
- ○ Disinfectant wipes
- ○ Bible-time costumes
- ○ Two 18" dowels
- ○ Two funnels that fit over the dowels
- ○ Duct tape
- ○ Small paper plates
- ○ "Time Stone" with symbols on it *(from the site)*
- ○ Clean stone for each child
- ○ Copies of the symbol for Site 2 *(page R.67)*
- ○ Craft glue
- ○ Masking tape
- ○ Permanent marker

SNACKS

- ○ French bread cut in cubes
- ○ Cheese cubes
- ○ Pewter or wooden plates and bowl
- ○ Tapestry table runner with pewter or wooden goblets *(optional)*
- ○ Apples, sliced
- ○ Pears, sliced
- ○ Plums, sliced
- ○ Seedless grapes, halved
- ○ Small doilies
- ○ Small disposable plates

CRAFTS

- ○ Poster board
- ○ Shield pattern *(page R.48)*
- ○ Washable tempera paints
- ○ Paint brushes
- ○ Newspapers
- ○ Paint shirts
- ○ Wipes
- ○ Masking tape
- ○ Copies of stained glass window pattern *(page R.49)*
- ○ Clear vinyl *(from fabric store)*
- ○ Black permanent marker
- ○ Crayons or colored pencils
- ○ Paint pens or permanent markers

TIME-STONE TRAVELERS™ VBS® TAKE-HOME PAGE

Today your child visited a medieval castle and heard the story of Jesus healing a crippled woman on the Sabbath, found in Luke 13 of the Bible. Your child learned that God deserves their worship.

Go online to **www.CookVBS.com** for more information about *Time-Stone Travelers™* VBS and what your child is experiencing each day.

FAMILY ACTIVITY AND CREATIVE BIBLE STORY ON BACK
SHARE WHAT YOU LEARNED TODAY WITH YOUR FAMILY!

"WORSHIP THE LORD." 1 CHRONICLES 16:29

COLOR YOUR OWN MURAL

S I T E T W O P R E S C H O O L

The QUEST CONTINUES

Core Concept:
God deserves our worship.

Child Response:
I will worship God.

Key Bible Passage

"Worship the LORD." — 1 Chronicles 16:29

Bible Passage:
Luke 13:10-17 *(Jesus Heals on the Sabbath);*
Exodus 20:7-8 *(Commandments 3, 4)*

Bible Story from Luke 13
At home, tell the Bible story with your child. Let your child choose to act out one of the characters in the story. You may use a towel draped over the head as a costume.

One day Jesus was at a church building called a synagogue. It was a special worship day called the Sabbath. Every week on this day, people were supposed to stop working and worship God.

Jesus was telling the people about God. One of the people listening was a woman. She was bent over and couldn't stand up straight and tall. She had been like that for 18 years.

When Jesus saw the woman, He asked her to stand in front of Him.

"Woman," He said, "I'm going to make you better. You can stand up straight now." Then Jesus put His hands on the woman. Right away, she stood up and praised God.

What a wonderful thing Jesus did for the woman! But not everyone thought it was wonderful.

There was a man in charge of the synagogue. He wasn't happy that Jesus had helped the woman. "There are 1-2-3-4-5-6 days for working," said the man. "People can come get healed on those days, not on our special worship day."

But Jesus said, "You know better than that. You give your animals food and water on our special worship day. Why shouldn't I help this woman? She has been bent over for so many years."

The man saw that he had been wrong. The woman was able to worship God. And the people were happy with all the things Jesus was doing.

The woman and the people knew they should worship God. We can worship God.

Family Activity

Worship Time
Take time for a family worship service. Let your child choose his or her favorite song to praise God. Follow the song by acting out the Bible story together. Say a short, simple prayer. Finish with a simple cheer, "I will worship God!"

ANCIENT LABORATORY

"Obey your parents."
— Ephesians 6:1

INFO for the TRIP

Why Kids Need to Understand that God Wants Them to Honor Their Parents

No honest parent feels worthy of their child's total honor and respect. And most kids aren't inclined to give it, no matter how much their parents may deserve it. God's fifth rule for living isn't built on parents' worthiness or children's' desires. It is a building block for the order and authority God desires for successful family-building.

God created the pattern for family life just as He wanted it. Parents function not just as caregivers for their offspring, but more importantly as models of the God-human relationship. As a child learns to obey, honor, and respect mom and dad, he or she learns that God also is to be honored, obeyed, and respected. Parents don't earn this respect—it's due them because that's how God created the family.

Our current society brings legitimate struggles to understanding how to apply this fifth commandment. Your students may wonder about the role of step-parents and other legal guardians such as grandparents. Children may fear a command to obey abusive or neglectful parents, and as a result may learn to mistrust God. Reassure your students that God's command is one of love and care, and children should seek help when they are in a dangerous or unloving home situation.

The concept of honoring and respecting isn't well developed in our society. Offer tangible ideas for how kids can honor their parents. Kids will get the idea as they begin using your suggestions at home and see positive results.

FACTOID

Alchemists were on a lifelong quest for inner purity as they sought to recreate the most pure metal—gold—from other imperfect metals. An alchemist's efforts were a combination of scientific, spiritual, and philosophical thought. Many great philosophers and religious leaders dabbled in alchemy, including Roger Bacon, Thomas Aquinas, Pope John XXII, and Isaac Newton. Many alchemists were monks who worked toward the salvation of the natural world.

GETTING MORE FROM THE BIBLE STORY

The narrative in Luke 2:41-51 takes place during the Jewish Passover celebration, which was in the spring and lasted a week. Families traveled together on foot to reduce their chances of being robbed along the way. On their way back to Nazareth after the Passover, Jesus' parents probably assumed that their son was elsewhere in the group. By the time they returned to the city, Jesus had been on His own for two days; then they searched for three days before they discovered Him.

As a Jewish, 12-year-old male, Jesus was nearly an adult. The temple school where He talked with the rabbis was the same seminary where Paul later studied (Acts 22). Because the Passover was such a significant gathering for the Jews, the most important and learned rabbis would have gathered at the temple where Jesus sat to listen and ask questions.

The end of the passage (Luke 2:49-50) is the first indication to us that Jesus knew He was God's Son. However, despite this declaration, He submitted to the authority of His earthly parents by obeying them. There's no other mention of Christ's youth or life until He commenced his ministry at age 30.

Core Concept

Honor and obey your father and mother as God commanded.

Key Bible Verse

"Obey your parents."
— **Ephesians 6:1**

Puppet Option

A Leader can operate FINNEGAN to help lead the children to different areas and interact spontaneously with the teacher and children. *(See puppet pattern for FINNEGAN on pages R.53-57.)*

Bible Passage

Luke 2:41-51 *(Boy Jesus at the Temple);*

Exodus 20:12 *(Commandment 5)*

Setting the Scene

Create an old laboratory setting. On one wall, draw an ancient laboratory scene using the transparency on page R.79. In front of the laboratory mural, place a wooden table piled high with thick books and sheets of parchment-looking paper, along with a stand over a paper fire *(similar to a Bunsen burner)* and some clear plastic containers. On a set of wooden shelves, place a

Schedule of Activities

5 minutes: Introduction	**10 minutes:** Snack Time
20 minutes: Hands-on Exploration	**15-20 minutes:** Game Time
10 minutes: Bible Story Time	**20 minutes:** Craft Time
10 minutes: Bible Memory Time	**5 minutes:** Application Time
10 minutes: Music Time	**10 minutes:** Time-Stone Take Off

bunch of jars and containers. In one corner of the room, create a simple altar by covering a small table with a white cloth and a candle in a simple holder. Have a pillow in front of the altar as a kneeler. From the ceiling, hang bunches of herbs or plants. Try to cover most of your floor with brown paper or cloth. Use a large sponge dipped in earth-tone paints to print stones on the paper or cloth. Set up a meadow in one corner of the room or just outside your room, and lay green paper or cloth here. If possible, dim the room by partially covering any windows with burlap. Be sure to include a large "Time-Stone" painted with the symbols from the reference section *(page R.67)*. You may also play laboratory sound effects from the CD.

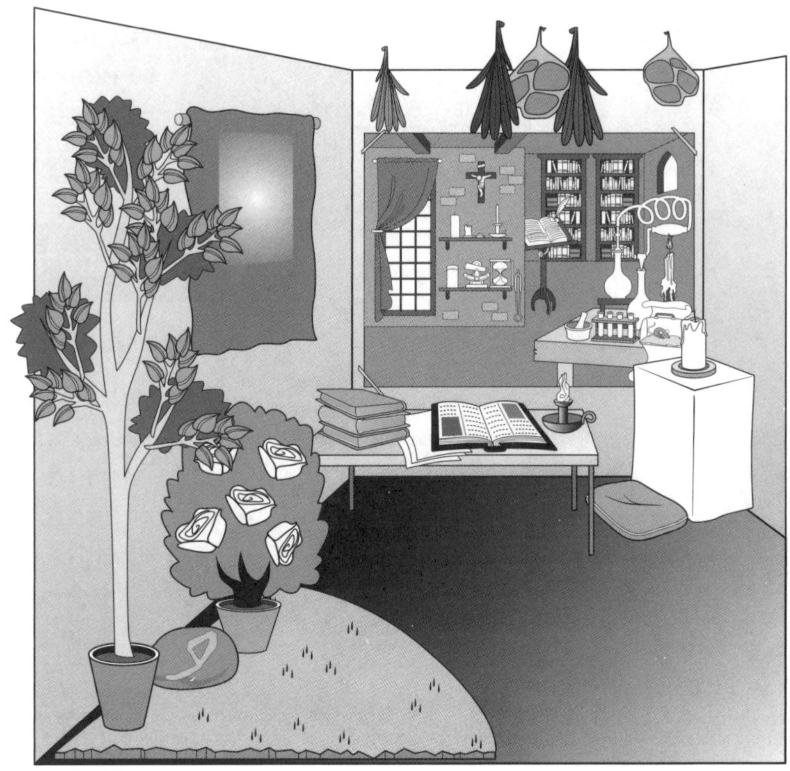

Introduction

(PA20) Supplies:

- ☐ **Laboratory sounds from** *Time-Stone Travelers*™ **CD**
- ☐ **CD or tape player**
- ☐ **Three mortar and pestle sets on a low table**
- ☐ **Three stools**

Advanced Preparation

COMMANDMENT
5

1. Have craft samples prepared in advance to show Travelers.
2. Be sure all supplies are gathered and your site is ready each day for Travelers to arrive.
3. Post the Schedule of Activities where Leaders and helpers can refer to it.
4. Address each other by site titles. Children should be referred to as Travelers.
5. After taking attendance, a Leader should tell those responsible for refreshments how many Travelers are present to be prepared for snack time.
6. You may wish to do some background research into the Bible story. Refer to Bible commentaries, encyclopedias, and dictionaries for additional information.

Have the laboratory sounds playing as the children enter and are seated on the stone floor in front of the low table.

(Josh, Ellen, and Will should enter and walk over to the stools. Josh should be scratching his thigh. Will should be mumbling something about going home because this is the worst time they have ever had. Ellen can be fanning herself with her hand.)

JOSH: *(Still scratching and sitting down on one of the stools.)* **Pardon me. I think I must be allergic to the wool in these pants.**

WILL: *(Sitting down on another stool.)* **Josh, I told you we shouldn't have come to this place. Look at all the stuff around here! This is a disaster!**

ELLEN: *(Sitting down at the last stool and beginning to grind with a mortar and pestle set.)* **Will, that's enough. Be glad you don't have to wear these long skirts. This laboratory of Pepik's is very interesting.**

Leaders Profile

Josh, Will, Ellen, Benjamin

Josh, Will, and Benjamin should be wearing long shorts that could pass for breeches and baggy white shirts. If possible, they should wear long, thick, white socks and leather shoes. Ellen should be wearing a baggy shirt and matching floor-length skirt. Ellen should also be wearing a pair of leather shoes.

JOSH: *(Beginning to grind with his mortar and pestle.)* **You're right Ellen.** *(Talks to the children.)* **We traveled to this laboratory of long ago. It's the home of a nice old man named Pepik and his nephew Benjamin. They work for the emperor, who is like a king. The emperor wants Pepik to put together different things to make gold. I think helping Pepik is really kind of cool.**

WILL: But we have to work very hard—and often at night, grinding different plants and making fires. Pepik's work is secret. No one can know what he is putting together. Benjamin helps him a lot, but I don't like this grinding. *(He starts grinding with the third mortar and pestle.)*

ELLEN: Pepik does all this work so that he can get closer to God. He spends a lot of time praying.

JOSH: I think this is my favorite trip so far. I really think this—

WILL: *(Interrupts.)* **You have a funny way of showing what you like. You haven't been listening very well to Pepik. I know that you're sorry when you don't listen, but we need to be respecting him.**

ELLEN: For helpers like us, we have to show respect and obey what Pepik tells us to do. Just as Benjamin respects and obeys his uncle. We don't want to mess up his work.

JOSH: *(Stops grinding.)* **It's like listening to our moms and dads. We need to respect and obey them. We'd like you to learn more about Pepik's laboratory. Then later you can meet Benjamin.**

Hands-on Exploration Centers

Have Leaders demonstrate the centers.

Laboratory Center 1
(PA21) Supplies:
○ Kitchen-size, white plastic trash bags *(to make lab coats)*
○ Table
○ Different sizes and shapes of plastic containers
○ Three large plastic tubs or basins
○ Water for each tub
○ Liquid food coloring
○ Old towels

In Advance: Create "lab coats" for the children to wear over their clothing to help them stay dry. For each lab coat, use a new kitchen trash bag. Cut an 8" slit in the middle of the seam of the closed end of the bag. Cut a 6" slit in each side seam, about 3" from the closed end. When the lab coat is put on, the head goes through the slit in the middle of the seam and the arms go through the slits in the side seams. Monitor the children closely so that their faces do not end up inside the bags.

Put the three tubs next to one another on a table. Add a couple inches of water and five to ten drops of food coloring to each tub. Make each tub a different color. Put towels on the floor to protect it from splashes of water.

Center Time: People with Pepik's job used different containers for their experiments. Each container helped do a different job.

Help the children put on their plastic bag lab coats. Encourage the children to pour the colored water into different containers. You may have them try mixing the colors. Give children time to explore how water can change to the shape of the containers as well as how different containers hold different amounts. Arrange your Helpers so that this center is always supervised.

Laboratory Center 2
(PA22) Supplies:
- ○ Plastic tablecloth
- ○ Plastic container lids
- ○ Small plastic containers *(cleaned)*
- ○ Empty film canisters *(cleaned)*
- ○ Baking soda
- ○ White vinegar
- ○ Craft sticks
- ○ Plastic bag lab coats
  (see instructions in Laboratory Center 1)
- ○ Dishpan for used materials

In Advance: At this center, the children will perform a simple, non-toxic chemical reaction. Measure one tablespoon of baking soda into each film canister. You will give these to the children during the center. Cover a table with a plastic tablecloth. Put a plastic lid at each spot as an experiment tray. Set a small plastic container on each lid. Lay a craft stick at each spot.

Center Time: Sometimes people with Pepik's job put two things together to make something else. Let's try a simple experiment to see if you'd like to be a helper to Pepik like Josh, Will, and Ellen were. Remember, you need to listen carefully and obey me.

Help each child put on a plastic bag lab coat. Pour 1/4 cup of white vinegar into each cup. Have the children describe how the liquid looks and smells. Don't let them taste it. Talk about how Josh, Will, and Ellen had been grinding powders. Explain that as helpers,

they will each be adding a powder to their liquid. Give each child a film canister. Count to three and have all the children dump their powder into their liquid at the same time. After the chemical reaction calms down, children can stir the liquid until all the powder dissolves. Have the children describe what happened

Meadow Area
(PA23) Supplies:
- ○ **Paper or silk flowers of different colors**
- ○ **Baskets**

In Advance: In the meadow of your site, scatter artificial flowers all over.

Center Time: Talk about how people with Pepik's job didn't go to the store to get what they needed. They sent their helpers to gather things, which Josh, Will, and Ellen did for Uncle Pepik. Today, as helpers, the children need to gather as many flowers in the baskets as they can. You can assign a specific color to each older preschooler.

# Bible Story Time

Luke 2:41-51 (*Boy Jesus at the Temple*); **Exodus 20:12** (*Commandment 5*)
(PA24) Supplies:
- ○ Bible
- ○ Bundle of firewood
- ○ Poster of the temple *(p. R.50)*

Gather the children together from the Hands-on Exploration Centers. Have them sit in a semicircle in front of the laboratory tables. There are two options for the story—one for older preschoolers and one for younger preschoolers. Use the option that best fits the children in your site each day.

Benjamin enters carrying a bundle of firewood and speaks to the kids: **Hi, I'm Benjamin. I live with my Uncle Pepik. You just learned a little bit about what life was like in** an old laboratory. I respect and obey my uncle just as if he were my dad because I live with him and he's in charge of me and takes care of me. Today we're going to hear a Bible story about Jesus and His mom and her husband, who was like His dad.** The Bible storyteller should continue now.

Bible Story Option for Older Preschoolers:

Our Bible story today comes from the part, or book, of the Bible called Luke. Show the children where Luke is in the Bible, and keep it open as you tell the story.

The Bible tells us about Jesus. Every year Jesus' parents went to the city of Jerusalem for a special worship time. When Jesus was 12 years old, He walked there with His mother, Mary, and with Joseph, who was like Jesus' father. Lots of their friends and family walked with them. Let's pretend to go to the city of Jerusalem with them. *(Have the children stand and follow the storyteller around the perimeter of the site. Occasionally pretend to be walking uphill. After taking one lap around the room, have the children stop and sit down.)*

It took more than a day for Jesus and His family and friends to get to Jerusalem. Let's stop and rest for a little while. *(Have the children lie down and pretend to rest.)*

It's the next day! Let's keep traveling! *(Have the children stand up and follow the storyteller around the room again. Keep going until the group gets to the altar area. Have the children stop and sit down.)*

(Show the poster of the temple.) **Jesus and His family went to a special church building called the temple. They worshiped God.** *(Have the children fold hands in prayer for a moment.)*

When they started walking back home, Jesus' family traveled with the large group of friends and family again. *(Leave the poster propped up against the altar. Have the children stand up and follow the storyteller halfway around the room.)* **Mary and Joseph thought that Jesus was with their friends and family in the group.** *(Ask the children to stop and sit down.)* **But that night, when Mary and Joseph looked for Jesus, they couldn't find Him anywhere! Jesus was missing! What should they do? They had to go back to Jerusalem!** *(Have the children stand up and follow the storyteller back the way they came, to the altar. Have the children sit.)* **Jesus' parents searched and searched.**

Finally, Mary and Joseph found Jesus. He was at the temple. *(Show the children the poster again.)* **Jesus was sitting with the temple teachers. He was listening to them, asking questions, and even answering their questions. Everyone who heard Jesus talking with the teachers was surprised. They were surprised because He knew so much about God. When Mary and Joseph found Jesus, they were surprised, too.**

Jesus' mom asked Him, "Why didn't You travel with us? We have been very worried about You. We didn't know where You were!"

Jesus told His mom, "You didn't have to worry about Me. I was here learning about God."

Then Jesus went back home with His mom and Joseph. *(Have the children follow the storyteller around the room two times, stopping once to lie down and rest.)* Jesus respected and obeyed Joseph and His mother. We can respect and obey our fathers and mothers, too.

Bible Story Option for Younger Preschoolers:

Our Bible story today comes from the part of the Bible called Luke. Show the children where Luke is in the Bible, and keep it open as you tell the story.

Every year Jesus' family went to the city of Jerusalem for a special worship time. When Jesus was 12 years old, He went with His family. Jesus' mommy was named Mary, and her husband, who was like Jesus' daddy, was named Joseph. Lots of Mary and Joseph's friends and family walked with them. Let's pretend to go to the city of Jerusalem. *(Have the children follow the storyteller halfway around the perimeter of the site. Then have the children stop and sit down.)*

It took more than one day to get to Jerusalem. Let's stop and rest for a little while. *(Have the children lie down and pretend to rest.)*

It's the next day! Let's keep traveling! *(Have the children stand up and follow the storyteller the rest of the way around the room. Keep going until the group gets to the altar area. Have the children stop and sit down.)*

(Show the poster of the temple.) Jesus and Mary and Joseph went to a special church building called the temple. They worshiped God. *(Have the children fold hands in prayer for a moment.)*

When they started walking back home, Jesus' family was with the large group of friends and family again. *(Leave the poster propped up against the altar. Have the children stand up and follow the storyteller partway around the room.)* Mary and Joseph thought that Jesus was with their other family and friends. *(Ask the children to stop and sit down.)* But when Mary and Joseph looked for Jesus, they couldn't find Him anywhere!

They had to go back to Jerusalem. *(Have the children stand up and follow the storyteller back the way they came, to the altar. Have the children sit back down.)* Mary and Joseph looked all over the city.

Mary and Joseph found Jesus. He was at the temple. *(Show the children the poster again.)* Jesus was with the teachers. He was listening to them, asking questions, and even answering their questions! Jesus knew a lot about God.

Mary and Joseph were surprised. Jesus' mommy said to Him, "We have been very worried about You. We didn't know where You were!"

Jesus told His mommy, "You didn't have to worry about Me. I was here learning about God."

Then Jesus went back home with His family. *(Have the children follow the storyteller back to the starting point, stopping once to lay down and rest.)* Jesus respected and obeyed His mommy and Joseph. We can respect and obey our daddies and mommies.

Bible Memory Time

(PA25) Supplies:

- Paper footprints set out in a path

Key Bible Verse

"Obey your parents." — Ephesians 6:1

Today we learned that Jesus respected and obeyed His mother and Joseph. Our Bible verse tells us to obey our mother and father. Say the verse slowly with the children.

Jesus, Mary, and Joseph traveled to Jerusalem. Let's travel down the path as we say our Bible verse. Have the children stand in a line and say the verse together as a class. Have the children walk down the path, saying one word from the verse with each step. Encourage the children to say the reference every fourth step.

Music Time

Obey, Obey

(PA26) Supplies:

- *Time-Stone Travelers*™ CD or tape copy of "Obey, Obey" *(Track 4)*
- CD or tape player
- Plastic containers and spoons *(one each per child)*
- FINNEGAN puppet *(optional)*

Say the words to the song for the laboratory one line at a time, with the children repeating it after you. Then play the song for the children.

Benjamin and his Uncle Pepik used different containers in their laboratory. Today we're going to use containers as drums. Have the children put the containers on the table so that the openings are facing down. Encourage the children to play their drums to the music as they listen to it a second time.

Snack Time

Creative Concoctions

(PS5) Supplies:

- Instant gelatin *(various flavors)*
- Whipped topping
- Various cake decorating sprinkles in fun shapes
- Clear plastic cups
- Disposable spoons

In Advance: Make gelatin as directed on package. Pour 1/3 cup into each cup. Chill until set.

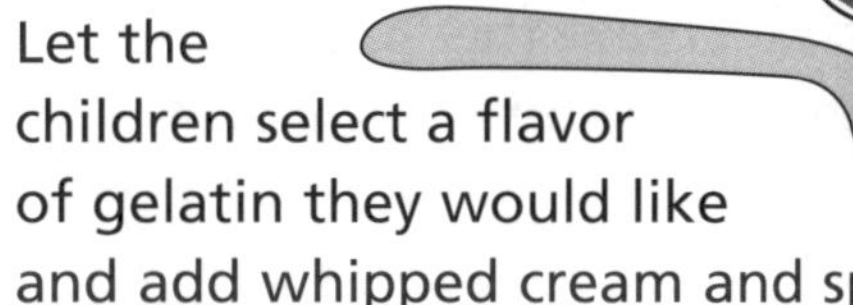

Let the children select a flavor of gelatin they would like and add whipped cream and sprinkles.

Flavor Experiments

(PS6) Supplies

- Animal cookies or other small shortbread or sugar cookies
- A variety of creative dipping toppings *(yogurt, whipped cream, flavored sauces, melted butterscotch chips, etc.)*
- Small disposable bowls
- Small paper plates
- Napkins

Set out each topping in its own bowl. Give each child a few cookies on a paper plate. Let the children try dipping their cookies in the different sauces and toppings to try various flavor combinations.

# Game Time

Use these games to give your preschoolers time to use some energy while still learning. Choose one or both options given, depending on your time and space.

Labyrinth

(PG5) Supplies:
- ○ Small chairs
- ○ Plastic tape or paper streamers
- ○ Small copy of the Ancient Laboratory mural (page R.79)

In Advance: Set out the chairs to create a simple maze. Connect the chairs with tape or paper streamers to create the "walls." Put the picture of the laboratory on the last chair or the wall.

Have Benjamin give the directions: **There are many laboratories near the emperor's castle. But the roads are small and confusing. Can you help me get through the streets to Uncle Pepik's laboratory?** Taking a few children at a time, have them work their way through the maze to the picture of the laboratory at the end. You could challenge older preschoolers to obey what an adult leader tells them to do as they go through the maze.

Get In the Box

(PG6) Supplies:
- ○ *Time-Stone Travelers* CD or tape
- ○ CD or tape player
- ○ Masking tape

In Advance: Use masking tape to outline three or four squares on the floor.

This game is a variation of "Musical Chairs." In this case, the children are trying to fit as many people as possible into the shapes.

Explain that the children are to pretend they are containers belonging to Benjamin's Uncle Pepik. As the music plays, the children can hop, jump, skip, or do another movement outside of the box. When the music stops, they need to all fit inside one of the boxes. Play the music for 15-30 seconds at a time. Encourage the children to work together so that all of them can fit in the boxes. Play several times so that children can move to different boxes.

Craft Time

Window Flower Vases

(PC5) Supplies:

- ○ Small water vials from a florist *(one per child)*
- ○ Silk flower bunches
- ○ Chenille stems of various colors
- ○ Iridescent pony beads
- ○ Small suction cups with hooks
- ○ Sandwich-size zipper-closure bags

In Advance: Separate the silk flowers so that each child will have one.

Show a vial to the children. **Uncle Pepik might have used a container that looked like this. We're going to use these containers to make a present for our parents.** You may want to show a completed craft hanging in a window to help the children picture what they are making.

Help each child wrap a chenille stem around a vial, threading three to four pony beads on the stem so that they are scattered around the vial. Show the children how to create a loop at the top of the vial so that it can be hung. A silk flower can go in each completed vase. Send the suction cup home in a bag so that it doesn't get lost.

Cool Chemistry Clay

(PC6) Supplies:

- ○ Suspension clay *(see recipe below)*
- ○ Liquid food coloring
- ○ Black permanent marker
- ○ Quart-size zipper-closure freezer bag
- ○ Duct tape

In Advance: Prepare enough clay so that each child has a portion of the recipe.

Suspension Clay Recipe:

1 1/2 cup cornstarch
 1/2 cup water

Put the cornstarch in a bowl. Slowly add the water while mixing with a spoon or your hands. Store the clay in a resealable bag. *(Makes enough for six children.)*

Note: This clay is really a chemical substance called a suspension. The cornstarch is suspended within the water molecules. When the clay is handled, the molecules heat up, creating a liquid. When the clay is left alone, the molecules cool, creating a solid.

Let's make a cool clay. We're going to mix together water and a white powder. When they are mixed together, they do some tricky things.

Put clay in a plastic bag for each child. Add drops of food coloring to the clay. Seal the bag completely, letting out most of the air. Put duct tape over the seal to help eliminate any leaks. Encourage the children to gently mix the food coloring into the clay. As they work with the clay, it should turn into a liquid. Then have them see what happens to the clay as it sits without being played with.

To teach colors, you could talk about combining primary colors as you add food coloring. (red + yellow = orange; yellow + blue = green; red + blue = purple) Let the children discover how the colors change as well as the clay.

Application Time

(PA27) Supplies:
- ○ Laboratory sounds from the *Time-Stone Travelers*™ CD
- ○ CD player
- ○ "Time Stone" with symbols on it *(from the site)*

Play the track of laboratory sounds from the CD to gather the children back together in a group.

ELLEN: It was amazing! There we were, watching Benjamin's Uncle Pepik heat up his experiment. All of a sudden, it started boiling. When everything was done, there was a stone in the container. I'm glad we obeyed everything Pepik told us as we were helping him.

JOSH: And then there was the story of Jesus. He traveled with His family to worship God. The Bible says that as Jesus was growing up, He obeyed His mom and Joseph. That's cool. Benjamin respected and obeyed his Uncle Pepik.

ELLEN: We can all do that. We can do what our Bible verse says and respect and obey our mommies and daddies. You can, too.

WILL: *(Moves things around the laboratory and then picks up the Time Stone.)* **Here's the Time Stone! We've had some exciting times in this laboratory, but this means it's time to go home.**

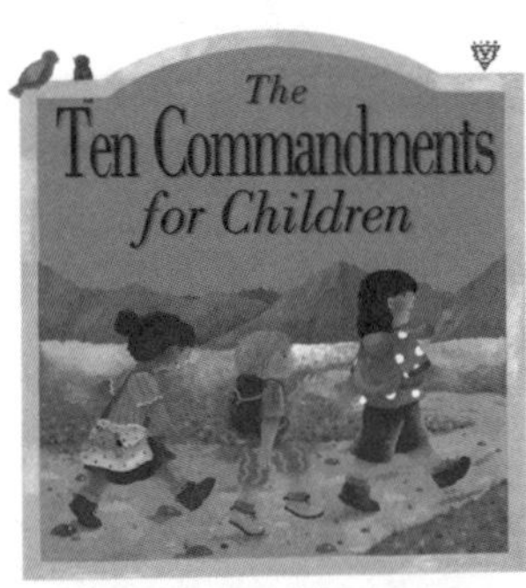

JOSH: Look at that symbol on the Time Stone that looks like the number nine. I remember Pepik talking about the number nine

with one of his experiments. So that symbol

will help me remember to respect and obey our parents.

WILL, ELLEN, JOSH: It's happening again! Everything is spinning. Let's hold hands—it must be time to go! *(Exit, holding hands.)*

Time-Stone Take Off

(PA28) Supplies:
- ○ Clean stone for each child
- ○ Copies of the symbol for Site 3 *(page R.67)*
- ○ Craft glue
- ○ Masking tape
- ○ Permanent marker
- ○ The Quest Continues

What did Josh say about the symbol that looks like a nine? *(It will help him remember to respect and obey his parents.)* **We can use the same symbol to help us remember to respect and obey our parents.**

Gather the children around a table, and help them all glue a Site 3 symbol on their stones. If this is the first day the stones have been

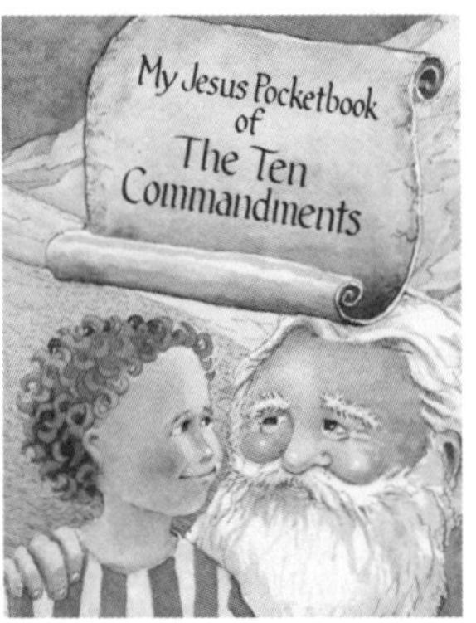

used, write each child's name on a piece of masking tape to put on the bottom. These stones will be added to at other sites during vacation Bible school. Have a helper bring the stones to the next site when the glue is dry.

Be sure to send home "The Quest Continues—Preschool" Take-Home Page and craft projects from the day. Go to www.CookVBS.com to find these additional materials.

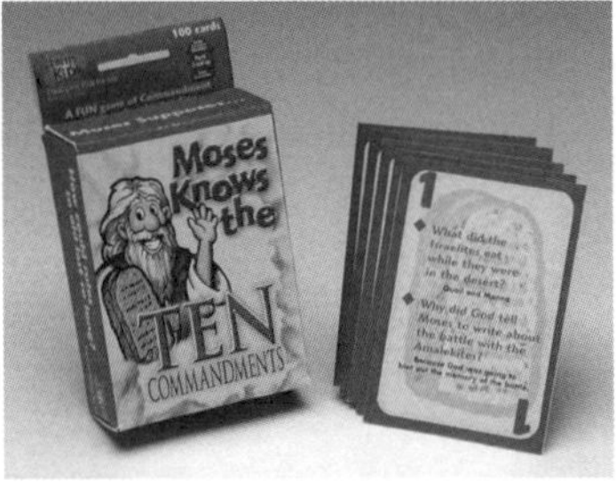

Site Supplies

GENERAL

○ Ancient Laboratory mural—Preschool version

○ *Time-Stone Travelers™* CD or tape copy

○ CD player or cassette tape player

○ FINNEGAN Puppet

○ Copy of "The Quest Continues—Preschool" student Take-Home Page *(pages P3.15-16)* for each child

GAMES AND ACTIVITIES

○ Three mortar and pestle sets on a low table

○ Three stools

○ Kitchen-size, white plastic trash bags *(to make lab coats)*

○ Table

○ Different sizes and shapes of plastic containers

○ Three large plastic tubs or basins

○ Water for each tub

○ Liquid food coloring

○ Old towels

○ Plastic tablecloth

○ Plastic container lids

○ Small plastic containers *(cleaned)*

○ Empty film canisters *(cleaned)*

○ Baking soda

○ White vinegar

○ Craft sticks

○ Dishpan for used materials

○ Paper or silk flowers of different colors

○ Baskets

○ Bundle of firewood

○ Poster of the temple *(page R.50)*

○ Paper footprints

○ Plastic containers and spoons *(one per child)*

○ Small chairs

○ Plastic tape or paper streamers

○ Small copy of the Ancient Laboratory mural *(page R.79)*

○ Masking tape

○ "Time Stone" with symbols on it *(from the site)*

○ Clean stone for each child

○ Copies of the symbol for Site 3 *(page R.67)*

○ Craft glue

○ Permanent marker

SNACKS

○ Instant gelatin *(various flavors)*

○ Whipped topping

○ Various cake decorating sprinkles in fun shapes

○ Clear plastic cups

○ Disposable spoons

○ Animal cookies or other small shortbread or sugar cookies

○ A variety of creative dipping toppings *(yogurt, whipped cream, flavored sauces, melted butterscotch chips, etc.)*

○ Small disposable bowls

○ Small paper plates

○ Napkins

CRAFTS

○ Small water vials from a florist *(one per child)*

○ Silk flower bunches

○ Chenille stems of various colors

○ Iridescent pony beads

○ Small suction cups with hooks

○ Sandwich-size zipper-closure bags

○ Suspension clay *(see recipe)*

○ Liquid food coloring

○ Black permanent marker

○ Quart-size zipper-closure freezer bag

○ Duct tape

Site 3 Notes

Today your child visited an ancient laboratory and heard the story, from Luke 2, of the boy Jesus in the temple. Your child learned the concept of respecting and obeying parents.

Go online to **www.CookVBS.com** for more information about *Time-Stone Travelers*™ VBS and what your child is experiencing each day.

FAMILY ACTIVITY AND CREATIVE BIBLE STORY ON BACK
SHARE WHAT YOU LEARNED TODAY WITH YOUR FAMILY!

"OBEY YOUR PARENTS." EPHESIANS 6:1

COLOR YOUR OWN MURAL

SITE THREE PRESCHOOL

The QUEST CONTINUES

Core Concept
Honor and obey your father and mother as God commanded.

Child Response
I will respect and obey my father and mother.

 ## Key Bible Verse

"Obey your parents." — **Ephesians 6:1**

Bible Passage
Luke 2:41-51 *(Boy Jesus at the Temple);*
Exodus 20:12 *(Commandment 5)*
Bible Story from Luke 2

At home, tell the Bible story while walking or hiking with your child. Let your child choose the route to travel to get to "Jerusalem." Stop at the end of each "day" in the story.

Every year Jesus' family went to the city of Jerusalem for a special worship time. His mom's name was Mary. Her husband, who was like Jesus' dad, was named Joseph. When Jesus was 12 years old, He went with His family and friends. Let's pretend to go to the city of Jerusalem with them.

It took more than a day for Jesus and His family to get to Jerusalem. Let's stop and rest for a little while.

Jesus and His family went to a special church building called the temple. They worshiped God.

When they went back home, Jesus' family was with a large group of friends and other family. Mary and Joseph thought that Jesus was with the others. So they stopped for the night. Let's pretend to stop here with the group.

Mary and Joseph started to look for Jesus. But they couldn't find Him anywhere! They had to go back to Jerusalem. They looked all over the city for Him.

Mary and Joseph found Jesus. He was at the temple. Jesus was with the teachers. He was listening to them, asking questions, and even answering their questions. Jesus knew a lot about God. Mary and Joseph were surprised to find Jesus at the temple.

Jesus' mom said to Him, "We have been very worried about You. We didn't know where You were!"

Jesus told His mom, "You didn't have to worry about Me. I was here learning about God."

Then Jesus went back home with His family. Jesus respected and obeyed His mom and Joseph. You can respect and obey your dad and mom.

Family Activity

Kitchen Lab
Turn your kitchen into a modern day laboratory. A lot of chemistry actually happens in baking and cooking. Choose a simple recipe to make together. As you work together, thank your child for obeying directions.

HAWK'S VILLAGE

"Love . . . thy neighbour." — **Luke 10:27**

INFO for the TRIP

Why Kids Need to Know That Kindness Is the Way to Treat Everyone

Kindness is not as easy as it sounds. Bullying has become a commonly discussed topic in communities, schools, and professional journals dealing with social issues. Some schools have adopted anti-bullying rules, holding special assemblies and promoting slogans to prepare kids to face bullying. What a statement this makes about how necessary it is for kids to learn that God commands us to treat one another with kindness.

Having been born sinners and with an innate sense of self-interest, each child needs to learn to tell the truth, control anger, maintain faithfulness in the covenant of marriage, and be honorable regarding the possessions of others. These commandments can be succinctly summarized as treating others kindly.

Some of the children at your VBS are growing up in situations not conducive to this mindset. Abuse and neglect may be hard to see, but they're widespread today. The only way the children will genuinely be able to learn to become like Jesus is to learn how to show kindness, not only to those whom they consider friends, but also to those to whom they have no relationship or allegiance. Your examples of kindness this week will be the starting point for some kids to "go and do likewise." Look for chances to go out of your way to show sincere kindness while the children are watching, not only to the kids themselves, but to other Leaders or any person.

FACTOID

The Ojibwa, also known as the Chippewa, were masters of the North American waterways. They excelled at building canoes from birch, white cedar, and spruce. Near the Great Lakes, just one birch tree could supply enough bark for a whole canoe. The bark was peeled off, or in winter the tree was cut down and had boiling water poured on it to thaw the wood. Roots of conifer trees were used to fasten the various canoe parts together.

GETTING MORE FROM THE BIBLE STORY

Jesus told this parable about a kind Samaritan when a Jewish lawyer in the audience sought to test Jesus' knowledge of Judaic law. The lawyer's question about inheriting eternal life was based on Moses' law in Deuteronomy 6:5 and Leviticus 19:18. The lawyer himself became a part of the parable's truth because he considered his question as a point of law, while Jesus showed that care for the person is the central point.

Interestingly, Jesus, who was Jewish, told a parable featuring a Samaritan, someone strongly disliked by the neighboring Jews. The Samaritan was the "good guy" in the story, which would have rankled those listening to Jesus. The Samaritans were a race of people of mixed heritage who were the result of intermarriage after the Hebrew exile between the Jews from the northern kingdom and other people groups. The Jews scorned this group.

By telling this particular story, Jesus was emphasizing that only one attitude toward others is acceptable to God: kindness motivated by love.

Core Concept

God wants us to treat others with kindness.

Key Bible Verse

"Love . . . thy neighbour."
— Luke 10:27

Puppet Option

A Leader can operate FINNEGAN to help lead the children to different areas and interact spontaneously with the teacher and children. *(See puppet pattern for FINNEGAN on pages R.53-57.)*

Bible Passage

Luke 10:25-37;
(The Good Samaritan);
Exodus 20:13-16
(Commandments 6, 7, 8, 9)

Setting the Scene

Create an Ojibwa village setting. On one wall, draw a village scene using the transparency on page R.80. In front of the mural, build a large fire ring by making a circle of big stones; pile logs in the middle and add tissue paper flames. Scatter animal hides or paper cutouts of animal hides in front of the mural. On one wall, paint a sky with a few clouds and blue water on the lower portion. Give the

<table>
<tr><td colspan="2">Schedule of Activities</td></tr>
<tr><td>5 minutes: Introduction</td><td>10 minutes: Snack Time</td></tr>
<tr><td>20 minutes: Hands-on Exploration</td><td>15-20 minutes: Game Time</td></tr>
<tr><td>10 minutes: Bible Story Time</td><td>20 minutes: Craft Time</td></tr>
<tr><td>10 minutes: Bible Memory Time</td><td>5 minutes: Application Time</td></tr>
<tr><td>10 minutes: Music Time</td><td>10 minutes: Time-Stone Take Off</td></tr>
</table>

appearance of a rocky shoreline by stuffing paper grocery bags with newspaper and taping them closed in irregular rock-like shapes. Scatter these "rocks" where you painted the water to make shoreline. If possible, put an empty canoe by the rocks. Be sure to stabilize the canoe so that it can't tip. You may want to paint trees on the other walls of your area. Use real or artificial bushy plants to create a forest scene. Try to cover most of the floor with green or brown carpet, felt, blanket, or artificial turf to represent the ground. Be sure to include a large "Time-Stone" painted with the symbols from the reference section *(page R.67)*. You may also play the forest sound effects from the CD.

Introduction

(PA29) Supplies:
- ○ Forest sounds from *Time-Stone Travelers*™ CD
- ○ CD or tape player
- ○ "Stone" arrowhead *(made from foam and painted)* tied onto a wood pole as a spear
- ○ Fishing net

Advanced Preparation

COMMANDMENTS 6, 7, 8, & 9

1. Have craft samples prepared in advance to show Travelers.
2. Be sure all supplies are gathered and your site is ready each day for Travelers to arrive.
3. Post the Schedule of Activities where Leaders and helpers can refer to it.
4. Address each other by site titles. Children should be referred to as Travelers.
5. After taking attendance, a Leader should tell those responsible for refreshments how many Travelers are present to be prepared for snack time.
6. You may wish to do some background research into the Bible story. Refer to Bible commentaries, encyclopedias, and dictionaries for additional information.

Have the forest sounds playing as the children enter and are seated in a circle around the fire ring.

(Josh, Ellen, and Will should be seated on animal hides from the site. Have a spear and net lying in front of them.)

JOSH: *(To kids.)* **I'm so glad you're here today. I'm Josh.**

WILL: **I'm Josh's brother, Will. We're getting ready to go fishing with our friend Hawk.**

JOSH: **This is my sister, Ellen.**

ELLEN: **I'm so glad you came today. Watch what is going on around you. It's exciting here.**

JOSH: **We have traveled to an Indian village, the way it used to be hundreds of years ago. The people here are very nice. But they have to work very hard to get their food.**

Leaders Profile

Josh, Will, Ellen, Hawk

Josh and Will should wear khaki shorts and T-shirts. Ellen should wear a khaki dress, which can be a simple boxy shape. Hawk should be dressed in traditional Indian clothing. All four should wear mocassins and a braided belt with a small, leather pouch hanging from it.

They can't buy it at a store. We're on our way to go fishing so that we can have some supper.

WILL: Josh and our friend Hawk are going to try fishing with a spear. I think that's a waste of time. I'm going to use this net.

JOSH: And you think you can do a better job than I can? What do you even know about fishing anyway?

ELLEN: *(Stands up and goes between Will and Josh.)* Would you two please stop fighting? You need to be kind to each other.

WILL: You're right, Ellen. I'm sorry, Josh. Let's see who can even catch a fish. I'm starving!

JOSH: That's okay, Will. I'm sorry too. This village is way too cool to spend time arguing. Let's help these kids find out more about Hawk's village before they meet him.

Hands-on Exploration Centers

Have Leaders demonstrate the centers.

Fishing Area

(PA30) Supplies:
- Black or gray craft foam
- 1" thick dowels
- Duct tape
- Magnetic tape cut in 1" strips
- 2 yards of brown netting fabric
- Craft glue
- Several sheets of craft foam
- Paper clips
- Blue or green tarp

In Advance: Make several "spears": From craft foam, cut arrowhead shapes three inches long. Use duct tape to fasten each arrowhead to a dowel. Put a 1" strip of magnetic tape near the tip of each spear.

Make several fishing nets by cutting the netting into two-foot squares. Use craft glue to fasten three strips of magnetic tape to the center of each net. Cut as many fish shapes as possible from the craft foam. They can be of various sizes. Put a paper clip at the mouth end of each fish.

Lay the tarp on the floor near the canoe or water area. Scatter the fish over the tarp.

Center Time: Talk about how the Indians used different ways to catch fish. Sometimes they threw a spear in the water. Sometimes they dragged a net through the water. Encourage the children to try different ways to catch fish. The magnetic tape will attract the paper clips on the fish.

If you are using the canoe, supervise the children as they sit in the canoe to catch fish.

Cooking Center

(PA31) Supplies:
- Several fist-sized rocks
- Large baskets *(not flat)*
- Sticks for stirring
- Play vegetables
- "Animal hides" from the site

In Advance: This center should be set up near the fire ring. Put the play vegetables on an "animal hide" near the fire with the baskets and fist-sized rocks nearby.

Center Time: The people in the Indian village didn't cook in a microwave or on a stove. They would heat rocks by the fire and then put them in baskets with the food. When they stirred hot rocks with the food, the food cooked.

Encourage the children to try making "soups and stews" in the baskets using the play food and rocks.

Indian Weaving

(PA32) Supplies:
- Two long sticks from trees, about 1 1/2" in diameter and 3' long
- Twine cut into 3' lengths
- 2 large baskets
- Weaving materials—thin strips of fleece or felt, bark, rushes, leather, etc.—each 2' long

In Advance: Make a simple loom by evenly tying each end of a length of twine to one of the sticks. The twine should be two inches apart. Suspend the top stick of the loom from ladders or the ceiling. The children should be able to easily stand at the loom. Evenly divide the weaving materials between the two baskets. Put a basket on each side of the loom.

Center Time: The people in the village had to make their own cloth for clothes. They would weave many things, including the covers for their houses. You can weave on this loom, which is like the ones that Indians used a long time ago.

Show the children how to weave by taking a strip of weaving material and moving it in and out through the twine. Let the children work on both sides of the loom weaving. It's fine if the strips of material are not close together or evenly woven. This is a skill that preschoolers are just beginning to learn.

 **Bible Story Time**

Luke 10:25-37 *(The Good Samaritan);*
Exodus 20:13-16 *(Commandments 6, 7, 8, 9)*
(PA33) Supplies:
- Bible
- Stand-up figures of the hurt man, priest, Levite, and Samaritan with his donkey *(pages R.49, 51-52)*

In Advance: Copy the five stand-up figures *(pages R.49, 51-52)* onto cardstock. Color the figures. Fold the tabs back so that each figure can stand.

Gather the children together from the Hands-on Exploration Centers, and have them sit in a circle around the fire ring. There are two options for the story. Use the option that best fits the children in your site each day.

The storyteller and Hawk should sit side by side on an animal hide from the site, where all the children can see them.

Hi, my name is Hawk. You just learned a little bit about what life was like in my village. Sometimes we sat in a circle around the fire ring, just as we are doing. The older people of our tribe told us stories. These stories helped us learn. Today, this wise person of our tribe is going to tell us a story from the Bible to help us learn to treat others with kindness. The Bible storyteller should take over telling the story.

Bible Story Option for Older Preschoolers:

Our Bible story today comes from a part, or book, of the Bible called Luke. Show the children where Luke is in the Bible, and keep it open as you tell the story.

One day a man asked Jesus a question. "Who is my neighbor? Do I have to be kind to everyone?"

To answer his question, Jesus told this story.

A man was walking down the road from the city of Jerusalem to the city of Jericho. *(Pat your knees for a walking sound.)* **Robbers attacked him. They beat him up, tore his clothes, took everything he had, and ran away. They left the man, hurt and alone, on the side of the road.** *(Put the figure of the hurt man in front of you.)*

Soon a man came down the road. *(Pat your knees for a walking sound.)* **He served God at the temple in Jerusalem. Surely he would stop and help.** *(Have the figure of the priest walk by the hurt man.)* **But when he saw the hurt man, the temple-worker walked by on the other side of the road.**

The next man walking down the road also worked at the temple. His job was to teach people about God. *(Pat your knees for a walking sound.)* **Surely he would stop and help someone who was hurt!** *(Have the figure of the Levite walk by the hurt man.)* **But when he saw the hurt man, the teacher walked past him too!**

Then a third man came walking down the road. *(Pat your knees for a walking sound.)* **He came from far away and was called a Samaritan. People who lived in Jericho and Jerusalem didn't think there was anything good about Samaritans.** *(Walk the figure of the Samaritan and donkey in front of you, stopping by the hurt man.)* **But when the Samaritan saw the hurt man, he stopped. He cleaned the man's cuts and bandaged them. The man was so hurt he couldn't walk. So the Samaritan put the hurt man on his own donkey.** *(Put the figure of the hurt man on the donkey and move the figures toward the side.)*

They didn't have hospitals, so the Samaritan took the hurt man to an inn and took care of him there. **When the Samaritan had to go, he gave the owner of the inn some money to keep on taking care of the hurt man.**

At the end of the story, Jesus asked, "Who was kind to the hurt man?"

The man listening to the story said, "The one who helped him."

We can be kind to others, too.

___

Bible Story Option for Younger Preschoolers:

Our Bible story today comes from the part of the Bible called Luke. Show the children where Luke is in the Bible, and keep it open as you tell the story.

One day a man asked Jesus a question. "Do I have to be kind to everyone?"

To answer his question, Jesus told this story:

A man was walking down a road. *(Pat your knees for a walking sound.)* **Bad men came and beat him up, tore his clothes, took everything he had, and ran away. The hurt man was left on the road.** *(Put the figure of the hurt man in front of you.)*

Soon a man came down the road. *(Pat your knees for a walking sound.)* **He worked at a church building. Would he stop and help?** *(Have the figure of the priest walk by the hurt man.)* **No, this man walked by on the other side of the road.**

Then another man came by. He was like a church teacher. *(Pat your knees for a walking sound.)* **Would he stop and help the hurt man?** *(Have the figure of the Levite walk by the hurt man.)* **No, this man walked right on by, too!**

A third man came walking down the road. *(Pat your knees for a walking sound.)* **He was called a Samaritan. Some people thought Samaritans weren't very nice. Would he stop and help the hurt man?** *(Walk the figure of the Samaritan and donkey in front of you, stopping by* *the hurt man.)* **Yes! The Samaritan stopped. He helped the hurt man. Then he put the man on his own donkey.** *(Put the hurt man on the donkey and move the figures toward the side.)*

The Samaritan took the hurt man to a place to take care of him. When the Samaritan had to go, he gave the man in charge some money to keep on taking care of the hurt man.

At the end of the story, Jesus asked, "Who was kind to the hurt man?"

The man who listened to the story said, "The one who helped him."

We can be kind to others.

Bible Memory Time

(PA34) Supplies: None needed

Key Bible Verse

"Love . . . thy neighbour." –Luke 10:27

Jesus told a story about being kind. When we are kind, we love our neighbor. Our Bible words say, "Love . . . thy neighbour. Luke 10:27."

Say the verse slowly with the children. **Sometimes Indians used actions instead of words to talk to others who didn't speak their language. Let's learn some actions to help us remember our Bible words.** Teach the following actions. As you say each word, do the action and have the children copy you.

Love *(Give yourself a hug.)*

thy *(Point to yourself.)*

neighbour *(Open arms wide.)*

Luke 10:27 *(Hold your hands open like a book.)*

Repeat saying the verse while doing the actions until all the children know it.

Music Time

Show Others Love

(PA35) Supplies:

- ○ *Time-Stone Travelers*™ CD or tape copy of "Show Others Love" *(Track 5)*
- ○ CD or tape player
- ○ A variety of different-sized drums or containers turned upside down that produce a good sound
- ○ FINNEGAN puppet *(optional)*

With the children in a group, say the words to the song for Hawk's village, one line at a time. Have the children say the words back to you. Then play the song for the children.

Hawk might have played a drum while others in his village sang. Let's play our drums while we sing. Play the song a second time with the children playing their drums. It's okay if they don't play on the beat. If you don't have enough drums for each child, repeat the song until everyone has had an opportunity to play a drum. Those waiting their turn for a drum may drum on their legs.

Snack Time

Fishin'

(PS7) Supplies:

- ○ **Fish crackers**
- ○ **Small, new fishnet** *(the kind used for scooping aquarium fish)*
- ○ **Large, clear, plastic or glass bowl**
- ○ **Clear plastic cups**

Place fish crackers in a big clear bowl to look like a fishbowl. Let the children use the fishnet to dip into bowl and scoop some fish crackers. Have the children empty their fish crackers into clear plastic cups ("mini fish bowls") to eat from.

Blueberry Muffins

(PS8) **Supplies:**

- Store-bought or homemade blueberry muffins
- Fresh or frozen blueberries in a bowl
- Small plates
- Hand wipes for blueberry stains

Serve blueberry muffins. Let the children pick a few fresh or frozen blueberries from a bowl to pretend they are picking blueberries in the forest around Hawk's Village.

Game Time

Use these games to help your preschoolers use some energy while still learning. Choose one or both options given, depending on your time and space.

Canoe Relay

(PG7) **Supplies:**

- Four 36" cardboard canoe paddles
- Eight paper canoe shapes
- Four small chairs
- Masking tape

In Advance: Cut four canoe-shaped paddles out of sturdy cardboard. From paper, cut out life-size side views of a canoe. Tape a canoe shape to the sides of two chairs, with one chair at the front and the other at the back of the canoe. Tape another canoe shape to the other sides of the chairs. Make four canoes and set them by the water.

Have Hawk give the directions. **In my village, we traveled on our big lake in canoes. Today you are going to practice paddling canoes. We held the paddle with one hand at the top and the other hand further down. Then we would work together and paddle.** Hawk should demonstrate how to hold a canoe paddle and stroke it.

Divide the children into pairs. Have one pair begin in each canoe, and help them carefully climb in. Give each child a paddle. With the group counting together, each pair should paddle their canoe 10 times. Then have them climb out and give another pair a turn. Once the children have practiced, you may have older preschoolers play in a timed relay of getting in the canoes, paddling 10 times, and getting back out.

Tree Tag

(PG8) **Supplies:**

- Three or four trees *(from the site)*

Choose one child to be "it." The other children should scatter around the playing area. "It" tries to capture as many other children as possible by running and tagging them. Once a child has been tagged, he or she helps tag others. To be safe from being tagged, a child can hug a tree *(or hold a branch of it)*. Those children hugging trees can't stay there longer than they can say to themselves, "I will be kind to others."

Craft Time

Drawstring Bags

(PC7) **Supplies:**

- Pouches
- Fabric markers
- Foam or wood shapes: cross, heart, Bible
- Newspaper
- Paint shirts
- Hand wipes

In Advance: Buy or make a small drawstring pouch for each child. Use a tan-colored, cotton fabric to make bags no larger than 3" x 5".

Be sure to have a Bible, a heart, and a cross for each child. If you need to cut out the foam shapes for the children, use a black rectangle for the Bibles. Write "The Bible" on one side using a fine-point gold or silver permanent marker. Their shapes should be larger than 1 1/2" but fit inside the pouches.

Have the children wear paint shirts. **Indians like the ones in Hawk's village used to wear little bags to carry special items. Today we're going to make little bags that you can each carry. First, we need to decorate our bags.** Encourage the children to decorate their bags with symbols that tell about themselves. After all the bags are finished, give each child the three symbols to put in their bags. Talk about what each can stand for. *(Cross—Jesus died for us; Heart—God loves us; Bible—Tells us about God.)*

Bible Verse Magnets

(PC8) Supplies:
○ 3" x 5" foam core rectangles *(one per child)*
○ Fine-point permanent marker
○ Small adhesive bandages
○ Adhesive magnetic tape, cut into 2" strips *(two per child)*

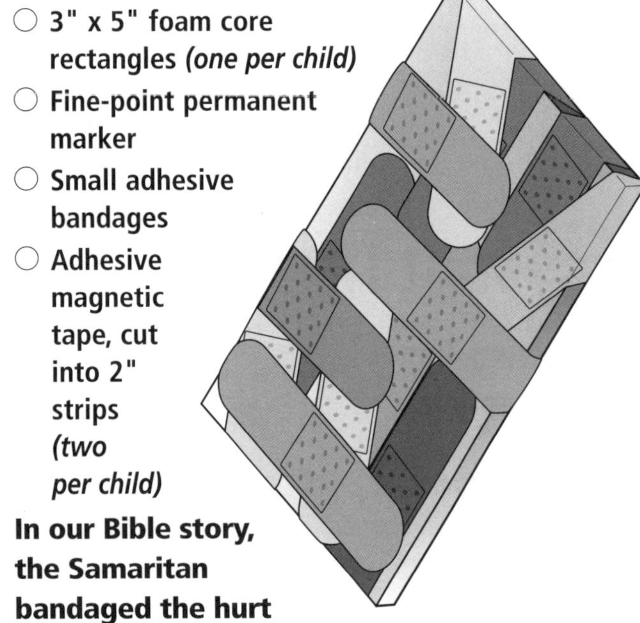

In our Bible story, the Samaritan bandaged the hurt man's cuts. We can use bandages to make a magnet that reminds us to be kind to others.

Have each child use an assortment of adhesive bandages to cover a foam core rectangle. On top of the rectangle print the Bible verse for today, "Love . . . thy neighbour. Luke 10:27," while saying it with each child. Help the children attach two magnets strips to the backs of the rectangles to finish the magnets.

Application Time

(PA36) Supplies:
○ Forest sounds from *Time-Stone Travelers*™ CD
○ CD player
○ "Time Stone" with symbols on it *(from the site)*

Play the forest sounds track from the CD to gather the children back together in a group.

JOSH: I never knew that I could paddle a canoe or fish with a spear. But Hawk taught me to think through something before I do it. That has helped me from hurting people by acting without thinking.

WILL: Remember the hurt man in the story? The Samaritan, the one who people thought wouldn't help, was the man who showed kindness. Jesus told the story to a man who learned that we can show kindness to others. That's one way to love our neighbor.

ELLEN: When we show kindness to others, we show that we love our neighbor.

WILL: *(Pretending to be watching something fly overhead, then tripping over the Time Stone. He picks it up.)* **It's the Time Stone! It's the Time Stone! Finding this means it's time to go home!**

JOSH: Already? Let me see it. See the symbol in the middle? That will help me remember that I will be kind to others.

WILL, ELLEN, JOSH: It's getting dark! The rocks are staring to shake. It must be time to go! *(Exit.)*

Time-Stone Take Off

(PA37) Supplies:
- ○ Clean stone for each child
- ○ Copies of the symbol for Site 4 *(page R.67)*
- ○ Craft glue
- ○ Masking tape
- ○ Permanent marker
- ○ Copies of stand-up figures for the Bible story *(one set per child, pages R.49, 51-52)*
- ○ The Quest Continues

Josh, Will, and Ellen's rock had a symbol on it that looked like a circle with a cross in the middle. It helped them remember that they will be kind to others. We're going to put the same symbol on our own rocks.

Gather the children around a table, and help them all glue a Site 4 symbol on their stones. If this is the first day the stones have been used, write each child's name on a piece of masking tape to put on the bottom of the rock. These stones will be added to at other sites during vacation Bible school. Have a helper bring the stones to the next site when the glue is dry.

Be sure to send home "The Quest Continues—Preschool" Take-Home Page, a copies of today's stand-up figures, and craft projects from the day. Go to www.CookVBS.com to find these additional materials.

Site Supplies

General

- Hawk's Village mural—Preschool version
- *Time-Stone Travelers™* CD or tape copy
- CD player or cassette tape player
- FINNEGAN Puppet
- Copy of "The Quest Continues—Preschool" student Take-Home Page *(pages P4.13-14)* for each child
- Bible

GAMES AND ACTIVITIES

- "Stone" arrowhead *(made from foam and painted)* tied onto a wood pole as a spear
- Fishing net
- Black or gray craft foam
- 1" thick dowels
- Duct tape
- Magnetic tape cut in 1" strips
- 2 yards of brown netting fabric
- Craft glue
- Several sheets of craft foam
- Paper clips
- Blue or green tarp
- Several fist-sized rocks
- Large baskets *(not flat)*
- Sticks for stirring
- Play vegetables
- Animal hides *(from the site)*
- Two long sticks from trees, about 1 1/2" in diameter and 3' long
- Twine cut into 3' lengths
- 2 large baskets
- Weaving materials—thin strips of fleece or felt, bark, rushes, leather, etc.—each 2' long
- Large, stand-up figures *(pages R.49, 51-52)*
- A variety of different-sized drums or containers turned upside down that produce a good sound
- Four 36" cardboard canoe paddles
- Eight paper canoe shapes
- Four small chairs
- Masking tape
- Three or four trees *(from the site)*
- "Time Stone" with symbols on it *(from the site)*
- Clean stone for each child
- Copies of the symbol for Site 4 *(page R.67)*
- Craft glue
- Permanent marker

SNACKS

- Fish crackers
- Small, new fishnet *(the kind used for scooping aquarium fish)*
- Large, clear glass or plastic bowl
- Clear plastic cups
- Store-bought or homemade blueberry muffins
- Fresh or frozen blueberries in a bowl
- Small plates
- Hand wipes for blueberry stains

CRAFTS

- Pouches
- Fabric markers
- Foam or wood shapes: cross, heart, Bible
- Newspapers
- Paint shirts
- Hand wipes
- 3" x 5" foam core rectangles *(one per child)*
- Fine-point permanent marker
- Small adhesive bandages
- Adhesive magnetic tape, cut into 2" strips *(two per child)*

TIME-STONE TRAVELERS™ VBS® TAKE-HOME PAGE

Today your child visited an ancient Indian village and heard the story of the Samaritan who showed kindness to the hurt man, found in Luke 10 of the Bible. Your child learned the concept of being kind to others.

Go online to **www.CookVBS.com** for more information about *Time-Stone Travelers™* VBS and what your child is experiencing each day.

FAMILY ACTIVITY AND CREATIVE BIBLE STORY ON BACK
SHARE WHAT YOU LEARNED TODAY WITH YOUR FAMILY!

"LOVE . . . THY NEIGHBOUR." LUKE 10:27

COLOR YOUR OWN MURAL

The **QUEST CONTINUES**

Core Concept

God wants us to treat others with kindness.

Child Response

I will be kind to others.

Key Bible Verse

"Love . . . thy neighbour." — Luke 10:27

Bible Passage

Luke 10:25-37 *(The Good Samaritan);*
Exodus 20:13-16 *(Commandments 6, 7, 8, 9)*

Bible Story from Luke 10

At home, let your child color the Bible story figures and cut them out. Tell the Bible story while your child uses the figures to act it out.

One day a man asked Jesus a question. "Do I have to be kind to everyone?"

To answer his question, Jesus told this story.

A man was walking down a road. Bad men beat him up, tore his clothes, took everything he had, and ran away. The man was left hurt on the side of the road.

Soon a man came down the road. He worked at a church building. Would he would stop and help? No, the man walked by on the other side of the road.

The next man walking down the road was like a church teacher. Would he would stop and help the hurt man? No, this man walked by on the other side of the road, too!

Then another man came walking down the road. He was called a Samaritan. Some people thought Samaritans weren't very nice. Would he would stop and help the hurt man? Yes, the Samaritan stopped. He helped the hurt man. Then he put the man on his own donkey.

The Samaritan took the hurt man to an inn and took care of him. When the Samaritan had to go, he gave the owner of the inn some money to keep taking care of the hurt man.

At the end of the story, Jesus asked, "Who was kind to the hurt man?"

The man said, "The one who helped him."

We can be kind to others.

Family Activity

Act It Out

As a family, talk about different people in your child's world who may be hurt or lonely or need something. How can your family show kindness to them? Plan to act out that kindness.

HAWAIIAN VOLCANO

"Take no thought for your life." — **Luke 12:22**

SITE FIVE PRESCHOOL

Why Children Need to Learn to Be Happy with What They Have

What child—or adult—hasn't felt a sag in their hearts when they see another person with something they wish were theirs? Coveting—having a strong desire to possess what belongs to someone else—is a sin everyone can relate to. God made this one of His 10 Commandments so that His people could attain spiritually glorifying and satisfying lives.

The human character, without God, can never be content. Some kids may be in a persistent state of "I wish I had" because the acquisition of possessions is so prevalent in North American culture. Don't heap guilt on the children for wanting what others have. Just help them see that this thought process or behavior isn't what God wants. Instead, He desires to fill them with love and security because He is their provider. Try turning kids' thoughts in the positive direction of being thankful for what they do have. Encourage them in learning to turn on their "coveting antennae," noticing when they're in the coveting mode instead of the thankful mode.

Coveting begins in the heart, so kids need to learn to recognize coveting in their thoughts so they can halt it before they act on their desires. Children who lack a nurturing family life, who are low in self-esteem, or who are part of a family culture that prizes possessions are some who might struggle more with big-time coveting troubles. All children can begin to quench their thirst for contentment by knowing God in a deeper, more fulfilling way.

FACTOID

Volcanic eruptions cause lava, ash, and gas to spew from volcanoes, ruining forests, filling lakes, and destroying cities. Seemingly simple ash, if erupting in large quantities, can create heavy rainfalls and even boiling mudflows that can move 60 miles per hour. However, mild ash falling can provide farmers with nutrient-rich fertilizer, and hardened lava forms rocks such as pumice that is used to grind and polish metal.

GETTING MORE FROM THE BIBLE STORY

Jesus' words in Matthew 6:25-33 are part of the Sermon on the Mount (Matt. 5–7). At this point in His ministry, Jesus was very popular and huge crowds followed Him around. These Jews traveled far—from Galilee in the north, Judea in the south, and east across the Jordan—because they desired Jesus' help and healing—and also His wise and comforting words. Matthew 7:28-29 explains that Jesus' teaching was appealing and "astonishing" because He taught with authority, unlike other religious teachers.

Jesus used the amphitheater effect of a mountainside to teach the large crowd. In this particular "sermon," Jesus covers topics that hit home with His listeners, subjects that affected their daily lives—hardship, religious law, relationships, prayer, money, and in this passage, worry. Jesus knew that worrying troubles most people. He wanted His listeners to let go of energy-draining anxiety and refocus their lives on the peace and security the Heavenly Father gives.

Jesus knew the importance of these truths and repeated them on other occasions. A shorter version of the Sermon on the Mount is found in Luke 6:20-49.

Core Concept

God wants us to be happy with what He has given us.

Key Bible Verse

"Take no thought for your life."
— **Luke 12:22**

Puppet Option

A Leader can operate FINNEGAN to help lead the children to different areas and interact spontaneously with the teacher and children. *(See puppet pattern for FINNEGAN on pages R.53-57.)*

Bible Passage

Matthew 6:25-33 *(Jesus Teaches Not to Worry);*

Exodus 20:17 *(Commandment 10)*

Setting the Scene

Create a South Pacific island setting. On one wall, make a volcano scene using the transparency on page R.81. At the base of the mural, build the bottom of the volcano out into the room by piling up wadded newspaper in a slope. Cover the paper wads with brown packing paper. Color the volcano in the mural to match. On one side of the volcano, make a black sand beach by using black paper or felt. The beach should

Schedule of Activities

5 minutes: Introduction	**10 minutes:** Snack Time
20 minutes: Hands-on Exploration	**15-20 minutes:** Game Time
10 minutes: Bible Story Time	**20 minutes:** Craft Time
10 minutes: Bible Memory Time	**5 minutes:** Application Time
10 minutes: Music Time	**10 minutes:** Time-Stone Take Off

meet an area of the floor that is the ocean. Use blue paper, fabric, or plastic wrap to make the water. Scatter some shells and plastic shellfish along the edge of the water. Create a tropical forest effect on the rest of the floor by laying out green carpet, felt, blanket, or artificial turf. You may want to paint trees on the other walls of your area. Use real or artificial bamboo and palm plants. Add tropical flowers. Be sure to include a large "Time-Stone" painted with the symbols from the reference section *(page R.67)*. You may also play the tropical island sound effects from the CD.

Introduction

(PA38) Supplies:

- ○ Tropical island sounds from *Time-Stone Travelers*™ CD
- ○ CD or tape player
- ○ Small basket

Advanced Preparation

1. Have craft samples prepared in advance to show Travelers.
2. Be sure all supplies are gathered and your site is ready each day for Travelers to arrive.
3. Post the Schedule of Activities where Leaders and helpers can refer to it.
4. Address each other by site titles. Children should be referred to as Travelers.
5. After taking attendance, a Leader should tell those responsible for refreshments how many Travelers are present to be prepared for snack time.
6. You may wish to do some background research into the Bible story. Refer to Bible commentaries, encyclopedias, and dictionaries for additional information.

Have the tropical island sounds playing as the children enter and are seated on the edge of the black sand beach.

(Josh, Ellen, and Will should be walking along the edge of the beach. Every once in a while Ellen should bend down and pick up a shell, putting it in her basket.)

JOSH: *(To kids.)* **Hi! I'm Josh. I have a secret to tell you. I wish I could do as well in school as my brother Will does. Maybe then I wouldn't have to spend so much time doing homework.**

WILL: I'm Josh's brother, Will. I have a secret to tell you, too. I wish I was good at playing sports, like my brother Josh. Maybe then

Leaders Profile

Josh, Will, Ellen, Pilikia (puh-LEE-kee-ah)

The boys should wear shorts, tropical shirts, and flip flops. Ellen should wear a simple knee-length dress in a tropical print, along with flip flops. A flower pinned into Ellen's hair will give a tropical look. Ellen could have on a shell anklet. Pilikia may dress similar to Ellen. Any of the characters could wear choker-length shell necklaces.

I would be stronger to help more when we go on these trips.

ELLEN: As your sister, Ellen, I can tell you both that you need to stop wishing for something you're not. You need to be happy with what you have. And just look around you! What a beautiful place to be—on a tropical island with our good friend Pilikia.

WILL: The only problem is that her village is on the side of a volcano. Think what would happen if it blew up!

JOSH: Stop worrying so much, Will. Let's have a good time learning how to surf, swimming in the ocean, and enjoying the good food.

WILL: I'm not so sure about this…

ELLEN: Let's enjoy being here.

WILL: You're right, Ellen. Let's find Pilikia.

Hands-on Exploration Centers

Have Leaders demonstrate the centers.

Surf's Up!
(PA39) Supplies:
- Four foam core boards
- Various colors of electrical tape
- Four wood strips 2" wide and 1" deep, cut in 3' lengths
- Duct tape

In Advance: Cut a surf board out of each piece of foam core, as big as possible. Use the electrical tape to decorate the boards. Tape a wood strip to the bottom of each surf board, centering it on the board.

Set the surf boards at the edge of the "ocean" in the site. Be sure to leave three to four feet between each board.

This center needs close supervision. There should be a Helper at each surf board.

Center Time: Talk about how surfing is a popular sport by the ocean. Explain that people try to stay balanced on the board while riding on top of the water. Talk about how surfers crouch on the board and then stand up.

Invite the children to try surfing on the surf boards. Be prepared to help them keep their balance. Encourage them to crouch down next to the board, then crouch on the board, and finally try to stand up, holding out their arms for balance.

Luau Center
(PA40) Supplies:
- Low table
- Small, green, paper plates
- Pineapple chunks
- Fresh coconut
- Honey ham cut in small bite-size pieces
- Rice pudding in bowls
- Disinfectant hand wipes

In Advance: Set up this center in the tropical forest area. The table should be low enough that the children could kneel at it. The food should be precut and set in large bowls at the table.

Center Time: The people in Pilikia's village had special feasts called a luau. They used the foods that grow on their ocean islands. Today we're going to try some of their foods.

After the children clean their hands with wipes, have them kneel at the table. Talk about each food. Pineapples and coconuts grow on island trees. The ham represents the pig, which would normally be roasted in a pit in the ground. The rice pudding is a substitute for *poi* which is a dish made from mashing roasted taro root. To try the poi, put a little on each plate. Have the children use their fingers to scoop it up and eat it. While it is a little messy, poi is eaten with bare hands.

Be sure to check food allergies of any child participating in this center.

Volcano Making

(PA41) Supplies:
- Wood or particle board base
- Film canister filled with baking soda
- Paper towel tube
- Wadded paper
- Window screening
- Tape
- Two batches of dough, one tinted green and one tinted red
- 1 cup vinegar tinted with red food coloring

In Advance: Make two batches of dough *(recipe follows)*. Tint one green and the other red.

To build the volcano frame, fill the film canister to the top with baking soda. Stand it in the middle of the board to serve as a base. Stand the paper towel tube around the film canister. Using wadded paper, build the sides of the volcano around the tube, being careful not to cover the open end of the tube. Lay the screening over the paper, taping it in place.

Dough Recipe:

2 c. flour
1 c. salt
4 Tbsp. cream of tartar
1 pkg. unsweetened dry drink mix for scent and color (use cherry for red and lime for green)
2 c. warm water
2 Tbsp. cooking oil

Stir over medium heat until mixture pulls away from sides to form a ball. Store in airtight containers. Makes enough for eight to ten children.

Center Time: In Pilikia's story the people built their village on the side of a volcano. A volcano is a mountain with a hole in it. Deep inside the volcano, rock melts. It gets hot and pushes up through the hole. Then it comes out of the hole. That is called an eruption. Let's make a model of a volcano to see how one works.

Have the children pat the dough into thin slabs and then put the slabs on top of the screening. Once the screening is covered with dough, pour the vinegar down the tube. It will react with the baking soda and come out the end of the tube.

# Bible Story Time

Matthew 6 *(Jesus Teaches Not to Worry);* **Exodus 20:17** *(Commandment 10)*

(PA42) Supplies:
- Bible

In Advance: Learn the hula hand motions and practice telling the story with them. Make the motions as flowing as possible. The person playing Pilikia also needs to be able to do the actions.

Have the children sit in a semi-circle around the base of the volcano. There are two options for the story—one for younger preschoolers and one for older preschoolers. Use the option that best fits the children in your site each day.

The storyteller and Pilikia should sit by each other between the volcano and the children. Pilikia speaks to the children first: **You just learned a little bit about the way we lived in my village. One way we told stories was called hula. Hula is using your hands in a beautiful way to act out words. Today, our storyteller is going to use hula to tell us a story from the Bible. Then, when I do the hula action, you do it with me. This story** teaches us to be happy with what we have.

The Bible storyteller should take over telling the story.

Bible Story Option for Older Preschoolers:

Our Bible story today comes from the book of the Bible called Matthew. Show the children where Matthew is in the Bible, and keep it open as you tell the story.

The Bible tells us many things about Jesus. The Bible tells us that Jesus was a good teacher. People followed Jesus wherever He went. They wanted to learn more about God.

One day Jesus climbed up the side of a big hill. *(Move your hands stepping above each other to motion climbing up steps.)* **Jesus asked His special helpers to sit down with Him.** *(Open your arms out wide and then make a circle with them.)*

Jesus began to teach. *(Put hands up to mouth and then bring out.)* **Jesus said, "Don't worry."** *(Move hands back and forth as a movement for no.)* **He knew that some of the people were worried. They worried about what food to eat or what clothes to wear. God didn't want them to worry about those things. Jesus knew God had a plan to take care of them.**

Jesus said, "Don't worry about what you will eat." *(Move hands back and forth as a movement for no.)* **He looked up in the sky.** *(Put hands above head then spread apart.)* **Jesus said, "See the birds in the sky?** *(Move arms up and down like wings.)* **They don't worry about what they will eat. They don't plant seeds or save food in a barn. God makes sure that they have food every day. God loves you much more than the birds.** *(Point up, then cross arms over chest.)* **Each day God will give you the food you need."** *(Point up, then pretend to eat.)*

Then Jesus said, "Do not worry about what clothes to wear." *(Have hands move back and forth as a movement for no.)* **He looked at the ground.** *(Point down with hands together then spread apart.)* **Jesus said, "See the plants? God helps them grow. He gives them beautiful flowers.** *(Pretend to pick and smell a flower.)* **You know how beautifully a king dresses in all his robes? Even a king doesn't look as beautiful as the flowers do!** *(Make a crown on your head.)* **If God dresses the flowers , He'll make sure you have clothes to wear. God loves you much more than the flowers.** *(Point up, then cross arms over chest.)* **Each day God will give you the clothes you need."** *(Point up, then rub hands down arms to represent sleeves.)*

Jesus taught that God will take care of you. *(Point up with both hands and then out to the children.)* **So don't worry about what you will eat.** *(Pretend to eat.)* **Don't worry about what you will wear.** *(Rub hands down arms.)* **Be happy with what you have.** *(Give yourself a hug.)*

Bible Story Option for Younger Preschoolers:

Our Bible story today comes from the part of the Bible called Matthew. Show the children where Matthew is in the Bible, and keep it open as you tell the story.

The Bible tells us that Jesus was a good teacher. People loved to listen to Him teach. One day Jesus climbed up the side of a big hill. *(Move your hands stepping above each other to motion climbing up steps.)* **Jesus asked His special helpers to sit down with Him.**

Jesus began to teach. He said, "Don't worry." *(Move hands back and forth as a movement for no.)* **"Don't worry about what you will eat." Jesus said, "See the birds in the sky?** *(Move arms up and down as if wings.)* **They don't worry about what they will eat. God makes sure**

that they have food every day. **God loves you much more than the birds.** *(Point up, then cross arms over chest.)* **Each day God will give you the food you need."** *(Pretend to eat.)*

Then Jesus said, "Don't worry about what clothes to wear." *(Have hands move back and forth as a movement for no.)* **Jesus said, "See the plants? God helps them grow. He gives them beautiful flowers.** *(Pretend to pick and smell a flower.)* **Even a king doesn't look as beautiful as the flowers do!** *(Pretend to put a crown on your head.)* **If God dresses the flowers and plants, He'll make sure you have clothes to wear. God loves you much more than the flowers.** *(Point up, then cross arms over chest.)* **Each day God will give you the clothes you need."** *(Point up, then rub hands down arms to represent sleeves.)*

Jesus taught that God will take care of you. *(Point up with both hands and then out to the children.)* **So don't worry about what you will eat.** *(Pretend to eat.)* **Don't worry about what you will wear.** *(Rub hands down arms.)* **Be happy with what you have.** *(Give yourself a hug.)*

 # Bible Memory Time

(PA43) Supplies:
○ Four plastic leis

Key Bible Verse:

"Take no thought for your life." — Luke 12:22

Jesus told a story about not worrying. We don't have to worry about what we eat or wear. Our Bible words say, "Take no thought for your life. Luke 12:22."

Say the verse slowly with the children. **Sometimes people in Pilikia's village gave each other flower necklaces called leis. We will use leis to help us learn our Bible words.** As the class says each word together, put a lei on one child, one for each word and the

reference, until the child is wearing all four. Repeat saying the verse together until every child has worn the leis.

If you have a large group of children, use additional sets of leis. Have other site Helpers put the leis on the children.

 # Music Time

Happy with What You Have
(PA44) Supplies:
○ *Time-Stone Travelers*™ CD or tape copy of "Happy with What You Have" *(Track 6)*
○ CD or tape player
○ FINNEGAN puppet *(optional)*

With the children in a group, say the words to the song for the island, one line at a time. Have the children say the words back to you. As a group, come up with a flowing hand movement for each line. Then play the song for the children. **Pilikia may have used hand actions like ours while someone sang a song. Let's sing our song and do the actions together.** Play the song a second time with the children doing the actions with you.

 # Snack Options

Dippin' Grapes
(PS9) Supplies:
○ Fruit wedges or grapes, cut in small pieces
○ Chilled fruit dip *(1 cup vanilla yogurt, 1 cup whipped topping, 1 teaspoon almond flavoring, 1/2 teaspoon lemon juice)*
○ Small plates

Give each child a small bunch of grapes with a tablespoon of fruit dip on a small plate. *(The above recipe makes about 32 tablespoons.)* If you have students with nut allergies, substitute the almond flavoring with another flavor.

Shish Kabobs

(PS10) Supplies:

- Pineapple chunks *(fresh or canned)*
- Grapes *(red and green)*, cut in half
- Skewers, K-bob sticks, or 4" toothpicks
- Disposable plates

Have the children thread a chuck of pineapple, a red grape, and a green grape on a skewer, repeating the pattern until the stick is full. Then let the children enjoy their "shish-kabobs." Prepare the snack ahead of time for younger preschoolers so they don't poke themselves with the skewers.

Game Time

Use these games with your preschoolers so they can use some energy while still learning. Choose one or both options given, depending on your time and space.

Lava Tube Crawl

(PG9) Supplies:

- Several large cardboard boxes
- Duct tape

In Advance: Tape the cardboard boxes together to create a long tube about 12' long. Cut holes in the top of the tube every three to four feet. The hole should be large enough for children to poke their heads through.

Have Pilikia give the directions: **Sometimes when a volcano erupts, the hot lava cools to make a special cave called a lava tube. Let's play with the lava tube by crawling through it. Sometimes there are holes in the tube. It's fun to look out of a tube and see what's around it.** One at a time, let the children crawl through the lava tube, exploring what they see as they move through it.

Coral Reef Hop

(PG10) Supplies:

- Pictures of starfish, coral, and other coral reef creatures
- Six to eight 1' x 1' squares of plywood or foam

In Advance: Set up this activity at the edge of the water. Put the squares of wood in a path with the squares about 10" apart. Scatter the pictures around the squares.

Talk about how the ocean moves in a way called tides. Discuss how the tides can uncover parts of the ocean where people can see starfish and other creatures. **Sometimes people hop from rock to rock to see what the tide uncovers. Let's hop on our rocks.** Have the children hop from square to square discovering the starfish and coral. Encourage older preschoolers to try hopping in different ways—with both feet, then on their left foot or right foot.

 # Craft Time

Leis

(PC9) Supplies:

- ○ Precut craft foam flowers
- ○ Large upholstery needle
- ○ Uncooked rigatoni pasta
- ○ Rubbing alcohol
- ○ Food coloring
- ○ Masking tape
- ○ 27" round shoelaces with plastic tips

In Advance: Use the needle to poke a hole in the middle of each flower. You will need 10 flowers for each child.

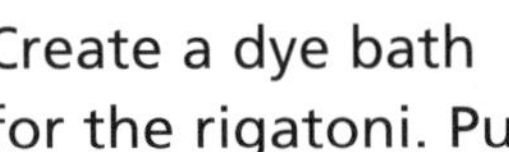

Create a dye bath for the rigatoni. Put 1 cup rubbing alcohol in a bowl. Add six to eight drops of food coloring, in the color combination you are making. Stir and add pasta making sure it is all covered by the dye. Let the pasta soak for no more than 20 minutes. Use more food coloring if a deep color is desired. Drain the pasta and let it dry completely on paper towels. You will need 11 pieces of dyed pasta for each child.

Give each child a shoelace. **The people in Pilikia's village used flowers to make necklaces called leis. We're going to use pasta beads and foam flowers to make leis.** Tape one end of each child's shoelace to the table. This will keep the beads from falling off. Encourage the children to use 10 flowers and 11 pieces of rigatoni to create leis. Some children may want to use a set pattern. When everything has been strung, tie the two ends of the lace together. Let the children enjoy wearing their leis.

Lava Painting

(PC10) Supplies:

- ○ 9" x 12" sheets of white construction paper
- ○ Washable tempera paints
- ○ Plastic cups
- ○ Plastic spoons
- ○ Marbles
- ○ Plastic dishpans or foil baking pans *(one per child)*
- ○ Paint shirts
- ○ Hand wipes

In Advance: Cut the construction paper so that each piece will lie flat in the bottom of a dish pan.

Fill each cup halfway with marbles. Add paint to a cup until all the marbles are covered. You may want to use an assortment of colors.

Have each child put on a paint shirt. Talk about how lava, the melted rock from a volcano, can have different colors as it flows. Today the children are going to paint with marbles to create different colors.

Give each child a dishpan or baking pan. After putting paper in the pan, let a child choose two colors to paint with. *(Adding more than two colors will create a lot of brown and muddy colors.)* Spoon out marbles coated with paint onto the paper. Encourage the children to tilt and move their pans so that the marbles move around just as molten lava moves.

Talk about the different colors that appear. Remove the paper and set it aside to dry. Children may want to make more than one.

Application Time

(PA45) Supplies:
- ○ Tropical island sounds from *Time-Stone Travelers*™ CD
- ○ CD player
- ○ "Time Stone" with symbols on it *(from the site)*

Play the track of tropical island sounds from the CD to gather the children back together in a group. Josh, Will, and Ellen should be sitting near the ocean part of the site.

JOSH: Look at how the water has broken up the lava to create this sandy beach.

WILL: It's amazing how the lava flowed down the volcano when it erupted. Everything in its path was covered!

ELLEN: And it was noisy and smelly. I'm glad that Pilikia's village is fine. They learned that they don't have to worry about what other people have. God takes care of them.

WILL: *(Looks down at the shore and picks up different rocks and shells.)* **We don't have to worry about stuff either. God gives us all the things we need.** *(Picks up the Time Stone.)* **It's the Time Stone! It's the Time Stone! When we find this it means it's time to go home!**

JOSH: Already? Let me see it. Look at this symbol on the Time Stone. *(Points to the symbol for this site on the Time Stone.)* **I'll use it to remind myself to be happy with what I have.**

WILL, ELLEN, JOSH: It's getting dark! The tide is coming in. It's time to go! *(Exit.)*

Time-Stone Take Off

(PA46) Supplies:
- ○ Clean stone for each child
- ○ Copies of the symbol for Site 5 *(page R.67)*

- ○ Craft glue
- ○ Masking tape
- ○ Permanent marker
- ○ The Quest Continues

Josh showed you a symbol on the Time Stone. It helped him and his brother and sister to remember that they will be happy with what they have. We're going to put the same symbol on our own stones.

Gather the children around a table, and help them all glue a Site 5 symbol on their stones. If this is the first day the stones have been used, write each child's name on a piece of masking tape to put on the bottom of the stone. These stones will be added to at other sites during vacation Bible school. Have a Helper bring the stones to the next site when the glue is dry.

Be sure to send home "The Quest Continues—Preschool" Take-Home Page and craft projects from the day. Go to www.CookVBS.com to find these additional materials.

Site Supplies

GENERAL

- Hawaiian Island mural—Preschool version
- *Time-Stone Travelers™* CD or tape copy
- CD player or cassette tape player
- FINNEGAN Puppet
- Copy of "The Quest Continues—Preschool" student Take-Home Page *(pages P5.13-14)* for each child
- Bible

GAMES AND ACTIVITIES

- Small basket
- Four foam core boards
- Various colors of electrical tape
- Four wood strips 2" wide and 1" deep, cut in 3' lengths
- Duct tape
- Low table
- Small, green, paper plates
- Pineapple chunks
- Fresh coconut
- Honey ham cut in small bite-size pieces
- Rice pudding in bowls
- Disinfectant hand wipes
- Wood or particle board base
- Film canister filled with baking soda
- Paper towel tube
- Wadded paper
- Window screening
- Tape
- Two batches of dough, one tinted green and one tinted red
- 1 cup vinegar tinted with red food coloring
- Four plastic leis
- Several large cardboard boxes
- Pictures of starfish, coral, and other coral reef creatures
- Six to eight 1' x 1' squares of plywood or foam
- "Time Stone" with symbols on it *(from the site)*
- Clean stone for each child
- Copies of the symbol for Site 5 *(page R.67)*
- Craft glue
- Masking tape
- Permanent marker

SNACKS

- Fruit wedges or grapes, cut in small pieces
- Chilled fruit dip *(1 cup vanilla yogurt, 1 cup whipped topping, 1 teaspoon almond flavoring, 1/2 teaspoon lemon juice)*
- Pineapple chunks *(fresh or canned)*
- Grapes *(red and green)*, cut in half
- Skewers, K-bob sticks, or 4" toothpicks
- Disposable plates

CRAFTS

- Precut craft foam flowers
- Large upholstery needle
- Uncooked rigatoni pasta
- Rubbing alcohol
- Food coloring
- Masking tape
- 27" round shoelaces with plastic tips
- 9" x 12" sheets of white construction paper
- Washable tempera paints
- Plastic cups
- Plastic spoons
- Marbles
- Plastic dishpans or foil baking pans *(one per child)*
- Paint shirts
- Hand wipes

Today your child visited a tropical island. Besides learning about volcanoes and tropical places, your child heard the story of Jesus teaching about not worrying from Matthew 6 in the Bible. Your child learned the concept of being happy with what he or she has.

Go online to **www.CookVBS.com** for more information about *Time-Stone Travelers™* VBS and what your child is experiencing each day.

FAMILY ACTIVITY AND CREATIVE BIBLE STORY ON BACK
SHARE WHAT YOU LEARNED TODAY WITH YOUR FAMILY!

"TAKE NO THOUGHT FOR YOUR LIFE." LUKE 12:22

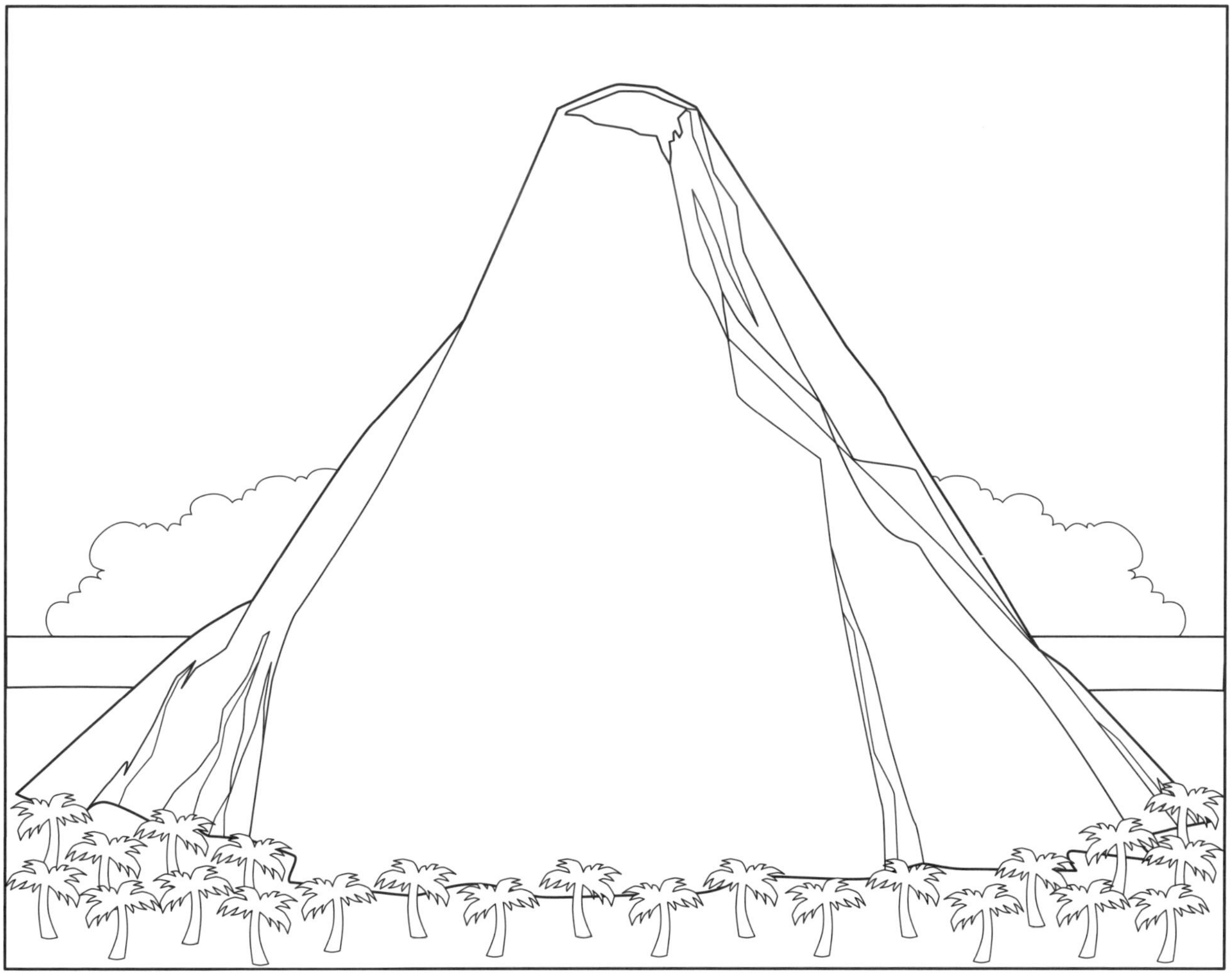

COLOR YOUR OWN MURAL

SITE FIVE PRESCHOOL

The QUEST CONTINUES

Core Concept

Be happy with what you have.

Child Response

God wants us to be happy with what He has given us.

 ## Key Bible Verse

"Take no thought for your life." — **Luke 12:22**

Bible Passage

Matthew 6:25-33 *(Jesus Teaches Not to Worry)*; **Exodus 20:3-4** *(Commandment 10)*

Bible Story from Matthew 6

Tell the story with your child at home. Let your child make up hand motions or actions to tell key points of the story.

The Bible tells us that Jesus was a good teacher. One day Jesus climbed up the side of a big hill. Jesus asked His special helpers to sit down with Him.

Jesus began to teach. He said, "Don't worry! Don't worry about what you will eat. See the birds in the sky? They don't worry about what they will eat. God makes sure that they have food every day. God loves you much more than the birds. Each day God will give you the food you need."

Then Jesus said, "Don't worry! Don't worry about what clothes to wear. See the plants? God helps them grow. He gives them beautiful flowers. Even a king doesn't look as beautiful as the flowers do! If God dresses the flowers and plants, He'll make sure you have clothes to wear. God loves you much more than the flowers. Each day God will give you the clothes you need."

Jesus taught that God will take care of you. So don't worry about what you will eat. Don't worry about what you will wear. Be happy with what you have.

 ## Family Activity

Service Project

Being satisfied can be a hard concept for young children to understand. Working together as a family to share items like food and clothing can help reinforce the idea. Talk about the food that God provides for your family. Talk about how you can all be happy with what God has given you to eat. Have your preschooler help you gather non-perishable food for a local food shelf. Deliver the food together.

Reproducible Resources

RESOURCES

VeBS® Budget Chart

CRAFT & GAME SUPPLIES

Item(s) Purchased	Cost $	Item(s) Purchased	Cost $
Item(s) Purchased ________	Cost $____	Item(s) Purchased ________	Cost $____
Item(s) Purchased ________	Cost $____	Item(s) Purchased ________	Cost $____
Item(s) Purchased ________	Cost $____	Item(s) Purchased ________	Cost $____
Item(s) Purchased ________	Cost $____	Item(s) Purchased ________	Cost $____
Item(s) Purchased ________	Cost $____	Item(s) Purchased ________	Cost $____
Item(s) Purchased ________	Cost $____	Item(s) Purchased ________	Cost $____
Item(s) Purchased ________	Cost $____	SUBTOTAL ITEM(S) PURCHASED $ ________	

CURRICULUM

Item(s) Purchased ________	Cost $____	Item(s) Purchased ________	Cost $____

PROMOTION

Item(s) Purchased ________	Cost $____	Item(s) Purchased ________	Cost $____
Item(s) Purchased ________	Cost $____	Item(s) Purchased ________	Cost $____
Item(s) Purchased ________	Cost $____	SUBTOTAL ITEM(S) PURCHASED $ ________	

PERSONNEL

Item(s) Purchased ________	Cost $____	Item(s) Purchased ________	Cost $____
Item(s) Purchased ________	Cost $____	Item(s) Purchased ________	Cost $____
Item(s) Purchased ________	Cost $____	Item(s) Purchased ________	Cost $____
Item(s) Purchased ________	Cost $____	SUBTOTAL ITEM(S) PURCHASED $ ________	

SNACKS

Item(s) Purchased ________	Cost $____	Item(s) Purchased ________	Cost $____
Item(s) Purchased ________	Cost $____	Item(s) Purchased ________	Cost $____
Item(s) Purchased ________	Cost $____	Item(s) Purchased ________	Cost $____
Item(s) Purchased ________	Cost $____	Item(s) Purchased ________	Cost $____
Item(s) Purchased ________	Cost $____	Item(s) Purchased ________	Cost $____
Item(s) Purchased ________	Cost $____	Item(s) Purchased ________	Cost $____
Item(s) Purchased ________	Cost $____	SUBTOTAL ITEM(S) PURCHASED $ ________	

DECORATIONS

Item(s) Purchased ________	Cost $____	Item(s) Purchased ________	Cost $____
Item(s) Purchased ________	Cost $____	Item(s) Purchased ________	Cost $____
Item(s) Purchased ________	Cost $____	Item(s) Purchased ________	Cost $____
Item(s) Purchased ________	Cost $____	Item(s) Purchased ________	Cost $____
Item(s) Purchased ________	Cost $____	SUBTOTAL ITEM(S) PURCHASED $ ________	

FOLLOW-UP

Item(s) Purchased ________	Cost $____	Item(s) Purchased ________	Cost $____

TOTAL

REIMBURSEMENT FORM

Name

$

Date   Amount spent (Include a copy of the receipt.)

What the money was spent on

Reimbursement given   Approved by

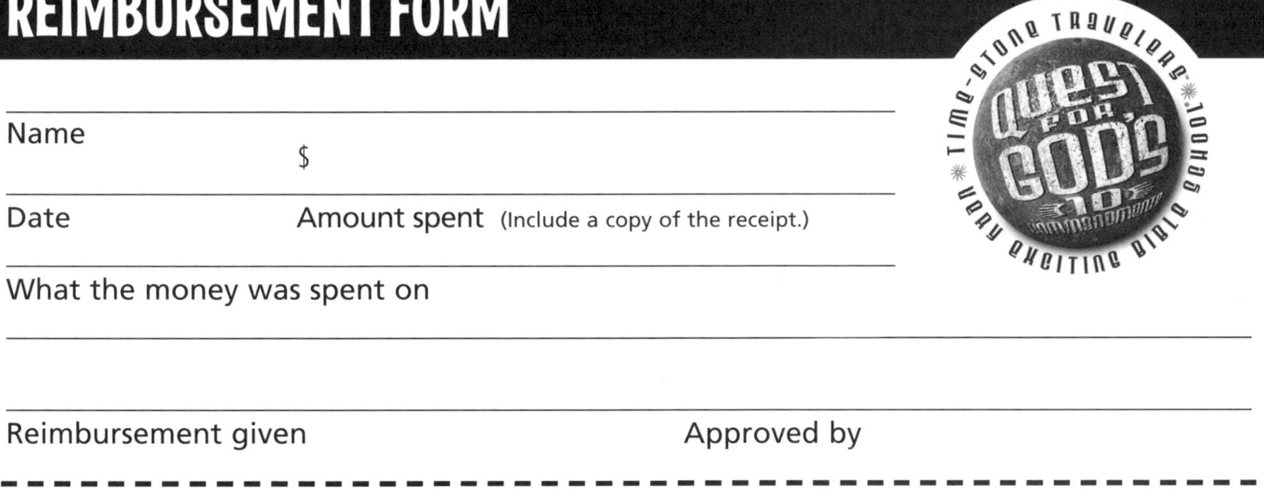

REIMBURSEMENT FORM

Name

$

Date   Amount spent (Include a copy of the receipt.)

What the money was spent on

Reimbursement given   Approved by

REIMBURSEMENT FORM

Name

$

Date   Amount spent (Include a copy of the receipt.)

What the money was spent on

Reimbursement given   Approved by

VeBS® REGISTRATION

Child's Name _______________________   Color Group Assignment _______

Birth Date _______________________   Age __________   Grade __________

Names of Siblings Attending VeBS® _______________________

Parents' Names _______________________

Address _______________________

City/State/Zip _______________________

Home Phone _______________   Work Phone _______________

Pager or Cell Phone _______________   Church Home _______________

Emergency Contact _______________   Relationship _______________

Phone _______________

Allergy/Health Conditions _______________

My child has my permission to attend and participate in *Time-Stone Travelers™ Quest for God's Ten Commandments* VeBS® program.

Parent Signature _______________________

Date _______________________

VeBS® REGISTRATION

Child's Name _______________________   Color Group Assignment _______

Birth Date _______________________   Age __________   Grade __________

Names of Siblings Attending VeBS® _______________________

Parents' Names _______________________

Address _______________________

City/State/Zip _______________________

Home Phone _______________   Work Phone _______________

Pager or Cell Phone _______________   Church Home _______________

Emergency Contact _______________   Relationship _______________

Phone _______________

Allergy/Health Conditions _______________

My child has my permission to attend and participate in *Time-Stone Travelers™ Quest for God's Ten Commandments* VeBS® program.

Parent Signature _______________________

Date _______________________

Group Color:

SITE NO.	SITE NO.	SITE NO.	SITE NO.	SITE NO.

Name	Dates Attended					Allergies/Notes
1						
2						
3						
4						
5						
6						
7						
8						
9						
10						
11						
12						

RESOURCES

I JOINED THE FUN!
TRAVELER'S NAME

I JOINED THE FUN!
TRAVELER'S NAME

I JOINED THE FUN!
TRAVELER'S NAME

I JOINED THE FUN!
TRAVELER'S NAME

I JOINED THE FUN!
TRAVELER'S NAME

I JOINED THE FUN!
TRAVELER'S NAME

I JOINED THE FUN!
TRAVELER'S NAME

I JOINED THE FUN!
TRAVELER'S NAME

DOORKNOB HANGERS (SCALE SHOWN 80%)

cut along lines
to create door hanger

cut along lines
to create door hanger

Announcing...
Very Exciting Bible School®
JOIN THE FUN!

PLACE

CONTACT

DATE & TIME

Announcing...
Very Exciting Bible School®
JOIN THE FUN!

PLACE

CONTACT

DATE & TIME

Announcing...
Very Exciting Bible School
JOIN THE FUN!
Time-Stone Travelers
QUEST FOR GOD'S 10 Commandments
Very Exciting Bible School
PLACE
CONTACT
DATE
TIME
SPECIAL

This Certificate is hereby awarded to

____

for the successful completion of the Time-Stone Travelers™ Program!

VeBS® Director **Date**

Announcing…
Very Exciting Bible School
JOIN THE FUN!
Time-stone Travelers
Quest for God's 10
Very Exciting
PLACE
DATE & TIME
CONTACT

Announcing…
Very Exciting Bible School
JOIN THE FUN!
Time-stone Travelers
Quest for God's 10
Very Exciting
PLACE
DATE & TIME
CONTACT

Announcing…
Very Exciting Bible School
JOIN THE FUN!
Time-stone Travelers
Quest for God's 10
Very Exciting
PLACE
DATE & TIME
CONTACT

Announcing…
Very Exciting Bible School
JOIN THE FUN!
Time-stone Travelers
Quest for God's 10
Very Exciting
PLACE
DATE & TIME
CONTACT

Prayer Reminder

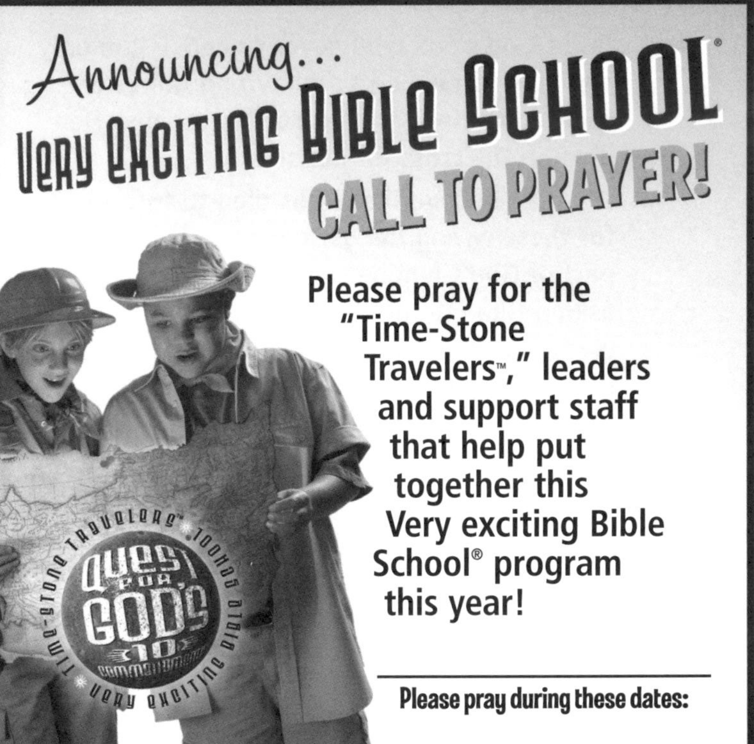

Volunteer Flyer

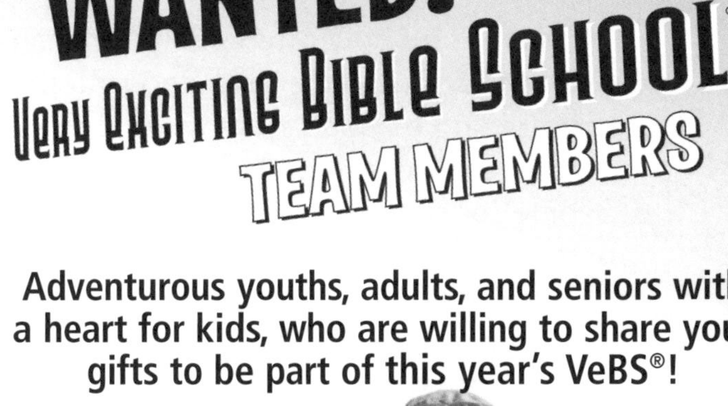

Name ______________________________

Address____________________________

Daytime phone______________________

Evening phone______________________

I am interested in:

❑ Organizing volunteers   ❑ Assistant Investigator

❑ Teaching   ❑ Crafts   ❑ Snacks

❑ Sewing puppets   ❑ Building sets

❑ Building relationships with kids

❑ Other: ______________________

____

Leader Hints

How to lead children to Jesus and into God's family

It's amazing how often adult Christians say that they first came to understand the unfolding of God's story when they were six to twelve years old. These years are a key time for children to make personal decisions for Christ and to begin their faith journeys. This decision is important, and we need to be very sensitive to children who are considering it.

When you have opportunities during VBS to talk with children about God's saving grace, keep in mind that no two children are at the same point of spiritual preparedness. Many children are not ready to trust in Christ—other children are. They are sensitive to their need for forgiveness and acceptance into God's family. Be open to the Holy Spirit's leading. Be available to answer questions, but let children decide themselves when the time is right to receive Christ. Here are a few tips:

○ It's good to be eager for children to trust Christ for salvation. Just be careful not to let your eagerness spur children to make that decision. A commitment to trust Christ for eternal life should not be made just to please an adult.

○ Usually it's best not to offer group invitations in which kids are asked to raise their hands. Kids are great conformists; they may respond to such an invitation just because everyone else is doing it.

○ Encourage children to talk privately with you about questions regarding salvation and what Jesus wants to do in their lives.

○ Have the child tell you in his or her own words what he or she wants.

○ If you feel the child understands the concept of salvation and is ready to receive Christ by faith, take a few minutes to pray with him or her. You and the child will want to talk with his or her parents about this decision to accept Christ. Unchurched parents may have questions about salvation, which opens the door for you to witness to them and invite them to your church.

○ Don't forget your important ministry of follow-up. Pray for the child and encourage discipleship and Christian growth.

The following suggestions may be helpful as you explain the message of salvation.

Help the child know the truths that are fundamental for all Christians. The child needs to know that:

1. God loves each of us, but we all have done things that displease Him.

2. Jesus, God's Son who never sinned, is the only one able to take away the wrong things we have done. He is able to do this because He died on the cross for our sins.

3. We must believe that Jesus died to forgive us for these wrong things so we can become a part of God's family—become a Christian—by asking Him into our lives.

4. We become Christians when we have Christ living in us. We become children of God and new people who want to follow Jesus when we receive Him by faith.

Let the Word of God prompt a child to come to Christ. Here are some verses relating to salvation:

○ John 1:12–"But as many as received him, to them gave he power to become the sons of God, even to them that believe on his name."

○ John 3:16–"For God so loved the world, that he gave his only begotten Son, that whosoever believeth in him should not perish, but have everlasting life."

○ **Romans 3:23**–"For all have sinned, and come short of the glory of God."

○ **Romans 5:8**–"But God commendeth his love toward us, in that, while we were yet sinners, Christ died for us."

○ **Romans 6:23**–"For the wages of sin is death; but the gift of God is eternal life through Jesus Christ our Lord."

○ **Romans 10:9-10**–"That if thou shalt confess with thy mouth the Lord Jesus, and shalt believe in thine heart that God hath raised him from the dead, thou shalt be saved. For with the heart man believeth unto righteousness; and with the mouth confession is made unto salvation."

○ **2 Corinthians 5:17**–"Therefore if any man be in Christ, he is a new creature: old things are passed away; behold, all things are become new."

○ **1 John 5:11-12**–"And this is the record, that God hath given to us eternal life, and this life is in his Son. He that hath the Son hath life; and he that hath not the Son of God hath not life."

Because many children still think concretely—they don't understand abstract concepts or symbolism—have the child explain to you the decision he or she has made. Then you can clear up any confusion.

How to help children understand the Bible

Some adults think they can't teach because they don't know the Bible well enough. No one can prepare to answer all the questions children have! So how do we handle those questions?

With humility: There's nothing wrong with saying, "I honestly don't know, but I'll do some studying and find out" (as long as you keep your promise). Don't avoid the challenge by saying something like, "Well, I guess you'll have to ask the pastor about that one."

With skill: Don't forget that, even though a child's question may throw you off guard, you're more prepared for the lesson than he or she is! Collect your thoughts and use your resources. Remember that one of those resources is the class as a whole. Why not repeat the question for the whole class to think about? Even though they're "just kids," the Holy Spirit can bring clarity and understanding to the group through the group.

With knowledge: Remember to use your knowledge of all Scripture when considering questions about interpreting a particular passage.

With love: Love of the Bible is a natural outgrowth of serious and sustained contact with it. Let love for kids and for God's Word interplay with each other. The more kids see that the Bible is part of what makes you who you are, the more they'll want to get into it on their own.

How to get children involved in discussions

Here are some suggestions on how to get children to discuss:

○ Respond to children in a warm, accepting, and non-threatening way so they can speak without fear.

○ Be open about yourself. You don't have to share intimate details, of course, but tell kids about your life to help them know you as a whole (albeit imperfect) person.

○ Ask questions of varying depth. The first level is the literal or "comprehension" question: What did the characters do? A little deeper is the interpretative question: Why did the characters act as they did? At the deepest level is the opinion question: Why do you think that happened? Try to balance all three levels. For interpretative and opinion questions, avoid giving the impression that there is only one "right" answer.

- Instead of asking a question that might be awkward or too personal, present a hypothetical situation and let children comment on that. Ask, "What should the girl in the story do?" rather than, "What would you do?"
- Don't be afraid of silence. If you want children to face a tough issue, give them plenty of time to think about it in silence or during silent prayer.
- Don't force "openness." Just as children should feel free to share, they should also feel free not to.

How to get children involved in more difficult activities

The Site Settings in this Very exciting Bible School® have children involved in a variety of learning activities. How do you get children involved in them?

Carefully: Children like challenges and will rise to the occasion more often than not. But even more than challenges, they like success. They'll play along with you if they have confidence in you and feel they'll succeed at the challenge. For children, the "payoff" shouldn't be too far away.

Positively: Introduce your project or activity with enthusiasm and a spirit of adventure. Make it clear that you're in this together, and you'll be there to give help when it's needed. When describing a project, explain the steps clearly and get feedback from kids as you go along to make sure they understand.

Respectfully: Try to involve as many children as possible, especially the shy or more introverted ones. But don't force involvement; encourage, but never demand participation. One quiet child may be resisting what you're trying to do, but another may be thinking deeply about what you've said.

How to help children understand abstract concepts and symbols

Children, especially younger ones, can't understand abstract concepts and expressions easily. Take care when this kind of language comes up.

- Don't assume anything. A Bible expression such as "born again" is widely used today, but that doesn't mean children understand it.
- When explaining a poetic term or abstract concept, use the simplest, most concrete language that you can.
- After you explain a concept, encourage children to put it into their own words. Listen carefully to see whether they really understand it.
- Watch children's facial expressions. You can usually tell when they're puzzled and need to have something presented in a different way.
- Avoid explaining one symbol by using another. For example, when Scripture refers to God's Word as "a lamp unto my feet," don't say it's like a flashlight that you'd use to find your way on a dark trail.
- Try explaining what a symbolic term does not mean. For example, when Jesus says, "I am the living bread . . . if any man eat of this bread . . . .," He is not really saying that He is a loaf of bread. After you've cleared the ground in this way, go on to explain what the term does mean.
- Always try to relate biblical teaching to the children's everyday lives. For example, if you're talking about "being born again," or if you're describing Jesus as the Good Shepherd, stop to ask yourself what that means for the children. What does rebirth into God's family mean when children feel lonely or sad? What kind of shepherd-like things does Jesus do for kids when they go through scary times or places?
- Don't be afraid to tell children that something may be difficult to understand. This can encourage them to really think. It makes them feel good about themselves when they struggle through to understanding.

How to play games with children

Children enjoy playing games. Here are suggestions for making games work with children:

○ Keep rules as simple as possible and think through your explanation in advance so you can present it quickly.

○ Be sensitive to children's ability levels. If you think that the skills necessary for a certain game might leave some children out, adapt it so everyone is included.

○ Allow enough time for a game so kids don't feel rushed, but be sure they don't get bored. Tell them when the last round begins so the end doesn't take them by surprise.

○ Think through how and where the game will be played. You don't want to start something, discover it won't work, and have to end it. Figure out how much noise will be made and how much room will be needed, in case you'll have to move.

How to help children feel needed and important

Children need to know how special and important they are. We need to show and tell them that they matter. How can we do this?

Non-verbally: Never underestimate the power of a smile, a wink, a touch on the shoulder, or a look that says, "I'm glad you're here."

Verbally: Children love it when you know and use their names. They also love it when you ask for their opinions and suggestions, especially if you listen well and take them seriously. Encourage them sincerely and frequently. Don't use or allow cutting remarks.

Physically: Children love it when you display their work at every opportunity. Sit down and make a list of every job you could delegate to them. Children love to do even menial tasks, and having them do these with a partner makes it extra special.

How to discipline

A well-prepared, organized classroom encourages positive behavior. Discipline means training and helping children with self-control; it doesn't only mean punishment.

○ Praise and affirm children for good behavior and things they do well. Don't wait for undesirable behavior before noticing a child.

○ Correct a child's behavior, not his or her person. Avoid statements like, "You never listen."

○ Children will misbehave if rules conflict. Be careful not to state a rule that cannot be enforced. Children know which rules are real.

○ Children may misbehave to vent frustration with some aspect of the learning experience or activity. Search for the cause rather than just punishing the misbehavior.

○ Children may misbehave because of boredom. Keep learning active and relevant. Be prepared and excited about what you are teaching.

○ Children may misbehave because of home situations. Be sensitive to the effect that family life can have on behavior in the classroom.

○ Decide in advance what your "or else" circumstances are going to be. Remember that the disruptive child is setting himself or herself against the group, not just against you. Deal with disruption the first time it happens by giving the child a warning.

○ Never give more than two warnings. If misbehavior persists, send the child to a "time-out" spot at the back of the room. By doing this, you're teaching that being allowed to sit with your friends is a privilege—a privilege you have to show you can handle.

R E S O U R C E S

- Never use physical punishment, ridicule, or empty threats. Don't wait until something becomes a problem to do something about it; think through trouble spots in advance. An ounce of prevention . . .
- Assume leadership. You're the teacher; let children know what you expect. Follow through consistently and fairly.
- Move freely about the classroom so that you can be close to all the children.

How to work with children of differing ages

Sometimes it's necessary to work with a group of children who range in age from 5 to 12 years old. If this is your situation, the following tips may help:

- Use older children in more responsible positions. These children feel good about themselves when they are able to help. Allow older kids to help younger ones with craft projects and activities. Older children also may be able to help give instructions and present or dramatize Bible stories.
- Incorporate a lot of visuals for the benefit of younger children!
- Sometimes if a difficult activity or one that takes a long time to complete is suggested, it may be appropriate to have a separate activity for younger children.
- Provide more challenging activities for older children who may complete work ahead of time.
- Recognize developmental differences in ages and provide for those differences in the equipment you use. If possible, have different sizes of chairs, crayons, tables, etc. *(See the charts of developmental characteristics on pages R.17–20.)*
- Incorporate various levels of questions for the levels of understanding children have.
- Have additional adults available.
- Provide opportunities for the younger children to "succeed." Often in mixed age groups, older kids dominate.

How to tell a story

Stories provide an exciting way for children to learn important truths. Special preparation by the storyteller helps children imagine that they are experiencing the story's events. Use the following guidelines:

1. Carefully and thoroughly read the entire story in advance.
2. Review the aims of the site so these can be emphasized throughout the telling.
3. Reread the story two or three more times. The more time you spend becoming familiar with it, the more naturally and effectively you will be able to present it.
4. Outline the main points of the story on note cards.
5. Practice telling the story using simple words and phrases with which you and the children will be comfortable.
6. Add hand gestures and actions that are natural for you to help the story come to life. Use of action words, good eye contact, and frequent pauses emphasize the meaning of the story.
7. Try to involve yourself emotionally with the events you're talking about.
8. Be sure to stay in character as long as you are dressed for the part.

Preschool Characteristics

Physical	Mental	Emotional	Social	Spiritual
• Small, but growing. • Active—needs frequent opportunity to use large muscles. • Learning to cut, color, sort, and string. • Boisterous and noisy. • Restless. • Loves repetition. • Susceptible to disease. • Sensitive eyes, ears, and voice. • Still needs lots of sleep.	• Single aspect thinker—focuses on one thing at a time. • Doesn't differentiate between fantasy and reality. • Learns through senses. • Learns by asking questions (usually "why" or "how"). • Learns by imitation. • Displays increased verbal ability. • Has wide scope of interests. • Engages in much imaginary play. • Curious. • Doesn't think symbolically, but in concrete terms.	• Has ups—joy, warmth, sympathy, love. • Has downs—fear, anger, anxiety. • Insecure. • Is a show-off. • Developing sense of humor. • Physically aggressive, sometimes rough and careless with toys.	• Egocentric. • Struggles with authority. • Home-centered. • Beginning to be interested in friends. • Still has imaginary playmates.	• Ideas about God are extensions of ideas about people (usually parents and teachers.) • Enjoys attending Sunday school. • Learning to pray. • Enjoys stories about Jesus. • Interested in God. • Gets Jesus and God confused.

RESOURCES

Early Elementary Characteristics
Kindergarten and 1st Grade

Physical	Mental	Emotional	Social	Spiritual
• Restless.	• Attention span increasing, up to 20 minutes, but varying according to interest.	• Shifts between emotional extremes.	• Shows loyalty, pride, and interest in family.	• Can grasp concept of God as Creator.
• Loves strenuous activity.	• Differentiates some between fantasy and reality.	• Needs routine, familiar surroundings.	• Attitudes vary toward brothers and sisters; may be bossy, jealous, proud, protective, or brutal.	• May ask questions—Who made God? Where is He?
• Works hard; often overdoes.	• Thinks in concrete terms.	• Many new feelings are emerging.	• Desires friends but does not get along well.	• May fear God because God sees everything he does.
• Tires easily.	• Just beginning to develop reasoning ability.	• Easily becomes angry at himself/herself, situations, others; younger early elementary may cry, have tantrums, become violent; kids on the older end of this age group may sulk.	• Has two or three best friends.	• Developing a concept of God as a real person.
• Is attempting to master a variety of new motor skills.	• Sphere of interest is widening.	• May set goals that are too high.	• Wants to win.	• Sees Jesus as a real person.
• Willing to try anything without regard for danger.	• Eager to learn.	• Ashamed of mistakes; irritated by failure.	• Tries to dominate in social situations by showing off, acting silly, bullying others.	• Limited awareness of who Jesus is.
• Often stumbles and falls; awkward in movements.	• Becomes excited about new learning tasks but may get discouraged in the middle and quit.	• May be defiant and rude, asserting independence from adult domination.	• Critical of other children's behavior; tattles.	• Can grasp simple explanation that Jesus is the Savior who died, came alive again, and someday will return to earth.
• Small-muscle and eye-hand coordination developing; enjoys coloring, cutting, pasting, painting, building, and creating with hands.	• Can shift from one activity to another.	• Responds negatively to direct demands, but benefits from reminders and verbal guidance.	• Desires attention; thrives on praise and approval.	• Understands that Jesus took the blame for our wrong-doings.
• Seems to look everywhere at once; easily distracted.	• Recognizes sequence.	• Often inconsistent, indecisive when making difficult choices; when a choice is made, may be uncompromising.	• Dislikes criticism.	• Limited understanding of sin; realizes one can choose right or wrong.
• Eyes easily strained from overuse.	• Has good memory when facts are presented in a meaningful context.		• Still quite self-centered.	• Recognizes Bible characters as real.
• Touches, handles, explores all materials within reach.	• Likes to listen to stories.		• Enjoys frequent and complex pretend play.	• Considers prayer important.
• Expresses himself/herself through movement.	• Learns best by active participation, self-activation, and dramatic assimilation.			

Middle Elementary Characteristics
2nd and 3rd Grades

Physical	Mental	Emotional	Social	Spiritual
• High activity level; interested in games and organized activities such as baseball. • Fondness for rough, boisterous games. • Expresses himself/ herself in variety of postures, gestures, and stunts; more self-conscious in expression than earlier. • Increasingly fluid and graceful in bodily movements. • Courage and daring in physical activity; frequent accidents. • Less easily fatigued than earlier. • Increased speed and smoothness in fine motor performance; improved manipulative ability; works very quickly and with increasing control. • Becoming better observer. • Interested in skill building; persistent in practicing complex motor skills. • Frequent repetition of enjoyed activities. • Drawing shows increasing awareness of body proportions; starting to draw in perspective; likes to draw figures in action. • Girls ahead of boys in physical development. • Able to take responsibility for personal hygiene.	• Capable of prolonged interest and concentration. • Expresses amazement and curiosity. • Beginning to see patterns, contexts, and implications; universe becoming less disconnected. • Sees similarities because two things share observable features or abstract attributes. • Likes to plan ahead. • Good at memorizing short sentences; remembers better if something is written. • Enjoys reading. • Likes stories of fantasy, adventure, travel, faraway places, humor; comic books are favorites. • Increasing independence. • Does not like to fail, but likes to be challenged; does not become upset when tasks are difficult; persistent in completing tasks. • Older pupils make up minds rapidly, definitely. • Starting to apply logical thought to practical situations; mostly unsystematic, trial-and-error approach. • Understands concept of money.	• Shows definite signs of empathy. • Widely variable emotional be-havior—shyness to boldness, morbid to cheerful, lethargic to excitable. • Likely to overextend oneself in thought and activities; when these become too much, retreats, leaving "a mess." • Often delays responses. • Anticipates with great eagerness; interest often short-lived; shifts rapidly. • Ready to tackle anything; likes challenges. • Feelings easily hurt; not given to pro-longed depression; seeks reconciliation after being hurt. • Sensitive to criticism from adults. • Likes orderliness and neatness. • Frequently complains, sulks, mutters, "lets off steam" as outlet for tension. • May fear dark, fights and physical injury, failing, not being liked; often will not admit fears, even to oneself. • Worries frequently, often in midst of pleasant experiences. • Seeks friendly relationships with adults.	• Prefers peer play to family outings. • May complain about assigned chores. • Hates playing alone; wants to have a best friend. • Learning to subordinate personal interests to group. • Developing self-discipline through responsibilities assigned by peer group and peer criticism; needs less constant adult supervision during play. • Enters group projects on extended basis; forms short-lived, loosely organized clubs; older children form more elaborate, purposeful, and lasting clubs. • Learning to give and take peer criticism constructively. • Admires and seeks friendships with older children. • Acquiring "company manners." • May show antagon-ism toward opposite sex; marked separation of sexes in play. • Growing conscious-ness of own racial, ethnic status. • Image of ideal self forming. • Feels tensions of pulling away from parental domination and achieving independence.	• Open to instruction about right and wrong; has ability to make deliberate choices regarding his/her actions. • Wants to be good; aware of urges to do good and bad. • Wants his/her goodness to be appreciated. • Older child is more concerned about what he/she has not done than about what he/she has done wrong. • Starting to feel the influence of conscience; feels wrongness of own sins; strives to be honest. • Capable of feeling shame; can admit wrongdoing; frequent excuses. • Has active interest in God. • Likes stories about Jesus; beginning to develop an understanding of history & Jesus' part in it. • Recognizes Jesus as God's Son. • Concepts of sin and salvation are more clearly understood. • Able to do Bible study because of growing reading skill and critical judgment. • Enjoys doing simple Bible map work.

Upper Elementary Characteristics
4th and 5th Grades

Physical	Mental	Emotional	Social	Spiritual
• High energy level. • Greater self-control and calmness in performing motor activities. • Improved ability to budget time and athletic ability greatly influence status with peers and self-concept. • Early physical maturing in boys and girls is related to more positive self-concept. • Girls begin pre-adolescent growth spurt; they are taller, heavier, often stronger than boys; often surpass boys in athletic prowess. • Girls start developing secondary sexual characteristics. • Quiescent growth period for boys.	• Alert, eager to learn; younger child may have short attention span. • Transitioning from concrete to abstract thinking. • Likes to identify facts, put items in order. • Likes to memorize. • Likes to read; enjoys stories. • Avid interest in history, people, current events, science, nature, and geography. • Beginning to do independent, critical thinking; can consider why Bible characters acted as they did and why God dealt with them as He did. • Can apply logic to solving problems; starting to form hypotheses and test things.	• Younger upper elementary kids are generally cheerful, content, carefree, relaxed. • Older kids in this range experience more emotional peaks, more variable moods. • Younger ones are oriented toward action rather than reflection, not self-conscious about feelings. • Older ones are aware of feelings but do not usually understand their causes. • Strong feeling related to likes and dislikes. • Older ones are sensitive to hurt feelings and criticism; subject to jealousy. • Occasional short-lived bursts of anger and violence. • Relieves tension through bodily movement. • Frequently bursts into laughter, especially when unsure of self.	• Wants many friends, but wants one best friend of same sex. • Girls prefer smaller, more intimate peer groups; boys want larger, less close-knit groups. • Shares "secrets" and personal information with friends. • Frequently fights and argues with peers. • Enjoys participating in gangs and clubs; spontaneous clubs are fluid in their organization. • Enthusiastically participates in teams and games. • Respects teachers, taking their word over parents'. • Thrives on certain amount of routine. • Exhibits best behavior away from home. • Loves teasing, chasing, pushing, hitting, nudging, poking, etc.	• Responsive to teaching about God's character. • Starting to realize he/she must follow his/her own convictions about Jesus. • Capable of understanding salvation and Jesus' part in it; able to confess belief in Jesus and accept Him as Savior. • Understands the purpose of prayer; makes up own prayers. • Draws heroes from the Bible. • Primarily concerned with Bible facts. • Values belong to group; anxious to join church and be part of group. • Basic understanding of ethical concepts. • Has strict moral code. • Capable of making value judgments about one's own actions. • Often puzzled about right and wrong.

Time-Stone Travelers

Words and Music by John H. Morton
Theme Song

Time-stone, Time-stone travelers.
Time-stone, Time-stone travelers.
Time-stone, Time-stone travelers.
Time-stone, Time-stone travelers.

Time-stone travelers, looking for adventure;
Time-stone travelers, get ready for the ride.
Time-stone travelers, learning from the Bible;
Time-stone travelers, the Lord will be our
    guide.

Time-stone travelers, looking for adventure;
Time-stone travelers, get ready for the ride.
Time-stone travelers, learning from the Bible;
Time-stone travelers, the Lord will be our
    guide.

Teach me, Lord, to follow Your ways.
Help me to understand.
I will keep Your law and obey.
I'll serve You to the end.

Time-stone, Time-stone travelers.
Time-stone, Time-stone travelers.

Time-stone travelers, looking for adventure;
Time-stone travelers, get ready for the ride.
Time-stone travelers, learning from the Bible;
Time-stone travelers, the Lord will be our
    guide.

I can know God through His Word,
all that He expects.
He is pleased when I choose right.
His Laws I will respect.

Time-stone, Time-stone travelers.
Time-stone, Time-stone travelers.

Time-stone travelers, looking for adventure;
Time-stone travelers, get ready for the ride.
Time-stone travelers, learning from the Bible;
Time-stone travelers, the Lord will be our
    guide.

Time-stone, Time-stone travelers.
Time-stone, Time-stone travelers.
Time-stone, Time-stone travelers.
Time-stone, Time-stone travelers.

Only One God

Words and music by John H. Morton
Site 1

There is only one God, and we worship Him
   alone.
He gives us strength and hope for life;
His power He's made known.
He is strong and mighty like a fort made out
   of stone.
There is only one God, and we worship Him
   alone.

There is only one God, and we worship Him
   alone.
He gives us strength and hope for life;
His power He's made known.
He is strong and mighty like a fort made out
   of stone.
There is only one God, and we worship Him
   alone.

First place is our lives is reserved for only
   Him.
We will choose to keep Him first, and He will
   help us win.

There is only one God, and we worship Him
   alone.
He gives us strength and hope for life;
His power He's made known.
He is strong and mighty like a fort made out
   of stone.
There is only one God, and we worship Him
   alone.

First place is our lives is reserved for only
   Him.
We will choose to keep Him first, and He will
   help us win.

There is only one God, and we worship Him
   alone.
He gives us strength and hope for life;
His power He's made known.
He is strong and mighty like a fort made out
   of stone.
There is only one God, and we worship Him
   alone.
There is only one God, and we worship Him
   alone.

God's Name Is Powerful

Words and music by John H. Morton
Site 2

God's name is powerful.
God's name gives life.
God's name is special.
Use His name, but use it right.

God's name is powerful.
God's name gives life.
God's name is special.
Use His name, but use it right.

If you're talking to Him or about Him, use
His name.
Any other way is disrespect.
We are held responsible each time we say
His name.
Be sure that how you use it is correct!

God's name is powerful.
God's name gives life.
God's name is special.
Use His name, but use it right.

God's name is powerful.
God's name gives life.
God's name is special.
Use His name, but use it right.

If you're talking to Him or about Him, use
His name.
Any other way is disrespect.
We are held responsible each time we say
His name.
Be sure that how you use it is correct!

God's name is powerful.
God's name gives life.
God's name is special.
Use His name, but use it right.

God's name is powerful.
God's name gives life.
God's name is special.
Use His name, but use it right.

Obey, Obey

Words and music by John H. Morton
Site 3

Obey, obey your parents.
This is the right thing to do.
Respect and honor your parents.
Then the Lord will give His blessing to you.

Obey, obey your parents.
This is the right thing to do.
Respect and honor your parents.
Then the Lord will give His blessing to you.

Though it's often hard work, I must obey.
My parents only want what's best.
They'll help me live the way God wants;
It's a great start on my life's quest.

Obey, obey your parents.
This is the right thing to do.
Respect and honor your parents.
Then the Lord will give His blessing to you.

Obey, obey your parents.
This is the right thing to do.
Respect and honor your parents.
Then the Lord will give His blessing to you.
Then the Lord will give His blessing to you.

Show Others Love

Words and music by John H. Morton
Site 4

Yah way, oh way yah, yah way a oh, way oh.
Yay zos, yah way oh.
Yah way oh way yah oh.

I will show others love just like the Lord
loves me.
Jesus, help me show love so others see You
through me.

I will show others love just like the Lord
loves me.
Jesus, help me show love so others see You
through me.

Happy with What You Have

Words and music by John H. Morton
Site 5

Lord, we have chosen to be thankful and
grateful, to be happy with what we have.
We will not chase after envy and desire,
but with contentment we will trust You,
Lord.

Don't worry 'bout your life.
God gives you all you need.
He will never leave you, He's near.
Think how you spend your life.
Think how you use your time.
Build character that won't disappear.

Lord, we have chosen to be thankful and
grateful, to be happy with what we have.
We will not chase after envy and desire,
but with contentment we will trust You,
Lord.

Don't worry 'bout your life.
God gives you all you need.
He will never leave you, He's near.
Think how you spend your life.
Think how you use your time.
Build character that won't disappear.
Build character that won't disappear.

Time-Stone Travelers

© 2005 John H. Morton, administrated by Music Precedent, Ltd. All rights reserved. Used by permission.
The original purchaser is granted permission to duplicate for ministry use. If you are a reporting CCLI member, please log copies.

F
C
Dm
stand.
pects.
I will keep Your law and o - bey. I ll
He____ is pleased when I choose right. His

C/G
G
C
Cm
serve You to the end.
Laws I will re - spect.
Time - stone,

Time - stone trav - el - ers. Time - stone, Time - stone trav - el - ers.

Cm
Fm6
Cm
Time - stone trav - el - ers, look - ing for ad - ven - ture; Time - stone trav - el - ers, get

G
Cm
Fm6
read - y for the ride. Time - stone trav - el - ers, learn - ing from the Bi - ble;

29 Cm G Cm
Time - stone trav - el - ers, the Lord will be our guide.
31
Time - stone, Time - stone trav - el - ers. Time - stone, Time - stone trav - el - ers.
35
Time - stone, Time - stone trav - el - ers. Time - stone, Time - stone trav - el - ers.

Only One God

Words & Music by
John H. Morton

Samba! ♩ = 118
There is on - ly one___ God, and we wor - ship Him___ a - lone.___ He
gives us strength and hope___ for life;___ His pow - er He s___ made known.___
He is strong and might - y like a fort made out___ of stone.___
There is on - ly one___ God, and we wor - ship Him a - lone.___
Repeat 1st time only

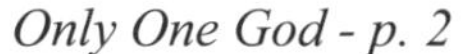

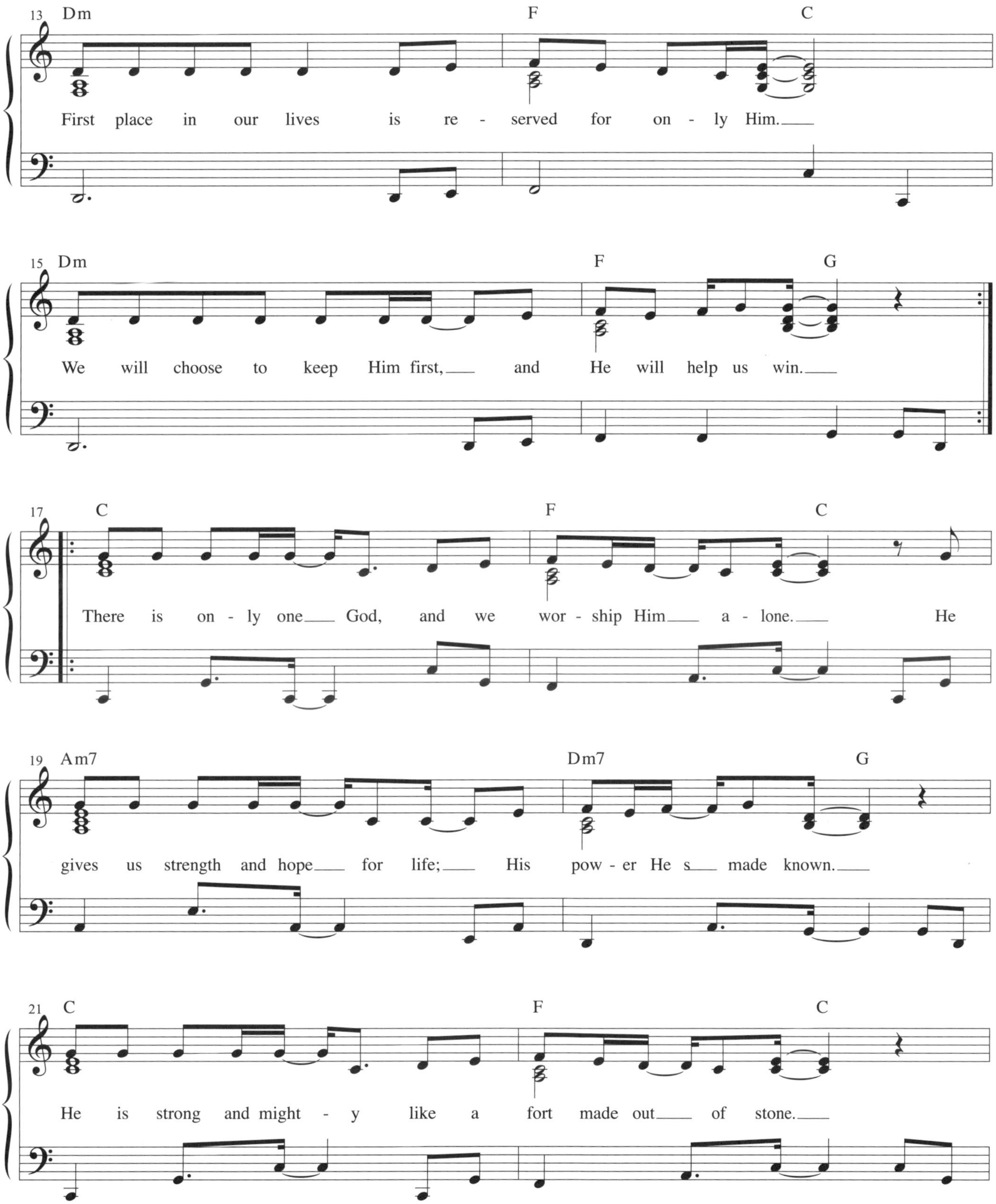
13 Dm F C
First place in our lives is re - served for on - ly Him.
15 Dm F G
We will choose to keep Him first, and He will help us win.
17 C F C
There is on - ly one God, and we wor - ship Him a - lone. He
19 Am7 Dm7 G
gives us strength and hope for life; His pow - er He s made known.
21 C F C
He is strong and might - y like a fort made out of stone.

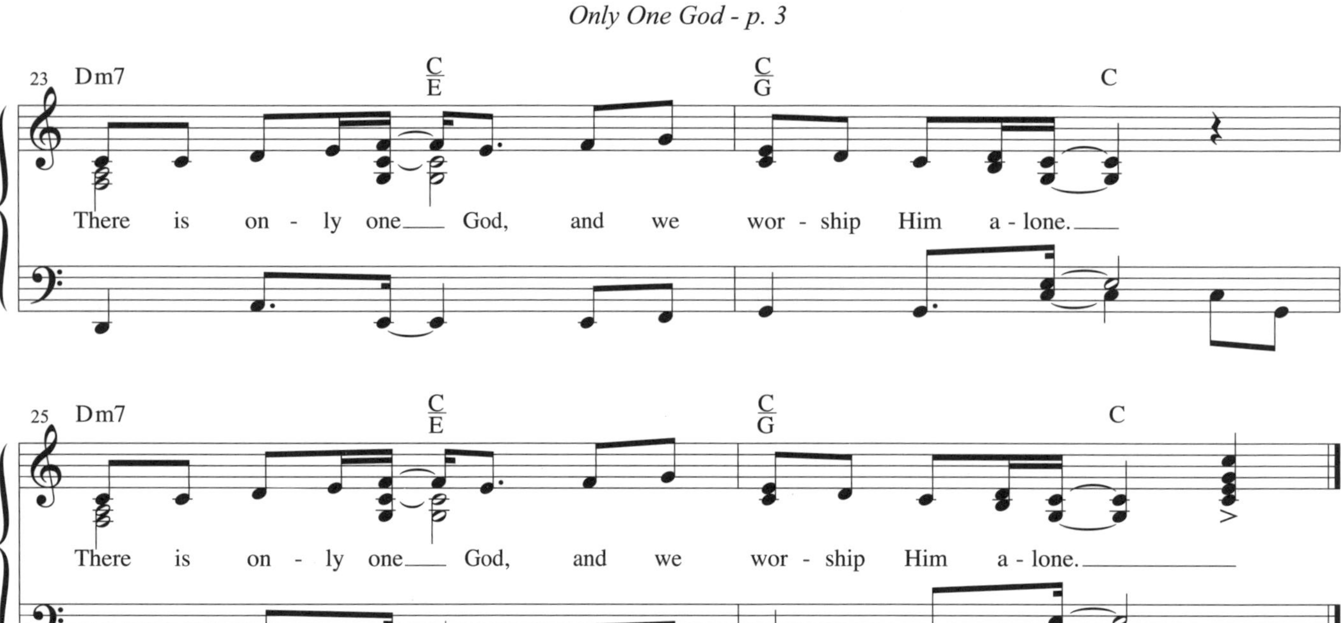
23 Dm7
C/E
C/G
C
There is on - ly one___ God, and we wor - ship Him a - lone.___
25 Dm7
C/E
C/G
C
There is on - ly one___ God, and we wor - ship Him a - lone.___

God's Name Is Powerful

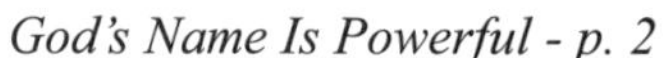

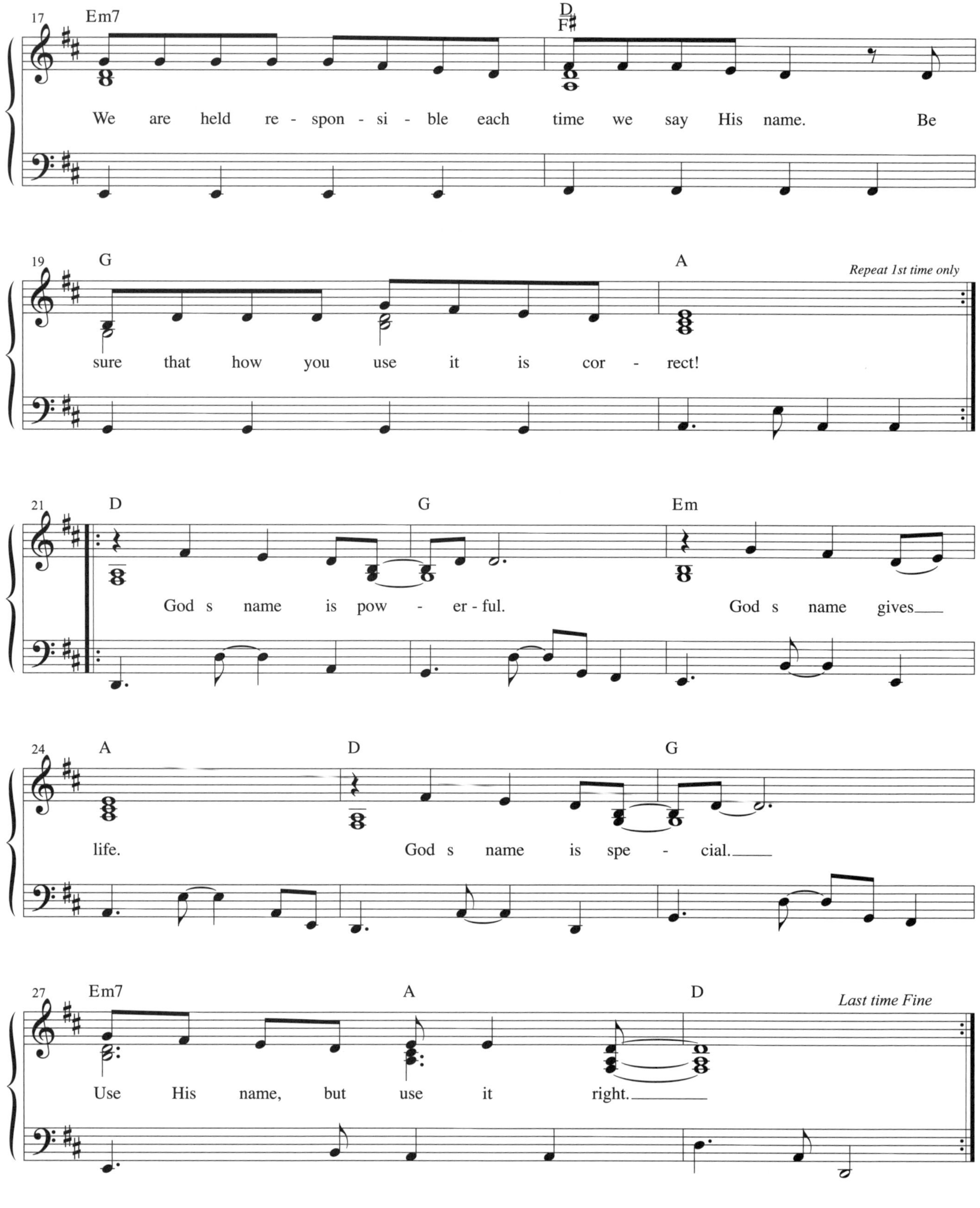
17
Em7
D/F♯
We are held re - spon - si - ble each time we say His name. Be
19
G
A
Repeat 1st time only
sure that how you use it is cor - rect!
21
D
G
Em
God s name is pow - er - ful. God s name gives
24
A
D
G
life. God s name is spe - cial.
27
Em7
A
D
Last time Fine
Use His name, but use it right.

Obey, Obey

Words & Music by
John H. Morton

15
Bb
Eb
best.
They'll help me live______ the way
17
Bb/D
Gm
Cm
Dsus
D7
God wants;______ it's a great start on my life's quest.
CODA
20
G
Em7
Am
D7
G
Then the Lord will give His bless - ing to you.______

Show Others Love

Words & Music by
John H. Morton

Happy with What You Have

© 2005 John H. Morton, administered by Music Precedent, Ltd. All rights reserved. Used by permission.
The original purchaser is granted permission to duplicate for ministry use. If you are a reporting CCLI member, please log copies.

He will nev - er leave you, He's near.
Think how you spend your life. Think how you use your time. Build
char - ac - ter that won't dis - ap - pear.
Build char - ac - ter that won't dis - ap - pear.

Announcing…
Very Exciting Bible School
JOIN THE FUN!

Come join in the fun and adventure as we discover the 10 Commandments! You'll love traveling back in time to exciting places that will help you understand God's Word.

You'll visit a Mayan jungle, a medieval castle, an ancient laboratory, a native American village, and a Hawaiian volcano as we dive into fun games, meaningful activities, Bible memory, cool crafts, and creative snacks—all with one purpose—to learn about God's good teachings in the Bible.

Children (and adults) ages _____ to ______ are invited to join the excitement for this Very exciting Bible School® program!

Keep your eyes and ears open for how to get involved and be part of the excitement!

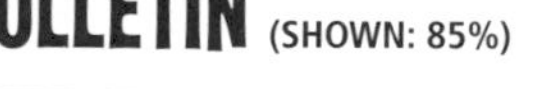

PLACE ______________________________

DATE & TIME ______________________________

CONTACT ______________________________

For Immediate Release

Church ____

Address ____

City, State, Zip ____

Contact Person _________________________________ Phone #___________________________
                                                                    (community)

is sponsoring a Very exciting Bible School® program for the kids of ___________________________________.

Being held____, from ___________________.
                              (dates)   (times)

Time-Stone Travelers™ is an interactive learning experience for children

ages _______ to ____ . Kids will learn about living for Jesus in five very different Discovery Sites.

For more information or to register for *Time-Stone Travelers,*™

call__________________________ at ______________________________________.
        (phone number)   (church name and/or director's name and best time to call)

For Immediate Release

Church ____

Address ____

City, State, Zip ____

Contact Person _________________________________ Phone #___________________________
                                                                    (community)

is sponsoring a Very exciting Bible School® program for the kids of ___________________________________.

Being held____, from ___________________.
                              (dates)   (times)

Time-Stone Travelers™ is an interactive learning experience for children

ages _______ to ____ . Kids will learn about living for Jesus in five very different Discovery Sites.

For more information or to register for *Time-Stone Travelers,*™

call__________________________ at ______________________________________.
        (phone number)   (church name and/or director's name and best time to call)

Family Evaluation

Thank you for allowing your child to participate in
Time-Stone Travelers™
Quest for God's Ten Commandments VeBS®

To help us provide the best VBS possible, please take a moment to fill
out this survey and return it to the church office.

Age(s) of child(ren) who participated: _______________________

Were you also part of the VBS staff? ❑ Yes ❑ No

Indicate how you feel each of these areas was handled:

	Excellent	Good	Fair	Poor
Registration	❑	❑	❑	❑
Record Keeping	❑	❑	❑	❑
Leaders & Helpers	❑	❑	❑	❑
Publicity	❑	❑	❑	❑
Daily Schedule	❑	❑	❑	❑
Assemblies	❑	❑	❑	❑
Discipline	❑	❑	❑	❑
Props/Sets	❑	❑	❑	❑
Crafts	❑	❑	❑	❑
Snacks	❑	❑	❑	❑
Lessons	❑	❑	❑	❑
Support from Church	❑	❑	❑	❑
Safety	❑	❑	❑	❑
Closing Program	❑	❑	❑	❑

How did you see God at work in the lives of your children?

What did you enjoy most about this VBS experience?

What could have been done to make this VBS experience easier?

What would you like to see changed for future VBS programs?

Do you regularly attend church services at this church? ❑ Yes ❑ No
Another local church? ❑ Yes ❑ No

Are you willing to help with follow-up of other families who
participated in VBS? ❑ Yes ❑ No
If Yes, how?

❑ To pray: Day/Time:_______________________

❑ To visit in their homes

❑ To invite a family to my home for a meal

❑ Other: _______________________

____

____

Staff Evaluation

An evaluation is the last important step of a successful VBS program.
Complete this form as soon as possible and hand it in to the church office.

Name: _______________________ **Phone Work:**_______________________

Address: _______________________ **Home Work:** _______________________

Age range of participating kids:_______________________

Were you also part of the VBS staff? ❑ Yes ❑ No

What was your role?_______________________

Indicate how you feel each of these areas was handled:

	Excellent	Good	Fair	Poor
Registration	❑	❑	❑	❑
Record Keeping	❑	❑	❑	❑
Leaders & Helpers	❑	❑	❑	❑
Publicity	❑	❑	❑	❑
Daily Schedule	❑	❑	❑	❑
Assemblies	❑	❑	❑	❑
Discipline	❑	❑	❑	❑
Props/Sets	❑	❑	❑	❑
Crafts	❑	❑	❑	❑
Snacks	❑	❑	❑	❑
Lessons	❑	❑	❑	❑
Support from Church	❑	❑	❑	❑
Safety	❑	❑	❑	❑
Closing Program	❑	❑	❑	❑

How did you see God at work in the lives of your children?

What did you enjoy most about this VBS experience?

What could have been done to make this VBS experience easier?

What would you like to see changed for future VBS programs?

Do you regularly attend church services at this church? ❑ Yes ❑ No
Another local church? ❑ Yes ❑ No

Are you willing to help with follow-up of other families who
participated in VBS? ❑ Yes ❑ No
If Yes, how?

❑ To pray: Day/Time:_______________________

❑ To visit in their homes

❑ To invite a family to my home for a meal

❑ Other:_______________________

Director's Evaluation

Please take a moment to fill out this questionnaire and send it back to us. This will help us to continue to meet your VeBS® needs and to create the best products to help you in your VeBS® ministry. Thank you!

Your Name _______________________________

Church Name _______________________________

Church Address _______________________________

____

Church E-mail Address _______________________________

Denomination _______________________________

What is the average attendance of your Sunday school?

❏ 0-50   ❏ 51-100   ❏ 101-150   ❏ 151-200   ❏ 201+

Please check the Children's Ministry programs your church provides.

❏ Children's Church/Worship

❏ Midweek Programs

❏ Children's Choir/Music Program

❏ Children's Drama Program

❏ Puppet Ministry to Children

❏ After-School Outreach Programs

❏ Other

What is your position with the church?

____

Who is responsible for choosing and purchasing your VBS curriculum?

❏ Director of Children's Ministry

❏ VBS Committee

❏ The Senior Pastor

❏ Other

How many children . . .

. . . attended your VBS?_______________________________

. . . were first time visitors of your church? _______

. . . accepted Jesus as Savior during VBS? _______

Did you . . . (check all that apply)

❏ reproduce the CD onto cassette? ❏ Yes ❏ No

If so, how many copies did you make? _______

❏ use the bonus materials from the CD?

❏ use the editable PDF files from the CD?

❏ use the puppet pattern to make puppets; if so, how many puppets did you make? _______________________________

What version of the VBS program did you use?

❏ NIV ❏ KJV

Please rate the following components of:

Time-Stone Travelers™
Quest for God's Ten Commandments

1 = Dissatisfied, 5 = Completely Satisfied

Up-front materials of the Director's Guide

Didn't Use   1   2   3   4   5

Comprehensive Supply List

Didn't Use   1   2   3   4   5

Reproducible Resources

Didn't Use   1   2   3   4   5

Time-Stone Travelers™ CD

Didn't Use   1   2   3   4   5

Promotional Materials

Didn't Use   1   2   3   4   5

Preschool Program

Didn't Use   1   2   3   4   5

Opening Skits

Didn't Use   1   2   3   4   5

Closing Program

Didn't Use   1   2   3   4   5

Project Share God's Treasure Missions Project

Didn't Use   1   2   3   4   5

Cook's VBS web site www.CookVBS.com

Never Visited   1   2   3   4   5

How we can improve the web site?

____

____

____

What was your favorite part of the program?

What would you change (if anything) about VeBS® curriculum for the future?

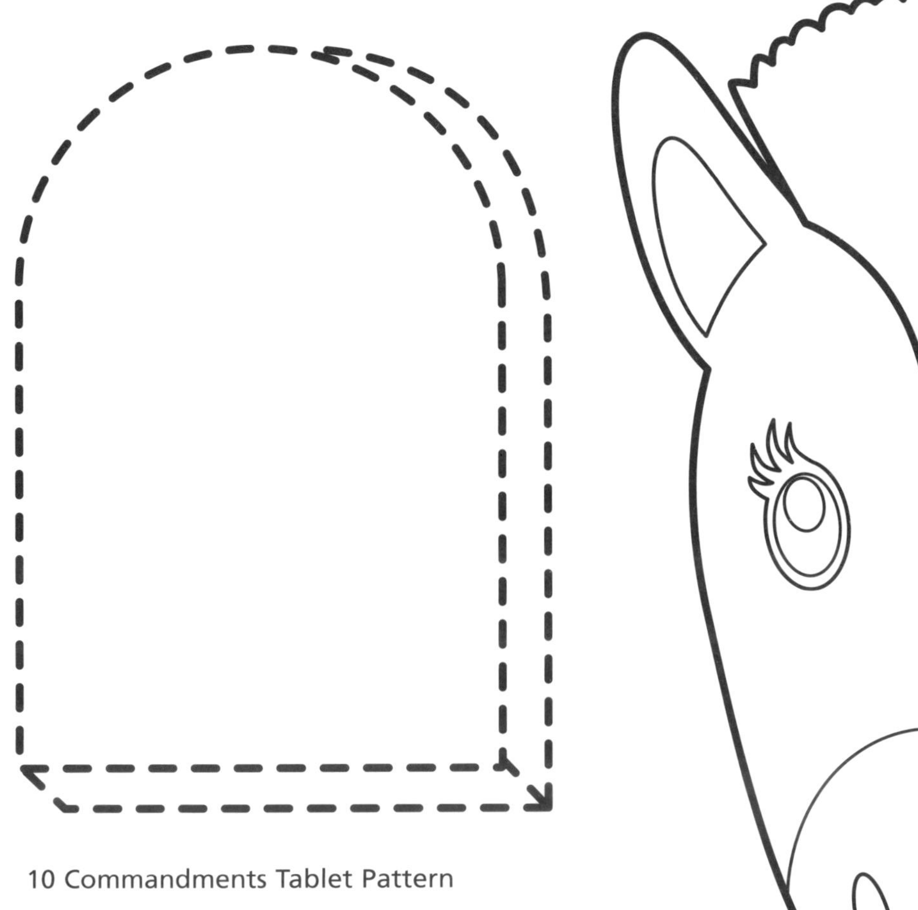

10 Commandments Tablet Pattern

All Sites

Preschool Site 2, Page P2.5

Horsehead

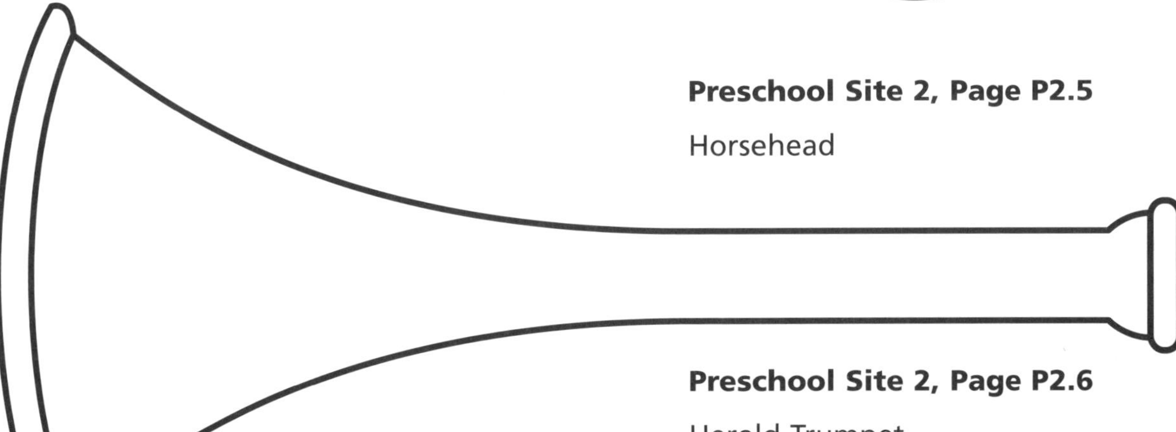

Preschool Site 2, Page P2.6

Herald Trumpet

CRAFT PATTERNS

Figures for Preschool Bible Story

Site 1, Page P1.6

Figures for Preschool Bible Story **Site 1, Page P1.6**

RESOURCES

CRAFT PATTERNS

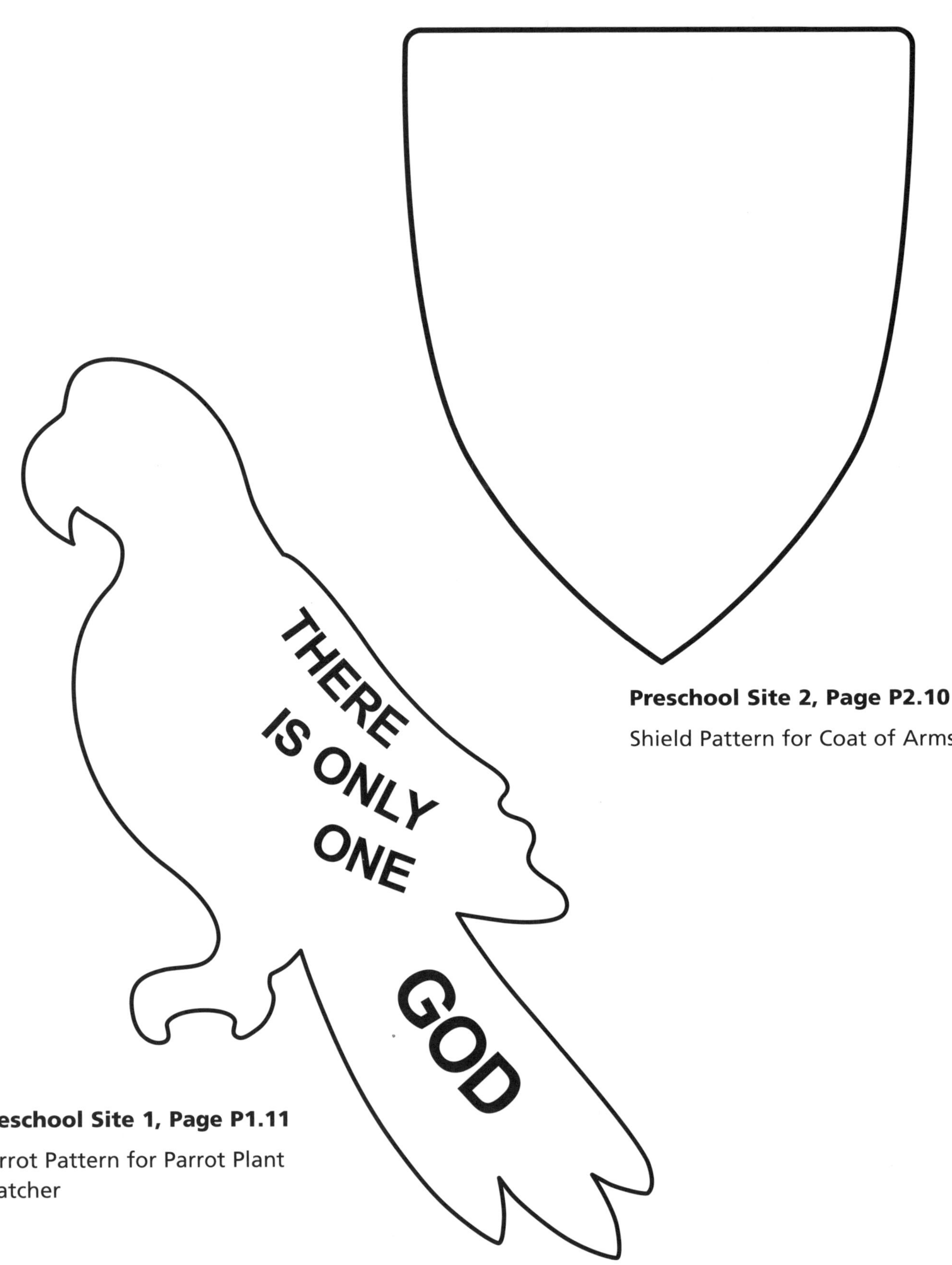

Preschool Site 2, Page P2.10

Shield Pattern for Coat of Arms

Preschool Site 1, Page P1.11

Parrot Pattern for Parrot Plant Watcher

Preschool Site 2, Page P2.10

Stained Glass Window Pattern for
Stained Glass Window Clings

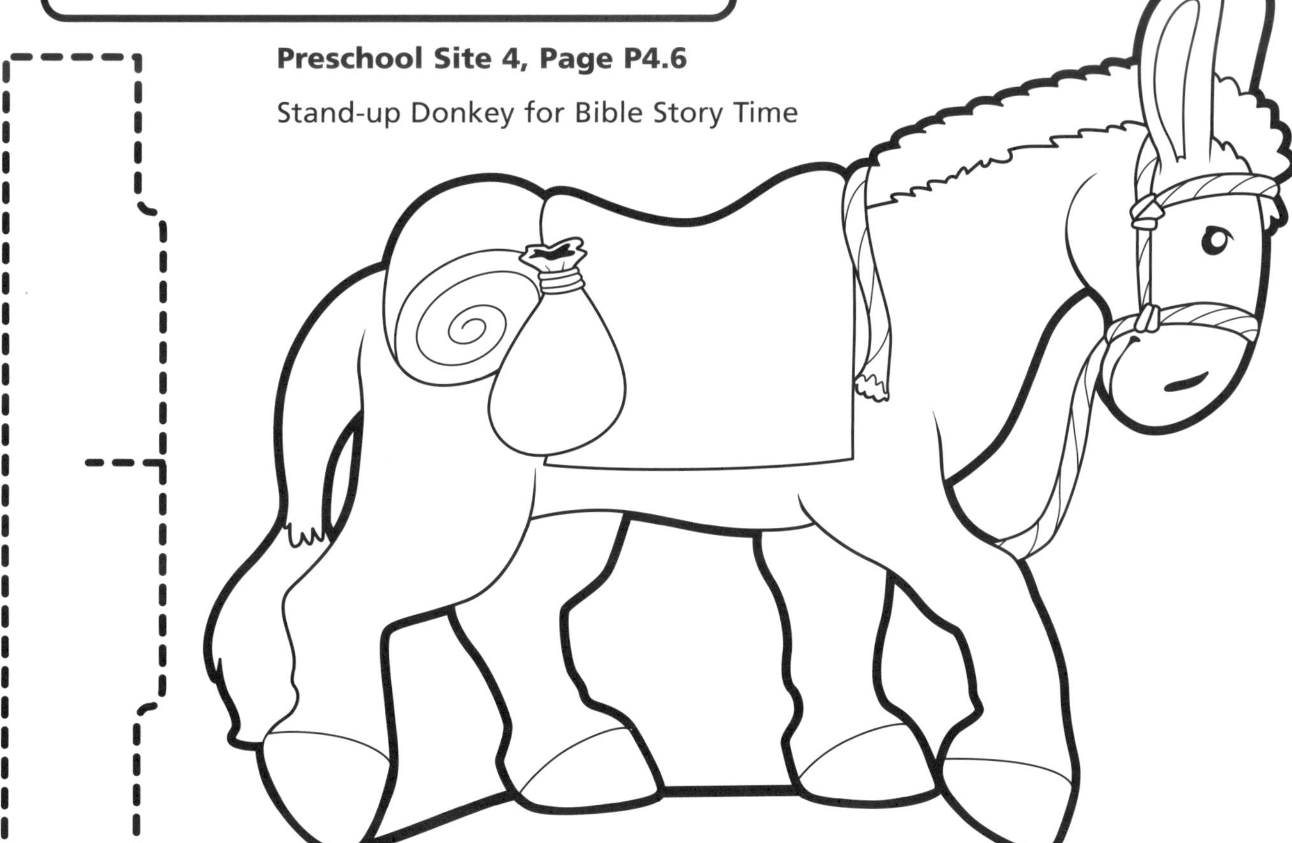

Preschool Site 4, Page P4.6

Stand-up Donkey for Bible Story Time

Preschool Site 3, Page P3.6

Temple Poster for Bible Story Time

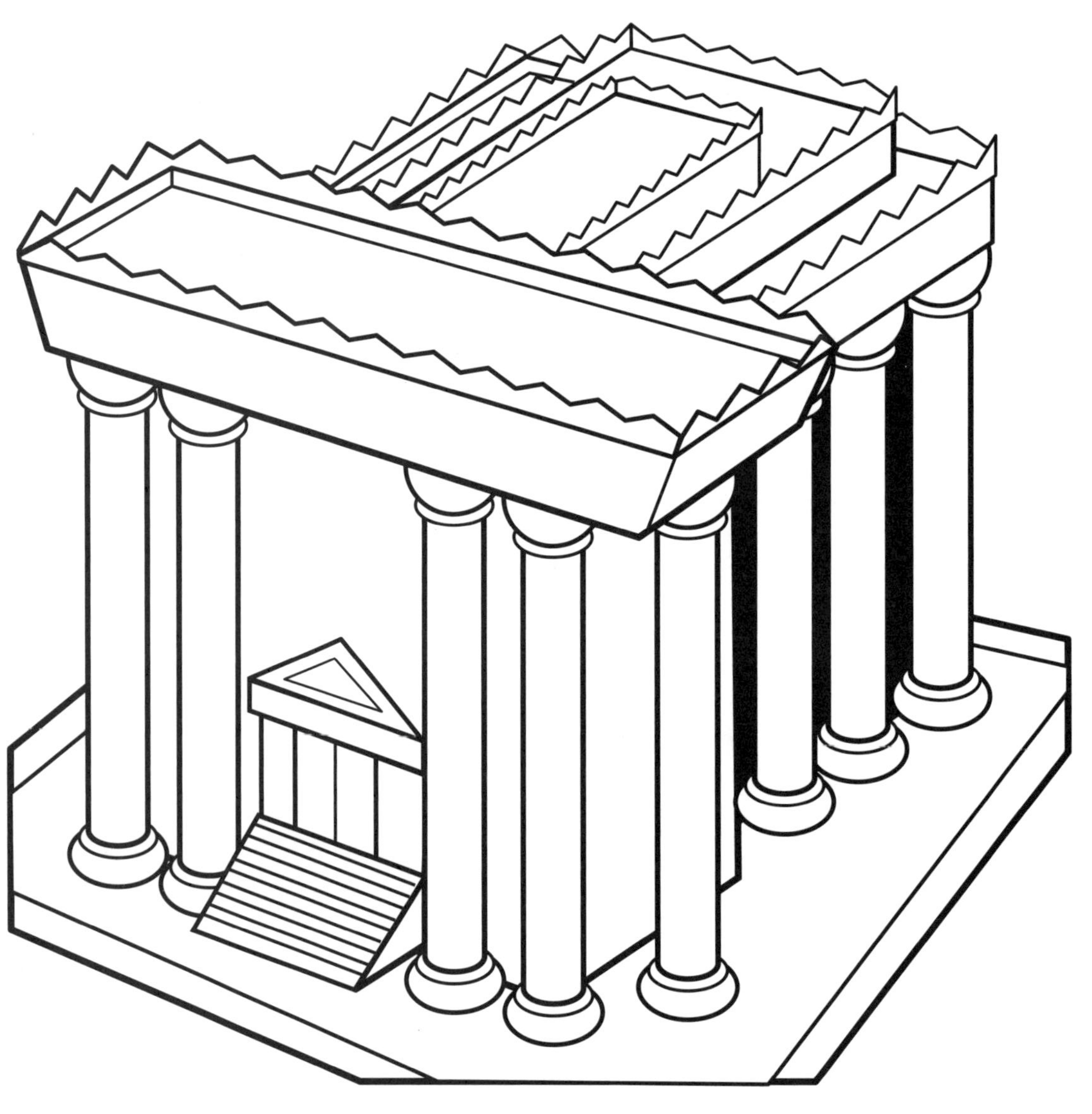

Bible Story Time Stand-up Figures **Preschool Site 4, Page P4.6**

RESOURCES

Bible Story Time Stand-up Figures **Preschool Site 4, Page P4.6**

FINNEGAN

THE GOLDEN RETRIEVER REPRODUCIBLE PATTERN

MATERIALS

1/2 yard golden-brown fake fur, scraps of peach felt for ear lining and eyes, black for inner mouth and eyes, and red for tongue. 1/8 yard denim or canvas fabric for backpack. 1and1/3 yards of 3/8-inch wide black grograin ribbon for bows and backpack straps. One small Velcro circle for backpack closure.

INSTRUCTIONS

Enlarge the pattern pieces. Arrange **Back 1, Front 2, Center Front 3, Back Forehead 4, Front Forehead 5** and **Ear 6** on wrong side of fur and outline with ballpoint pen. Mark large dot of **Back 1**, dart lines and mouth corner point of **Front 2** and pleat lines of **Ear 6**. Mark all notches. Cut out pieces 1,2,3,4,5 and 6. Cut Ear **Linings 7** and **Eyes 12** from peach felt. Cut **Inner Mouth 8, Nose 10** and **Eyes 11** from black felt. Cut **Tongue 9** from red felt. Arrange **Backpack 13, Side 14** and **Flap 15** on wrong side of denim. Cut out pieces 13, 14 and 15. Mark all notches. Sew all seams with 1/4 inch seam allowance unless otherwise noted.

FINNEGAN

Pin and then sew eye darts on **Front 2**. Slash along line to mouth corner points. Pin **Ears 6** to **Ear Linings 7**, easing Ear to match notches on lining. Sew together. Clip curves. Turn right side out. Form pleat on outside by matching fold line to tuck line. Lining up top edges of Ear and Ear lining, pin pleat in place thru all thicknesses. Baste together. Pin **Front Forehead 4** to **Back Forehead 5**, matching notches. Sew together. Pin ears to forehead at seam line, right sides together, matching placement lines. Baste in place. Pin **Back 1** to **Front 2** at side seam, matching notches. Stitch together. Pin Forehead sections to Back and Front center seams, matching notches and large dot on **Back 1**. Stitch together. The seam will be very thick at the ear placement, stitch slowly. Pin **Fronts 2** to **Center Front 3**, right sides together. Sew. Clip curves. Pin **Inner Mouth 8** to upper and lower snouts, right sides together, matching mouth corner points. Sew with 1/8th inch seam. Pin center seam on Back matching large dot. Sew together. Clip curves. Turn right side out. Fold up bottom hem 1/2 inch and sew. **Glue Eyes 12** to **Eyes 11**. Glue completed eyes above eye darts centering on forehead seam. Glue nose on upper snout. Glue tongue to inner mouth. Cut two 16-inch pieces of ribbon. Tie each one around an ear at forehead seam line forming a bow.

Continued on back

FINNEGAN - **Reproducible Pattern** *Continued*

BACKPACK

Pin **Flap 15** sections, right sides together, matching notches. Sew, leaving double notched edge open. Clip curves. Turn right side out and press. Cut two 8-inch pieces of ribbon. Position one end of each ribbon to small dots on **Flap 15** aligning raw edges. Sew in place. Pin **Flap 15** to one **Backpack 13** section, right sides together, matching small dots, making sure ribbon is sandwiched in between. Sew. Position remaining ends of ribbon to large dots on same section of **Backpack 13** aligning raw edges. Sew in place. Pin remaining **Backpack 13** section to **Side 14**, right sides together, matching notches. Sew. Fold down top hem 1/4 inch and topstitch. Pin **Backpack section 13** with attached **Flap** to **Side 14**, matching notches. Stitch together making sure ribbon is sandwiched in between. Clip curves. Turn right side out. Glue Velcro at placement markings on underside of Flap and front of backpack.

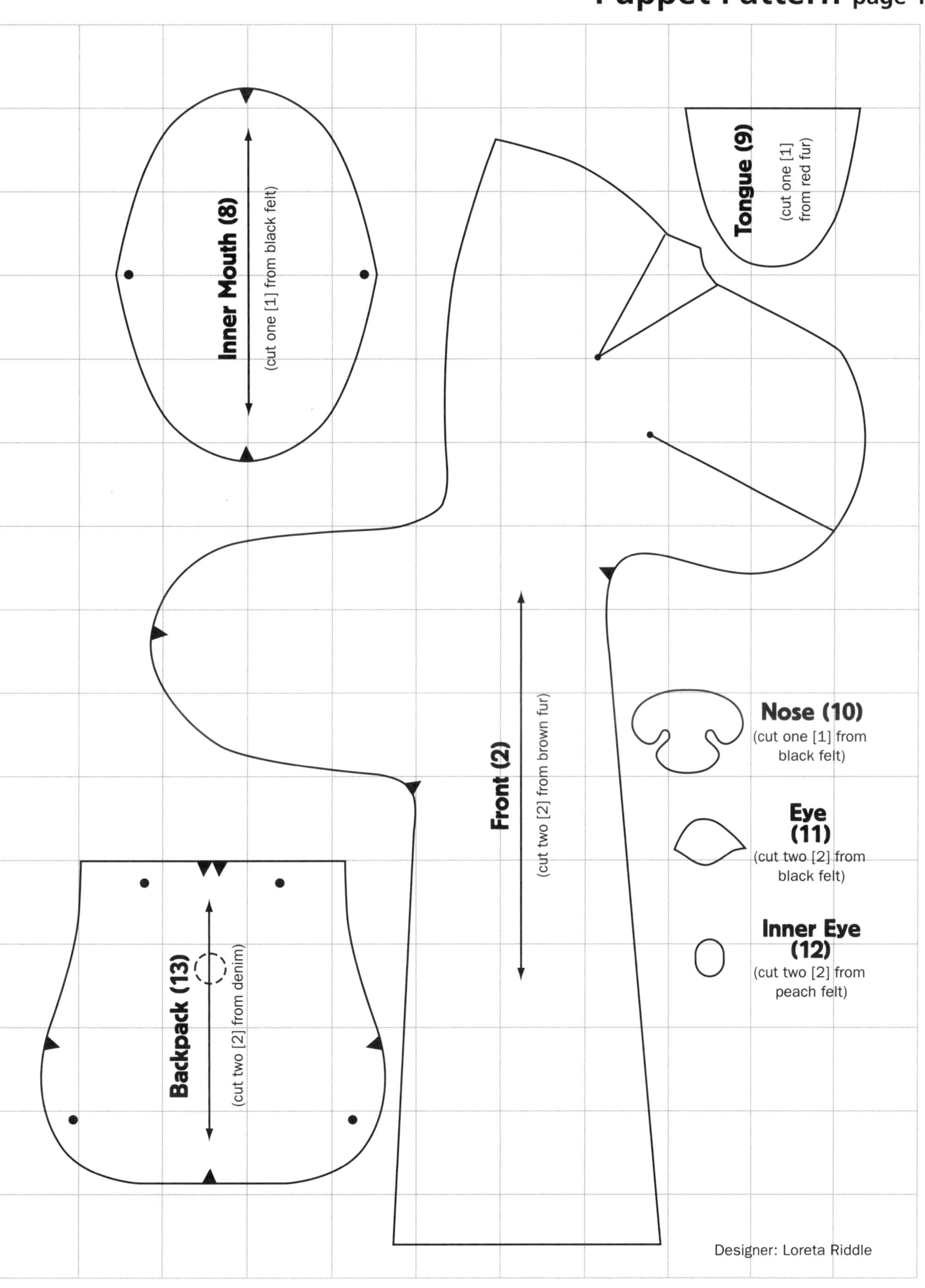

Inner Mouth (8)
(cut one [1] from black felt)
Tongue (9)
(cut one [1] from red fur)
Front (2)
(cut two [2] from brown fur)
Nose (10)
(cut one [1] from black felt)
Eye (11)
(cut two [2] from black felt)
Inner Eye (12)
(cut two [2] from peach felt)
Backpack (13)
(cut two [2] from denim)
Designer: Loreta Riddle

Puppet Pattern page 2

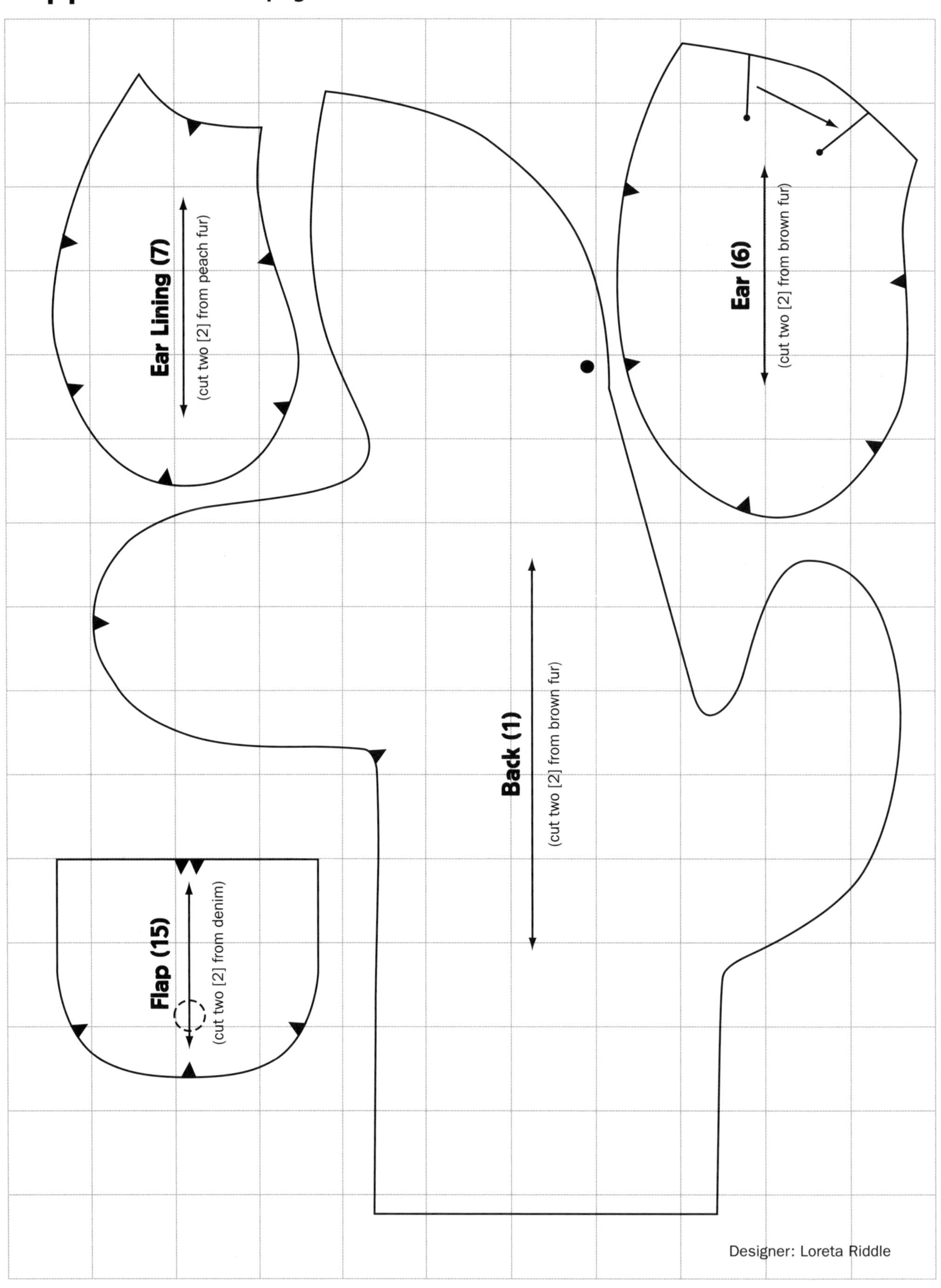

Front Forehead (5)
(cut one [1] from brown fur)
Back Forehead (4)
(cut one [1] from brown fur)
Center Front (3)
(cut one [1] from brown fur)
Side (14)
(cut one [1] from denim)
Designer: Loreta Riddle

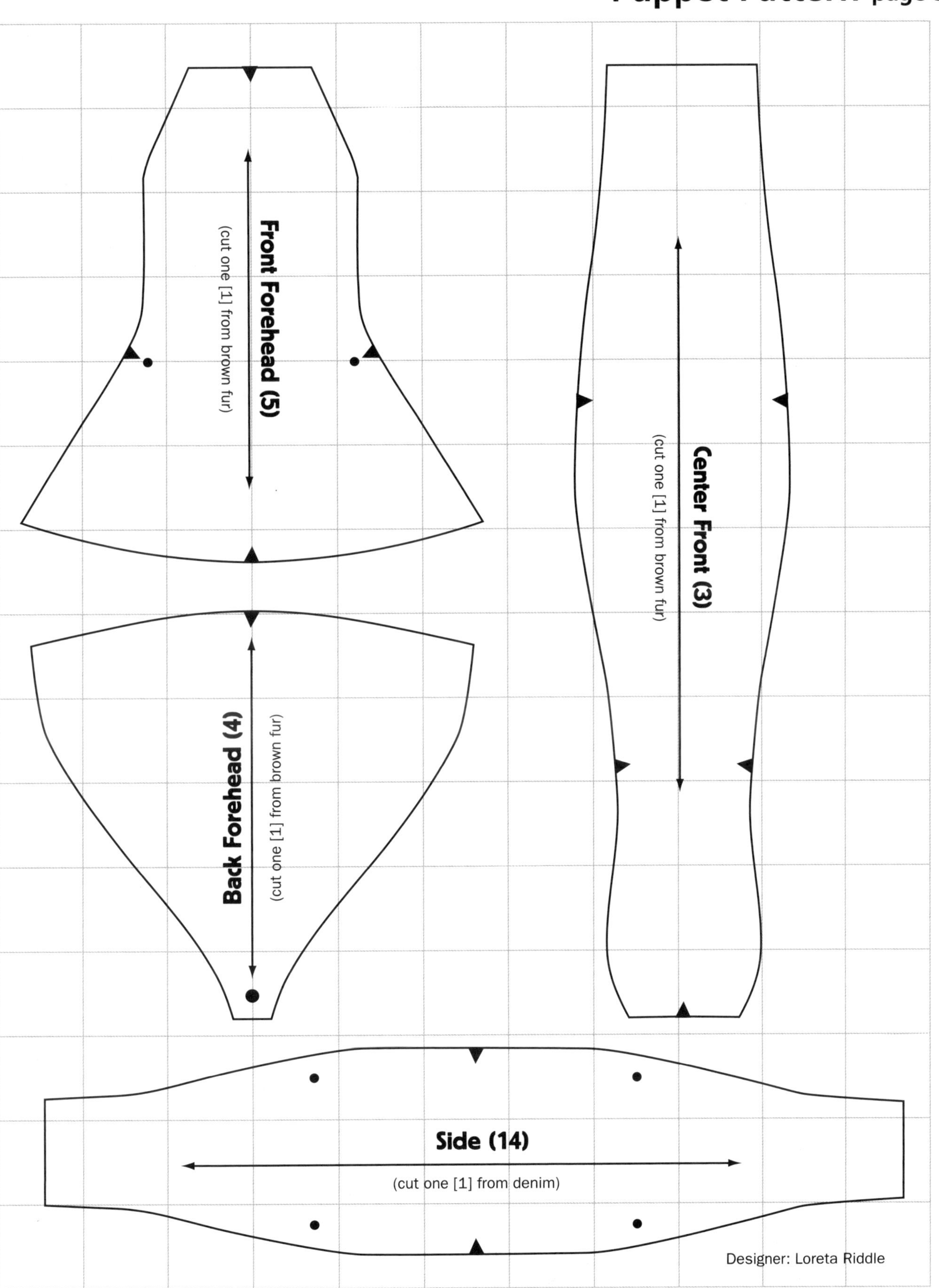

R E S O U R C E S

Key Verse Cards

Photocopy and cut out cards. Place a "hinge" of tape at the top of the card, and adhere it to page 7 of each Traveler's Journal. Starting at the bottom of the page, layer each card so that the Site Icon shows. Early-elementary verse in bold type.

"My soul, wait thou only upon God; for my expectation is from him. **He only is my rock and my salvation: he is my defence; I shall not be moved."** —Psalm 62:5-6

SITE 1

MAYAN JUNGLE

"There remaineth therefore a rest to the people of God. **For he that is entered into his rest, he also hath ceased from his own works, as God did from his."** — Hebrews 4:9-10

SITE 2

MEDIEVAL CASTLE

"Children, obey your parents in the Lord: for this is right." — Ephesians 6:1

SITE 3

ANCIENT LABORATORY

"Therefore I say unto you, **Take no thought for your life,** *what ye shall eat; neither for the body, what ye shall put on.* **The life is more than meat, and the body is more than raiment."** — Luke 12:22-23

SITE 5

HAWAIIAN VOLCANO

"Thou shalt **love the Lord thy God with all thy heart,** *and with all thy soul, and with all thy strength, and with all thy mind;* **and thy neighbour as thyself."** — Luke 10:27

SITE 4

HAWK'S VILLAGE

 OFFICIAL **TRAVEL PASSPORT**

This is to certify that

____

Name

has completed the time-travel journeys to the Mayan Jungle, a Medieval Castle, an Ancient Laboratory, Hawk's Indian Village, and a Hawaiian Volcano and is now an official Time-Stone Traveler™.

____

Signed (Leader or Assistant Leader)

____

Date

____

Church Name

Time-Stone Travelers™ Quest for God's 10 Commandments VeBS® program
© 2005 Cook Communications Ministries. www.cookministries.com

SITE 1
MAYAN JUNGLE

DIRECTIONS: You're trapped in the jungle! Find your way out by deciding if the sentences are true or false.

FIND YOUR WAY OUT OF THE JUNGLE

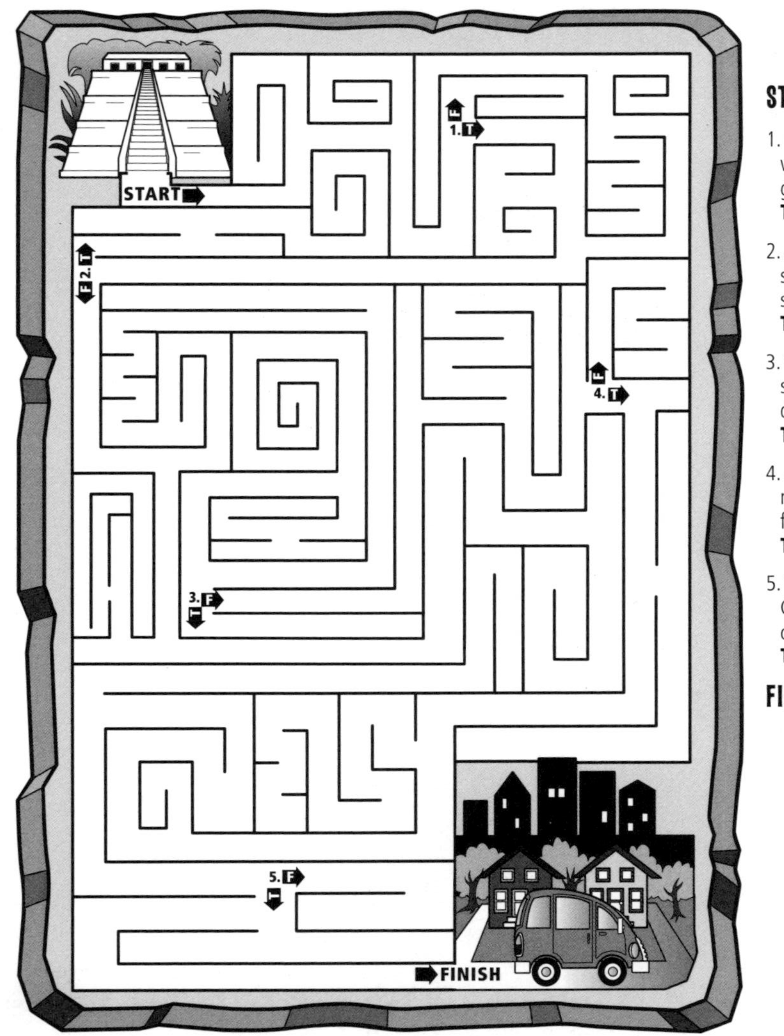

START

1. God says don't worship any other gods.
T or F?

2. An idol is only something made of stone or gold.
T or F?

3. Worshiping God is something you do only in church.
T or F?

4. An idol can be money, clothes, food, or friends.
T or F?

5. We show we love God by worshiping only Him.
T or F?

FINISH

Commandments for Site 1: Exodus 20:3-4 Commandments 1, 2

"My soul, wait thou only upon God; for my expectation is from him. He only is my rock and my salvation: he is my defence; I shall not be moved." — Psalm 62:5-6

KEY VERSES PAGE

DIRECTIONS: Using a "hinge" of tape, attach each of the key verse cards below. Start at the bottom of the page and layer the cards as you go up the page.

Tape verse 5 here

Tape verse 4 here

Tape verse 3 here

Tape verse 2 here

Tape verse 1 here

SITE 3
ANCIENT LABORATORY

LABORATORY SEARCH

DIRECTIONS: Using the verse at the bottom of the page, find the words of the memory verse in the lab beaker puzzle. Words can go forward, backward, up, down or at an angle.

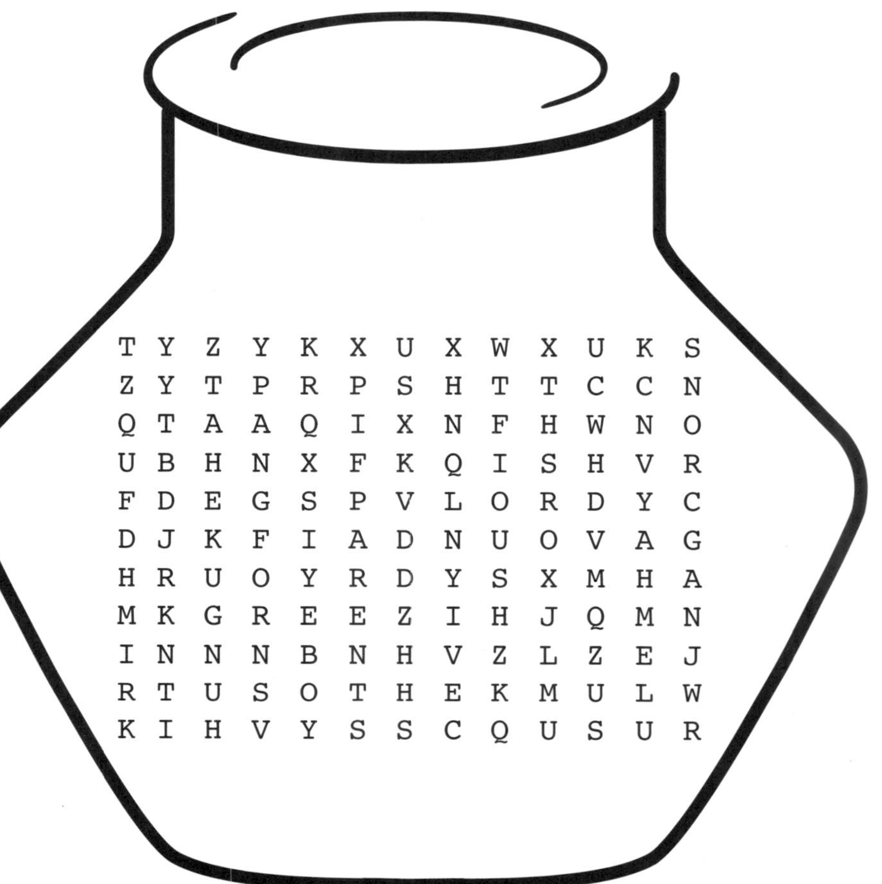

Commandments for Site 3: Exodus 20:3-4 Commandments 1, 2

"Children, obey your parents in the Lord: for this is right." — Ephesians 6:1

SITE 4
HAWK'S VILLAGE

SCRAMBLED MESSAGE

DIRECTIONS: Unscramble each word, and write it on the line. Find where each unscrambled word belongs in the memory verse, and write it in. Quiz a friend to see if they know the verse. Help each other finish memorizing it.

grentths _______________
tearh _______________
nidm _______________
slou _______________
voel _______________
refsloyu _______________
broghein _______________

"_________ the Lord your God

with all your _________ and

with all your _________ and

with all your _________ and

with all your _________ ; and,

Love your _________ as

_________." – Luke 10:27

Commandments for Site 4: Exodus 20:13-16 Commandments 6, 7, 8. 9

"Thou shalt love the Lord thy God with all thy heart, and with all thy soul, and with all thy strength, and with all thy mind; and thy neighbour as thyself." — Luke 10:27

SITE 5
HAWAIIAN VOLCANO

VOLCANIC VERSE

DIRECTIONS: Cut out words and pictures from a magazine to create one phrase of the memory verse. Glue them here. (Or draw each word creatively and artistically.) When done, have a friend or leader "read" your verse.

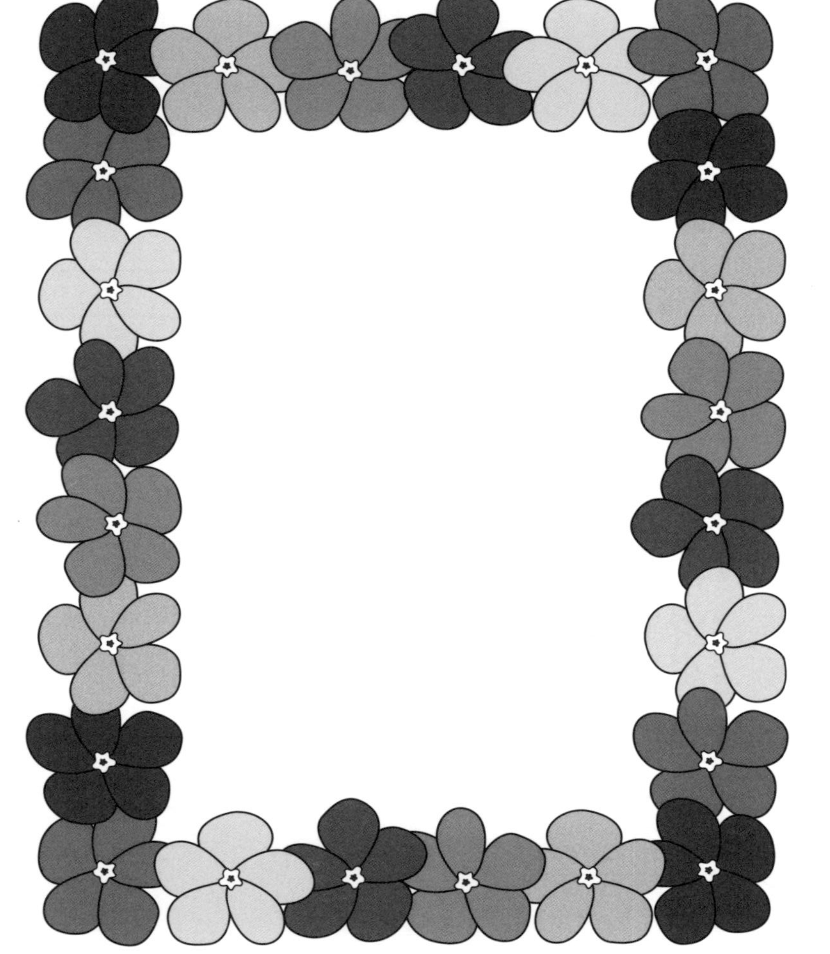

Commandments for Site 5: Exodus 20:17 Commandments 10

"Therefore I say unto you, Take no thought for your life, what ye shall eat; neither for the body, what ye shall put on. The life is more than meat, and the body is more than raiment." — Luke 12:22-23

SITE 2
MEDIEVAL CASTLE

NAMES OF GOD

Fortress
King of Kings
Rock

Mighty Warrior
Bread of Life
Shield

Good Shepherd
Light

DIRECTIONS: Make a collage of drawings about God's names. A collage is a group of pictures that don't go in any order and look beautiful bunched together. See how creative you can be as you think about what these names say about your Heavenly Father.

Commandments for Site 2: Exodus 20:7-8 Commandments 3, 4

"There remaineth therefore a rest to the people of God. For he that is entered into his rest, he also hath ceased from his own works, as God did from his." — Hebrews 4:9-10

OFFICIAL TRAVEL PASSPORT

This is to certify that

____

Name

has completed the time-travel journeys to the Mayan
Jungle, a Medieval Castle, an Ancient Laboratory,
Hawk's Indian Village, and a Hawaiian Volcano and
is now an official Time-Stone Traveler™.

____

Signed (Leader or Assistant Leader)

____

Date

____

Church Name

Time-Stone Travelers™ Quest for God's 10 Commandments VeBS® program
© 2005 Cook Communications Ministries. www.cookministries.com

YOUNGER ELEMENTARY VERSION

Traveler's Name:

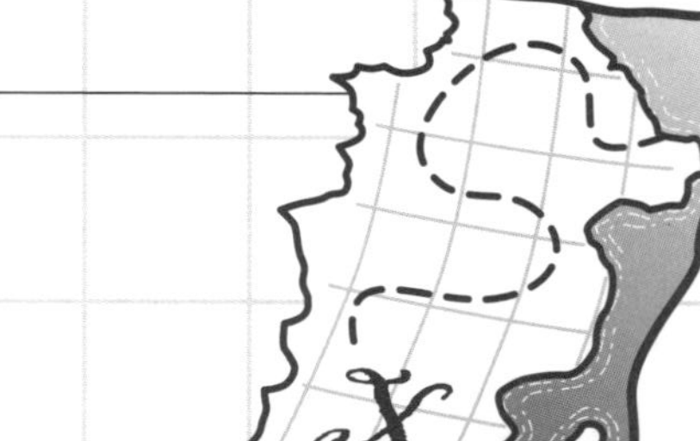

MAYAN JUNGLE

JUNGLE SURPRISES

DIRECTIONS: Look in the jungle for animals or plants with letters on them. Then look for that animal or plant under the lines. Write the letter on the line that matches the animal or plant. Then read what it says!

"[God] only is my rock and my salvation: he is my defence; I shall not be moved." — Psalm 62:5-6

KEY VERSES PAGE

DIRECTIONS: Using a "hinge" of tape, attach each of the key verse cards below. Start at the bottom of the page and layer the cards as you go up the page.

Tape verse 5 here

Tape verse 4 here

Tape verse 3 here

Tape verse 2 here

Tape verse 1 here

SITE 3
ANCIENT LABORATORY

SECRET MESSAGE

DIRECTIONS: Try to find this message in the puzzle. Start by circling the letter at the arrow. Move clockwise around the circle. With your pencil, draw a circle around every third letter to find the hidden message. When you have circled the letters, write them in order starting on the lines below.

— — — — —

— — — — —

— — — — — — — — — —

Commandments for Site 3: Exodus 20:3-4 Commandments 1, 2

"Children, obey your parents in the Lord, for this is right." — Ephesians 6:1

SITE 4
HAWK'S VILLAGE

WHAT HAPPENED NEXT?

DIRECTIONS: These six pictures show parts of the Bible story. But they are not in order. Choose which picture shows what happened first. Write a number 1 in the small square of that picture. Choose what happened next. Write a 2 in the small square. Keep going until all the pictures are numbered in the correct order. Tell a friend the Bible story using these pictures.

Commandments for Site 4: Exodus 20:13-16 Commandments 6, 7, 8. 9

"Love the Lord thy God with all thy heart . . . and thy neighbour as thyself." — Luke 10:27

SITE 5
HAWAIIAN VOLCANO

VOLCANO TREASURE

DIRECTIONS: Look for seven hidden things: (car, bicycle, monkey, soccer ball, doll, dog, skateboard). Find the pictures and color them. Then color the rest of the picture.

Commandments for Site 5: Exodus 20:17 Commandments 10

"Take no thought for your life . . . .

The life is more than meat and th body more than rainment." — Luke 12:22-23

SITE 2
MEDIEVAL CASTLE

DIRECTIONS: We can honor and respect God's name. We can use Bible names for Him. Read the name of God in the first column. Draw a line from it to the matching picture in the second column.

NAMES OF GOD SYMBOLS

Fortress

King of Kings

Rock

Mighty Warrior

Bread of Life

Shield

Good Shepherd

Light

Commandments for Site 2: Exodus 20:7-8 Commandments 3, 4

"For he that is entered into his rest, he also hath ceased from his own works, as God did from his." — Hebrews 4:9-10

Creating Time-Stones

Supplies:
- Smooth rocks (like river rock or equivalent) approximately 3" to 4" in length
- Photocopies of the symbols at the bottom of this page (one set per child)
- White, washable school glue
- Small containers large enough to hold one rock (one per child)
- Permanent markers
- Scissors

In Advance: Wash the rocks to remove any dirt particles. Let dry completely.

On the first day of this project, give each child a container. With a permanent marker write names on the sides of the containers. (You can have a Helper do this in advance if you prefer.) If your children are moving from site to site each day, assign a Helper to be sure to move the rocks in their containers to the next site each day.

Let each child choose a rock. On the first day, give out symbol #1 to each child. Have the children cut out their symbols. Using the school glue, ask each child to glue the first symbol on the left end of the rock they have chosen. The rocks should be placed back into the containers so each child can easily identify their rock. On each successive day, give out the next symbol, cut out the symbols, and glue them on the rocks. By the last day each child should have the five symbols glued onto the rocks.

On the last day, after the fifth symbol is dry, the children will put a coating over the entire top of the rock. Have them carefully drizzle glue over the top of the rock. Then have the children carefully smooth the glue over the rock so that all of the symbols are again coated with glue. Allow the glue to dry. This should take 10 to 15 minutes. (You may want to make a rock in advance to test the time. Each climate is somewhat different.)

| Site 1 | Site 2 | Site 3 | Site 4 | Site 5 |

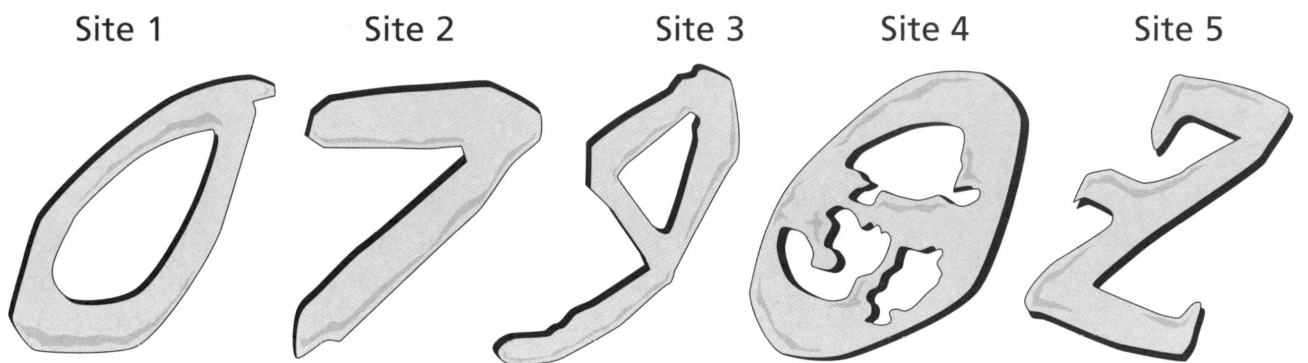

R E S O U R C E S

Creating Discovery Sites

Creating your VBS Discovery Sites is easy when you use these Mural Transparencies. You can simply trace and color a backdrop or create an elaborate environment—all using the traceable art figures and suggestions in this section. Use your imagination and have fun!

You will find the following inside this section:
- ○ **Five background murals (one for each site)**
- ○ **Two pages of site-related art to create additional props**

HOW TO USE THE ART IN THIS SECTION

Create an environment where your kids can learn and have fun! Simply follow these three easy steps and make each site as elaborate or as simple as you desire. For ideas on how to set up your room for each site, see the "Site/Introduction" section for sites 1-5. The Director's Guide section also contains tips for recruiting people to help create decorations.

Step 1: Choose images for each site.

There is a mural and many related objects to be used at each of the sites. First you will need to choose which art scenes and objects you will use based on the space you have and your room setup. You will probably want to begin with the mural as your most basic decoration and then build from there. Other objects can be used as add-ons to the mural to create a 3-D effect, such as stand-up figures and room decorations. (See subsequent pages for more ideas.) Once you have chosen your transparencies, remove them from the book.

Step 2: Set up your work area.

The use of transparencies allows you to make your murals as large as your space allows. To simply trace and color your mural, hang newsprint, table covering paper, white

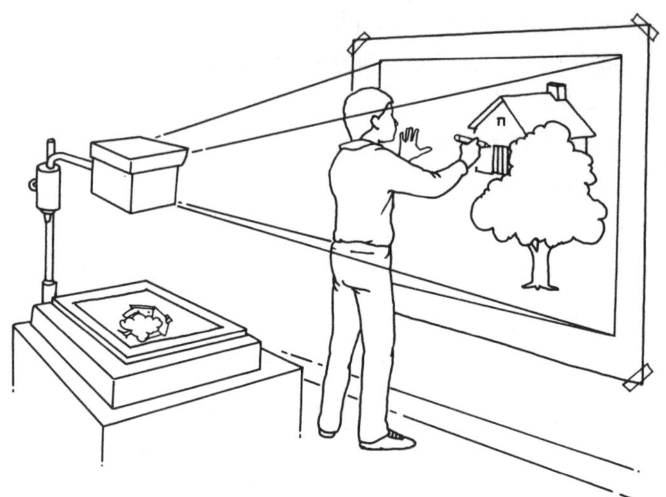

bed sheets, craft paper, poster board, tag board, or lightweight cardboard on a wall. Set up an overhead projector so that the image you want is projected onto the mural material on the wall. If you have a number of people working on this project, you may want to duplicate the transparencies and use more than one projector. You can adjust the size of the images by moving the projector closer to or farther away from the wall.

Step 3: Trace the images.

Once you are satisfied with the shape and size of the image, trace the figure with pencil or marker. Next, color the murals and/or figures as much or as little as you wish. For coloring figures and adding background details, consider using crayon, marker, colored pencils, chalk, or paint. Larger, less detailed images can be traced onto and cut out of colored paper or poster board.

CREATING STAND-UP FIGURES

Add some fun to your site by creating stand-up figures! To do this, follow the previous steps for tracing the images but be sure to use cardboard, foam core, or other sturdy material. Carefully cut out the figure using sharp scissors, a razor blade, or a utility knife. Then brace the figure by attaching a rectangular piece of cardboard to the back.

CONSTRUCTING FLATS, OR FRAMES

If you have the budget and the labor, you can easily create "flats" or frames for the backdrops of your set. Each flat will be a little over four feet wide by eight feet tall. Depending on your space, you may choose to use two or more of these flats to create an interesting corner—a focal point for your activities. Besides a hammer, drill, nails or screws, here is what you will need to build each flat:

- ○ **Three 8' x 1" x 2" boards (1 x 2's). Have one of the boards cut down to two 4-foot pieces.**
- ○ **One 4' x 9' sheet of 1/2" thick foam insulation.**
- ○ **Four 8" 90-degree triangle corner braces cut from plywood (Fig. B) OR four steel corner braces. You'll need two extra braces when forming a corner with two flats.**

1. **Lay two 8-foot 1 x 2's parallel to each other, about 4 feet apart, broad side down. These will be the sides of your frame. (Fig. A)**
2. **Place the two 4-foot boards broad side down, between the side boards, at the top and bottom of the frame. (NOTE: Four optional steel "L" brackets on the inside corners will help add stability, and make joining each of the corner pieces easier. See Fig. C.)**
3. **Position a triangle corner brace at each corner and secure with nails or screws. (Fig. B)**
4. **Flip the frame over (triangles on the floor) and glue or nail the sheet of foam insulation to the frame.**

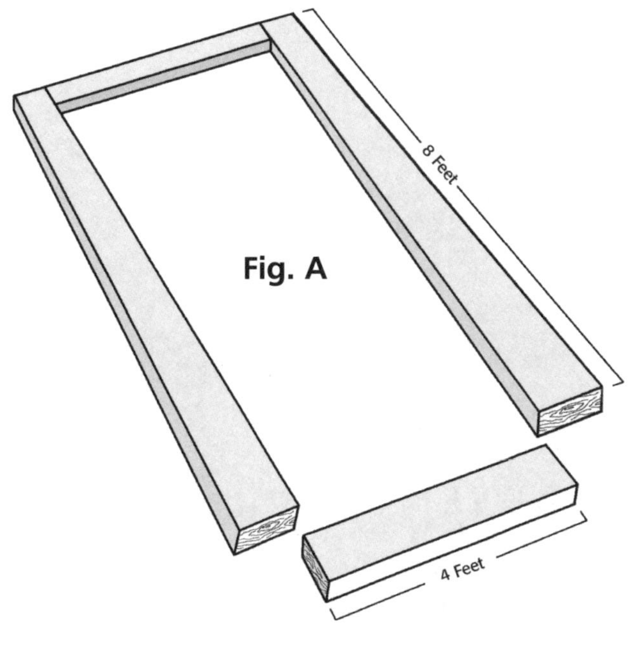

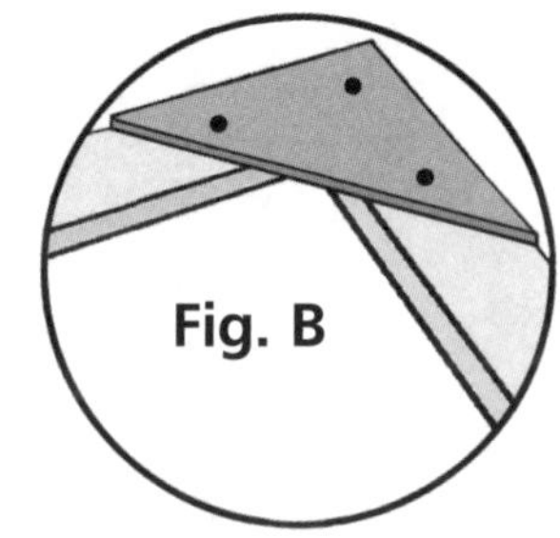

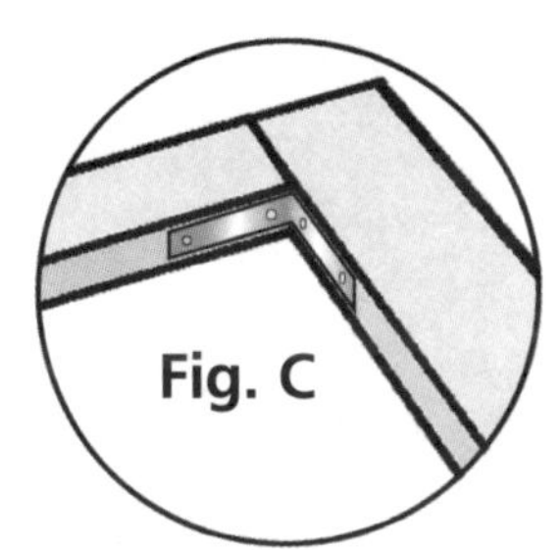

5. **Repeat the process for the second flat. After allowing enough time for the glue to dry, stand the flats up and position them next to each other, forming a corner at a 90-degree angle. To secure the corner shape, nail or screw triangle corner braces in place on top and bottom of the flats.**

If a larger set is desired, attach more flats using 1 x 2's for braces. Position a 1 x 2 across the top of two frames, connecting them. Nail or screw in place. Repeat at the bottom.

Now the fun begins! Cover the foam insulation using rolls of brightly-colored art paper or paint with a non-gloss paint (gloss paint will reflect glare). If you choose to paint the flats, you should first cover the seams neatly with wide tape, such as packing or drywall tape.

RESOURCES

Discovering Jesus as Your Savior

1 God loves us, but He does not like our sin. The Bible teaches that all people have sinned or disobeyed God (Rom. 3:23).

Have you sinned by disobeying God?

2 The Bible says that our sin separates us from God (Rom. 6:23). There is only one way that we can be connected to God and live with Him forever. We must be forgiven by God.

Do you want to know how to be forgiven by God?

3 Jesus has made the way for us to be forgiven by God. Jesus is God's perfect Son. Jesus died on a cross to take the consequences for our sins (John 3:16). Because Jesus died for us, our sins can be forgiven.

Do you believe that Jesus died on the cross to forgive you of your sins?

4 Jesus didn't stay dead. The Bible tells us that He rose from the dead and is alive today. So we can talk to Him right now. If we believe that Jesus died on the cross to take the consequences for our sins (Romans 10:9-10), we can ask Him to forgive us of our sins. The Bible promises that if we ask Jesus to forgive us, He will (1 John 1:9).

Would you like to ask Jesus to forgive you of your sins?

5 Once we have asked Jesus to forgive us, our sins are forgiven. Jesus saves us from the result of our sins. When we trust Jesus as our Savior, we are part of God's family forever (1 John 5:11-12).

Because we are part of His family, we are to live in ways that please God and do things that help us learn more about Him (Colossians 1:10).

What are some ways you can learn more about Jesus?

Now that you are forgiven and part of God's family (John 1:12), you will want to share your decision with others.

WHO WILL YOU TELL ABOUT YOUR DECISION TO TRUST JESUS AS YOUR SAVIOR?

"Discovering Jesus as Your Savior."

Use the other side of this page to talk with kids who express interest in discovering Jesus as Savior. See Page D•9 for more about this resource.

Step 1 This is the necessary first step. Sorrow for our sin is appropriate (2 Cor. 7:10). God loves us even though we sin (Rom. 5:8). We must recognize that we deserve God's punishment, and His love is a free gift (Rom. 6:23).

Step 2 We must truly believe in God and want to be forgiven by Him (Heb. 11:6). Without sincere desire, we will not find God.

Step 3 We must declare our belief in Jesus and God's gift of salvation (Rom. 10:9-10). Without belief there is no forgiveness.

Step 4 Asking in words that are meaningful to us is required. Once we ask in faith, we can celebrate new life in Christ and trust in God's faithfulness (1 John 1:9).

Step 5 Reading the Bible, praying, and coming to church to learn about God are ways to learn more. God wants us to "grow in grace, and in the knowledge of our Lord and Saviour Jesus Christ" (2 Pet. 3:18).

Step 6 It is important to let children express their decision in their own words. It will ensure that they understand what has happened and prepare them to share the Good News with others. Jesus teaches us to tell others about Him (Matt. 10:32; 28:19).

DEAR PARENTS

Today at VBS your child expressed his or her desire to accept Jesus Christ as Lord and Savior. After hearing the Bible truths and explanations printed on the other side of this paper, your child responded to the questions presented and prayed for salvation.

Please give your child the opportunity to tell you about his or her decision in his or her own words. The following questions may help guide your conversation.

- **Why did you decide to ask Jesus to be your Savior?**

- **What does this decision mean to you?**

- **How will you learn more about Jesus and what He wants you to do?**

- **Do you have any questions right now about God, or what it means to believe in Jesus as your Savior?**

If you'd like help answering your child's questions, talk with the leaders of the church where your child is attending VBS.

If you are seeking God's free gift of salvation for yourself, the leaders and members of the church where your child attends VBS would be happy to talk with you about how to receive forgiveness and become part of God's family.

Learn God's Word with pictures!

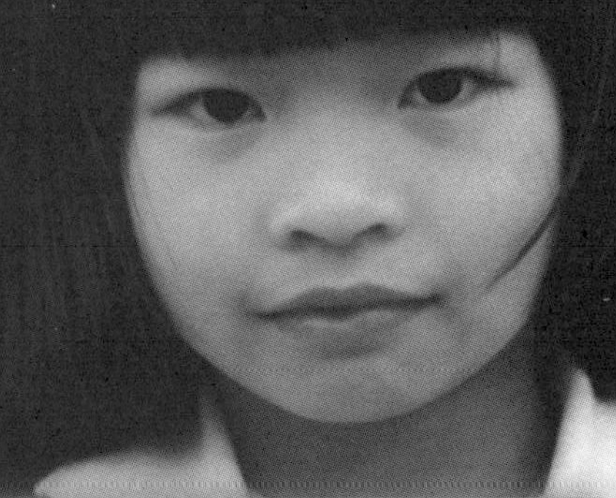

Scripture Pictures Series

Bring the Bible to Life
with 52 Visually-Interactive
Bible Stories for Kids!

Every lesson is easy to teach—in English or Spanish! You'll love the flexible design—the built-in easel makes it easy to use with your kids. Use it alone or as an extra resource for your Sunday school class or midweek program. All 52 age-appropriate Bible stories will inspire your kids to walk through the Old Testament and discover more about God. Each lesson comes with Bible Background that helps the teacher prepare, engaging Application Questions, and a fun Review Activity.

52 pages, 4-color Bible art, 52 pages of Bible story material
17 x 11, Spiral bound

NEW! Exploring the Miracles and Parables of Jesus
#103992
ISBN: 0-78144-201-X

A Journey Through the Old Testament
#103433
ISBN: 0-78144-074-2

Experiencing the Life of Christ
#103247
ISBN: 0-78144-032-7

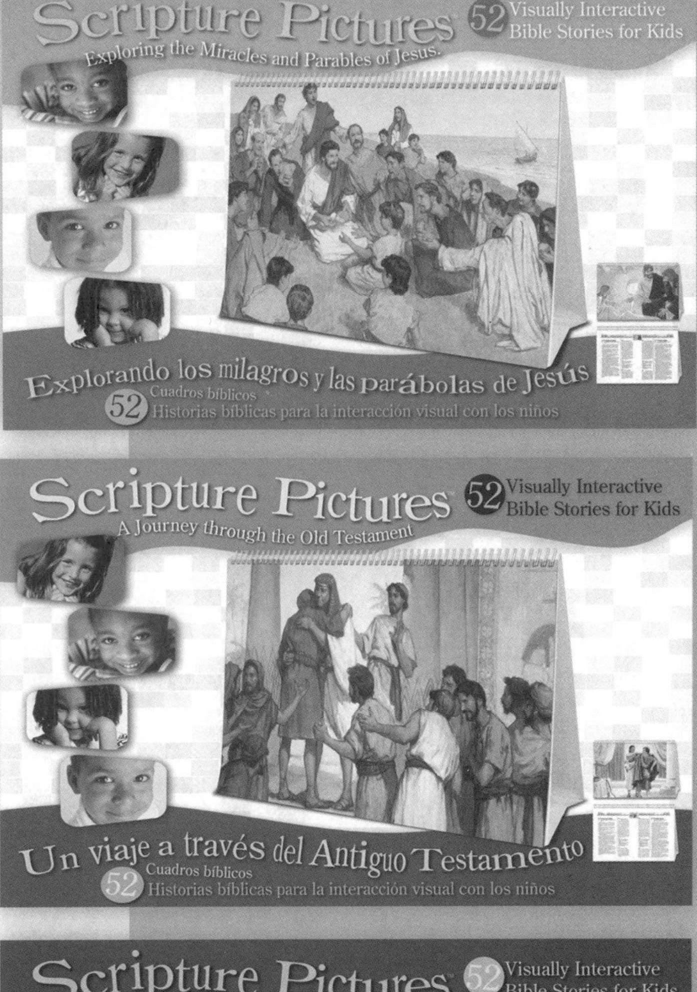

Fun-filled ways to learn God's Word!

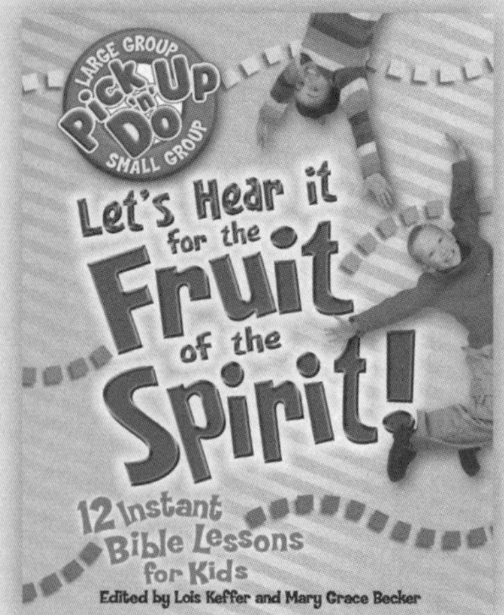

Let's Hear it for the Fruit of the Spirit!
ISBN: 0-78144-066-1; Item #: 103325

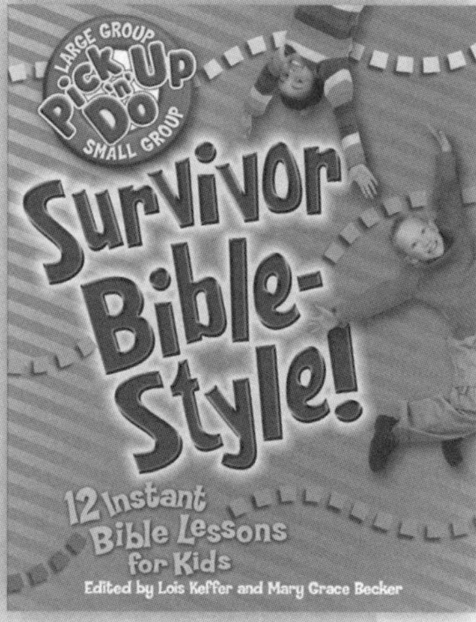

Survivor Bible-Style!
ISBN: 0-78144-068-8;
Item #: 103323

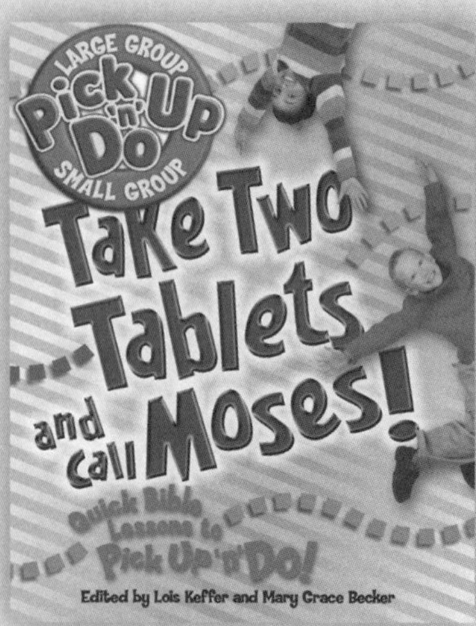

Take Two Tablets and Call Moses!
ISBN: 0-78144-067-X; Item #: 103324

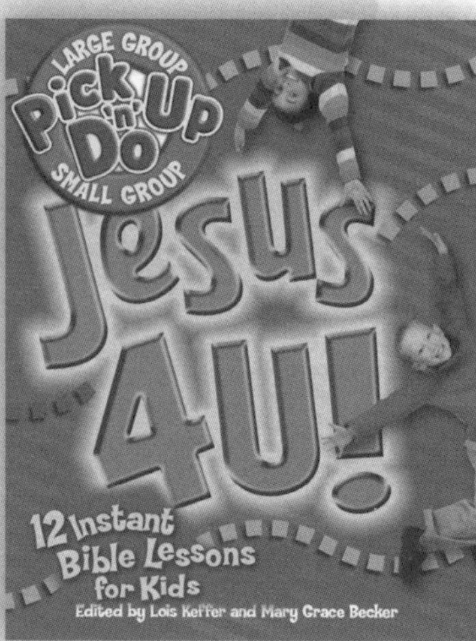

Jesus 4U!
ISBN: 0-78144-069-6;
Item #: 103326

Pick Up 'n' Do Series

12 Instant Bible Lessons for Kids

This all new resource is cost-effective and totally class-efficient! An entire quarter of Sunday School (twelve lessons) in one book! This economical new concept in elementary curricula gives your kids in-depth Bible teaching and serious discipleship without hours of preparation or lots of staff. Here's why you and your kids will love Pick Up 'n' Do:

- Instant fun-filled dramas take a unique approach to the Bible stories.
- Engages knowledgeable students while giving kids who are new to God's Word a solid foundation of Biblical truth.
- Perfect for the ministry with large group sessions and small group shepherding time!
- Copy "n" go handouts bring the lessons to life.
- Optional hands-on workshops stretch each lesson with a craft, science or food activity.

Take control of your children's ministry without all the hassle of writing your own curriculum from the ground up. Pick Up 'n' Do and you've got it all!

128 pages; 8.5 x 11

Exciting ways to learn God's Word!

Bible FUNStuff Series

Excellent resources for children and teachers

Children's ministry can be fun and meaningful when you use these incredible creative resources from Godprints. Every activity comes with a Godprint, Bible Truth and Bible Verse to help kids learn what God is like and how to become more like Him! Build your own lesson from these creative options, or use them as a supplement! 8.5 x 11

 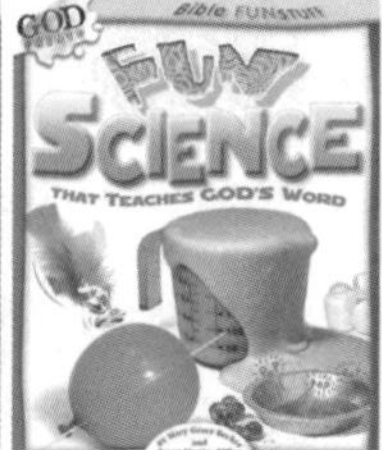

Down in Front Children's Sermons
ISBN: 0-78144-083-1
ITEM #: 103452 112P

Fun Science That Teaches God's Word
ISBN: 0-78144-081-5
ITEM #: 103450 112P

Folder Games for Children's Ministry
ISBN: 0-78143-961-2
ITEM #: 102364 140P

The Official Puppet Ministry Survival Guide
ISBN: 0-78143-841-1
ITEM #: 101782 112P

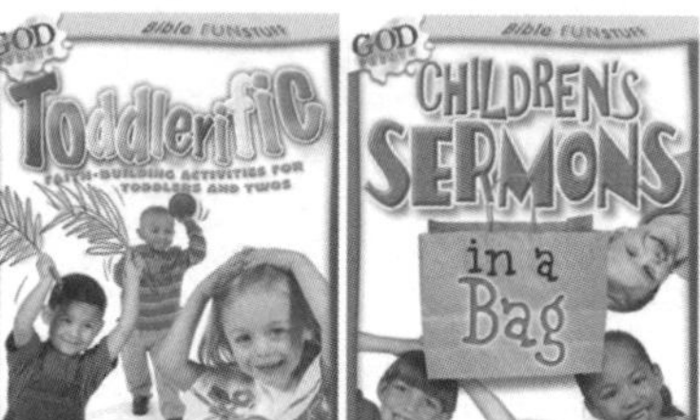

Toddlerific
ISBN: 0-78144-082-3
ITEM #: 103451 112P

Children's Sermons In a Bag
ISBN: 0-78143-958-2
ITEM #: 102361 112P

Seasonal Pageants and Skits
ISBN: 0-78143-959-0
ITEM #: 102362 112P

Teaching Off the Wall: Interactive Bulletin Boards
ISBN: 0-78143-837-3
ITEM #: 101779 112P

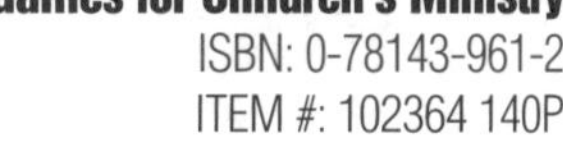

Every Season Kid Pleasin' Children's Sermons
ISBN: 0-78143-839-X
ITEM #: 101780 112P

FUNtastic Kid Crafts
ISBN: 0-78143-838-1
ITEM #: 101777 112P

Wiggle Worms Learn the Psalms
ISBN: 0-78143-960-4
ITEM #: 102363 112P

NEW! Spur of Moment Preschool Activiites
ISBN: 0-78144-230-3
ITEM #: 104153 112P

Paper Capers
ISBN: 0-78143-836-5
ITEM #: 101778 112P

A Gaggle of Giggles and Games
ISBN: 0-78143-840-3
ITEM #: 101781 112P

NEW! If ands & Buts Children's Sermons
ISBN: 0-78144-206-0
ITEM #: 104025 112P

NEW! Bible Crafts for all Seasons
ISBN: 0-78144-205-2
ITEM #: 104024 112P

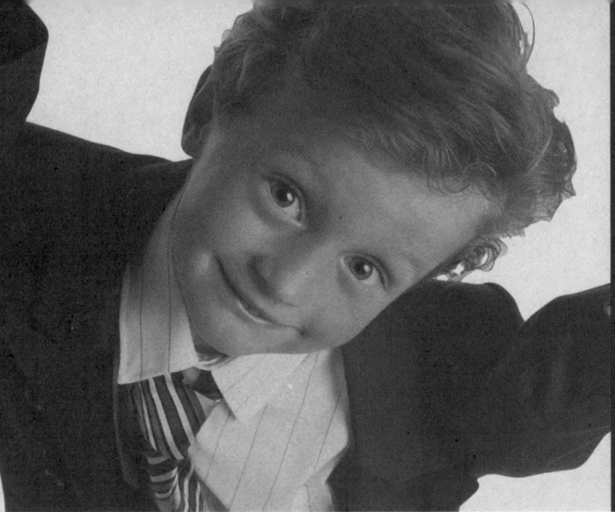

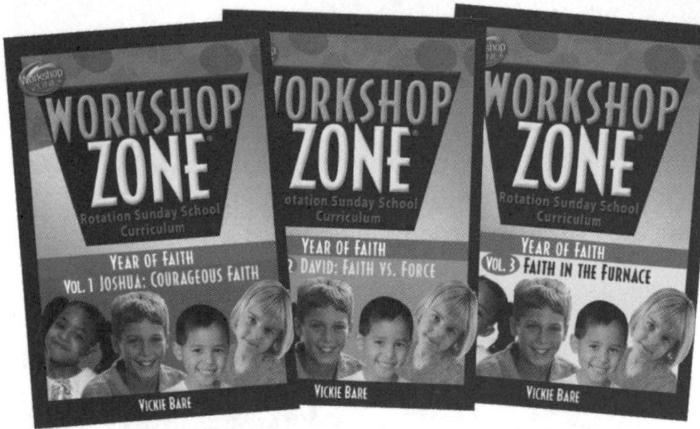

Workshop Zone®

The Ultimate Christ-Centered, Bible Based Rotation Sunday School Curriculum!

Workshop Zone is Sunday school reborn—it's the ultimate kid-friendly Sunday school adventure **for Grades 2-5.**. Rich, Bible-based lessons focus on the **Deep Truth** of God's Word, generate a **Bold Faith,** and lead to **Changed Lives.** And Workshop Zone is friendly on teachers, too. Makes recruitment of volunteers easy cause each teacher teaches to their strengths and giftings. And teachers prepare just once a month. Each CD contains a month's worth of Bible-based, experiential lessons that minister to the whole child. **Kids are gently and thoughtfully shepherded through captivating, innovative workshops, such as:**

- **Good Shepherd's Inn**: *Bible Story/Food Activity.*
- **StarGazer Theater**: *Drama*
- **Game Zone**: *movement*
- **Seaside Studio**: *Art.*
- **Mountaintop Productions**: *Video.*
- **Salt & Light Shop**: *Science*
- **The Temple Court**: *missions/out-of-the-box Bible study*
- **Faith In Action**: *Movement/Missions/Outreach*

Year one—The Year of Faith—Contains Nine CDs
Provide 36 Weeks of Lessons (Four Weeks per CD)

The Year of Faith

Vol 1—**Joshua: Courageous Faith**, ISBN: 0-78144-213-3, Item # 104049
Vol 2—**David: Faith vs. Force**, ISBN: 0-78144-214-1, Item # 104050
Vol 3—**Faith in the Furnace**, ISBN: 0-78144-215-X, Item # 104051
Vol 4—**Faith Finds the Messiah**, ISBN: 0-78144-216-8, Item # 104052
Vol 5—**Daniel: Faith Faces Lions**, ISBN: 0-78144-217-6, Item # 104053
Vol 6—**A Lame Man Healed: Faith Goes Through the Roof**, ISBN: 0-78144-218-4, Item # 104054
Vol 7—**Peter: Faith with Wet Feet**, ISBN: 0-78144-219-2, Item # 104056
Vol 8—**Resurrection Faith**, ISBN: 0-78144-220-6, Item # 104057
Vol 9—**Faith in Philippi**, ISBN: 0-78144-221-4, Item # 104058

Other Workshop Zone® Resources

ISBN: 0-78144-226-5, Item #104079

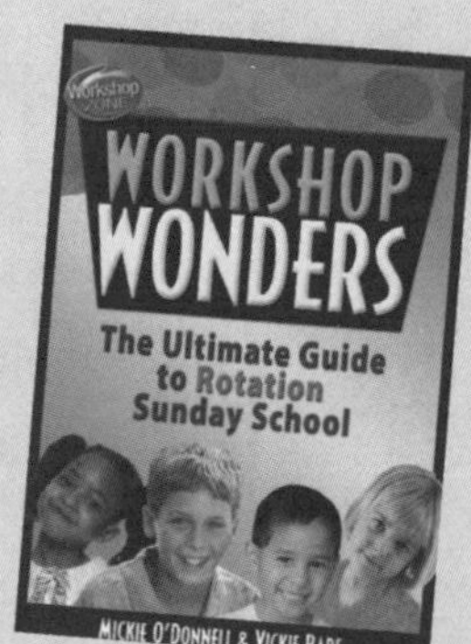

ISBN: 0-78144-208-7 Item #104032